Vernaculars in an Age of World Literatures

Cosmopolitan–Vernacular Dynamics in World Literatures

The four books in this limited series are an outcome of a major Swedish research project called "Cosmopolitan–Vernacular Dynamics in World Literatures," the aim of which has been to intervene – not least methodologically – in the current disciplinary development of world literature studies. The series is united by a common introductory chapter and approaches the vernacular in world literature across a range of fields, such as comparative literature, postcolonial literature, and literary anthropology.

More information on the research project can be found at Worldlit.se. The books in this series are available as open access through the Bloomsbury Open Access programme and are available on www.bloomsburycollections.com. They are funded by the Riksbankens Jubileumsfond.

Series Editor
Stefan Helgesson

Volumes in the Series
Claiming Space: Locations and Orientations in World Literatures
Edited by Bo G. Ekelund, Adnan Mahmutović and Helena Wulff
Literature and the Making of the World: Cosmopolitan Texts, Vernacular Practices
Edited by Stefan Helgesson, Helena Bodin and Annika Mörte Alling
Northern Crossings: Translation, Circulation and the Literary Semi-periphery
By Chatarina Edfeldt, Erik Falk, Andreas Hedberg, Yvonne Lindqvist, Cecilia Schwartz and Paul Tenngart
Vernaculars in an Age of World Literatures
Edited by Christina Kullberg and David Watson

Vernaculars in an Age of World Literatures

Edited by
Christina Kullberg and David Watson

BLOOMSBURY ACADEMIC
NEW YORK • LONDON • OXFORD • NEW DELHI • SYDNEY

BLOOMSBURY ACADEMIC
Bloomsbury Publishing Inc
1385 Broadway, New York, NY 10018, USA
50 Bedford Square, London, WC1B 3DP, UK
29 Earlsfort Terrace, Dublin 2, Ireland

BLOOMSBURY, BLOOMSBURY ACADEMIC and the Diana logo
are trademarks of Bloomsbury Publishing Plc

First published in the United States of America 2022
Paperback edition published 2023

Volume Editors' Part of the Work © Christina Kullberg and David Watson, 2022
Each chapter © Contributors

For legal purposes the Acknowledgements on p. ix constitute
an extension of this copyright page.

Cover design by Namkwan Cho
Cover image © Shutterstock.com

This work is published open access subject to a Creative Commons Attribution-NonCommercial-NoDerivatives 3.0 licence (CC BY-NC-ND 3.0, https://creativecommons.org/licenses/by-nc-nd/3.0/). You may re-use, distribute, and reproduce this work in any medium for non-commercial purposes, provided you give attribution to the copyright holder and the publisher and provide a link to the Creative Commons licence.

Bloomsbury Publishing Inc does not have any control over, or responsibility for, any third-party websites referred to in this book. All internet addresses given in this book were correct at the time of going to press. The author and publisher regret any inconvenience caused if addresses have changed or sites have ceased to exist, but can accept no responsibility for any such changes.

A catalog record for this book is available from the Library of Congress.

ISBN: HB: 978-1-5013-7405-0
       PB: 978-1-5013-7409-8
       ePDF: 978-1-5013-7407-4
       eBook: 978-1-5013-7406-7

Series: Cosmopolitan–Vernacular Dynamics in World Literatures

Typeset by Integra Software Services Pvt. Ltd.

To find out more about our authors and books visit www.bloomsbury.com
and sign up for our newsletters.

Contents

Notes on contributors　vi
Acknowledgements　ix
Series introduction – The cosmopolitan–vernacular dynamic: Conjunctions of world literature　*Stefan Helgesson, Christina Kullberg, Paul Tenngart and Helena Wulff*　x

Introduction: Theorizing the vernacular　*Christina Kullberg and David Watson*　1

1　Contextualizing the vernacular: Signposts from African languages, writing, and literature　*Moradewun Adejunmobi*　25
2　Vernacular resistance: Catalan, Basque, and Galician opposition to Francoist monolingualism　*Christian Claesson*　51
3　The modern adventures of Kanian Poongundranar, classical Tamil poet: Reflections on literatures of the world, vernacularly speaking　*S. Shankar*　81
4　Vernacular soundings: Poetry from the Lesser Antilles in the aftermaths of hurricanes Irma and Maria　*Christina Kullberg*　101
5　From *Fesiten* to *Fesibuku*: Shifting priorities in the Saamaka vernacular　*Richard Price and Sally Price*　127
6　Cosmopolitan and vernacular dynamics in modern Chinese fiction and Lao She's satirical novel *Cat Country*　*Lena Rydholm*　153
7　Worldly themes and vernacular literature: Aino Kallas on gender, ethnicity, and class　*Katarina Leppänen*　181
8　Specters of the vernacular: Neoliberalism, world literature, and Marlon James's *A Brief History of Seven Killings*　*David Watson*　203
9　Vernacular imagination and exophone reconfiguration in Francophone Chinese diasporic literature　*Shuangyi Li*　223

Vernacular lessons: Dante, Cavafy, Gombrowicz (Instead of an afterword)　*Galin Tihanov*　251

Index　261

Contributors

Moradewun Adejunmobi is a professor in the African American and African Studies Department at the University of California, Davis. She is the author of two books: *JJ Rabearivelo, Literature and Lingua Franca in Colonial Madagascar* (1996) and *Vernacular Palaver: Imaginations of the Local and Non-Native Languages in West Africa* (2004). She is also a co-editor (with Carli Coetzee) of the *Routledge Handbook of African Literature* (2019).

Christian Claesson is Associate Professor of Hispanic Literatures at Lund University. He received his Ph.D. in Romance Languages at Harvard University in 2009, and has mainly worked on Spanish contemporary postcrisis literature and on the intersection of Spanish, Catalan, Basque and Galician literatures. He is the editor of *Narrativas precarias: Crisis y subjetividad en la cultura española actual* (2019) and the forthcoming *España pluriliteraria Literatura, lengua y política en la cultura contemporánea*.

Christina Kullberg (editor) is Professor of French at Uppsala University, specializing in contemporary Caribbean literature and early modern travel writing. Her publications include *The Poetics of Ethnography in Martinican Narratives* (2013) and *Lire l'Histoire générale des Antilles de J.-B. Du Tertre* (2020). She is part of the steering committee to the research program "Vernacular and Cosmopolitan Dynamics in World Literature."

Katarina Leppänen is Professor of Intellectual History at the Department of Literature, History of Ideas, and Religion at the University of Gothenburg, Sweden. Her research focuses on transnational feminism in the mid-twentieth century, ecological feminism, social movements, nationalism and internationalism, and regionalism. She combines intellectual history and literary studies and has published on diverse topics such as women and political violence, literature and nationalism, and the trafficking of women.

Shuangyi Li is Lecturer in Comparative Literatures and Cultures at the University of Bristol. His first monograph, *Proust, China and Intertextual Engagement: Translation and Transcultural Dialogue* (Palgrave Macmillan, 2017), won the

International Comparative Literature Association Anna Balakian Prize 2019. Shuangyi received his Ph.D. at the University of Edinburgh and studied at l'École Normale Supérieure (Paris). He worked as a Research Fellow at Lund University (2017–2021), funded by the Swedish Research Council (VR).

Richard Price's books include *First-Time* (1983, 2002), *Alabi's World* (1990), *The Convict and the Colonel* (1998, 2006), *Travels with Tooy: History, Memory, and the African American Imagination* (University of Chicago Press, 2008), and with Sally Price, *Maroons in Guyane* (University of Georgia Press, 2022). The Prices' website is www.richandsally.net.

Sally Price's books include *Co-Wives and Calabashes* (1984, 1993), *Primitive Art in Civilized Places* (1989, 2001, published in eight languages), *Paris Primitive: Jacques Chirac's Museum on the Quai Branly* (University of Chicago Press, 2007), and with Richard Price, *Saamaka Dreaming* (Duke University Press, 2017).

Lena Rydholm is Professor of Chinese at the Department of Linguistics and Philology at Uppsala University. Her research interests include classical and modern Chinese literature, mainly poetry and fiction, and literary theories, such as Chinese theories of literature, fiction, genre and style, and transcultural literary theories.

S. Shankar is a novelist, literary and cultural critic, and translator. He is Professor and Chair in the Department of English at the University of Hawai'i at Mānoa. Shankar's most recent book is his third novel, *Ghost in the Tamarind* (2017). His most recent critical book is the award-winning *Flesh and Fish Blood: Postcolonialism, Translation, and the Vernacular* (2012). His scholarly essays and cultural journalism have appeared in the United States, India, and Europe.

Galin Tihanov is the George Steiner Professor of Comparative Literature at Queen Mary University of London. He is the author of five books, most recently *The Birth and Death of Literary Theory: Regimes of Relevance in Russia and Beyond* (2019), which won the 2020 AATSEEL Prize for "Best Book in Literary Studies." His work in intellectual history and on cosmopolitanism, world literature, and exile has been widely translated. He is currently completing *Cosmopolitanism: A Very Short Introduction* for Oxford University Press.

David Watson (editor) is Associate Professor in the Department of English at Uppsala University, where he specializes in American literature and culture. He has published on nineteenth-century and modernist American poets, nineteenth-century and contemporary novelists, and issues in transnational and translation studies. Currently, he is completing a monograph on *The National Security Aesthetic: Twenty-First-Century American Fiction and the Governance of Contingency*. His most recent research is on neoliberalism, finance, and the contemporary American novel, as well as nineteenth-century vernacular writing.

Acknowledgements

This book is available as open access through the Bloomsbury Open Access programme and is available on www.bloomsburycollections.com. The open-access edition of this text was made possible by Riksbankens Jubileumsfond.

Series introduction
The cosmopolitan–vernacular dynamic: Conjunctions of world literature

Stefan Helgesson, Christina Kullberg, Paul Tenngart and Helena Wulff

"World literature is not an object, it's a *problem*." This was Franco Moretti (2000: 55), famously, in 2000. But what is the problem of world literature today, two decades later? In broad strokes, the disciplinary challenge would seem to be the same: to devise methods and reading practices that offer alternatives to entrenched national and civilizational frameworks. Scholarship within world literature shares a fundamentally *comparative* urge, whereby different instantiations of literature are considered in conjunction. But "conjunction" is in fact the nub of the problem, as this is supposedly not just an older version of comparative literature under a new name. Instead, conjunction can be conceptualized through a wide number of temporalities, scales, geographies, generic constellations, languages and ideological perspectives—all of them susceptible to historical change.

Moretti proposed a world-systemic model, inspired by Immanuel Wallerstein, which has since developed into a strong but by no means exclusive or uncontested methodological premise of world literature. Deep-time approaches focusing on imperial formations, translation-based approaches, Alexander Beecroft's (2015) ecologies of literature—all offer distinct ways of investigating conjunction and connection. What they do not always offer is mutual compatibility. Instead, the most productive way to delineate world literature today might be to consider it as a set of procedures and methods rather than a coherent body of theory. As a scholarly field, it provides in the first instance a space of conversation and intellectual exchange *across* specializations that may also enable reconfigured empirical and critical investigations within those specializations.

This give-and-take among different disciplinary locations has shaped the work leading up to the four volumes presented here. Emerging from a long-running project based in Sweden, and involving researchers from comparative literature, anthropology, intellectual history and a range of language departments, the basic methodological wager of our work differs from much else that has been published in the field of world literature. Avoiding hard-wired systemic, deterministic or "global" claims, what we call the *cosmopolitan–vernacular dynamic* (which can also be read as *vernacular–cosmopolitan*) offers itself not as a distinct theory, but as a methodological starting point—akin to an *Ansatzpunkt* in Erich Auerbach's (1952) sense—from which to explore the resonances and connections between widely diverse literary texts and cultures.

To explain the motivations behind such a methodology, we need to make a detour into the current state of world literature studies. Undergirding this sprawling field is the political and ethical intuition that literary knowledge in our crisis-ridden, globalized and racialized world—even in its (anticipated) post-Covid-19 shape—requires new modes of scholarly attention. To speak from our own contemporary vantage point in Scandinavia, it is clear that the joint impact of the cultural Anglosphere, migration from Europe, the Middle East, Africa and Asia, the cultural policies of the EU and the ubiquitous presence of digital media not only weaken the explanatory value of the nation state and the national language as the privileged loci of the production and reading of literature in Sweden today, but also invite reconsiderations of an earlier literary history in the region. Similar shifts in the production of literature and in the literary imagination can be registered elsewhere across the world, shifts that prompt us to rethink how we read and contextualize literature. The road to such a revised conception of literary studies leads, however, to a garden of forking paths. This is one important lesson to be learned from the twenty-odd years since Moretti's lively provocation in the year 2000.

Common to the turn-of-the-millennium interventions by Moretti and David Damrosch (2003) (less so Pascale Casanova, whose concern was consecration) was an emphasis on circulation—quite literally on how texts move and are received in diverse contexts. This deceptively simple perspective counters what Jerome McGann (1991: 7) once called "textual idealism," which treats texts as if they were just magically "there." Instead, the circulational perspective allows us to engage the material, spatial and historical unconscious of literature as texts in movement. This approach has been developed by Beecroft (2015), Venkat Mani (2017), Sandra Richter (2017) and Yvonne Leffler (2020), among others. Increasingly, as in contributions to Stefan Helgesson and Pieter Vermeulen's (2016) *Institutions of World Literature* or in Ignacio Sánchez-Prado's (2018) study of Mexican literature, this tends towards studies of market dynamics and, not least, the sociology of translation (Heilbron 1999, 2020, de Swaan 2001, Sapiro

2008, Buzelin and Baraldi 2016). However, the most rigorous large-scale studies of circulation are to be found within computational literary studies (CLS) which involves an even more fundamental shift towards quantitative methods than the sociology of translation. Not surprisingly, given his coinage of "distant reading," CLS has become Moretti's (2000: 56–8) main field of activity at the Stanford Literary Lab. Even as the merits and drawbacks of CLS are being debated (Da 2019), the achievements in all these interlinked areas of investigation attest firmly to the *complexity* of studying world-literary circulation. This knowledge is not just readily available, nor does it amount merely to an external study of literature, but it is rather of crucial relevance both to the empirical and theoretical understanding of how literary cultures evolve.

Having said that, a striking alternative development over the last ten years has been the proliferation of interpretive, qualitative methods in world literature studies. Often on the basis of strong theorizations of the world-concept, and sometimes pitched polemically against the circulation approach, researchers have attempted to read "the world" through specific literary works, rather than through Morettian "distant reading" (which is ideally suited for digital methods). The epistemic assumption in these interpretive models follows the synechdochal logic of *pars pro toto*, or the part standing in for the whole. Eric Hayot (2012) was early to embark on this path in *On Literary Worlds*, an ambitious but all too brief attempt to bring world literature studies—understood as a global extension of literary studies—to bear on, in principle, *any* given work of literature, regardless of origin or period. Emily Apter's (2013) much publicized *Against World Literature* instead championed linguistic specificity—coded as the "Untranslatable"—as the normative locus of a worldly reading. A related tendency has been the regionally or linguistically restricted conception of literature X *as* world literature, with the francophone *littérature-monde* as a high-profile example, but also evident in many (not all) titles in Bloomsbury's "Literatures as World Literature" series. Building on Moretti's world-systemic inclination, the Warwick Research Collective (WReC) has elaborated a significantly different conception of world-literature (with a hyphen) as the aesthetic registration of combined and uneven development in the capitalist world-system—but this, too, has issued in a mode of close interpretive attention to literary texts, rather than distant reading. Other, more or less distinct examples of this interpretive turn in world literature studies can be cited, such as Francesca Orsini's (2015) concept of the multilingual local, pitched in opposition to systemic approaches, Debjani Ganguly's (2016) work on the global novel, Ottmar Ette's (2016) "transarea" approach, Pheng Cheah's

(2016, 2017) phenomenology of 'worlding literature" and Birgit Neumann and Gabriele Rippl's (2017) notes on world-making. A point of relevance to our work is that while the most rigorous systemic approaches, represented here by WReC, speak of world-literature in the singular, the implication of, for example, Hayot's, Apter's or Orsini's perspectives is to consider *literatures* as an inevitably plural phenomenon—even in contexts of exchange and translation. At stake here, ultimately, is the relative theoretical weighting of determinacy and contingency in interpretive practices. Our work does not collectively pursue one or the other of these angles, but most contributions tend to side with contingency and hence the plural conception of literature.

Having said so, it must be stressed that each volume in this series has a distinct methodological profile of its own. As its title indicates, *Northern Crossings* deals with aspects of circulation to and from Sweden—understood in structural terms as a semi-periphery rather than a reified national space. It is in that sense the most systemically oriented volume in this series. *Claiming Space*, by contrast, approaches the narrative inscription of places around the world mainly through interpretive methods. *Literature and the Making of the World* configures its object of inquiry as "literary practice" (both intra- and extratextual) and combines for that reason text-focused readings with book-historical and anthropological methods of inquiry. *Vernaculars in an Age of World Literatures*, finally, with its focus on the concept of the vernacular, combines interpretive readings with large-scale historical analyses.

As mentioned, it is the working hypothesis of the cosmopolitan–vernacular dynamic that brings these studies together. In the simplest and most general terms, this assumes that literature in different times is shaped through a combination of cosmopolitan and vernacular orientations. Indeed, the cosmopolitan–vernacular dynamic, we claim, *is precisely what is at stake in the world literature field*: not just the outward success or failure of certain texts, genres or literary languages, nor just the "refraction" of *national* literatures (Damrosch 2003: 281), but rather the always situated negotiation of cosmopolitan and vernacular orientations in the temporal unfolding of literary practice. The further implication—which extends beyond our contributions—is that such a methodology might allow for the articulation of "universality" after the collapse of "universalism" (Messling 2019).

Just as importantly, however, the cosmopolitan–vernacular dynamic should be understood as a falsifiable postulation: in the hypothetical case of Beecroft's (2015: 33) "epichoric," or strictly local, literary ecology it would hardly be meaningful to talk of a cosmopolitan orientation. The opposite point, that there might be texts, genres and modes of writing without any vernacular connection at all, is harder to make—but it is the case, for example, that standard Arabic or *fusha* can function as a cosmopolitan written standard that runs parallel to local (spoken) Arabic dialects (Tageldin 2018). We are not claiming, in other words, that the cosmopolitan–vernacular dynamic *must* apply in all literary contexts. Even more importantly, it does not operate in just one mode, nor is it necessarily always successful. To speak of the cosmopolitan–vernacular dynamic is an open proposition, in the sense that it does not prescribe in advance any particular weighting of cosmopolitan or vernacular tendencies. Although the cosmopolitan–vernacular dynamic is fundamentally a question of how literary values are shaped, just *how* these values should be understood and assessed can only be discovered by examining the particular case.

In adopting the cosmopolitan–vernacular perspective, we acknowledge our debt to Sheldon Pollock (2006), whose magisterial macro-historical analysis of pre-modern literary cultures in South Asia and Europe in *The Language of the Gods in the World of Men* offered a path-breaking comparison not just of the cosmopolitan literatures of Sanskrit and Latin, but more importantly of the historical constructedness of vernacular literatures. *Contra* the Romanticist assumption of vernacular authenticity and immediacy, Pollock (and Beecroft after him) argued that a historical approach to vernacular literatures will show how they tend to be elite projects shaped in reaction against a dominant cosmopolitan Other (such as the literate cultures of Latin and Sanskrit). To *literize* (standardize through writing) and *literarize* languages coded as vernaculars are to be understood as deliberate, politically motivated actions (Pollock 2006: 4–5).

Illuminating though such an explanatory model is, it should not be taken at face value as a transhistorical constant, nor need it be restricted to macro-historical analyses but can be applied equally to closer textual study. Contrary to Pollock's pre-modern focus, our four volumes engage with literature from the last 200 years (about half of the primary sources are contemporary), an epoch which marks a radical new departure in literary history. This is when *Weltliteratur* was conceptualized in the wake of the accelerating commodification of print literature, the emergence of comparative philology and the entrenchment of (and resistance to) European nationalism and imperialism. It is, hence, an era when cosmopolitan and vernacular orientations in literature have been reconfigured drastically in relation not least, if not only, to the cultural authority of "the West." An important aspect of this process has been the accelerating *vernacularization* of languages and literatures in all parts of the world. This needs to be understood in two ways. First, vernacularization entails the positioning of named languages, registers of language or local knowledges as inferior in the field of power, as for instance Aamir Mufti (2016) discusses in the context of India and Pakistan. But, secondly, vernacularization also involves the deliberate elevation of vernaculars, including what we more broadly call the "domain of vernacularity," as a resource for the construction of national or socially distinct literatures. Given the constitutively relational nature of vernacularization, this process needs to be thought of as unstable: it can change over time (an obvious example being how European vernaculars such as English and French became cosmopolitan, imperial languages), as well as shift momentarily across space (Spanish being transformed into an immigrant vernacular in the United States). Or, as has often been the case in Africa, a *literary* vernacularity has had to be crafted through adopted, formerly imperial languages.

With its connections to comparative philology and the German romantic aesthetics of Herder, Goethe, Schlegel and Schleiermacher, among others (for more on this see Noyes 2015, Bhattacharya 2016, Mufti 2016, Ahmed 2018), post-eighteenth-century vernacularization is a deeply ambivalent affair: its value-coding can be programmatically positive yet grounded in untenable essentializations of race and ethnicity. A particularly effective challenge to this legacy has been the interrogation of language boundaries and "artefactualized" languages (Blommaert 2010: 4), along with the critique of the "monolingual paradigm" (Yildiz 2012; see also Bauman and Briggs 2003, Heller-Roazen 2005, Sakai 2009, Minaard and Dembeck 2014, Stockhammer 2015, Gramling 2016, Tidigs and Huss 2017, Helgesson and Kullberg 2018). These debates are relevant to our work, not least since discourses of the vernacular have often been a tool for establishing a monolingual paradigm that effaces translingual conceptions of language (Adejunmobi 2004). Our heuristic employment of the term allows, however, for an alternative take on mono- and multilingualism. If the vernacular indicates a *relation*, it may entail a heteroglossic or translingual register "within" a named language (vernacular varieties of English, say), as much as an identity as a separate language vis-à-vis a dominant other (which, for example, was the position of Wolof in relation to imperial French). The social dimension of the vernacular also draws our attention to the relativity of communities of comprehension—the intimacy of a vernacular to one group will be perceived as opacity by others. Such fluidity in the definition and nature of the vernacular chimes well with the critique of linguistic "bordering" (Sakai 2009), but—and this is important—it also factors the wholly contextual dimension of social hierarchies into the analysis. This has two consequences. One is that it acknowledges the de facto importance of artefactualized language, particularly within literature, despite its *theoretical* untenability. In the world of publishing, the authority of standard varieties of English, French or Arabic—including their publishing infrastructures—cannot be wished away. Hence, when terms such as "centre" and "periphery" are used in *Northern Crossings* in the context of translational exchanges, this is not a normative judgement, but rather an attempt at descriptively conceptualizing a given state of affairs.

The other consequence is that a social conception of language opens up towards a wider frame of analysis. As argued in *Vernaculars in an Age of World Literatures* and elsewhere in our volumes, the vernacular is not "just" a linguistic matter, but implies rather an entire domain of vernacularity. This can be understood in metonymic terms as that which relates to proximate, intimate, domestic or local experiences and sensibilities, particularly in their linguistic registration. It has tremendous aesthetic as well as persuasive potential, but is also ideologically ambiguous. As Moradewun Adejunmobi's important work on West Africa shows, it is naive to assume that promotions of the vernacular are always "intrinsic and unproblematic exemplars of minority politics" (2005: 179). On the contrary, what she calls "discourses of the vernacular" have, intermittently, justified asymmetries of power under colonialism, as well as supported the political aspirations of subordinated groups, notably by those "at the forefront of interaction with the dominant foreign culture" (ibid.: 191). The dynamics of the vernacular will, in brief, always be strictly context-sensitive. From this it follows that an assessment of its political tenor can only be issued a posteriori.

If, when we embarked on this project, we found that the vernacular was an ignored or undertheorized term in world literature studies, this has changed to some extent in recent years. An important line of questioning in this regard concerns the extent to which the very term "vernacular" is possible to use outside of its particular European-latinate genealogy. Tageldin (2018: 115), for one, has observantly noted the instability of the term's field of reference—it is "terminological quicksand"—but her account of Arabic supports rather than refutes the heuristic value of using the term "vernacular" comparatively: it is often the case, we find, that when the vernacular transforms into a deliberate literary project, "middle registers" of writing which fixate the flux of spoken language abound. In literary practice, that is to say, the vernacular oscillates between being a medium and being a citation within the medium. Interestingly, this need not work very differently in oral or performative modes of verbal art, which also exhibit the qualities of craftedness and quotability (see Barber 2007). Against this backdrop, the value of a "comparativist assessment of vernacular styles and political practices across the globe," as Sieglinde Lemke (2009: 9) puts it, should be evident. And this is precisely what numerous case studies carried out in these four volumes demonstrate.

We should note here that much of the critique *against* world literature as a field of study has argued that the vernacular is what world literature leaves behind. If the basic motivation for world literature as a disciplinary commitment could be described in terms of a cosmopolitan ethics, this has, in turn, often been accused of being an elitist, Eurocentric or politically aloof concern. There is by now an entire sub-field of debates in this vein whose most common articulation has been that of postcolonialism "versus" world literature (Rosendahl Thomsen 2008, Hitchcock 2010, Huggan 2011, Shankar 2012, Spivak 2012, Young 2011, Boehmer 2014, Helgesson 2014, Slaughter 2014, Mufti 2016, Tiwari and Damrosch 2019 and 2020, Sturm-Trigonakis 2020). The more recent contributions to this discussion tend, however, also to identify points of convergence between these positions. Our take on this is that if postcolonialism is ideologically primed to speak on behalf of the vernacular (whose proximity to concepts such as the subaltern or indigeneity should not pass unnoticed), an actual attention to vernacular orientations also shows their relevance far beyond strictly postcolonial concerns. We are, in other words, claiming that the cosmopolitan-vernacular optic engages the postcolonial perspective, without effacing or supplanting it.

At this point, however, it is of some urgency also to address the cosmopolitan dimension of our methodology. As mentioned, world literature and cosmopolitanism were revived as concerns in academia more or less in tandem in the post-1989 phase: if world literature is underwritten by a fundamentally cosmopolitan ethos of openness towards the other, it also offers the more philosophical concerns of cosmopolitanism an empirical field of study. Even more importantly, the gradual turn from such philosophically normative approaches to a descriptive conception of cosmopolitanism as "a characteristic and possession of substantial social collectivities, often nonelite collectivities that had cosmopolitanism thrust upon them" (Robbins and Horta 2017: 3) offers yet further scope for its coupling with world literature. Not unlike Pollock (2000: 593), who considers cosmopolitanism as something people "do rather than something they declare, as practice rather than proposition," our own work in these volumes is informed not by any a priori definition of what a cosmopolitan space or stance is, but, again, by a relational premise: terms such as "cosmopolitan," "cosmopolitanism" and "cosmopolitanization" have meaning only insofar as they set themselves off against other modes of belonging, or, better, other orientations. But to complicate things further, cosmopolitan orientations, insofar as they are verbalized, must have a *specific* linguistic signature; this signature, in turn, might more often than not be positioned as vernacular. Conversely, vernacular orientations may, under the right conditions (such as an attachment to a global language) have a cosmopolitan appeal. An example of the latter could be the Antillean French of Patrick Chamoiseau's Goncourt-winning novel *Texaco* (1992). An example of the former is Rabindranath Tagore's ([1907] 2015) famous lecture in 1907 on world literature, held in the late colonial period when Tagore's Bengali—a formidable language of literature and erudition—was still regarded by the British as a vernacular. It is in other words crucial to think of the cosmopolitan and the vernacular orientations as *different* but not as mutually exclusive *opposites*, in a schematic sense. Homi Bhabha (1996), not least, has inspired such a view by speaking of vernacular cosmopolitanism (Werbner 2006). To grasp how these orientations might interact, it is therefore imperative to emphasize that the cosmopolitan–vernacular dynamic is also, and fundamentally, a matter of translation—which could be illustrated by how Tagore's lecture is only accessible to us who are writing this introduction in its English version. As with the vernacular, however, the cosmopolitan tendencies are also ambiguous when translation enters the picture. If cosmopolitan orientations are at work whenever transnational structures or agents—be it Anglophone, French, Chinese or any other cross-cultural exportation of literature—exercise their power over less well-endowed literary spaces, it may equally be the case that the cosmopolitan orientation of translational practice creates intercultural channels and mindsets that challenge isolationist tendencies. As Robbins and Horta (2017) explain, cosmopolitanism has always both a positive and a negative definition. In positive terms, it embraces a wider humanity; in negative terms, it fosters detachment. This duality also applies to literary modes of cosmopolitanism, which indicates how *location* must always be factored into the cosmopolitan–vernacular analysis, even if it is a negatively conceived locality (as a consequence of detachment). There is, strictly speaking, no "world space," no vaguely conceived orbit "out there" where world literature exists in its separate realm. Instead, any postulation or imaginary of a wider world necessarily implies a particular "here." This premise is made explicit in *Claiming Space*, whose readings are organized by way of the two terms "location" and "orientation," and in *Literature and the Making of the World*, where the focus on literary practice links the textual and fictive aspects of literature to the emplaced and linguistically inflected work of writers, editors or, in one case, a maker of scrapbooks. The word "world" emerges here as double-coded, as both the life-world once theorized by Hannah Arendt ([1958] 1998) and others, and as an imagined world with a wider scope—and this imagined world, it turns out, is typically nurtured by modes of writing, much as Don Quixote once mistook his romances for the world.

The world, then, can be made and sustained through literary practice, a perspective which also offers a particularly strong motivation for our incorporation of anthropological approaches to literature in our volumes. Not only is the immediate relevance of anthropology evident when engaging terms such as "vernacular," "cosmopolitan," and "world," but we also claim that the defamiliarizing gaze of anthropology on the literary domain helps literary scholarship to move beyond excessive textualism. The work of Karin Barber (2007) serves as a rich source of inspiration, but there is also a long-running debate on the relation of literature to ethnography (Coundouriotis 1999, Desai 2001, Debaene 2010, Kullberg 2013, Izzo 2019) as well as a subfield of literary anthropology which has grown rapidly in recent years (Rapport 1994, Cohen 2013, Wulff 2017, Hemer 2020, Uimonen 2020). In the latter instance in particular, there has been a consistent development of methods for cultural, temporal and biographical contextualization of literary texts relating vernacular–cosmopolitan dynamics. A central idea here is that the anthropologist and the author are fellow intellectuals and thus the author's commentary is key to understanding issues such as choice of topic, the writing process, the literary career, the publishing industry and the literary market, as well as the circulation of books. This, juxtaposed with the anthropologist's ethnographic observations, can reveal analytical aspects of world literature that are not obvious from the texts alone. It is for this reason that our volumes integrate contributions that build on anthropological methods, such as ethnographic observations during literary festivals, readings and book launches, combined with extensive in-depth interviews of authors.

Our four volumes will appear in staggered fashion in 2021 and 2022, so depending on when exactly you as reader are encountering this general introduction, not all of them may yet be available. Regardless, we will end by briefly describing their profiles.

As already indicated, *Claiming Space*'s contribution to our larger project is its specification of the cosmopolitan and vernacular vectors in terms of "location" and "orientation." This enables a refined analysis of spatial imaginaries in literature. This volume pays attention to language, forms of aesthetic worlding and processes of translation and distribution, while its edge is turned towards the spatial and territorial politics involved in literary practices and works in the late twentieth and early twenty-first centuries. Locations, we argue, are inhabited or claimed by means of vernacular or cosmopolitan strategies, choices that are also visible in the orientations bound up with these sites. In dialogue with the critical geopolitics of culture, with sociology and anthropology, our attention to literary locations and orientations brings spatial particularity into the reckoning of vernacular and cosmopolitan relationality. Explicitly expressed or implied, manifesting itself sometimes as *dis*location and *dis*orientation, the claiming of space by any symbolic means necessarily is revealed as a constant effect of literary practice.

Vernaculars in an Age of World Literatures attempts to theorize the vernacular. As indicated in the discussion above, our point of departure is that the vernacular is always plural: not limited to language alone but comprising various types of expressions, material objects, people and environments. Moreover, its significance and value change with time and context. From a European point of view, it has been identified with the consolidation of national literatures, but in other contexts it has been associated with diaspora and movements of the marginalized or else, like in early twentieth-century China, it needs to be adapted to a specific literary and linguistic tradition to be useful as a concept. Sometimes, but not always, it works as an expression of resistance to the hegemony of cultural centres. Yet this seemingly inherent heterogeneity and variability is precisely what makes the vernacular a productive concept for rethinking world literature today. In nine case studies approaching a select number of narratives from the long twentieth century, from more or less marginal contexts, the volume explores how the concept may be put into practice and demonstrates how vernaculars operate within different literary, critical, cultural and political circumstances.

In the collectively authored *Northern Crossings* we analyse cosmopolitanizing and vernacularizing translational processes from the point of view of the literary semi-periphery. Literary traffic to and from Swedish displays a nuanced palette of diverse intercultural relations. The world literary system has hitherto been predominantly described from a binary centre–periphery perspective. A focus on the semi-periphery makes visible other important phenomena in the formation of interlingual literary flows. Our studies show that the logic of integration into new literary cultures does not follow one set of principles or a single pattern. The strategies employed by publishers, translators and other intermediaries in adapting the foreign text to a new literary culture always put the cosmopolitan–vernacular dynamic into play, but exactly what processes are implemented depends on a wide range of variables, such as genre, narrative technique, literary style, textual and authorial position in source and target cultures, publishing agendas, translator profiles and overall relations between specific literary cultures.

Literature and the Making of the World, finally, engages the cosmopolitan–vernacular dynamic by focusing on a range of literary practices and materialities. In its first section, "Worlds in texts," the world-making potential of place, genre and language is explored in readings of, among other things, French nineteenth-century novels, Lu Xun's "A Madman's Diary" and Siberian exile writing. The second section, "Texts in worlds," looks at literary journals, the profession of travel writers, the social world of a scrapbook keeper in Harlem and the trajectory of a contemporary novel in the Indian language Kannada with a view to fleshing out, in an anthropological spirit, the "world" of world literature as an experiential and embodied category. In contrast to macro-scale varieties of world literature studies, the empirically fine-grained contributions to this volume bring close reading, book history, ethnography and historical contextualization to bear on its selected instances of literary practice.

References

Adejunmobi, M. (2004), *Vernacular Palaver: Imaginations of the Local and Non-native Languages in West Africa*, Clevedon: Multilingual Matters.

Adejunmobi, M. (2005), "Major and Minor Discourses of the Vernacular: Discrepant African Histories," in F. Lionnet and S. Shih (eds), *Minor Transnationalism*, 179–97, Durham, NC: Duke University Press.

Ahmed, S. (2018), *Archaeology of Babel: The Colonial Foundation of the Humanities*, Stanford, CA: Stanford University Press.

Apter, E. (2013), *Against World Literature: On the Politics of Untranslatability*, London: Verso.

Arendt, H. ([1958] 1998), *The Human Condition*, Chicago, IL: Chicago University Press.

Auerbach, E. (1952), "Philologie der Weltliteratur," in W. Henschen, W. Muschg and E. Staiger (eds), *Weltliteratur: Festgabe für Fritz Strich zum 70. Geburtstag*, 39–50, Bern.

Barber, K. (2007), *The Anthropology of Texts, Persons and Publics*, Cambridge: Cambridge University Press.

Bauman, R. and C. Briggs (2003), *Voices of Modernity: Language Ideologies and the Politics of Inequality*, Cambridge: Cambridge University Press.

Beecroft A. (2015), *An Ecology of World Literature*, London: Verso.

Bhabha, H. (1996), "Unsatisfied: Notes on Vernacular Cosmopolitanism," in L. Garcia-Morena and P. Pfeifer (eds), *Text and Nation*, 191–207, London: Camden House.

Bhattacharya, B. (2016), "On Comparatism in the Colony: Archives, Methods, and the Project of *Weltliteratur*," *Critical Inquiry*, 42: 677–711.

Blommaert, J. (2010), *The Sociolinguistics of Globalization*, Cambridge: Cambridge University Press.

Boehmer, E. (2014), "The World and the Postcolonial," *European Review*, 22 (2): 299–308.

Boehmer, E. (2018), *Postcolonial Poetics*, Cham: Palgrave Macmillan.

Buzelin, H. and C. Baraldi (2016), "Sociology and Translation Studies: Two Disciplines Meeting," in Y. Gambier and L. Van Doorslaer (eds), *Border Crossings: Translation Studies and Other Disciplines*, 117–39, Amsterdam: John Benjamins.

Casanova, P. (1999), *La République mondiale des lettres*, Paris: Seuil.

Cheah, P. (2008), "What Is a World? On World Literature as World-Making Activity," *Daedalus*, 13: 26–38.

Cheah, P. (2016), *What Is a World? On Postcolonial Literature as World Literature*, Durham, NC: Duke University Press.

Cheah, P. (2017), "Worlding Literature: Living with Tiger Spirits," *Diacritics*, 45 (2): 86–114.

Cohen, M., ed. (2013), *Novel Approaches to Anthropology: Contributions to Literary Anthropology*, New York: Lexington Books.

Coundouriotis, E. (1999), *Claiming History: Colonialism, Ethnography, and the Novel*, New York: Columbia University Press.

Da, N. (2019), "The Computational Case against Computational Literary Studies," *Critical Inquiry*, 45: 601–39.

Damrosch, D. (2003). *What Is World Literature?* Princeton, NJ: Princeton University Press.

Debaene, V. (2010), *L'Adieu au voyage. L'ethnologie française entre science et littérature*, Paris: Gallimard.

Desai, G. (2001), *Subject to Colonialism: African Self-Fashioning and the Colonial Library*, Durham, NC: Duke University Press.

De Swaan, A. (2001), *Words of the World: The Global Language System*, Cambridge: Polity Press.

Ette, O. (2016), *TransArea: A Literary History of Globalization*, trans. Mark W. Person, Berlin: De Gruyter.

Ganguly, D. (2016), *This Thing Called the World: The Contemporary Novel as Global Form*, Durham, NC: Duke University Press.

Gramling, D. (2016), *The Invention of Monolingualism*, New York: Bloomsbury.

Hayot, E. (2012), *On Literary Worlds*, Oxford: Oxford University Press.

Heilbron, J. (1999), "Book Translation as a Cultural World-System," *European Journal of Social Theory*, 2 (4): 429–44.

Heilbron, J. (2020), "Obtaining World Fame from the Periphery," *Dutch Crossing: Journal of Low Countries Studies*, 44 (2): 136–44.

Helgesson, S. (2014), "Postcolonialism and World Literature: Rethinking the Boundaries," *Interventions*, 16 (4): 483–500.

Helgesson, S. and C. Kullberg (2018), "Translingual Events: World Literature and the Making of Language," *Journal of World Literature*, 3 (2): 136–52.

Helgesson, S. and P. Vermeulen, eds (2016), *Institutions of World Literature: Writing, Translation, Markets*, New York: Routledge.

Heller-Roazen, D. (2005), *Echolalias: On the Forgetting of Language*, New York: Zone Books.

Hemer, O. (2020), *Contaminations and Ethnographic Fictions: Southern Crossings*, Cham: Palgrave.

Hitchcock, P. (2010), *The Long Space: Transnationalism and Postcolonial Form*, Stanford, CA: Stanford University Press.

Huggan, G. (2011), "The Trouble with World Literature," in A. Behdad and D. Thomas (eds), *A Companion to Comparative Literature*, 490–506, Oxford: Blackwell.

Izzo, J. (2019), *Experiments with Empire: Anthropology and Fiction in the French Atlantic*, Durham, NC: Duke University Press.

Kullberg, C. (2013), *Poetics of Ethnography in Martinican Narratives: Exploring the Self and the Environment*, Charlottesville, VA: University of Virginia Press.

Laachir, K., S. Marzagora and F. Orsini (2018), "Significant Geographies: In Lieu of World Literature," *Journal of World Literature*, 3 (3): 290–310.

Leffler, Y. (2020), *Swedish Nineteenth-Century Literature and World Literature: Transnational Success and Literary History*, Gothenburg: Göteborg University.

Lemke, S. (2009), *The Vernacular Matters of American Literature*, Basingstoke: Palgrave Macmillan.

Mani, B. V. (2017), *Recoding World Literature: Libraries, Print Culture, and Germany's Pact with Books*, New York: Fordham University Press.

McGann, J. (1991), *The Textual Condition*, Princeton, NJ: Princeton University Press.

Messling, M. (2019), *Universalität nach dem Universalismus: über frankophonen Literaturen der Gegenwart*, Berlin: Matthes & Seitz.

Minaard, L. and T. Dembeck (2014), "Introduction: How to Challenge the Myth of Monolingualism?," *Thamyris/Intersecting*, 28: 9–14.

Moretti, F. (2000), "Conjectures on World Literature," *New Left Review*, 1: 54–68.

Mufti, A. (2016), *Forget English! Orientalisms and World Literatures*, Cambridge, MA: Harvard University Press.

Neumann, B. and G. Rippl (2017), "Anglophone World Literatures: Introduction," *Anglia*, 135 (1): 1–20.

Noyes, J. (2015), *Herder: Aesthetics against Imperialism*, Toronto: University of Toronto Press.

Orsini, F. (2004), "India in the Mirror of World Fiction," in C. Prendergast (ed.), *Debating World Literature*, 319–33, London: Verso.

Orsini, F. (2015), "The Multilingual Local in World Literature," *Comparative Literature*, 67 (4): 345–74.

Pollock, S. (2000), "Cosmopolitan and Vernacular in History," *Public Culture*, 12 (3): 591–625.

Pollock, S. (2006), *The Language of the Gods in the World of Men*, Berkeley, CA: University of California Press.

Rapport, N. (1994), *The Prose and the Passion: Anthropology, Literature and the Writing of E.M. Forster*, Manchester: Manchester University Press.

Richter, S. (2017), *Eine Weltgeschichte der deutschsprachigen Literatur*, Munich: Bertelsmann.

Robbins, B. and P. Horta (2017), *Cosmopolitanisms*, New York: New York University Press.

Rosendahl Thomsen, M. (2008), *Mapping World Literature: International Canonization and Translational Literatures*, London: Continuum.

Sakai, N. (2009), "How Do We Count a Language? Translation and Discontinuity," *Translation Studies*, 2 (1): 71–88.

Sánchez-Prado, I. (2018) *Strategic Occidentalism: On Mexican Fiction, the NeoliberalBook Market, and the Question of World Literature*, Evanston, IL: Northwestern University Press.

Sapiro, G., ed. (2008), *Translatio: le marché de traduction en France à l'heure de la mondialisation*, Paris: CNRS éditions.

Shankar, S. (2012), *Flesh and Fish Blood: Postcolonialism, Translation, and the Vernacular*, Berkeley, CA: University of California Press.

Slaughter, J. (2014), "World Literature as Property," *Alif*, 34: 39–73.

Spivak, G. (2012), "The Stakes of a World Literature," in G. Spivak, *An Aesthetic Education in the Era of Globalization*, 455–66, Cambridge, MA: Harvard University Press.

Stockhammer, R. (2015), "Wie deutsch ist es? Glottamimetische, -diegetische, -pithanone, und -aporetische Verfahren in der Literatur," *Arcadia*, 50: 146–72.

Sturm-Trigonakis, E., ed. (2020), *World Literature and the Postcolonial*, Berlin: Springer.

Tageldin, S.M. (2018), "Beyond Latinity, Can the Vernacular Speak?," *Comparative Literature*, 70 (2): 114–31.

Tagore, R. ([1907] 2015), "Vishva Sahitya," trans. R. Das and M. R. Paranjape, in D. Benerjii (ed.), *Rabindranath Tagore in the 21st Century*, 277–88, New Delhi: Springer.

Tidigs, J. and M. Huss (2017), "The Noise of Multilingualism: Reader Diversity, Linguistic Borders and Literary Multimodality," *Critical Multilingualism Studies*, 5 (1): 208–35.

Tiwari, B. and D. Damrosch, eds (2019 and 2020), Special issues on world literature and postcolonial studies, *Journal of World Literature* 4 (3) and 5 (3).

Uimonen, P. (2020), *Invoking Flora Nwapa: Nigerian Women Writers, Femininity and Spirituality in World Literature*, Stockholm: Stockholm University Press.

Warner, M. (2002), "Publics and Counterpublics," *Public Culture*, 14 (1): 49–90.

Warwick Research Collective (WReC) (2015), *Combined and Uneven Development: Towards a New Theory of World-Literature*, Liverpool: Liverpool University Press.

Werbner, P. (2006), "Vernacular Cosmopolitanism," *Theory, Culture & Society*, 23 (2–3): 496–8.

Wulff, H. (2017), *Rhythms of Writing: An Anthropology of Irish Literature*, London: Bloomsbury.

Yildiz, Y. (2012), *Beyond the Mother Tongue: The Postmonolingual Condition*, New York: Fordham University Press.

Young, R. J. C. (2011), "World Literature and Postcolonialism," in T. D'haen, D. Damrosch and D. Kadir (eds), *The Routledge Companion to World Literature*, 213–22. Oxon: Routledge.

Introduction: Theorizing the vernacular

Christina Kullberg and David Watson

> ... *the great angst of the vernacular is its spatio-temporal entropy.*
> —Sheldon Pollock, "Cosmopolitan and Vernacular in History"

It may already be too late for the vernacular. Sheldon Pollock begins the epilogue to *The Language of the Gods in the World of Men: Sanskrit, Culture, and Power in Premodern India* (2006)—his magisterial study of the cosmopolitan and vernacular—by warning the reader about the gradual disappearance of vernacular languages. The globalization of English, he argues, is resulting in a homogenization of language and culture, a "reduction of diversity in the cultural ecosystem" (567) comparable to the global decline in biological diversity during the last decades. Consequently, we are facing a stark choice between a homogenous globalism, and a violent alliance between nationalism and vernacular cultures intent on policing and excluding difference (568). From this perspective, two futures, both cruel, remain open to vernacular cultures: to dissolve into a globally deployed yet uneven neoliberal culture, or to become complicit with a reassertion of exclusionary national and group formations.

More than a decade later, we are now well into the millennium that would put an end to the vernacular. At first glance it seems like both cruel versions of Pollock's prophecy have been realized. Even languages such as French that were considered to be dominating thirty years ago have lost prestige and function under the pressure of global English. Nationalism along with violent populism expand across the world, paradoxically enough often by means of global English used on social media platforms. One could even add to the dark scenario by suggesting that this is indeed also the closure of the literary millennium and the end of the book. Yet, apocalyptic images such as these rarely give the whole picture. Is it so that accounts heralding the end of the vernacular or suspecting it of allying itself with a resurgent nationalism

(Kymlicka 2001) reflect a certain blindness in theory and method to account for it in an operative, productive way?

Our argument here is that it is not too late for the vernacular, which is to say we should neither view it solely as a residual formation that is fading away quickly, nor solely associate it with often-reactionary, populist political cultures. On the contrary, given the precarious historical moment that we now experience to various degrees of acuteness, critical engagements with literature in the world—what is generally referred to as world literature—prompts a theorization of the vernacular. Our time, shaped by a long century of decolonization, new imperial formations, and emergent new technologies, is indeed an age that requires a different take on the vernacular. We cannot, as was arguably the case when Goethe famously coined the notion of world literature, take the West, or the "canon" or even print culture and the world market as points of departure for thinking literature in the world. Climate crises, rising economic inequalities, platform capitalism, growing populisms and activisms spur new attention to the active role of the local, the indigenous, the minor, and the peripheral in international literary flows and exchanges. This is where our volume wants to make a contribution by rethinking the vernacular through its various practices, functions, and meanings. The case studies brought together here explore the vernacular in different places, cultures, and historical moments. By means of different methodologies from literary studies, anthropology, linguistics, and history of ideas, they testify that the vernacular is not just one thing. It is always plural and shifting. And as a protean category, the vernacular should not be dismissed too quickly as if we always already know what it signifies, but should instead be rethought and explored time and time again for what it tells us about the variegated, uneven globe we inhabit and its cultures.

Such a project runs into an immediate problem. The development of the still emergent field of world literary studies is to a large extent inimical to an exploration of vernacular formations. From David Damrosch and Franco Moretti, world literature, whether it is understood as a network of texts, as a "mode of reading" or as an intellectual discourse (Tihanov 2018: 468), puts the emphasis on texts that "gain in translation" in a broad sense (linguistically, thematically, culturally) and therefore are marketable and circulate easily (Damrosch 2003: 281). Despite accurate criticism, notably from postcolonial scholars, that world literature could as well be called "literature for the West" (D'Haen 2013: 2–3), researchers within the field continue to equate world literature with cosmopolitanism. It is said to belong nowhere and everywhere—"at home in any place; free from local attachments or prejudices"—and as such it is the literary expression of a world citizen, a cosmopolitan subject belonging everywhere and nowhere. The problem here is not so much the characterization of world literature as being "homeless" in the world, but that the equation builds on a binary opposition between the cosmopolitan and the vernacular and emphasizes, as well, exchanges between center and periphery, forgetting and occluding other circuits of circulation and modes of being in the world, and eliding thereby the place of the vernacular from discussion within world literary studies. This has consequences for *what* is being considered world literature and *how* we read these texts. Studying the evolution of the contemporary novel, Rebecca Walkowitz (2015), for instance, shows how politics of translation and global English impact on novels with worldly ambitions; they are "born translated" and thus more internationally marketable. Walkowitz continues to argue that the high commercialization of literatures of the world does not pass unchallenged, partly due to individual authors from peripheral places, often working between languages, who infuse their globally exchangeable prose with differences and to the fact that global English itself multiplies and is provincialized as it spreads across the world. In an attempt to shift the focus from circulation and the "born translated," Emily Apter (2013) famously argued *against* world literature by insisting on the untranslatability of certain textual dimensions. But to identify the vernacular too quickly with what remains untranslatable in today's world literary field is to risk reducing it to an object or expression of difference, and equating it too easily with the local, the "exotic," or the national—formations easily considered anachronistic today. In this framework, put bluntly, either literature from small places and languages must adopt a form and style that abide by rules set by an English-speaking market or else it can resist these demands by remaining local. The premise and risk remain the same: the local is separated from the global, elite cosmopolitanism from popular or regional vernaculars.

In theorizations that do engage more overtly with the vernacular, particularly when examining the consolidation of a specific (national) literature, the vernacular is often only considered as a step toward a cosmopolitan language within which it is subsumed. Pascale Casanova's now classic account of the emergence of French as the language of the "World Republic of Letters" (2004) is a paradigmatic instance of such a move. The problem is that this approach captures the cosmopolitan destiny of the vernacular, not necessarily the vernacular as a concept in itself. As Pollock puts it, the vernacular is understood as a "response to a specific history of domination and enforced change, along with a critique of the oppression of tradition itself, tempered by a strategic desire to locate resources for a cosmopolitan future in vernacular ways of being themselves" (2000: 624). In other contexts, the vernacular is analyzed as an expression of resistance to the hegemony of cultural centers, as occurs, for example, when multilingual literature mobilizes a defense of local languages against the homogenizing pressure of imposed colonial languages and global English. Here, too, the vernacular is not the starting point for analysis but is framed as a reaction to cosmopolitan domination and relegated to a secondary position within the literary field.

Our contention is that this glossing over of the vernacular hides problematic tendencies within studies of world literature. A consequence of the expectations surrounding the proper object of world literature—the globe, its colonial geography, and so on—is that small-scale circulation, from one small language to another, for instance, goes under the radar. Moreover, while contemporary literary criticism may be leaving the vernacular behind it is also the case that recent fiction by authors ranging from James Kelman to Marlon James and Patrice Nganang are saturated with different vernaculars and that more authors in West Africa for example chose to write in vernacular. It is also the case that an increasing number of local publishing houses have surfaced in places like the Caribbean and publish local authors for regional audiences even while establishing new global networks. Moreover, it is indisputably the case that histories of migration and diaspora have resulted in the global dissemination and transformation of vernacular traces of the local, as notably research on African-American literature has demonstrated (Lemke 2009). The international success of hip-hop sufficiently shows how vernacular expressions reach well beyond locality and are transformed when received in another context.

This volume argues that the vernacular can and does indeed intervene productively in the shaping of world literature as an aesthetic strategy, in terms of a mode of reading, and as a global network of texts. Even more so, it poses serious questions to the field. Can theories and methods of world literature encompass the opposite of the cosmopolitan? And if that is indeed the case, as we suggest here, how can we theorize the vernacular, in time, space, and language, in a manner that interacts with, and contributes to, world literature studies? It is the ambition of this volume to calculate what this inclusion would mean for how we think about world literature, and, in the obverse, how accounts of world literature force us to rethink and reimagine the vernacular. We seek to bring out the vernacular as an operative and analytical *concept*, in itself containing manifold versions of itself, rather than as a thing in and of itself, a category that functions as a short-hand for national literatures as is often the case within the European literary field. This is challenging in so far as the set of terms used to carry out this investigation is broadly Western (European) and thus, as Shaden Tageldin (2018) warns, does not always operate in accordance with the material or their spatio-temporal contexts. However, as chapters in this volume dealing with China and West Africa demonstrate, even if there might not be a vernacular equivalent to "the vernacular," the concept may nonetheless be useful as a critical tool for reading, or misreading productively, temporal and spatial layers in a text, for reading tensions between scripts and orality, between languages of power.

In many ways the concept of the vernacular we seek to activate productively in this volume is indebted to some of the oldest ways of thinking about it. Etymologically, the word derives from learned Latin *vernaculus*, referring to slaves born in the house. It is defined as *particular to a country, to its habitants; synonymous with native, domestic, indigenous*; a language spoken by the people, often equated with the mother tongue and vulgar language. The implicit association with slavery has made it particularly useful in conceptualizing those subordinate peripheral formations and modes of circulation that are often obliterated in world literature theories. At the same time, the second connotation of the term—the domestic—highlights a sense of attachment to a place or a community, suggesting a resistance to universalizing claims of any theory of literature. Yet looking at Dante Alighieri's *De vulgari eloquentia*, it becomes clear that the domestic connotation is intimately tied to the shifting character of what he called vulgar languages. Exiled from his local Florence, Dante perceived the language spoken by people in their everyday life as mobile as opposed to stagnated "grammar" or Latin. Here the vernacular is understood in terms of orality rather than written language, in the sense that it is the first language we hear when we begin to distinguish sounds—a definition that echoes in African literatures where the term "mother tongue" is often used (Warner 2019). It is a language acquired without instruction, whereas "grammar" needs to be taught following set rules rather than life. Dante thus reversed the dominant reasoning around languages by eulogizing the vernacular as an expression of a universal and natural *human* quality:

> Of these two kinds of language, the more noble is the vernacular: first, because it was the language originally used by the human race; second, because the whole

world employs it, though with different pronunciations and using different words; and third, because it is natural to us, while the other is, in contrast, artificial.

(1996: 3)

The vernacular acquires value here not from being extremely local but from the fact that everyone speaks it, an insight that would later allow for particular instances of the vernacular to be reframed as national, perhaps even proto-democratic, forms of language. Dante himself does not distinguish one vernacular language from others but considers *the* vernacular, which translates into the human ability to speak and acquire a language. He defines it in relation to speech (*locutione*), to body, and to practice. In the vernacular, sound (senses) and meaning (reason) merge as an expression of distinctively and perfectible human qualities. The plurality of languages across the world is an expression of the richness of that perfectibility.

For Dante, then, even within one vernacular, languages multiply: there are different languages for different arts and crafts (one for architects, one for masons, etc.). Language is thus valued in terms of communication, practice, and creativity; it is the means by which human beings get by in everyday life, cultivate gardens, and construct worlds. These functions both deterritorialize *and* locate the vernacular. It is a language that *works* precisely because it is not set by rules, but evolves as it adapts to the situation. In this perspective—and contrary to the logic of contemporary nationalisms—the vernacular would not hold the promise of stability, nor would it be inimical to circulation. Rather, it would be a language between a person and her immediate surroundings, between practitioners in a particular context determined by time and purpose. As such the vernacular, due to the mobility of the speakers propelling new linguistic circumstances, would be transforming and include all kinds of expressions, not only linguistic. Curiously, then, Dante's ever emerging vernacular recalls a process of creolization or language mixing, transforming through time, whereas grammar is presented as a bordering performance that singles out *a* language. Italian, French, and Spanish were long considered to be "corrupt" versions of Latin, a description historically used for explaining the emergence of Creole languages too (Bachmann 2013). The vernacular, as it were, is a language that cannot be counted, to rephrase Naoki Sakai (2009); it is shifting because it opens up to other languages.

We thus understand the vernacular as a concept that would not refer to a specific object but rather capture a precodified status of language and culture undergoing the fraught, contested process of becoming *a* language or *a* culture.

The meaning and function of vernacular changes with time and place, and depends on a range of factors such as actors, media, and oppositional forces. This conceptualization of the term allows for discussing language and culture *in statu nascendi*, thus better capturing the variety of aesthetic engagements with the vernacular in different contexts and in different times. It can be used as an identity marker in nationalist formations. It can also be an instrument for subaltern resistance. As seen in Kamau Brathwaite's "jazz-novel," the vernacular may reach well beyond language as an object and include non-verbal expressions, sensibilities, and rhythm. In the current state of global warming, vernacular literary explorations extend to engagement with the non-human world, as in Patrick Chamoiseau's novel *Les Neuf consciences du Malfini* (2009) which is narrated from the perspective of a bird and attempts to account for the local Caribbean experience of climate crisis. As such it may open up new modes of reading literature in the world that draws attention to the co-production of literature and the world rather than to a pre-established canon of texts or map of the globe. To put this otherwise, to view the vernacular as the *statu nascendi* of literary language provides this volume with the means to analyze the world literary trajectory of a text.

As will be demonstrated in the case studies, the vernacular can be used as a pluriform concept rather than as a thing in itself. It will thus mean different things and do different things depending on context and methodology, leaving it open for constant negotiations. In order to situate our conceptualization of the term, what follows in the rest of this theoretical introduction is an account of how it has been used within world literary studies, first on a temporal scale in regard to the deep-history of the field and to the rise of nation-formations, which is imbricated in the notion of world literature, and second, on a spatial scale where we discuss the concept in relation to minor, sub-altern, and diasporic movements. Perhaps counterintuitively, it is precisely because of the tensions between the different uses and interpretations of the vernacular that we propose it as an operative concept for reading literatures in the world.

The vernacular in global deep histories and in the rise of the nation-state

The recent critical turn toward world literary studies has necessitated the rethinking of the vernacular in various ways. It has rendered legible the importance of the vernacular to literary history across millennia by extending deep into the past the study of vernacular formations, and, thereby, necessitating a comparative analysis of the concept of the vernacular. In doing so it has also shifted attention for such an investigation away from European history, secular modernity, and the formation of the nation-state. Christian Høgel (2018) for instance argues for the term trans-imperialism to do better justice for how literature circulated in earlier periods. In this and many other accounts of literary circulation and formation beyond the modern nation-state, it becomes obvious that the connection between power and politics, language and literature is still there, only it is not the West that is taken as a point of departure or a model for explanation. The decolonization of world literature by means of a *longue durée* perspective is thus not a de-politicization of the term. Quite to the contrary, language and literature are considered in terms of power struggles, which in turn entails that vernacular and cosmopolitan languages emerge in relation to one another.

When a language, through various means, is then constituted and articulated in relation to another dominant language it enters into a process of *vernacularization*. This is the term used by Alexander Beecroft, Pascale Casanova, and Sheldon Pollock, in different contexts, to describe the consolidation of a language with regard to time and space and, ultimately, in literature that differentiates itself from a cosmopolitan language. Pollock, for instance, identifies a connection between increasing movements among peoples simultaneously in southern Asia and western Europe around the eighth century AD, which, following on a cosmopolitan epoch, saw the emergence of vernacular languages and literary cultures, and assisted in inaugurating the early modern period. It is here that he localizes the vernacular millennium, which is now supposedly brought to a close.

Leaving aside the anxieties imbuing Pollock's account, part of the significance of his work for our understanding of the vernacular is that he explores it by rethinking the time frame and temporal scale within which vernacular languages and literatures are to be investigated. Within the enlarged frame proposed by his study the premodern and modern are interlinked, and the vernacular emerges as the subject of a continuous history stretching across a millennium. It is clear that Pollock's "vernacular millennium" shares in the turn within the emergent field of world literary studies toward new enlarged time frames or scalar expansions. In his critique of this turn in "Prolegomena to a Cosmopolitanism in Deep Time" (2016), Bruce Robbins identifies three discreet reasons for the new methodological investment in expanded time frames: a movement initially occurring within postcolonial studies to engage as Pollock does with cultures and texts predating modernity, attention to ecological degradation and the enlarged time frames such a project requires, and the international indigenous movement which has drawn attention to non-European colonial ventures. And indeed, such an expanded frame could widen and deepen our understandings of the cosmopolitan and vernacular dynamics in East Asia where literary Chinese, *wenyan*, was, in Denecke's and Zhang's terms, the *scripta franca* (Denecke and Zhang 2015: vii–viii) and the main medium of communication between the elites for almost two millennia up until the twentieth century. Japan, Vietnam, and Korea had adopted the Chinese script and the Chinese literary language although it was pronounced in local, "vernacular" languages. Chapter 6 of this volume discusses how China underwent radical language reforms in the first half of the twentieth century with the creation of a modern vernacular Chinese in which the oral *baihua* and the scriptural *wenyan* was fused. In Chapter 9, we see how this language reform, along with the linguistic effects of Mao's cultural revolution, mark even contemporary literature, written in French by Chinese authors in exile.

The methodological investment in enlarged timescapes, or "deep time" as Robbins puts it, has shaped recent inquiries other than Pollock's into the vernacular and its literatures. For instance, Beecroft's exploration of vernacular literature in his *An Ecology of World Literature: From Antiquity to the Present Day* (2015) situates this literature within a time frame dwarfing even the vernacular millennium. According to him, vernacular literature developed in a series of consecutive historical waves, "beginning with the emergence of ancient Near Eastern vernaculars about three thousand years ago, followed by the emergence of a series of vernaculars in Europe and the Mediterranean between the third century BC and the fourth century AD, and then by Pollock's vernacular millennium beginning around the eight century AD" (148). Each one of the vernacular ecologies, to use his term, is preceded by a cosmopolitan tradition, which it emulates and transforms. In the long history Beecroft is narrating, once the vernacular has supplanted the cosmopolitan it too gives way to a different literary ecology: 'when the era of the coexistence of cosmopolitan and vernacular came to an end, it was a specifically European ecology that was to take its place," he argues, "that of the national literature" (193). Indeed, national literature plays a similar role in Beecroft's account as the globalization of English does in Pollock's history, with both signaling if not the end of the history of the vernacular then certainly a transformation in its status as the dominant literary ecology of an epoch.

Ecological metaphors such as Beecroft's are absent in Casanova's *The World Republic of Letters* (2004). She reads instead the constitution of languages and the flows of literature through a grid borrowed from Pierre Bourdieu's sociology. Consequently, rather than referring to organic constellations, she insists on the institutional dimension of the relationship between the vernacular and the cosmopolitan. Vernacularization understood in political terms translates as a struggle for recognition: it is the process by which a local language gains in value so that it can compete with another, cosmopolitan, language's dominance. Literature is crucial in Casanova's model, since print culture makes it possible for a language to intervene in the formation of knowledge and ultimately in the shaping of politics. This leads her to conclude that even national literatures are a global affair, as they are "constructed through literary rivalries, which are always denied, and struggles, which are always international" (36). Accordingly, it was because Joachim du Bellay's *La Deffence et illustration de la langue francoyse* (1549) marked "the first time that a national literature had been founded in a complex relation to another nation and, through it, another language, one that moreover was dominant and apparently indomitable, namely Latin" (46), that it became the foundation of the world republic of letters, not because it eulogized France or the French language. Nonetheless, the effect of Du Bellay's treatise was that France reversed the power balance in a century and a half and became the dominant literary power of Europe, to the extent that Paris, according to Casanova, still holds its central place as the cultural capital of the world, even if English is the global language and the economic power resides elsewhere.

This model is somewhat nuanced in *La Langue mondiale: traduction et domination* (2015). Here Casanova points out the impossibility of localizing a moment in time when French took over Latin for instance, citing Lodge's contention that standard language is a dialect among other dialects (25). She concludes that a language only becomes prestigious once its users (*les locuteurs et les scripteurs*) give it prestige and significance beyond the communicative function of language (29). The transition from vernacular into a prestigious language was, in the case of French, supported by a conscientious strategy that had little to do with regional attachment. The Renaissance authors of the Pléiade-group to which Du Bellay belonged validated French by borrowing from the Ancients (51). Put differently: the vernacular became a literary language by means of plagiarism. Reading between the lines, Casanova seems to adopt a French libertine conception of language: as a language enters into the grammar of sociability, its arbitrary quality increases, it becomes artificial. In this process, vernacularization "denaturalizes" local language by turning it into a cosmopolitan language and distinguishing it from other languages viewed as vernacular. Not only does vernacularization produce a travesty of another language, but also far from the authenticity and the naturality often implied in the idea of the mother tongue, its *originality* (in the double sense of the term) lies in a construction: the lexical, topical, and phraseological borrowings are converted into something characteristic of that vernacular.

Casanova's demonstration sharply proves that equating the vernacular with authenticity is historically inaccurate and theoretically suspect. If the vernacular is interpreted as an expression of cultural authenticity, it is charged with a particular political meaning occluding that it is in itself a construction. But as old regimes fell and new state formations emerged in Europe in the late eighteenth century and all through the nineteenth century, language became the bearer of the nation and by extension the people. The standardization of vernaculars through the establishment of academies of letters and dictionaries since the seventeenth century became a principle for unifying the people under the state. The process almost mirrors vernacularization around the eighth century AD: now the vernacular, which had become cosmopolitan, turns inward to seal a pact between its speakers, the space of belonging, and the space of power. Yet, as we can see by studying peripheral regions like the Baltic, discussed in Chapter 7, this process did not follow a neat evolutionary chronology. The case of Aino Kallas' Estonian novels from the 1920s also show that the presumably local sources of inspiration for constructing a vernacular literature for the new nation-state were indeed multicultural and even written in languages of foreign powers that had been dominating the region.

However, this inward turn produced by the alliance between language and nation-building projects should not lead us to overlook that the re-vernacularization of cosmopolitan languages that occurred in the nineteenth century and onward came about in part as a result of globalization and colonization. It is in this light that John K. Noyes (2015) reads the key thinker of place, language, and literature as foundation of that collective identity that forms the modern nation-state, the German philosopher Johann Gottfried Herder. It must be said that the influence of Herder's thoughts on the importance of the vernacular language can hardly be overstated. It planted the seeds for the growth of a truly cosmopolitan phenomenon—the nation-state—and the incessant philological activity that accompanied it put the study of literature at the service of power and paved the way for the scholarly literary disciplines divided by language as well as for comparative literature. As problematic as Herder is, Noyes manages to rescue him from the far-right and reads his investment in the local as a critical response to globalization during the colonial expansion of the second half of the eighteenth century. Imperialist expansion made the European intellectual discover the infinite diversity of the world, but also that imperialism, in its brutal exploitation, was a threat to that very diversity. According to Noyes, it was the knowledge about the horrors of imperialism that motivated Herder to develop an attachment to locality and language in terms of anti-imperialist thinking. In this context he developed the notion of *Volk*, "people," referring to more than just the inhabitants of a place. *Volk* implied an ethnic and cultural community, carried by a common language so that it became interwoven with or even synonymous to the nation. If the *Volk* was to survive and prosper, it had to search for its own, particular soul instead of following cosmopolitan standards, including writing in cosmopolitan languages. This did not necessarily mean closing in on the region. On the contrary, other vernaculars were mobilized in the articulation of *Volk* culture; Herder found inspiration in faraway languages, such as Peruvian oral poetry (Tihanov 2018: 476–7). Its stance is thus global but in terms of an exoticizing of other languages. And in this turn, language becomes an expression of authenticity and origins.

We may fruitfully contrast this account with that of Benedict Anderson on the nation as an "imagined community." He conceives of the nation as a community or "sociological organism moving calendrically through homogenous, empty time" (1983: 26). In Anderson's reasoning, the possibility to imagine the nation came when three fundamental conceptions began losing their grip: the idea that a particular script language offered privileged access to ontological truth, precisely because it was an inseparable part of that truth; the belief that society was naturally organized under sovereigns ruling by divine dispensation; and third, a conception of temporality in which cosmology and history were indistinguishable, the origins of the world and of people essentially identical. The slow decline of these certainties was caused by economic change, social and scientific discoveries, and the development of increasingly rapid communications. But the stark alliance between nation, people, and language identified by Anderson as taking the place of these certainties denies the vernacular the ability to transform, excludes it from mobility, and denies it temporal "coevalness," to use anthropologist Johannes Fabian's term (Fabian 2014). The modern nation-state thus seems to impose a particular time frame onto the vernacular languages of the world, either by forcing them to enter into modernity by means of cultural and linguistic assimilation with the nation-state or by refusing them entry into modernity.

Juxtaposing Herder and Anderson, it seems like the imagined community of the nation-state is built upon a fundamentally contradictory relationship to vernaculars. On the one hand, the world's cultural and linguistic diversity is revealed and used as an argument against the centralization of power under one monarch in one place. As such the thought of the nation state appears as an incitement to anti-imperialism which was the case in Latin America and the Spanish islands of the Caribbean in the late nineteenth century. Still using the language of the imperial power—Spanish—Cuban authors turned to native Caribbean mythology and African diasporic songs and storytelling to challenge Spain's authority in the Americas. This would in the twentieth century explode into a vernacular literary language where Spanish was fused with Creole, Afro-Cuban and indigenous cultural expressions in the work of Alejo Carpentier and José Lezama Lima, for example, that questioned the post-independence dictatorships. On the other side of the spectrum, the standardization of language within the Western modern nation-state, a language that made it possible to imagine a community, occurred at the expense of linguistic diversity. Chapter 2 in this volume makes this point clear by investigating the complicated process behind the construction of Castilian as the language of Spain under Franco. The dictatorship forcefully struck down the other languages of the country. Yet, as the chapter shows, this linguistic repression was not monolithic but adapted to the situation and to the particularity of the different languages in Spain. The vernacular is situated here in a precarious position within a modernity in which language, culture, and the nation-state enter into an often-exclusionary alliance. At the same time, in other contexts, such as East Asia, where a cosmopolitan language, literary Chinese, had for almost two millennia been coexisting with various local languages, the link between vernacularization and the emergence of nations was built on a long history of complicated linguistic negotiations (Zhou 2011: 129–30).

It is undoubtedly the romantic understanding of the vernacular as a vehicle for a specific locality, culture, and authenticity that has prevailed in European thought and thus framed much of how the vernacular has been opposed to and subjugated under the cosmopolitan in world literary theory. As argued in Chapter 3, this has further consequences for literatures deemed vernacular in a Eurocentric partition of the literatures in the world, which has been at the basis of world literature since Goethe. Working through and practicing translations, the chapter demonstrates how the romantic-nationalist reading eschews complex spatial and temporal trajectories within a literature—in this case Tamil classics. Another example of other processes of vernacularization beyond both the nation and the cosmopolitan destiny would be the Saamaka maroon community discussed in Chapter 5. Leaning on international law, the community won the right to both their territory and language over the Surinam government and Chinese multinational companies in 2007. At the same time, parts of Saamaka culture risk being lost as young Saamaka are today spread across the globe and the chapter offers an anthropological approach to how Saamaka history is passed on to new generations. Our volume accounts for different temporal trajectories of the term vernacular, thus clearly showing that vernacularity as an expression of the local and of "authenticity" is not "natural"; it is a product of a particular time and place. This insight should not, however, belittle the fact that the political consequences of such a construction of the vernacular in complicity with the rise of the nation-state have been far-reaching, even violent, and still affect us today.

Vernacular mobilities in the diaspora and the post-colony

Once the language of the nation-state was imposed onto speakers of other languages by means of universal education, the spread of print culture, and of political administration, it became a strong force of domination over other peoples. For this reason, postcolonial scholars in particular have wondered what an account of the vernacular that is oriented more towards complex interlinkages between national and imperial as well as cosmopolitan and vernacular formations—formations frequently threaded together by an unprecedented increase in human mobility, willing or unwilling—would look like. For instance, by the turn of the millennium, Homi K. Bhabha (2000) framed the postcolonial subject in terms of a "vernacular cosmopolitanism," who despite colonial oppression and inequalities could enter into global exchanges as a citizen of the world. Here, as previously in *Location of Culture* (1998), Bhabha is primarily interested in interrogating the liminality of the (postcolonial) contemporary subject, caught between the local and the global. Vernacular is associated with subalternity to put it simply. Yet implicitly this means that it is only by adapting a cosmopolitan posture that the vernacular, or its subject, can be relevant to the world, while another type of vernacular, the one that stays at home, remains excluded from modernity. As S. Shankar argues in *Flesh and Fish Blood* (2012), the emphasis on hybridity and up-rootedness within postcolonial studies has made the field "suspicious of any robust idea of the local or the vernacular" (20); it has failed to acknowledge vernacular modes of knowledge "oriented away from the transnational, the modern, and the hybrid and toward the local, the traditional, and the culturally autonomous" (1).

Taking his examples from the Indian context, Shankar defines the vernacular in terms of local languages and literatures. Rather than tracing a sense of belonging, as in Pollock's reading of vernaculars in the deep history of Chinese literature, Shankar detects global concerns in these texts. The postcolonial vernacular would thus be a local expression of the anxiety of modernity. In other words, the vernacular becomes a way to question the frames in which we usually think of the world be it from the point of view of the nation or that of the cosmopolitan. In an interesting turn, Shankar reaches beyond the postcolonial moment by reading the vernacular in light of universalism and humanism. Vernacular humanism, he claims, is marked by an anxiety; it does not assume its own humanness, but redefines the human from their own particular perspective and in so doing articulates a "conflicted approach to the universal that is not yet ready to relinquish an orientation toward the rooted, the culturally autonomous, and the local" (100). In comparison with Casanova's model of prestige and consecration within the world literary system, Shankar's local angle suggests that the vernacular does not necessarily seek to take the place of a dominant language. It can be understood as an assertion that questions the exclusionary grounds of universalism and humanism alike.

Voices critical of the postcolonial approach, or rather its inability to approach the vernacular, have also been raised in African contexts. In *Vernacular Palavers: Imaginations of the Local and Non-Native Languages in West Africa* (2004), Moradewun Adejunmobi suggests that it is necessary to get rid of the presupposition that using colonial language is a matter of decolonial struggle or is indicative of a desire for recognition. History shows that the promotion of local languages has also been a tool for asserting power over colonial subjects in West Africa. Adejunmobi problematizes the common assumption that "a return to the mother tongue would imply a remedy to alienation" (viii) caused by colonial suppression. The response to alienation is here instead to open up towards the world as if the mother tongue is not a language but an expression of practice that articulates itself by finding resonance in other contexts. Focusing on the vernacular reveals a different pattern where colonial and postcolonial subjects alike have adjusted to a polyglot life. In Chapter 1 in this volume, Adejunmobi extends this discussion in relation to Afrobeat, showing that the vernacular is not necessarily equivalent to a traditional expression, or to writing in either the mother tongue or the colonial language, but serves to distinguish between the local and the non-local in a particular context.

In the African diaspora, however, the meaning of the local has undergone a significant shift. In *The Vernacular Matters in American Literature* (2009), Sieglinde Lemke argues that the vernacular should be identified with the "expressions of culturally excluded people," whether by virtue of race, class, or gender, and that its usage "signals a lack of cultural capital" (3), in part because the vernacular is often understood as being synonymous with the popular. The vernacular participates then in a politics of recognition attuned to cultural difference and different processes of exclusion and marginalization. In the context of transatlantic slavery, the etymological roots of the vernacular obviously come out with particular force and frame it within an urgent contemporary politics. Grant Farred approaches the vernacular, or what he terms vernacularity, in a similar albeit more radical fashion than Lemke in his *What's My Name: Black Vernacular Intellectuals* (2003). According to Farred, vernacular speech signifies economic and political disenfranchisements, it is politicized "minority discourse" (17) that is "characterized by its informality, its nontraditional grammatical structures, its discursive hybridity, and its proclivity for drawing on and incorporating other cultural formations, even other languages" (18). As already politicized discourse, vernacular utterances are often political themselves and substitute for other modes of engagement in the public sphere and civil society. Farred and Lemke are writing from a critical tradition in which vernacular expression is associated with the language of the disenfranchised, dispossessed, and social movements. The vernacular signifies for them cultural differences and political contestations. Moreover, it is understood as embodying a diversity—that of languages, culture, and the population—that exists in tension with the nation-state and its regular disavowal of such forms of difference.

As this perhaps suggests, one feature that has attached itself to critical treatments of vernacular formations we may very well gloss by using the notion of cultural survival. In his "On Cultural Survival" (2004), Gil Anidjar explains that what is at stake in the notion of cultural survival is the "community 'as it is,' mastering and controlling its past and its future, rather than living its changes in its intricate connections with alterities that can no longer be thought as simply *exterior*" (7–8). The notion of cultural survival encodes, then, something about the contingencies faced by different cultures, the temporalities of risk, endurance or extinction that come into play once a cultural formation becomes intent on reproducing itself into a future identical with its present. Chapter 4 in this volume investigates how poetry from the Lesser Antilles mediates such a mode of cultural survival in the wake of hurricanes Maria and Irma in 2017. The vernacular here is not necessarily located in linguistic terms but in rhythm and sound language. Another, similar mode of survival is at stake when Vicente Rafael details in his *Motherless Tongues: The Insurgency of Language amid Wars of Translation* (2016) how the language policies of the United States both at home, especially in relation to immigrants, but also within imperial contexts, such as its occupation of the Philippines, have regularly resulted in the suppression of vernacular languages in favor of American English. He describes this process as a form of "repression that amounts to an act of translation, transforming a train of possible expressions into a grammatically correct and stylistically recognizable discourse" (1). Speaking of the Philippines, he argues that the repression of local languages and vernaculars in favor of English "turned natives neither into Filipinos nor Americans but into failed copies of the latter" (30). Rafael's depiction of Filipinos as sent "ontologically adrift by English" (30) serves as a stark reminder of what is at stake in the survival of vernacular formations in imperial and national contexts. But as Rafael notes, the desire for a shared, singular language, for a disavowal of linguistic plurality, also stems from a desire for cultural survival. He argues that "signs of linguistic difference," of different languages and vernaculars, are often experienced as a "cultural assault" (93) to be readdressed by an assertion of monolingualism. The desire for cultural survival emerges here as a shared currency circulating between, for instance, migrant communities, colonized subject, as well as the nation-state.

One mode of survival, of course, relies on the circulation of the vernacular. Arguing that African American literature should be considered as a diasporic and not a national formation, Wai Chee Dimock reads this literature as a "linguistic force—articulated in the vernacular rather than in formal speech—and as bearing witness to the global migration of tongues, the mixing of syntax and phonemes across continents" (2006: 142). Drawing on linguistic studies of the black vernacular as a creole form incorporating traces of an African past into standard English, Dimock argues that the vernacular produces and testifies to routes and pathways stretching across centuries and interlinking Africa, the Caribbean, and the United States. In this account, the expanded time frame within which Dimock situates African American literature is not exactly the result of a methodological choice made by the critic, as it is for Pollock and Beecroft. Rather, it is in a sense produced by instances of the vernacular itself, by acts of language that summon forth past histories and suggest the consanguinity of distant places. In other words, the vernacular houses and memorializes a long history stretching back across slavery, the Middle Passage, and the African beginnings of this diasporic literary formation. In this respect Dimock's work, as she acknowledges, is indebted to that of such Caribbean authors as Wilson Harris. Harris, in his *The Womb of Space: The Cross-Cultural Imagination* (1983), identifies what he terms "primordial resources within a living language" that, once activated, produce an experience of "simultaneity in the imagination of times past and future" (1983: x). Dimock, like Harris, invites us to imagine a vernacular language as a heterochrony, a collection of slices of time that carries traces of the past into the present and future, and undulates its own non-linear, expansive temporality. To put this more concretely, the vernacular continues to bear witness to a "global migration of tongues," as she glosses the violent acts of enslavement and expulsion making up the history of the Black Atlantic. Chapter 8 in this volume continues this exploration of the "migration of tongues" focusing on Marlon James' *A Brief History of Seven Killings*, the circulation of vernacular tongues and cultural forms in the hemispheric Americas, and the cultural and social impact of neoliberalism on Jamaica and its relation to the United States.

Moving away from the concerns of the American empire and back to the question of world literature that concerns us here, the "culturally excluded" would translate into that which passes unnoticed by center–periphery theories. This is the point made by Françoise Lionnet and Shu Mei Shih in *Minor Transnationalism* (2005) where they argue for the need for examining relationships among different margins, instead of studying the relationship between center and periphery in binary terms. Similarly, in *Vernacular Worlds, Cosmopolitan Imagination* (2015), Stephanos Stephanides and Stavros Karayanni explore the idea of *vernacular worlds* arising from "more scattered and less scripted" contexts. There are spaces of circulation and exchange that warrant further attention as they suggest that the vernacular operates regardless of the cosmopolitan. Or else, the vernacular may work *through* the cosmopolitan. An example in point would be indigenous, locally bounded literatures written in what Ronne Moberg and David Damrosh call "ultra-minor" languages that have reached well beyond their local origin thanks to translations into cosmopolitan English. Here, as in the work of Lionnet and Shih and some scholars of African American vernaculars, the tensions between margins and centers are conceptualized through Gilles

Deleuze and Félix Guattari's philosophy of language, more precisely the concept of minor literature (1991). It is not necessarily a literature of rootedness written by minorities, but a literature that cannot belong anywhere *because* it is minor. There is thus a crucial difference between minor and cosmopolitan literature as well. The former exists everywhere by virtue of its minor status, while the latter is the circumscribed domain of the elite, the powerful, the dominant. This allows for entering the local–global dynamics differently. Ultraminor vernaculars like Sámi literature may via cosmopolitan languages connect to other ultra-minor vernaculars without losing their vernacularity. The vernacular is thus not lost in translation, but gains political force by using the cosmopolitan as vehicle. Such rethinking of global dynamics adds yet another dimension to the complexity of the concept that motivates this volume. The vernacular is not only a language or a thing such as an expression of the local, rather it refers to certain potentiality of language to become something else; it is a pre-coded language that may be politically, aesthetically, or culturally charged.

Rethinking the vernacular

Where do all of these different histories and theorizations of the vernacular leave us? For one thing we may conclude that if the vernacular is on the path to extermination or is only an expression of narrow-minded and violent nationalisms, it clearly still sparks critical debate. It may be that the vernacular—in contrast to a reified, even exoticized, conception of the local—is best understood *in relation* to more expansive milieus such as the nation, the cosmopolitan, and the planet. To advance this argument requires a conception of the vernacular that associates it with different even conflicting vectors in the circulation of languages and cultures. Such an account would pay heed to Beecroft's contention that within European modernity the vernacular, whether as language or literature, is subsumed by and incorporated within the national, while also considering the fact that within this modernity imperial rule, settler colonialism, slavery, class struggles, and the movements of peoples and cultures have resulted in the production of regional, subnational vernacular formations (Jones 1999; Miller 2010; Rafael 2016) that remain at odds with official and national formations. But such an account would also pay attention to what Pollock describes as the "dialectic between cosmopolitan and vernacular that creates them both" (2000: 616).

Rather than attending to the tense situation of the vernacular in relation to the national we advance that it is necessary to explore the different flows and circulations constitutive of the vernacular. It may, for instance, become necessary to understand Franco Moretti's thesis concerning the history of the modern novel as naming one trajectory within Pollock's dialectic—the European form of the novel is *vernacularized* within the peripheries of the literary system when it is made to accommodate local content, including vernacular languages. Or in a contrastive vector, we may find in Casanova's account of the "Faulknerian revolution" (2004: 327) the resources to imagine the feedback loops whereby vernacular literatures modify cosmopolitan literary systems. William Faulkner's vernacular modernist aesthetic is indissociably bound to his project of giving expression to the numerous vernacular cultures and languages of the American South. Yet, in Casanova's account, in doing so he provides a model for writers in Algeria, the Caribbean, and Latin America as to how to activate the vernacular within literary forms also inhabiting the world literary system. Finally, we may consider whether the works of authors such as the African American modernist and anthropologist Zora Neale Hurston do not inhabit vernacular flows and circuits anterior to the cosmopolitan milieu of European modernity and world literature. Ostensibly engaging with the legacy of slavery in the United States, her *Their Eyes Were Watching God* (1937), much of it written in Haiti, incorporates the African American dialect alongside modernist narration, and moreover, alludes to West African cultural traditions she first encountered in the Caribbean (Pavlić 2004). In doing so the novel maps a diasporic terrain, and asks of us to resituate the drift of vernacular cultures within the circuits and coils of the Black Atlantic and the Middle Passage.

Such instances suggest that the vernacular is not simply to be equated with the local, but that it should be understood in relation to its mediations by the cosmopolitan and the national, how it transforms these in turn, and even in relation to vectors of the vernacular operative underneath European modernity. We argue, then, that the vernacular becomes visible within and is constituted by flows, forces, and antagonisms unleashed when the local is set flowing within the nation, the cosmopolitan, or across the globe. From such a vantage point the concept would have no pre-established ontological claim, as if existing outside and prior to other larger-scale formations, but would be constituted by the contact between different and uneven language and cultural formations. After all, we recognize the vernacular when it appears to be a subordinate peripheral formation within a larger system, which it may then transform or which may transform it in turn. Following on, to reintroduce it as a concept within world literary studies may very well be to reorient ourselves towards the fate of the peripheral and subordinate within such a system, which may include the transformation of the system itself.

As we have seen from the discussion above the vernacular goes well beyond literature as a form. It may respectively refer to "sensibilities," to "ways of belonging," to oral literature, to music, to culture in general with an attachment to locality or to a marginalized position. We must not forget that vernaculars operate in everyday life, where it is not first and foremost an instrument in a battle over power. The majority of language users remain untouched by language struggles in their daily lives and switch unproblematically between languages. Literature reflects this reality too. We may also conclude that the vernacular is always political, but not necessarily in the ways that we think. In some situations, it is a tool for contesting the current linguistic order. In others, it might be a way to make room for maneuver. It may express a sense of belonging to a place or a culture in order to consolidate a community against the surrounding world or in order to better communicate with other communities across the globe. Again, the notion of plurality is foregrounded not only in regard to the various types of expression, but also to the observation that the vernacular seems to emerge in multilingual situations. There are then a range of reasons to stretch the concept even further and think it beyond pre-established political formations and beyond a specific language, as a certain sensibility and a way of being in the world.

How can it be otherwise? If there is one thing to be learned from the history of the vernacular it is that the term contains a multiplicity, and is constituted by the various ways it has mediated the forces of the nation and empire, and has circulated across cosmopolitan milieus. That strange thing the vernacular is a conjunctural formation, transforming, retreating, advancing, and shapeshifting in relation to the uneven system of languages and cultures it inhabits and refracts. For this reason, we may wonder about prognoses worrying about the demise of the vernacular. The contemporary global linguistic landscape can hardly be understood solely in terms of an Anglo-globalism is which English accompanies the global unrolling of the neoliberal economy. Within contemporary neoliberalism, language is linked to entrepreneurship, personal enterprise, and profit (Rojo 2018). While many languages are viewed as subordinate to English in such a system, the acquisition of a new language, online services in multiple languages, and, related, multilingual work at, for instance, call centers or within tourist industries are all ways in which issues of language and mediation are connected with the global economy (Pujolar 2018). It may be that such an environment, perhaps best described as a hierarchical multilingual milieu, fosters rather than inhibits the growth of new vernacular formations.

Note: This theoretical introduction is the result of a collective work by the members of the "Vernacularities" group in the research program "Vernacular and Cosmopolitan Dynamics in World Literatures." The critical discussions with Christian Claesson, Elisabeth Herrmann, Katarina Leppänen, Shuangyi Li, Lena Rydholm, and Irmy Schweiger have been crucial for the writing of this chapter. Our special gratitude goes to Gahlin Tihanov for his perspicacious reading of the text and for his engagement with our project.

References

Adejunmobi, M. (2004), *Vernacular Palaver: Imaginations of the Local and Non-Native Languages in West Africa*, Bristol: Multilingual Matters.

Anderson, B. (1983), *Imagined Communities: Reflections on the Origin and the Spread of Nationalism*, New York: Verso.

Anidjar, G. (2004), "On Cultural Survival," *Angelaki. Journal of the Theoretical Humanities*, 9 (2): 5–15.

Appiah, K. A. (2005), *The Ethics of Identity*, Princeton, NJ: Princeton University Press.

Apter, E. (2013), *Against World Literature: On the Politics of Untranslatability*, New York: Verso.

Bachmann, I. (2013), "Creoles," in M. Maiden, J. C. Smith, and A. Ledgeway (eds), *Cambridge History of the Romance Languages* (CHRL), 400–44, Cambridge: Cambridge University Press.

Beecroft, A. (2015), *An Ecology of World Literature: From Antiquity to the Present Day*, New York: Verso.

Bhabha, H. K. (1998), *The Location of Culture*, New York: Routledge.

Bhabha, H. K. (2000), "The Vernacular Cosmopolitan," in F. Dennis and N. Khan (eds), *Voices of the Crossing: The Impact of Britain on Writers from Asia, the Caribbean, and Africa*, 133–42, London: Serpent's Tail.

Biti, V. (2013), "The Fissured Identity of Literature: The Birth of National Literary History Out of International Cultural Transfers," *Journal of Literary Theory*, 7 (1): 1–30.

Casanova, P. (2004 [1999]), *The World Republic of Letters*, trans. M. DeBevoise, Cambridge, MA: Harvard University Press.

Casanova, P. (2015), *La Langue mondiale: traduction et domination*, Paris: Éditions du Seuil.

Chamoiseau, P. (2009), *Les Neuf consciences du Malfini*, Paris: Gallimard.

Dante, A. (1996), *De vulgari eloquentia*, trans. S. Botterill, Cambridge: Cambridge University Press.

Damrosch, D. (2003), *What is World Literature?* Princeton, NJ: Princeton University Press.

Damrosch, D. and B. Moberg (2017), "Defining the Ultraminor," *Journal of World Literature*, 2 (2): 133–7.

Deleuze, G. and F. Guattari (1991), *Kafka: Pour une littérature mineure*, Paris: Les Éditions de Minuit.

Denecke, W. and L. Zhang, (2015), "Series Editors' Foreword" to East Asian Comparative Literature and Culture Series, in J. A. Fogel (ed.), *The Emergence of the Modern Sino-Japanese Lexicon*, v.i–ix, Leiden: Brill.

Dimock, W. Ch. (2006), *Through Other Continents: American Literature Across Deep Time*, Princeton, NJ: Princeton University Press.

Du Bellay, J. (1549), *La Deffence et Illustration de la langue francoyse*, Paris: Arnoul L'Angelier.

Fabian, J. (2014 [1983]), *Time and the Other: How Anthropology Makes its Object*, New York: Columbia University Press.

Farred, G. (2003), *What's My Name Black Vernacular Intellectuals*, Minneapolis: University of Minnesota Press.

D'Haen, T. (2013), "Major Histories, Minor Literatures, and World Authors," *Comparative Literature and Culture*, 15 (5): https://doi.org/10.7771/1481-4374.2342.

Harris, W. (1983), *The Womb of Space: The Cross-Cultural Imagination*, Westport: Praeger.

Hurston, Z. N. (2006 [1937]), *Their Eyes Were Watching God*, New York: Amistad.

Høgel, C. (2018), "World Literature Is Trans-Imperial: A Medieval and a Modern Approach," *Medieval Worlds*, 8 3–21.

Jones, G. (1999), *Strange Talk: The Politics of Dialect Literature in Gilded Age America*, Berkeley: University of California Press.

Kymlicka, W. (2001), *Politics in the Vernacular: Nationalism, Multiculturalism, and Citizenship*, Oxford: Oxford University Press.

Lemke, S. (2009), *The Vernacular Matters in American Literature*, London: Palgrave.

Leonhardt, J. (2013), *Latin: Story of a Language*, Cambridge, MA: Harvard University Press.

Lionnet, F. and S-m, Shih, eds. (2005), *Minor Transnationalism*, Durham, NC: Duke University Press.

Miller, J. L. (2010), *Accented America: The Cultural Politics of Multilingual Modernism*, Oxford: Oxford University Press.

Moradewun, A. (2004), *Vernacular Palavers: Imaginations of the Local and Non-Native Languages in West Africa*, Clevedon: Multilingual Matters.

Mufti, A. (2018), *Forget English! Orientalism and World Literatures*, Cambridge, MA: Harvard University Press.

Noyes, J. K. (2015), *Herder: Aesthetics against Imperialism*, Toronto: University of Toronto Press.

Pavlić, E. M. (2004), "'Papa Legba, Ouvrier Barriere Por Moi Passer': Esu in 'Their Eyes' & Zora Neale Hurston's Diasporic Modernism," *African American Review*, 38(1): 61–85.

Pollock, S. (2000), "Cosmopolitan and Vernacular in History," *Public Culture*, 12(3): 591–625.

Pollock, S. (2006), *The Language of the Gods in the World of Men: Sanskrit, Culture, and Power in Premodern India*, Berkeley: University of California Press.

Pujolar, J. (2018), "Postnationalism and Language Commodification," in J. W. Tollefson and M. Pérez-Milans (eds), *The Oxford Handbook of Language Policy and Planning*, 486–504, Oxford: Oxford University Press.

Rafael, V. (2016), *Motherless Tongues: The Insurgency of Language amid Wars of Translation*, Durham, NC: Duke University Press.

Robbins, B. (2016), "Prolegomena to a Cosmopolitanism in Deep Time," *Interventions*, 18 (2): 172–86.

Rojo, Luisa Martín (2018), "Neoliberalism and Linguistic Govermentality," in J. W. Tollefson and M. Pérez-Milans (eds), *The Oxford Handbook of Language Policy and Planning*, 545–64, Oxford: Oxford University Press.

Sakai, N. (2009), "How Do We Count a Language? Translation and Discontinuity," *Journal of Translation Studies*, 2: 71–88.

Shankar, S. (2012), *Flesh and Fish Blood: Postcolonialism, Translation and the Vernacular*, Los Angeles: University of California Press.

Stephanides, S. and S. Karayanni, eds. (2015), *Vernacular Worlds, Cosmopolitan Imagination*, Leiden: Brill.

Tageldin, S. (2018), "Beyond Latinity: Can the Vernacular Speak," *Comparative Literature*, 70 (2): 114–31.

Tihanov, G. (2018), "The Location of World Literature," in W. Fang (ed.), *Tensions in World Literature: Between the Local and the Universal*, 77–99, Singapore: Springer.

Walkowitz, R. (2015), *Born Translated: The Contemporary Novel in an Age of World Literature*, New York: Columbia University Press.

Warner, T. (2019), *The Tongue-Tied Imagination: Decolonizing Literary Modernity in Senegal*, New York: Fordham University Press.

Zhou, G. (2011), *Placing the Modern Chinese Vernacular in Transnational Literature*, New York: Palgrave Macmillan.

1

Contextualizing the vernacular: Signposts from African languages, writing, and literature

Moradewun Adejunmobi

This chapter considers the evolving functions and status of ideas about the vernacular as an expression of what Sheldon Pollock (2000: 591–2) famously called an attachment to "the smaller place" rather than "the larger world." And it does so from the perspective of African interactions with the idea of the vernacular. Speaking about Europe and the Indian subcontinent, Pollock (1998a: 41) further described the accompanying project of vernacularization as "a process of change by which the universalistic orders, formations, and practices of the preceding millennium were supplemented and gradually replaced by localized forms." Pollock (1998a: 45) associates this process with a deliberate turning towards languages that do not travel as the predominant languages of the ensuing political unit that he calls the vernacular polity. In reflecting on what the vernacular is and signifies in the context of African societies in this chapter, special attention will be given to the ways in which African conceptions of vernacular literacy and developments in literary writing from the mid-twentieth to the early twenty-first century do or do not appear to instantiate a process of vernacularization. The chapter will also weigh the degree to which such attachments to the smaller place are manifested in a foregrounding of vernacular languages and vernacular writing, and the degree to which commitments to vernacular languages factor into the international circulation of African literature and textual forms more broadly.

My principal argument is that if we think of vernacularization as the course of renouncing the larger place for the smaller place as Pollock (2000: 592) puts it, then this is indeed a process that we see unfolding in political terms in several sites on the African continent in the early twenty-first century. And yet, the ramifications of vernacularization for initiatives intended to bolster vernacular literacy and thus vernacular literature have been far from predictable. In general, support for smaller polities has not often been accompanied by a commitment to policies and practices advancing the interests of languages that distinguish the smaller political unit from larger political units. At the same time and since the mid-twentieth century, writing in the vernacular has continued to grow for several African languages.[1] However, much of this literature does not enter into the mainstream of African literature, let alone the mainstream of world literature, or if it does, it does not do so in vernacular languages.[2] Still, the notion of the vernacular remains eminently useful even for those African authors whose works circulate internationally and usually in non-native languages, under the banner of world literature. This is because affiliations with the vernacular often serve to authenticate distinctive cultural provenance. Nonetheless, vernacular languages seldom function as the principal medium through which the most prominent literary texts circulate in written form even within a singular African country, let alone within the African continent as a whole, and beyond the African continent. But a strong or tenuous connection with vernacular languages almost always strengthens the cultural claims made for a work that circulates internationally. Support for these observations will be provided in what follows in the rest of the chapter.

Defining the vernacular

To start with, one might ask, what exactly is the vernacular? In recognition of the many competing definitions of the vernacular, Shaden Tageldin says the vernacular is "terminological quicksand" (2018: 115). In a similar vein, S. Shankar had earlier remarked that the "*vernacular* has multiple meanings"

---

[1] Much of this writing occurs in languages that are official languages like Kiswahili or Amharic, or in languages that are spoken by a significant majority in particular countries, such as Hausa and Yoruba in Nigeria, or Zulu in South Africa, or Setswana in Botswana.

[2] Many of these African-language texts are published by relatively small presses within individual countries that make the published texts available mainly for students in primary and secondary schools as well as universities. For reasons that will be discussed in further detail later in the chapter, these texts rarely circulate beyond an individual country and beyond literate native speakers of the language of the text within that country. This does not necessarily mean that these texts are inward looking. For example, Mwangi (2017) says: "African-language texts published by small firms and for local audiences grapple with the issues of cosmopolitanism and hospitality to the foreign, especially borrowing metaphors from translation practices" (6). Similarly, Karin Barber (1997) remarks that the authors of three Yoruba language novels written during the colonial period were not "narrowly parochial" and addressed "readers as *representatives* of a much larger constituency: a community of all 'eniyan dudu' (Africans/black people), present and future—a 'we' that reaches beyond the horizon" (115; emphasis in original).

(2012: 133). Citing the dictionary, Tageldin further proposes that we might define the vernacular as "native or indigenous, non-literary, nonstandard, spoken or oral, colloquial, everyday, nonspecialized" (2018: 114).

Among African creative writers, the term vernacular has often been understood as a reference to another language-related concept that attracts special reverence, namely the concept of the mother tongue. The Senegalese writer, Cheikh Aliou Ndao, described the mother tongue as "'the language that nurses you' [làmmiñ wi nga nàmp]" (Warner 2019: 214). The Tanzanian author, Shaaban bin Robert, likewise mobilizes mammary metaphors when he describes the mother tongue "as his mother's breast, a 'titi la mama'" (Mwangi 2017: 48). There are, however, other ways of understanding what the vernacular might be in an African context. For example, the sociolinguist, Chege Githiora characterizes Sheng, a variety of Kenyan Swahili, as a Kenyan vernacular, as a way of alluding to the ease with which mostly younger Kenyans would default to speaking in Sheng, even when it was not a mother tongue. From this perspective, Githiora argues that "[a] significant population of Kenya speaks Sheng as their 'vernacular', that is as a variety of language used for spontaneous, natural expression by members of a speech community" (2018: 19). In describing Sheng as a Kenyan vernacular here, Githiora is not necessarily implying that the language functions as an avatar of irreducible nativeness. To the contrary, he has also underscored Sheng's cosmopolitan potential, pointing out that it is often deployed as a "pan-ethnic variety of Swahili attuned to global black culture" (172).

My own earlier definitions of the vernacular in discussions of African literature bring us back to the question of the mother tongue and stem from an awareness of the continuing preoccupation with mother tongues among African creative writers who advocate for writing in African languages. It is for this reason that I invoked the term vernacular to "describe language in its specific function as a mother tongue" (Adejunmobi 2004: 2). Given the significant levels of multilingualism and polyglotism registered in many African communities, I found it useful in thinking about literature and language in an African setting to distinguish between the varied functions of a language, in its capacity as lingua franca or language of wider communication for example, in contrast to deployment as mother tongue. This is a distinction that is critical for understanding the actual languages in which texts circulate when they travel beyond a community of native speakers of a given language. As noted further in this chapter, it is not always clear whether advocacy for writing in a language described as the vernacular among African writers is actually advocacy on behalf of a lingua franca or whether what is at stake is the possibility of writing in a mother tongue that is not also a lingua franca.

Given the tendency to conflate the mother tongue and the lingua franca in discussions about the vernacular, it is worth pointing out that Pollock's own reference to the rejection of universalistic orders for more localized forms does not necessarily imply adoption of a mother tongue by vernacular polities. What is more likely is that premodern (and indeed contemporary) vernacular polities often reverted to a local language that did not have as wide a reach as the language of universalistic orders, but which had the highest probability of sustaining an independent sphere of communication and creativity among all the local languages spoken within the polity. In that vein, I would further posit that invocations of the vernacular are above all claims to localness that principally matter for distinguishing between the local and the non-local.[3] What is presented as the vernacular may or may not have a long history in a particular region, as long as it serves to distinguish between the local and the non-local in a given context. This is a point that I will return to later when I discuss the example of Afrobeats.

There are other African authors who have also endorsed the principle of writing in an African language, or using an African originated script. The Ghanaian Ayi Kwei Armah's plea for writing in Egyptian hieroglyphics is one example (Mwangi 2017: 8). This too can be understood as a plea for a vernacular, distinguishing between an expansive sense of the local encompassing the entire African continent, and a non-local corresponding to the non-African, but does not necessarily equate to writing in either a first language or a mother tongue for any Africans alive today. In contrast, the call by the Kenyan writer Ngũgĩ wa Thiong'o for writing in African languages has often been misunderstood as a call for writing in all African languages when it was in fact a call for writing specifically in mother tongues envisioned as the true vernaculars for African writers. As made clear in Adejunmobi (2004: 21), African advocates for writing in African languages have not been consistent in distinguishing between writing in an African language that had become a lingua franca like Kiswahili and writing in an African language that had not become a lingua franca. Thus, Tanzania was sometimes presented as an example of a country that under its first president had encouraged citizens to write in their mother tongues. But what Julius Nyerere, Tanzania's first president in fact did was make Kiswahili—a language that was

---

[3] As noted by Adejunmobi, there is a need to move away "from the tendency to see the local and the foreign as fixed categories, exemplified inter alia, in choices to be made between using indigenous and non-native languages. On the contrary, these are classifications whose scope of application is in constant flux and always subject to revision" (2004: 134).

for the majority at that time, a second or third language—the official language of the country and the language of education.⁴ When some African writers like Wole Soyinka called for writing in African languages, what they had in mind was the elevation of a single African language like Kiswahili as the sole and unifying language of writing for all Africans.⁵ For many others, however, Ngũgĩ included, writing in an African language meant writing in one's mother tongue.

Against this backdrop, we can see that Ngũgĩ's position on writing in African languages actually differs from that of the Tanzanian author Shaaban, who described Kiswahili, the language in which he wrote, as his mother tongue, though as Mwangi (2017: 48) has indicated, Shaaban's first language was Yao, not Kiswahili.⁶ Shaaban's willingness to identify with a language that was not his first language is certainly in keeping with historical trends in Africa before the twentieth century. As Carola Lentz observes with respect to identities on the African continent in the past: "Communities could be based on neighbourhood, kinship and common loyalties to a king, but this did not absolutely have to include notions of a common origin, a common language or a common culture" (2000: 411). Friederike Lüpke echoes Lentz in noting that traditionally "African societies were and are not organized along ethnic and linguistic boundaries" (2021: 2). Notwithstanding this history, and as noted by Mwangi (2017: 48), both Ngũgĩ and Shaaban mobilized their divergent understandings of the concept of the mother tongue as a way of defining their respective homelands as a space preferably reserved for the speakers of the designated mother tongue, and not for the non-African residents who did not speak either Gikuyu (in Kenya) or Kiswahili (in Tanzania).

Renouncing the larger place, embracing the vernacular?

In postcolonial Africa, renouncing the larger unit for the smaller space has more often been accompanied by an association with a regionally distinctive language than with a commitment to promoting a mother tongue as the

---

⁴ In electing to make Kiswahili, which was already an emergent lingua franca, the national language, Nyerere, whose own mother tongue was not Kiswahili, exemplified the practice mentioned on the preceding page of choosing a local language that did not travel as widely as the language of universalistic orders, but which had the highest probability of sustaining an independent sphere of communication and creativity among all the local languages spoken within the polity.
⁵ See Soyinka (1988) for more on this
⁶ At that point, Kiswahili was a lingua franca in Tanzania, but rarely a mother tongue.

language of state or language of education, and especially higher education. For countries in North Africa that use Arabic, which is not the language of a recent colonizing power as the language of state and education, this is an idiom that is shared with several other countries in Africa and in the Middle East. Arabic is of course a distinctive language, but one of a vast pan-Arab region rather than of an individual country. This selection is also a choice that overlooks numerous first languages spoken in some of these North African countries such as the Berber languages and the non-standardized varieties of spoken Arabic. And for countries like Ethiopia, Eritrea, and Tanzania that do use a language that is distinctive to the nation as the language of state, the language selected is not the mother tongue of substantial segments of the population in each country. The selected languages also have a regional presence beyond the individual country. In these instances, then, the turn towards a distinctive language for the smaller space of a would-be nation-state is not associated with investing in a first language or a mother tongue, though the elevation of one or more languages above other languages might be justified by describing the selected languages as vernaculars. Certainly, the claim could be made that the indigenous language selected as a country's distinctive language offers a more authentic representation of the country, and, in that sense, is entitled to be considered a vernacular in a way that imperial languages like English, French, or Italian could never be. Such claims might be viewed as all the more justified given the selected language's longer history in the country and region, as well as the fact that the selected language or languages were already spoken by a more substantial number of citizens than might be the case for the languages of recent colonizing nations. Maneuvers of this kind on the part of some African governments since at least the mid-twentieth century point to a divergence between governments and many creative writers when it comes to defining what the vernacular is and what its role should be. In some instances, these divergent interpretations of the vernacular have opened up a gap leading to tensions between the multilingual nation-state's adoption of a distinctive language as an official language intended to unify the country, and the individual writer's commitment to producing literature in their own mother tongue.[7]

---

[7] For examples of the tensions between the language of the state and the languages of regions within a multilingual nation-state, see Marzagora and Kebede's discussion of the interactions between writing in Amharic and writing in Oromo in Ethiopia.

The notion of a firm equivalence between language and nation or ethnos as described by Pascale Casanova (2004: 78) would appear to be fairly recent on the African continent. Still, it is true that in the current era, ethnic groups across Africa now like to distinguish themselves by language even when the existence of the group as a singular cultural and political unit is quite recent (Lüpke 2020; Adejunmobi 2004). In such cases too, the now acknowledged language of the ethnic group will be described as their vernacular language. Strangely enough, though, several of the politically oriented ethnic nationalisms in colonial and postcolonial Africa have not often come into existence in conjunction with a commitment to using the ethnic group's claimed distinctive language in official statements and in writing.[8] For example, for the Igbo of southeastern Nigeria during the late colonial period and early post-independence years, awareness of belonging to a distinct group was connected with the notion of a distinctive language; nonetheless, after the introduction of Roman script, what van den Bersselaar (2000) calls a vernacular readership coalesced around texts written in English rather than in Igbo. In fact, van den Bersselaar (2000) goes so far as to describe the popular literature that emerged in English in the Igbo-speaking areas of Nigeria in the mid-twentieth century, popularly known as Onitsha Market Literature, as the "vernacular literature" of the Igbo despite the fact that it was written in English.

Developments in the twenty-first century reveal the continued salience of the notion of the vernacular for African communities as well as its changing functions. The languages identified by diverse African ethnic groups as their vernaculars can no longer be described as languages that do not travel in the way in which Pollock envisioned the vernacular. Given the pace of global migration, speakers of these languages are now distributed around the world. However, and because these languages rarely serve as languages of wider communication uniting speakers of different mother tongues, they do not often serve as vectors for what Pollock calls "universalistic orders." Instead, they may be associated with nationalist movements that are transnational and regional in their membership.

---

[8] I refer here to claimed languages since the languages that some ethnic groups would later claim to be their distinctive language was a language that earlier generations did not recognize as their language. As van den Bersselaar (1997) makes clear with respect to the language of the Igbo ethnic group, members of the ethnic group now described as Igbo did not see themselves as speaking the same language until the second half of the twentieth century, and after successive interventions by missionaries to persuade the Igbos that they were speakers of a single shared language. For other instances in Africa where identification with the standardized language was slow to come, see Adejunmobi (2004: 56–61).

Indeed, a new regionalism that is often transnational in its membership is at play around Africa in the early twenty-first century. There are newer nationalist movements emerging in different African countries pursuing political autonomy on behalf of units smaller than the larger world of the existing states. But these movements, too, do not seem particularly committed to advancing the ideal of literacy in a distinctive language, let alone a mother tongue.

Consider, for example, the many separatist movements that have emerged across Nigeria since 2000. Some of the best known include MASSOB (Movement for the Actualization of the Sovereign State of Biafra) founded in 2000, and IPOB (Indigenous Peoples of Biafra) established in 2012. Both movements are following in the footsteps of the secessionist movement that attempted to break away from Nigeria in the late 1960s in the leadup to the Nigerian civil war. As currently imagined, the territory of a future Biafra would encompass much of southeastern Nigeria as well as substantial parts of what is called the "South South" geopolitical zone, which is home to well over fifty ethnic groups speaking different languages.[9] While the diverse separatist movements in Nigeria have been associated with ethnic nationalisms (Duruji 2012), and those in southeastern Nigeria are seen as mainly expressions of Igbo ethnic nationalism, this is not an ethnic nationalism that focuses on promoting a distinctive language as a future language of state and education. For instance, and on the website of IPOB's radio station, Radio Biafra,[10] virtually all materials are in English. Even on the broadcasts on the radio station, most of the spoken language is in English occasionally interspersed with phrases in Igbo. It is not just that the language used by these movements is not their self-identified mother tongue; even more importantly, it is not a language that distinguishes the nation that is being willed into existence from other nations in Africa.

The distance between desires for the smaller place and commitment to writing in a distinctive language is even greater for the separatist movements that are now active in Cameroon. In 2016, a full-scale protest movement culminating in calls for secession erupted in the region of the Republic of Cameroon formerly known as the British Southern Cameroons and often described today simply as anglophone Cameroon. Supporters of this protest and increasingly militant movement are calling for the creation of a separate country, to be named

---

[9] Nigeria is currently divided into six geopolitical zones. The Southeast and what is called the South South are two of the six geopolitical zones of the country.
[10] For more on Radio Biafra, see: https://radiobiafra.co/.

Ambazonia. While the tensions between anglophone Cameroonians and the Cameroonian government cannot be reduced to matters of language alone, language and the expectation that all interactions with government officials should be in French has been a major flashpoint.[11] Indeed, a demand for Cameroonian authorities to stop appointing Francophone judges who spoke no English to the anglophone areas of Cameroon was the catalyst for the protests that broke out in 2016. This was soon followed by the resurgence of militant groups demanding independence, a development that has led the Cameroonian government to declare a state of emergency in the anglophone Cameroon. The forces calling for the independence of a country to be named Ambazonia are undoubtedly motivated by nationalist impulses. Still, it is interesting to note that what the multiethnic and multilingual residents of the proposed country have in common is a history of British colonial rule, opposition to the French dominated Republic of Cameroon, and a desire to live in a country where the language of bureaucracy and state would be English rather than French. Since the events unfolding in the anglophone Cameroon involve renouncing the larger space for a smaller space, they can indeed be called vernacularization as Pollock defines it. But this is not a process undertaken with an intent to advance the interests of a mother tongue. In addition, the language of the separatist movement itself, English, is not one that distinguishes this smaller place from other countries on the African continent, though it does distinguish Ambazonia from French-speaking Cameroon.[12]

In sum and in twenty-first century Africa, if the examples of Biafra and Ambazonia are anything to go by, there would seem to be fewer opportunities for the kind of vernacularization accompanied by the privileging of distinctive languages that unfolded in early modern India and Europe to occur. What we have here is vernacularization as a political process without a commitment to the vernacular either as distinctive language or mother tongue. In matters pertaining

---

[11] This region in Cameroon had previously been a German colony until World War I, becoming a British colony in 1914. Denied the opportunity of becoming an independent nation, residents voted to join the French Cameroons in 1960. The country was initially administered as a federal republic allowing for the use of English in the former British territory. However, and as successive governments have become more autocratic in Cameroon, the rights of residents in this part of the country to use a language other than French in public settings has become increasingly contested.

[12] For more on the language and culture divide in the anglophone Cameroons, see volume 14, number 2 (2020) of the *Journal of the African Literature Association*, titled "Fragmented Nation or the Anglophone-Cameroon Problem in Cameroon," and edited by Juliana Makuchi Nfah-Abenyi and Gilbert Doho. Also see: "History Explains Why Cameroon is at War with Itself over Language and Culture," https://theconversation.com/history-explains-why-cameroon-is-at-war-with-itself-over-language-and-culture-85401.

to language, the primary challenge facing twenty-first-century nationalist movements in Africa is not so much the fact that the communities purportedly represented by the movements are multilingual though this undoubtedly represents a challenge. What the movements for regional autonomy and indeed independence in both southeastern Nigeria and in anglophone Cameroon have in common is the fact that both emerged in an age where political leaders can no longer assume that claiming any one language as a country's "vernacular" and imposing that language as the country's distinctive language on a multilingual population will not be met with sustained opposition.[13] Thus, we have side by side in contemporary Africa political movements dedicated to advancing the interests of smaller spaces, often coupled with an avoidance of explicit interventions designed to elevate one distinctive language above other languages or other vernaculars spoken within those spaces.

Vernacular literacies, scripts and languages

Despite the fact that processes of vernacularization on the African continent have not been supported by increased investment in vernacular literacy since the end of the twentieth century, writing in vernacular languages continues to grow and spread in different regional contexts. Writing has a longer history than is often acknowledged in Africa. There are many indigenous scripts on the continent, some of which are quite old (Abdelhay, Asfaha, and Juffermans 2014: 4–5). Among the older scripts that Abdelhay, Asfaha, and Juffermans identify, one might mention scripts like Geʻez in Ethiopia, and Tifinagh in Morocco that are still in use. These are vernacular literacies in the sense proposed by Barbara Trudell and Anthony Klass, who write that, "Vernacular literacy is not simply literacy in the community's own language; it is distinctive in its lack of official recognition, institutional use, and political prestige" (2010: 124).

Ajami, or the use of Arabic script to write African languages, is one of the most widely distributed forms of vernacular writing in Africa today. Ajami script is used across much of West Africa in communities with long-established Muslim traditions. Texts written in Ajami can be found all the way from Senegal on the western end of West Africa to northern Cameroon as well as in East

---

[13] The post-Apartheid governments in South Africa resolved this conundrum by declaring eleven of the country's more than thirty languages as official languages of the country.

Africa. Adoption of Ajami has been documented for languages like Wolof, Pulaar, Hausa, and Yoruba among others. In Senegal, where a vibrant practice of writing Wolof using Ajami continues till the present time, it is known as Wolofal. Wolof in Ajami script dates back to at least the seventeenth century (Lüpke and Bao-Diop 2014: 101). As a form of writing, Ajami has traveled widely, even if the languages or varieties of the languages written in Ajami script are not always as widely spoken as the script itself is used. Notwithstanding the widespread use of Ajami, texts written in Ajami are not often translated and seldom enter into the international flow of cultural goods and textual forms emanating from the African continent. This is at least in part because the practice of Ajami often involves writing in a non-standardized script.

If we describe the vernacular as highly localized forms of expression, then non-standard forms of writing are some of the most vernacular forms of writing. Tageldin's association of the vernacular with the "native or indigenous, non-literary, nonstandard" comes to mind here (2018: 114). These non-standardized scripts have spread in the absence of institutionally sanctioned forms of writing and because individuals across the continent want to be able to express themselves in writing and in images even where local institutions do not have the means or willingness to promote standardized forms of writing. Some languages like Wolof and Hausa have acquired a standardized form in Roman script (Ngom 2010: 10), but as McLaughlin (forthcoming) points out for Wolof, the standardized Roman script is less frequently used than the non-standardized Ajami script. While not displacing languages such as English and French in Roman script from their entrenched positions, writing in indigenous languages appears to be gaining in popularity in at least some African contexts. However, and as Lüpke observes, "the standard orthographies devised for West African languages by missionaries and linguists are barely used. Yet other regimes of writing are thriving in the area: some of them have exploded with the advent of social media and mobile phones, and some of them have long predated colonial times" (2018: 129). Along the same lines, Warner (2019: 151, 213) reports that in Senegal, Wolof in Romanized script is now ubiquitous, though more frequently written in nonstandard orthographies than in the officially approved orthography.

If during the colonial period missionaries could develop orthographies for African languages and then, working in tandem with the colonial authorities impose those orthographies through the school system, the situation is more complicated today. With the exception of the handful of African countries where a distinctive language has been selected as official language, most African governments exhibit considerable ambivalence when it comes to enforcing an orthography for any one of the many vernaculars spoken in the country. On the one hand, and as reported by Ohiri-Aniche (2007), Olúmúyìwá (2013), and Bourlet (2019), it is not uncommon for government-backed committees to be established to update or finalize the orthography for particular vernacular languages. On the other hand, the authorities in what are typically multilingual states often do not have much incentive or the wherewithal to enforce adoption of an orthography for the languages in use within the country. As suggested by Lüpke (2018) in her observations about writing African vernacular languages, a growing sense of comfort with non-standardized scripts appears to be fueling more and more writing in African languages, especially on social media. However, the implications of these trends for the circulation of literary texts beyond the groups of people who speak a particular vernacular and can read the language in a particular kind of script remain to be seen. To the extent, then, that we can speak of vernacularization with respect to writing happening today on the African continent, we are referring to a process that almost always entails developments occurring outside the scope of initiatives backed by the full force of the state. Under the circumstances and given the fact that standardized forms of writing vernacular languages appear to be less well established in many parts of Africa, we would not be far off the mark in describing much of the continent as a zone where multiple and intersecting forms of vernacularity thrive. Yet only infrequently do these forms of vernacularity stand in contrast to a standard form of a given language whose dominance has been settled.

Even as non-standardized forms of writing African languages appear to be proliferating, so also do disagreements over orthography, standardization, and even the choice of script for individual languages. Recent examples include the campaign to privilege Roman script over Arabic script among marginalized ethnic groups in Sudan (Abdel Rahim Mugaddam and Ashraf Abdelhay 2014) as well as in Mauritania (Bourlet 2019), and disagreements over standardization and orthography for the Berber languages (Amazigh) in Morocco (Abderrahman El Aissati 2014). One might also mention here the debates over an appropriate orthography for Wolof in the early years after independence in Senegal (Warner 2019: 123–8, 144–7). This was a debate that pitted creative writer against creative writer, Birago Diop against Ousmane Sembene, and Leopold Senghor, the writer and president, against Ousmane Sembene, the writer. Even for languages that supposedly have an official orthography, arguments continue over the appropriateness of the orthography, at a time when non-standardized forms of writing the languages in question are becoming more widespread especially among the youth. As an example, in August of 2020 the British Museum in London hosted a two-day symposium on how to write Yoruba, one of the African languages with the largest number of speakers, and whether to reject non-standard forms of writing Yoruba. The symposium was marked by fierce and lively disagreement among scholars, creative writers, and editors, with some panelists insisting that only the standardized forms of writing Yoruba were acceptable, while others pleaded for a more lenient approach towards non-standardized forms of writing. And, as reported by Olúmúyìwá (2013), far from being a recent phenomenon, such disputations over how best to write Yoruba go back at least a hundred years or more.

All of this has implications for the circulation of texts written in non-standardized scripts beyond the immediate locality where the script is in use in conjunction with a specific language. All things being equal, established publishers are less likely to invest in publishing a work written in a language for which there is not yet an agreed-upon orthography or where non-standardized scripts have become entrenched. In other words, the circulation of a text written in a non-standardized script beyond the community of those who use that script and are fluent in the variety of the language in question will likely be fairly restricted. The critic and creative writer Mukoma wa Ngugi (2018: 1) could lament the fact that Chinua Achebe's celebrated *Things Fall Apart* had not been translated into and published in Achebe's mother tongue, Igbo, without knowing that Achebe's own ventures in writing in Igbo had attracted criticism from other Igbo scholars for failing to use what was considered the standard but also often contested orthography for the language (Ohiri-Aniche 2007: 425). Lüpke and Bao-Diop (2014: 111) maintain that Ajami remains popular in a country like Senegal despite its lack of standardization. However, the texts written in a specific vernacular that can and do travel beyond the communities of those who are fluent in the vernacular in question are those that are produced in standardized script since standardization allows for translation and the creation of zones of commensurability between texts in different languages and different scripts.[14] I would not necessarily go so far as to say that by virtue of being infrequently translated, these non-standardized vernacular forms of writing

---

[14] This would more likely be the case for texts written in standardized forms of languages like Yoruba, or Isizulu, though as I point out subsequently in this chapter, even when texts are written in standardized forms of African languages, they are not translated into other languages as frequently as one might expect.

"resist translation" in the way that Shankar (2012: 138) does, since that suggests some degree of agency. But I would suggest that these non-standardized scripts tend to be highly opaque to outsiders of a community who are not already fluent in the vernacular and familiar with the specific script used.

African vernacular literatures and the world's literatures

World literature is often understood as a classification that seeks to acknowledge and accommodate the literatures of the world in their diversity. Some scholars, like S. Shankar, come to the discussion about world literature from a perspective that privileges acknowledgement of the "literatures of the world" (Shankar 2012: 135) in their variety, whether or not those literatures are read beyond the communities where they were produced. By contrast, and in David Damrosch's famous formulation, world literature encompasses "all literary works that circulate beyond their country of origin either in translation, or their original language" (2003: 4). In effect, this would amount to a mere subset of what Shankar calls "literatures of the world." Nonetheless, and within this expansive grouping of works on the move, writing in a vernacular tends to function as a proxy for the different cultural units in the world that could be acknowledged within the compass of the term. Furthermore, and according to Aamir Mufti, world literature operates as a *"plane of equivalence,* a set of categorical grids and networks that seek ... to render legible as literature a vast and heterogeneous range of practices of writing from across the world" (2016: 11). For such a category aiming at equivalencies, translation is essential. The different points of emphasis underscored by Shankar, Damrosch, and Mufti are all relevant to our understanding of the intersections between African literature, African vernaculars, and the category of world literature.

The grouping of literary texts that is commonly referred to as African literature initially emerged from and still largely functions as an expansive domain of vernacularity, or what I have described elsewhere as a "zone of affinity" (Adejunmobi 2004: 68–9), albeit a zone where the constituents do not share the same mother tongues, though they all claim affiliation with the same geographical unit. Since the stakeholders for this grouping of texts and its attendant field of interactions (such as writers and critics) often owe their primary allegiance to this special conjunction of literature with geography

(Africa), rather than a conjunction of literature with particular languages such as Hausa or Shona for example, their ability to sustain this grouping depends to a large extent on a process of continuous translation or communication using a limited number of languages.[15] Historically, the opportunities and facilities for translation in this domain of vernacularity have been rather limited, with the result that the major languages through which this field of interactions has operated have been English or French, though and as I have explained elsewhere (Adejunmobi 2004: 66), there is no reason why one or two African languages cannot also serve the same purpose.

Notwithstanding this history, several African languages do in fact have established traditions of vernacular-language literary writing.[16] Literary vernacularization has happened for several languages and is perhaps even accelerating without the benefit of vernacularization at the level of language policy, with particular consequences for the ways in which the texts do, or do not, circulate. For one thing, these vernacular-language texts are only infrequently translated into the languages of adjacent communities speaking other languages, let alone languages of wider communication that would enable the text to travel further from home within the same country or within a region of the continent. For example, and among Yoruba creative writers who rose to fame starting in the mid-twentieth century, relatively few have had their works translated into any language. None of the Yoruba-language plays and novels by Ọládèjọ Òkédiji have ever been translated into other languages. Among his many works, only two of the plays of Akínwùmí Ìṣọ̀lá have ever been translated into English, namely, the very successful play, *Efúnsetán Aníwúrà, Ìyálóde Ìbàdàn*, and his second historical drama, *Tinúubu, Ìyálóde Ègbá*.[17] Daniel Fagunwa's *Ògbójú Ọdẹ nínú Igbó Irúnmọlẹ̀*, the first lengthy prose work in Yoruba published in novel form in 1938, was not translated into English until 1968. *Itan Igbesi-Aiye Emi "Ṣegilola, Ẹleyin'ju Ẹgẹ", Ẹlegbẹrun Ọkọ L'Aiye*, the first lengthy work of fiction in

---

[15] Although this may appear counter-intuitive, I maintain that many of the advocates for creative writing in African languages owe their primary allegiance to the entity of African literature rather than to a grouping defined by language. Indeed, authors like Ngũgĩ who have called for writing in African languages, appear to be more committed to ensuring the authenticity of "African" literature than to fostering the independent growth of literature in African vernaculars.

[16] For an overview of creative writing in selected African languages, see for example: Albert Gérard (1981), Graham Furniss (1996), Innocentia Mhlambi (2012), Karin Barber (2012), Xavier Garnier (2013), Mélanie Bourlet (2014), Sara Marzagora (2015), and Sara Marzagora and Ayele Kebede (2019).

[17] Please see Pamela Olúbùnmi Smith (2005) for details of the translation.

Yoruba serialized in a Nigerian newspaper from 1929 to 1930, did not receive its first full and annotated translation until 2012.[18]

This pattern, and the fact that African vernacular-language texts are rarely translated into other languages, helps to explain the more limited circulation of these works, even within individual countries, and across the African continent as a whole. With the exception of languages such as Kiswahili, Amharic, and, to a lesser extent, languages like Hausa, many African vernacular-language texts are written in languages that are not often spoken as second languages and do not function as languages of wider communication. As a result, and in the absence of translation, such texts are usually available only to mother-tongue readers of the vernacular in question. Within the same country, researchers and critics of African literature who are not mother-tongue speakers of the vernacular in which the text is written will usually be unable to access the text. Furthermore, the small presses that publish these vernacular-language texts often do not have a distribution network that is wide enough to enable distribution of the text beyond the sections of a school system where the text has been assigned.[19] If, against this background, translation happens infrequently for texts written in languages like Yoruba, for which standardized scripts exist, the situation is likely more dire for literary texts rendered in non-standardized scripts. It is patently difficult to achieve Mufti's plane of equivalence and thus a full accounting of the world's literatures (to borrow Shankar's terminology) when dealing with and attempting to translate texts initially written in non-standardized languages and scripts. We are not dealing here, then, with works that are likely to circulate in translation beyond their country of origin in the ways that Damrosch anticipated for world literature.

Unfortunately, however, the challenges for African vernacular literatures do not end with the occasional translation of the African language literary work into other languages. Indeed, when African-authored texts written in a vernacular language are translated into global languages of power, they tend to have unusual circulation trajectories. In the case of Okot p'Bitek's *Song of Lawino*, publication of the English-language translation preceded publication of the Acholi language source text, *Wer pa Lawino* by three years (Mwangi 2017: 60; Adejunmobi 2004: 76). Following in the same pattern, a translation of *Wer pa Lawino* into

---

[18] Please see Karin Barber (2012) for details.
[19] For Mélanie Bourlet, just tracking down actual literature books written in Pulaar took on the character of a treasure hunt that spread over multiple cities in multiple countries over several years.

Luganda, one of the major languages of p'Bitek's native country, Uganda, was not published until 2016 (Gikandi 2016: 1196). That the translation into Luganda was based on the English language version of the volume rather than on Acholi language source text points to yet another pattern in the circulation of African vernacular language literary texts: these texts become accessible to non-native speakers of the vernacular used mainly by first being translated into a global language. In short, and no matter the language in which the African authored text was composed or will be read, circulation often occurs through the medium of a global language whenever the text travels beyond a community of native speakers of the vernacular used. Similarly, Cheikh Aliou Ndao's Wolof-language novel, *Buur Tillen*, was first published in a French translation (or adaptation as the author calls it) because the author could not find a publisher to publish the Wolof-language text. The Wolof-language source text would not be published for thirty years after it was initially written (Warner 2019: 153). But even in instances where publication of the translation into a global language did not precede publication of the source text in an African language, the circulation trajectories of the translation could still be constructed in such a way as to subordinate the African language source text to its translation in a global language. Such was the case for Daniel Fagunwa's Yoruba-language novel, *Ògbójú Ọdẹ nínú Igbó Irúnmọlẹ̀*, translated into English in 1968 by Wole Soyinka, who was already a writer of some acclaim in English at the time though he was still decades away from winning the Nobel Prize in literature. As reported by Abiola Irele, publishers of the translation arranged their presentation of the work in such a way as to foreground the translator who owed his fame to texts written in English, while leaving the vernacular-language author in the background:

> In the translation of Fagunwa's novel, *Ogboju Ode*, prepared by Wole Soyinka and published by Nelson, the title page and blurb are designed to relegate Fagunwa into the background as much as possible, and to bring the translator into focus; obviously Nelson are more interested in having Soyinka on their list (with the prospect of good sales that this entails) than in giving the wider world a taste of Fagunwa's creative genius. The cynical attitude of Fagunwa's original publishers with regard to his work is seen at its height in one advertisement of Soyinka's translation I have seen in which they have gone so far as to suppress Fagunwa's name altogether.
>
> (1981: 176)

To be sure, there are African-authored texts in what can be described as vernacular languages that appear to circulate internationally without requiring translation. As an example, one might mention Afrobeats, a popular music genre identified with both Nigeria and Ghana, that draws inspiration from global hip-hop, has a global reach, and often relies on mixed registers of individual languages and a mixing of languages.[20] On the one hand, and for Oloruntoba-Oju, Afrobeats is a "global-local or glocalized phenomenon" (2018: 187). On the other hand, however, this "glocalized phenomenon" as he describes it, is attached to a "conscious Africanity" (198) and signals the rediscovery of an "indigenous heritage" appropriated for "a glocal practice" (182). In Afrobeats, then, we have speech forms that are positioned as vernacular and distinctive of a particular region, coupled with a musical genre that is perceived as global in its style. This clearly domesticated genre confirms a point made by Adejunmobi (2004: 153) with respect to the jazz-influenced music of Fela Anikulapo-Kuti, the Nigerian popular singer from the 1970s who pioneered a style of music that he called "Afrobeat."[21] In instances where author/producer/artists like Fela in the 1970s and Afrobeats stars in the early twenty-first century creating new and stylistically foreign-inspired orientations for local culture find themselves in competition with cultural outsiders within the borders of their own home territory, they often have an incentive to advertise the local credentials of their art form by invoking their connections to "tradition" or to distinctive languages even when such languages are not mother tongues. In such cases, the artists stand to benefit by aligning their unusual stylistic choices with practices that they can characterize as vernacular or locally inspired.

It is worth noting here that the urban youth languages used in Afrobeats correspond to the kinds of mixed spoken registers that Lüpke (2020: 386) has observed in several African countries, and which Oloruntoba-Oju (2018: 182) describes as a hybrid form of language. In fact, Oloruntoba-Oju (2018: 188) goes so far as to characterize language use in Afrobeats as an instance of "mixilingualism" rather than code-switching.[22] For fans of Afrobeats, this admixture of expressions from multiple languages further heightens the genre's

[20] While English is one of many languages used in Afrobeats, the dominant language of Afrobeats is in fact Nigerian Pidgin English. Under the circumstances, it is preferable, like Oloruntoba-Oju, to describe language use in Afrobeats as one that involves hybridity, and multiple types of mixing rather than the term creolization which would require the making of more technical distinctions between Pidgins and Creoles.
[21] Fela's style known as Afrobeat in the 1970s is to be distinguished from the hip-hop inflected Afrobeats of the twenty-first century.
[22] For Oloruntoba-Oju, code-switching as envisioned by Carol Myers-Scotton in *Duelling Languages* suggests an alternation between two languages, while Oloruntoba-Oju finds that Afrobeats music often involves alternation between as many as six languages in a single song.

pan-ethnic, continent-wide, and cosmopolitan appeal. At the same time, and with lyrics mixing as many as six different languages, these hybrid speech forms are nonetheless highly localized forms of speech, and in that sense true vernaculars. Like Sheng in Kenya, and as argued by Githiora, the mixed register of Afrobeats is seen as a distinctive youth language in parts of West Africa. Thus endowed with various dimensions of vernacularity, these expressive forms can circulate both locally and internationally as quintessentially African creations.

If the trajectory of Afrobeats is anything to go by, international circulation is not incompatible with claims to locality and the vernacular. It is not just that the speakers of African vernacular languages are distributed around the world in ever greater numbers, but also that digital technologies and social media now enable a different type of cultural circulation that is transnational in scope rather than global, and which serves primarily to connect dispersed speakers of particular vernacular languages with each other. Thanks in particular to digital technologies, an alternative circuit of international distribution for African vernacular-language texts has come into existence, one that works to the advantage of shorter texts like those that Stephanie Bosch Santana has called "blog or Facebook fiction," but also excerpts of texts as well as brief video clips.[23] It is worth noting that the African vernacular-language texts circulating transnationally tend to belong to the world of popular culture rather than that of high literature. The ease with which Afrobeats, as one example, circulates transnationally and globally can also not be dissociated from the fact it is a performative textual form where the beats matter more than the meanings of lyrics, and which, therefore, does not require full intelligibility as would be the case with a lengthy written text. Above all, these are vernacular-based practices that are not "in need of translation" (Shankar 2012: 137–8) because they are often directed at a community comprising mainly native speakers of particular vernaculars.

Unlike performative texts, however, lengthier written texts often require some level of intelligibility in order to be read either locally or abroad by those who are not conversant with the language of the text. The principal way that a lengthy text written in a vernacular that is not a global language will be read beyond a community of speakers of the language used tends to be by being translated

[23] For more on this, see Stephanie Bosch Santana (2018, 2021). Like the Afrobeats singers discussed in this chapter, some authors of what Santana calls "new media literature" write in a mixture of African vernaculars and English that is mainly accessible to members of local communities (Santana 2021: 447).

into a global language of power which then opens the door for translation into other languages. In theory, any text could be translated into a global language; in practice, this option tends to be available for only a fraction of African vernacular language works. Increasingly, the African vernacular-language literary texts that are most likely to be translated into global languages and to circulate around and beyond the African continent are those written by authors who already have works composed and circulating in such global languages. This is the case for both Ngũgĩ wa Thiong'o and Boubacar Boris Diop. Ngũgĩ's *Mũrogi wa Kagogo* was translated into English as *Wizard of the Crow* while Boris Diop's *Doomi Golo* (2003) was translated into English in 2016 as *Doomi Golo: The Hidden Notebooks*. Having previously written in English and French respectively, both authors already had significant visibility on world literature platforms. But it is probably also the case that because their literary works written in global languages of power were already circulating beyond their individual nations and the African continent, their works written in the vernacular could be taken as commensurate types of texts that could easily be admitted into a representative repository of the world's literatures (Warner 2019: 22; Shankar 2012: 135).[24] The idea of the vernacular attached to selected texts by these authors thus allows for claims of commensurability but also of authenticity.

Other than as a means for confirming the authenticity of the African-authored text that continues to circulate locally and internationally mainly in global languages, African writers who have deliberately turned from writing in English and French to writing in African vernaculars have not, however, shown much interest in other potential functions of vernacular language literary texts. They have not, for example, spoken of writing literature in vernacular languages as a means for advancing standardization of their chosen vernaculars. Indeed, advocates for literary vernacularization in Africa almost never acknowledge the existence of multiple varieties of the languages under consideration and often seem to imply that every language has a singular fixed form. For these authors, demonstrating that writing in an African vernacular is even possible or has a history in a specific setting, usually provides the primary motivation for writing in the vernacular, given the preponderance of African-authored texts written in global languages within the grouping of texts known as African literature.

---

[24] In this respect, Warner writes for example: "When an argument breaks out about what *language* literature ought to be written in, a great feat of commensurability has already been performed. At the point at which language becomes the issue, the nature and equivalence of *literature* is increasingly being taken as a given" (2019: 22).

Furthermore, and if authors like Ngũgĩ and Diop have often ended up translating their own vernacular-language texts into global languages, it is not so much in a bid to highlight the gap between the global language and African vernaculars, or to showcase the untranslatables within African vernacular languages, but in order to prove that as an entity, African literature takes shape not only in global languages, but also in African vernaculars. In a sense, then, their commitment to writing in the vernacular cannot be separated from a desire to ensure that literatures in African vernaculars have as much visibility as African literatures that circulate in global languages.

For African-authored texts, composition in the vernacular helps to distinguish between the local and the non-local, a distinction that is sometimes obscured when the text is composed in a language of global power. Being able to point to the fact that works by African authors like Ngũgĩ and Diop were written in an African language clears up this area of tension for African-authored literary works that circulate internationally under the rubric of world literature. In the case of authors like Ngũgĩ and Diop, the claim can now be made that the languages in which the works circulate internationally are not the languages in which they were initially written, thus conforming to the usual pattern for works from other regions of the world also assembled within the framework of world literature. But the standing of such works as true vernacular texts may matter more for the ways in which they are perceived when they enter into the realm of world literature than it does for how these texts are read on home turf. For Diop's *Doomi Golo*, Warner concludes this Wolof-language work could not be considered an instance of "Wolof literary activism in any kind of self-evident or transparent way" (2019: 221). As Warner further (2019: 229) recounts, it was important for the translators of Diop's novel into English to point out that the novel was initially written in Wolof, even though the English-language translation was actually based on the French-language version of the text. Likewise, the fact that Ngũgĩ's *Wizard of the Crow* was written in Gikuyu mattered more for the book's circulation in English than it did for Gikuyu readers since the single-volume novel was first published and circulated in English before the final installments of the multi-volume source text, *Mũrogi wa Kagogo*, were published in Gikuyu (Mwangi 2017: 60). What careful attention to the circulation trajectories of African language works suggests, therefore, is that one cannot fully assess the implications of writing in the vernacular for the circulation of African-authored works without setting the experience of world-famous authors like Ngũgĩ and Diop alongside the experience of authors like Akínwùmí Ìṣọ̀lá and Ọládẹ̀jọ

Òkédiji. For the latter authors whose creative writing occurred mostly or entirely in their mother tongues, their works were seldom translated into any language and attracted virtually no engagement whatsoever within the field of criticism of world literature. Their works belong within the large storehouse of Shankar's "literatures of the world" but not within the more restricted grouping of world literature as understood by Damrosch.

A number of small-scale experiments with African vernacular language writing and translation has been attempted in recent years. One such experiment involved the publication of a multilingual anthology of romance stories by a Nigeria based publisher, Cassava Republic under its Ankara Press imprint in 2015.[25] Each of the seven stories available for download in the 2015 anthology was written in English and translated into another (usually African) language accompanied by an audio recording of each story read both in English and the language into which the story had been translated.[26] This pattern of translation made it possible for the stories to be available to literate and non-literate speakers of individual African languages in which the texts were composed, but also to circulate within the larger ecosystem of African literature, a zone of affinity where participants are bound together, not by shared vernaculars, but by a shared geography, and where the predominant languages of interaction have been English and French.

Notwithstanding such experiments translating short prose texts into African languages, relatively few African authors already writing in English or French and whose works circulate in the world-literature space have followed in the footsteps of Ngũgĩ and Diop. This is in part because African-authored texts become visible within the domain of African literature itself mainly when they are composed in or translated into global languages. And for understandable reasons: participants in the field of African literature continue to rely on selected languages of wider communication which happen to be global languages for most of their interactions. But it is also in large part because African-authored texts rarely show up in world literature lists as works identified with any one African language. Rather, they show up most frequently as works identified with geopolitical constructs, the African continent itself or a specific African country,

---

[25] For more on this, see, e.g., Adejunmobi (2017: 139).
[26] Although, as of 2021, the text for the romance stories is no longer available for download from Ankara Press as a PDF, the audio recordings of the stories in English and the languages into which they were translated can still be accessed at: https://soundcloud.com/ankara-press/sets/valentines-day-anthology-2015.

but not language. In discussions of world literature, Ngũgĩ appears simply as an African author, not as a Gikũyu-language author. Diop shows up in those discussions simply as an African author, not as a Wolof-language author. In general, literatures specifically attached to African vernacular languages have little to no salience in world-literature spaces, almost certainly because these literatures are often invisible even within the domain of vernacularity signified by the more narrowly defined term of African literature. This is the trend for works by authors who write only or predominantly in African languages. However, and for African writers whose initial presence and reputation in world literature spaces already rests on texts written in global languages, there is a rationale for affiliating their texts that circulate in global languages with African vernacular language writing.

By way of conclusion, I will note that as a political project mostly detached from policy initiatives focused on language, vernacularization has continuing appeal across Africa in the twenty-first century. In dysfunctional postcolonial polities, the appeal of the smaller space as an alternative to unwieldy bigger spaces continues to grow. So also does the trend towards a kind of literary vernacularization that is detached from vernacularization at the level of language policy or a commitment to vernacular literacy. At the same time, the circulation of vernacular-language texts by African authors who write only in the vernacular rarely extends beyond the community of literate mother tongue speakers of the vernacular in question whether they reside at home or are dispersed around the world. Still, and for African authors whose works written in global languages are already well positioned in the stream of international literary flows, writing in the vernacular accompanied by translation remains a sign of irreducible cultural difference with high value within that stream.

References

Abdelhay, A., Y. Mesfun Ashafa, and K. Juffermans (2014), "African Literacy Ideologies, Scripts and Education," in K. Juffermans, Y. Mesfun Ashafa, and A. Abdelhay (eds), *African Literacy Ideologies, Scripts and Education*, 1–62, Newcastle upon Tyne: Cambridge Scholars Publishing.

Adejunmobi, M. (2004), *Vernacular Palaver: Imaginations of the Local and Non-native Languages in West Africa*, Clevedon: Multilingual Matters.

Adejunmobi, M. (2017), "Native Books and the English Book," *PMLA* 132 (1): 135–41.

Barber, K. (1997), "Time, Space, and Writing in Three Colonial Yoruba Novels," *The Yearbook of English Studies* 27: 108–29.

Barber, K. (2012), *Print Culture and the First Yoruba Novel: I. B. Thomas's 'Life Story of Me, Ṣẹgilọla' and Other Texts*, edited and translated by Karin Barber, Leiden: Brill.

Bourlet, M. (2014), "Mobilité, migrations et littératures en reseaux: Exemples des romans poulâr," *Cahiers d'Études africaines*, 213–14: 309–40.

Bourlet, M. (2019), "Cosmopolitanism, Literary Nationalisms and Linguistic Activism: A Multi-local Perspective on Pulaar," *Journal of World Literature* 4: 35–55.

Casanova, P. (2004), *The World Republic of Letters*, trans. M. B. DeBevoise, Cambridge, MA: Harvard University Press.

Damsrosch, D. (2003), *What Is World Literature?* Princeton, NJ: Princeton University Press.

Diop, B. B (2003), *Doomi Golo*, Dakar: Editions Papyrus.

Diop, B. B. (2006), *Doomi Golo: The Hidden Notebooks*, trans. V. Wülfing-Leckie and El Hadji M. Diop, East Lansing, MI: Michigan State University Press.

Diop, B. B. (2009), *Les Petits de la guenon*, Paris: P. Rey.

Duruji, M. M. (2012), "Resurgent Ethno-Nationalism and the Renewed Demand for Biafra in South-East Nigeria," *National Identities*, 14 (4): 329–50.

El Aissati, A. (2014), "Script Choice and Power Struggle in Morocco," in K. Juffermans, Y. Mesfun Ashafa, and A. Abdelhay (eds), *African Literacy Ideologies, Scripts and Education*, 147–77, Newcastle upon Tyne: Cambridge Scholars Publishing.

Fagunwa, D. (1938), *Ògbójú Ọdẹ nínú Igbó Irúnmọlẹ̀*, Edinburgh: Thomas Nelson.

Fagunwa, D. (1968), *The Forest of a Thousand Daemons: A Hunter's Saga*, trans. Wole Soyinka, London: Nelson.

Furniss, G. (1996), *Poetry, Prose, and Popular Culture in Hausa*, Edinburgh: Edinburgh University Press.

Garnier, X. (2013), *The Swahili Novel: Challenging the Ideas of Minor Literature*, Suffolk: James Currey.

Gérard, A. (1981), *African Languages Literatures: An Introduction to the Literary History of sub-Saharan Africa*, London: Longmans.

Gikandi, S. (2016), "Introduction: Another Way in the World," *PMLA*, 131 (5): 1193–206.

Githiora, C. (2018), *Sheng: The Rise of a Kenyan Swahili Vernacular*. Suffolk: James Currey.

"History Explains Why Cameroon Is at War with Itself over Language and Culture," *The Conversation*, October 15, 2017, https://theconversation.com/history-explains-why-cameroon-is-at-war-with-itself-over-language-and-culture-85401.

Irele, A. (1981), *The African Experience in Literature and Ideology*, London: Heinemann Educational Books.

Ìṣọ̀lá, A. (1970), *Efúnsetán Aníwúrà, Ìyálóde Ìbàdàn*, Ibadan: Ibadan University Press.

Ìṣọ̀lá, A. (1983), *Olú Ọmọ*, Ibadan: Onibonoje Press.

Lentz, C. (2000), "Settlement Histories and Ethnic Frontiers," *Berichte des Sonderforschungsbereichs*, 411–13, 268: 14.

Lüpke, F. (2018), "Escaping the Tyranny of Writing: West African Regimes of Writing as a Model for Multilingual Literacy," in C. Weth and K. Juffermans (eds), *The Tyranny of Writing: Ideologies of the Written Word*, 129–47, London: Bloomsbury Academic.

Lüpke, F. (2020), "The Writing's on the Wall: Spaces for Language-Independent and Language-Based Literacies," *International Journal of Multilingualism*, 17 (3): 382–403.

Lüpke, F. (2021), "Standardization in Highly Multilingual National Contexts: The Shifting Interpretations, Limited Reach, and Great Symbolic Power of Ethnonationalist Visions," in W. Ayres-Bennett and J. Bellamy (eds), *Cambridge Handbook of Language Standardization*, 1–26, Cambridge: Cambridge University Press.

Lüpke, F. and S. Bao-Diop (2014), "Beneath the Surface? Contemporary Ajami Writing in West Africa, Exemplified through Wolofal," in K. Juffermans, Y. Mesfun Ashafa, and A. Abdelhay (eds), *African Literacy Ideologies, Scripts and Education*, 88–117, Newcastle upon Tyne: Cambridge Scholars Publishing.

Marzagora, S. (2015) "Literatures in African Languages," *Journal of African Cultural Studies* 27: 1–6.

Marzagora, S. and A. Kebede (2019), "Literary Networks in the Horn of Africa: Oromo and Amharic Intellectual Histories," in M. Adejunmobi and C. Coetzee (eds), *Routledge Handbook of African Literature*, 88–117, Abingdon: Routledge.

McLaughlin, F. (forthcoming) "*Ajami* Writing Practices in Atlantic Africa," in F. Lüpke (ed.), *The Oxford Guide to the Atlantic Languages of West Africa*, Oxford: Oxford University Press.

Mhlambi, I. J. (2012), *African Language Literatures: Perspectives on Isizulu Fiction and Popular Black Television Series*, Johannesburg: Wits University Press.

Mufti, A. (2016), *Forget English! Orientalisms and World Literature*, Cambridge, MA: Harvard University Press.

Mugaddam, A. R. and A. Abdelhay (2014), "The Politics of Literacy in the Sudan: Vernacular Literacy Movements in the Nuba Mountains," in K. Juffermans, Y. Ashafa, and A. Abdelhay (eds), *African Literacy Ideologies, Scripts and Education*, 178–205, Newcastle upon Tyne: Cambridge Scholars Publishing.

Mwangi, E. (2017), *Translation in African Contexts: Postcolonial Texts, Queer Sexuality, and Cosmopolitan Fluency*, Kent, OH: Kent State University Press.

Ndao, C. A. (1972), *Buur Tilleen: Roi de La Médina*, Paris: Présence Africaine.

Ndao, C. A. (1993), *Buur Tillen*, Dakar: IFAN Cheikh Anta Diop.

Nfah Abbenyi, J. and G. Doho, eds. (2020), "Fragmented Nation or the Anglophone-Francophone Problem in Cameroon," Special Issue, *Journal of the African Literature Association*, 14 (2): 171–2.

Ngom, F. (2010), "Ajami Scripts in the Senegalese Speech Community," *Journal of Arabic and Islamic Studies*, 10: 1–23.

Ngugi, M. (2018), *The Rise of the African Novel: Politics of Language, Identity, and Ownership*, Ann Arbor, MI: University of Michigan Press.

Ngũgĩ wa Thiong'o (2006), *Wizard of the Crow*, New York: Pantheon.
Ngũgĩ wa Thiong'o (2007), *Mũrogi wa Kagogo: Mbuku ya Kana, Gatano na Gatandatũ* (*Wizard of the Crow*: books 4, 5, and 6), Nairobi: East African Educational Publishers.
Ohiri-Aniche, C. (2007), "Stemming the Tide of Centrifugal Forces in Igbo Orthography," *Dialectal Anthropology*, 31: 423–36.
Oloruntoba-Oju, T. (2018), "Contestant Hybridities: African Urban Youth Language in Nigerian Music and Social Media," in E. Hurst-Harosh and F. Kanana Erastus (eds), *African Youth Languages: New Media, Performing Arts and Sociolinguistic Development*, 181–203, New York: Palgrave Macmillan.
Olúmúyìwá, T. (2013), "Yoruba Writing: Standards and Trends," *Journal of Arts and Humanities*, 2 (1): 40–51.
p'Bitek, O. (1966), *Song of Lawino*, Nairobi: East African Publishing Company.
P'Bitek, O. (1969), *Wer pa Lawino*, Nairobi: East African Publishing Company.
Pollock, S. (1998), "India in the Vernacular Millennium: Literary Culture and Polity, 1000-1500," *Daedalus*, 127 (3): 41–74.
Pollock, S. (2000), "Cosmopolitan and Vernacular in History," *Public Culture*, 12(3): 591–625.
Radio Biafra. https://radiobiafra.co/
Santana, S. Bosch (2018), "From Nation to Network: Blog and Facebook Fiction from Southern Africa," *Research in African Literatures*, 49 (1): 187–208.
Santana, S. Bosch (2021), "Navigating Digital Worlds: African Digital Forms in the Digital Age," in O. George (ed.), *A Companion to African Literatures*, 439–53, Hoboken, NJ: Wiley Blackwell.
Shankar, S. (2012), *Flesh and Fish Blood: Postcolonialism, Translation, and the Vernacular*, Los Angeles: University of California Press.
Smith, P. (2005), *Efúnsetán Aníwúrà, Ìyálóde Ìbàdàn and Tinúubu, Ìyálóde Ègbá, Two Yorubá Historical Dramas*, Trenton, NJ: Africa World Press, Inc.
Soyinka, W. (1988), "Language as Boundary," in W. Soyinka (ed.), *Art, Dialogue and Outrage*, 132–45, Ibadan: New Horn Press.
Tageldin, S. (2018), "Beyond Latinity: Can the Vernacular Speak?" *Comparative Literature*, 70 (2): 114–31.
Trudell, B. and A. Klaas (2010), "Distinction, Integration and Identity: Motivations for Local Language Literacy in Senegalese Communities," *International Journal of Educational Development*, 30 (2): 121–9.
Van Den Bersselaar, D. (1997), "Creating 'Union Ibo': Missionaries and the Igbo Language," *Africa: Journal of the International Africa Institute*, 67 (2): 273–95.
Van Den Bersselaar, D. (2000), "The Language of Igbo Ethnic Nationalism," *Language Problems and Language Planning*, 24 (2): 123–47.
Warner, T. (2019), *The Tongue-Tied Imagination: Decolonizing Literary Modernity in Senegal*, New York: Fordham University Press.

2

Vernacular resistance: Catalan, Basque, and Galician opposition to Francoist monolingualism

Christian Claesson

In July of 1936, the conservative wing of the Spanish army initiated a coup d'état against the Republic and its democratically elected government. It was supposed to be a swift takeover of power but quickly evolved into a gruesome civil war with international implications, where the rebels enjoyed the military support of Nazi Germany and Fascist Italy, and the Republic had the backing of international brigades of anti-Fascists and, to a lesser extent, the Soviet Union. After three years of conflict, half a million people had lost their lives, millions were forced into exile, and the democratic government was replaced by a military dictatorship, forged into the image of the man who assumed the military leadership in the beginning months of the war: General Francisco Franco. One of the first measures of the Franco regime was to take control over language. By January of 1937, in the beginning of the war, a Delegation for Press and Propaganda was created, following the model of Nazi Germany and Fascist Italy. The delegation took to redefining the ideological charge of language: the Civil War was thus called a *crusade*, the coup d'état became *the uprising*, Franco, *el Caudillo* or *Generalísimo*, the insurgents, *the Movement*, and the enemies of Franco—including conservatives serving under the Republic and its democratically elected government—simply dismissed as *Communists, reds* or *barbaric hordes*. The insurgents called themselves *nacionales*, in order to enforce the idea that the Republic was in fact was being ruled by foreign and separatist forces. In Francoist discourse, words like *class, cohabitation, spirit, nation, Fatherland, destiny, history, liberty, sacrifice, work, will, faith, justice, progress,* and *unity* were all ideologically redefined to serve the purposes of the new regime (Veres 2010). At the Madrid book fair in

May of 1939, a month after the end of the war, a massive book burning was organized in order to erase the ideological trace that recalled the losing side (Sinova 1989: 38).

However, it was not only the semantics of language that underwent strict government control but also *which* language was to be used under the new regime. During the years of the Republic (1931–36), Catalan and Basque had been granted semi-official status in the respective regions, for example, as languages of instruction in the school system (Herreras 2010), but when Franco came to power, the use of any language other than Castilian was severely repressed. In the first years after the war, all public use of Catalan, Basque and Galician was prohibited, including in schools, social and cultural associations, printed material (books, magazines, and newspapers), religious ceremonies, and radio broadcasts. Mass book burnings were organized, non-Spanish first names were prohibited or had to be "translated," and tombstone inscriptions and funeral markers had to be removed. Priests were even chastised for pronouncing Latin with a non-Castilian accent (Conversi 1997: 81, 113; Solé i Sabaté and Villarroya 1995: 45). Thus, while the vernacular languages had had a short-lived spring in the 1930s, now the so-called imperial language had to be employed: per official decree, noticeboards urging citizens to speak *el idioma del imperio* were hung in public places throughout Catalonia (Conversi 1997: 110; Sueiro Seoane 2009: 182). In this New Spain, vernacular languages had to be eradicated in order to ensure the unity of the nation.

The aim of this chapter is to study how the different language communities resisted the prohibition, censorship, and asphyxiation of vernacular cultures during the almost four decades of Franco dictatorship, from 1939 to 1975. Even though the language communities were under duress throughout Franco's reign, the situation changed greatly during the years of the dictatorship, from violent repression in the beginning to a more permissive attitude in the end. As I will show in this chapter, the protection of the regional languages inscribed in the Constitution of 1978, written during the transition, existed even in the last years of the dictatorship—in fact, in some ways the Constitution shows less consideration for the regional languages than the dictatorship, at least during its final years. Through a comparative study of the Catalan, Basque, and Galician language communities, I will examine how the different strategies of resistance reflected the varying contexts of the different vernacular cultures and how these strategies changed according to the shifts of language policy within the Franco regime.

The language situation in Spain

In order to understand the language situation of Spain in the 1930s, and by extension even today, it is illuminating to contrast its linguistic and political development with that of comparable countries. By the end of the eighteenth century, around one fifth of the population in France spoke and understood standard French, while as little as 2.5 percent of the Italian population spoke Tuscan, which later became standard Italian, by the time of the unification (Beecroft 2015: 207 n. 20).[1] In contrast, in the same period more than 80 percent of the population of Spain knew and used Castilian (Moreno Fernández 2005: 173).[2] In spite of this uneven relationship, while French became the sole official language of France and Italian the national language of Italy,[3] Castilian has never enjoyed the same unquestioned superiority in Spain, and the question of the linguistic minorities has been central to Spanish politics from at least 1898—when the last Spanish overseas colonies were lost—until today.

Why, then, has this development been so different in Spain in comparison to the other two large, Romance-language countries? José Álvarez Junco (2001: 549–65) points out three fundamental areas in the nineteenth century where Spain failed to follow France in order to carry out a national integration: education, military service, and national symbols. Due to lack of funding and political will, the Spanish state did not make a decisive effort to create a system of public schools where a Spanish sense of national identity could be created; instead, it let the religious private schools dominate. These religious schools were more interested in propagating the doctrine of Catholicism than that of the newly founded nation—Spain's first Constitution is from 1812—and often taught pupils in the vernacular languages where those had a stronger popular presence. Catalans, Basques, and Galicians never went to national schools and had no need to communicate with Spaniards from other parts of the country; thus, they only expressed themselves in their own languages and rarely in Castilian. Equally important was the lack of a universal military service. This service, so important

---

[1] Beecroft also states (2015: 207) that the number of Castilian speakers in Spain roughly equaled that of Tuscan speakers in Italy by the time of the French Revolution, which, following the number from Moreno Fernández above, would be very far removed from the truth.
[2] It should be added that the language diversity of those countries is, even today, much higher than in Spain: there are twenty-four autochthonous languages in France and as many as thirty-four in Italy.
[3] French was declared the official language of France by the time of the Revolution, while Tuscan was declared Italy's national language with the unification in 1870; however, in practice, the regional languages retained a strong position in non-official contexts well into the twentieth century.

in the transformation of the citizens of France from "peasants into Frenchmen," as Eugen Weber (1976) puts it, suffered not only from a lack of funding but also from a lack of political will. As the case of France shows, a universal military service may break the regional isolation of young men by forcing them to live in other parts of the country and speak the common language, while subjecting them to nationalist indoctrination. However, in Spain, military service was quite easily eschewed by the upper classes, which made service and sacrifice a question of social status rather than nationality. As for the lack of powerful and common national symbols—flags, anthems, commemorative ceremonies, monuments, street names, and other symbols and rites created to give an illusion of the national collective's glorious past—this, too, was a result of failing political will. The Spanish state, where conservatives were more loyal to Church and Crown than to the Nation, was too divided to implement a full-scale national project in the nineteenth century.

At the turn of the twentieth century, in 1898, Spain entered an unprecedented national crisis. The loss of the American colonies between 1810 and 1824 put an end to the once-grand Spanish Empire, but those overseas territories were perceived as belonging to the Crown rather than to the people. However, when Cuba, Puerto Rico, and the Philippines were lost as a result of the swift and devastating Spanish–American War, "this was perceived as a national disaster, affecting all citizens" (Labanyi 2013: 27). It was only at this time "that one can really talk of Spain as a nation-state in the full modern sense of the term: that is, as a national collective whose members feel a sense of shared values" (27). At the same time, the cultural movements of the non-Castilian language collectives had adopted decisively political ambitions, ranging from regional autonomy to full-fledged independence from what was seen as a moribund and obsolete state. In the first decades of the century, while the Spanish-speaking intelligentsia searched for the country's soul in Castile—the region that was once at the center of military and cultural dominion of the peninsula, as well as of the imperial enterprise in the New World—peripheral national collectives, especially Catalans and Basques, sought to enhance as much as possible their autonomy and eschew centralist power. There was a wide range of political experiments during the years of the Second Republic, between 1931 and 1936, but the statutes of autonomy for Catalonia and the Basque Country were definitely among the most daring. The consequences of these experiments during the Civil War and the ensuing dictatorship would be severe and reach all the way to the transition to democracy and current-day politics.

Francoist monolingualism in practice

The Franco regime may have been one of the longest dictatorships in Western Europe in the twentieth century, but under its unified and totalitarian façade it underwent constant changes and reshufflings, due to internal divisions and political changes in the outside world. The dominant Francoist slogan, coined during the heyday of the Republic by JONS leader Onésimo Redondo, was *Una, grande y libre*. Besides referencing the Holy Trinity and contemporary Fascist slogans, it summarized the Francoist idea of Spain quite well. *Una* referred to what was seen as the indivisible unity of the country, in contrast to the regional autonomies of Catalonia and the Basque Country during the Republic; *grande* pointed to the former grandeur of the Spanish overseas empire, spreading the Spanish language and the Catholic faith all over the American continent; and *libre* reinforced that the country was free from foreign intervention, especially Communists, Jews, and, somewhat peculiarly, Freemasons. Since the interest of this volume is on the vernacular as a concept, it is worth considering, first, its opposites. Francoism rejected the perceived cosmopolitan ideals of its foes and cherished the idea of empire: although some Falangists dreamed of a new Spanish empire, the main focus of the utterly conservative Francoist ideology, obsessed with the concept of an "eternal Spain," was the imperial dominance of the Spanish Golden Age in the sixteenth and seventeenth centuries (see, e.g., Sueiro Seoane 2009). To a large extent, the dreams of the past fueled the ambitions of the present.

Inimical to the imperial imaginary was the presence of the vernacular. As already noted, the nationalist ambitions of Catalans and Basques had been one of the major reasons for the coup d'état, and during the war the anti-separatism of National Catholicism was declared:

> A central element of this ideology, in addition to anti-Marxism, anti-liberalism and anti-Semitism, was an aggressive and exclusive Spanish nationalism, which postulated the absolute supremacy of Castilian and the subordination or marginalization of "regional dialects"—also called "vernacular languages"—since, as Jaime Solá argued in 1937 in the magazine *Vida Gallega* "under the innocent defense of vernacular languages lurks the grim intentions of separatism."[4]

---

[4] *Elementos centrais desa ideoloxía, ademais do anti-marxismo, o anti-liberalismo e o anti-semitismo, era un nacionalismo español agresivo e excluínte, que postulaba a supremacía absoluta do castelán e a subordinación ou marxinación dos "dialectos regionales" —tamén chamados "linguas vernáculas"—, xa que, conforme argumentaba en 1937 Jaime Solá na revista Vida Gallega "debajo de la inocente defensa de las lenguas vernáculas acechan las torvas intenciones del separatismo"* (Monteagudo 2021: n.p.).

The term *vernacular languages* is thus used negatively by the regime's ideologues, in parallel with the equally derogatory term *regional dialects*, in a clear contrast to the imperial stateliness of Castilian. In the eyes of the Catholic Church, of course, all Romance languages may be seen as vernaculars, but in the particular thinking of National Catholicism, it could be said that Catalan was to Spanish what Spanish had been to Latin: a bleak and vulgar tongue, estranged from the loftiness of the divine and eternal language. In addition, behind the supposedly innocent defense of those vernaculars lurked separatist intentions, a threat to the very existence of the Spanish nation, and as such, it needed to be suppressed in favor of Spanish:

> After the fall of Catalonia under Franco's boot, the newspaper *La Vanguardia* published an editorial entitled "Speak like Franco," in which a threat was made: "All Spaniards must do three things: think like Franco, feel like Franco and speak like Franco, who, speaking, of course, in the national language, has imposed his Victory."[5]

Think like Franco, feel like Franco, speak like Franco: the totalitarian aspirations of the Spanish dictator, imbued with religious resonances, have rarely been invoked in this way: to shape Spaniards in his own image and likeness. The mind of the new citizen must be colonized, and, perhaps most importantly, the language spoken must be that of the dictator, already endowed with divine and imperial qualities. The regional languages, dismissed as lowly vernaculars in relation to the language of victory, had no place in the new state formation.

The control over language and literature was asserted in the beginning of the Civil War, in the areas controlled by the rebels. Six months after the outbreak of the war, the Junta issued an order that would have far-reaching consequences: "The production, trade and circulation of newspapers, magazines, brochures and all kinds of pornographic prints and engravings, as well as socialist, communist, libertarian, and, in general, solvent literature are declared illegal."[6] An order issued the following year specified the jurisdiction in some further detail, prohibiting any publication containing "subversive

---

[5] *Despois da caída de Cataluña baixo a bota franquista, o xornal La Vanguardia publicaba un editorial titulado "Hablar como Franco," en que se ameazaba: "Todos los españoles debemos hacer tres cosas: pensar como Franco, sentir como Franco y hablar como Franco, que hablando, naturalmente, en el idioma nacional, ha impuesto su Victoria"* (Monteagudo 2021: 297).

[6] *Se declaran ilícitas la producción, el comercio y la circulación de periódicos, revistas, folletos y toda clase de impresos y grabados pornográficos o de literatura socialista, comunista, libertaria y, en general, disolventes* (in Abellán 1984: 158).

ideas, immoral concepts, propaganda of Marxist doctrines and everything that means disrespect for the Dignity of our glorious Army, attacks on the Unity of the Nation, contempt for the Catholic Religion and anything that opposes the meaning and purposes of our National Crusade."[7] Since this study explores in part the suppression and prohibition of regional languages in Spain under Franco, I have tried to trace this repression back to the original documents. Where and when, exactly, does the Franco regime state the prohibition of the regional languages of Spain? The answer is that no laws or unequivocal regulations seem to have existed. At least in the Spanish case, the censorship itself was by nature evasive—to the point that we can talk about "censura de la censura" (the censoring of the censorship) (Torrealdai 1998: 8)—and would do anything to erase its traces. What we have, then, are two vague wartime orders and the actions that they spurred. The orders themselves are certainly open for interpretation but nonetheless sufficiently clear for regional and local authorities in the period: as we have seen, the Fascist rhetoric of the time drew a clear line between language and separatism, so the fact that the "subversive ideas" and the "attacks on the Unity of the Fatherland" were to be chastised could only mean that local languages had to be repressed.

In spite of the vagueness of the language of the proclamations—or even because of that vagueness—the local authorities took their task extremely seriously, to the point that they were, as Solé i Sabaté and Villaroya phrase it, "*más papistas que el papa*" (more Catholic than the Pope) (1995: 48). The first step was, of course, not so much to stop book production but to hinder their dissemination and "purge" the books already circulating. At first, people were urged to hand over books in Catalan, Basque, and Galician voluntarily, but then, shops, libraries, and private collections were raided, and the books were burned in the streets of Madrid, Barcelona, and Bilbao (Perriam et al. 2000: 5). The archives of Catalanist politician Antoni Rovira i Virgili or the invaluable library of Pompeu Fabra, the engineer and linguist behind the standardization of Catalan in the 1920s, were thrown into the flames (Abellán 1984: 161). However, there were a few cracks in the regime's attitude towards the languages. Dionisio Ridruejo, director of propaganda and a convinced Falangist, was shocked by the

---

[7] *Ideas disolventes, conceptos inmorales, propaganda de doctrinas marxistas y todo cuanto signifique falta de respeto a la Dignidad de nuestro glorioso Ejército, atentados a la Unidad de la Patria, menosprecio de la Religión Católica y de cuanto se oponga al significado y fines de nuestra Cruzada Nacional* (in Abellán 1984: 158).

repression when a truckload of propaganda leaflets in Catalan was stopped from entering Barcelona. To him, content trumped language; to the regime, it was the opposite.

After the war was over, with much of the purging already achieved, the regime moved to control production. At this point, the regime did not so much prohibit different social activities but, rather, obligated citizens to request prior authorization, as an *a priori* form of repression (Solé i Sabaté and Villarroya 1995: 52). This measure created an effective form of self-censorship among many authors and publishers. In general, what was striking about the Spanish censorship at the time was its sheer arbitrariness: "The most totalitarian feature was inconsistency and arbitrariness as methods of state terror: the unpredictability of censorship was often based on exemplary prohibitions and on the display of its discretionary character. The contradictions of its opinions, the apparent capricious nature of its decisions, the diversity of censors could give the impression of a permissiveness that did not exist" (Gracia and Ródenas 2011: 24).[8] The "double censorship," regarding both language and content was felt by regional writers and publishers (De Blas 1999: 296).

At the same time, the regime magnified the social status of Castilian at the expense of the regional languages. By order of the Ministry for National Education the *Catecismo Patriótico Español* was required reading in all Spanish schools in 1939, making the governing attitude clear:

- Why do you say that the Spanish language will be the language of the civilization of the future?
- The Spanish language will be the language of the civilization of the future because English and French, which could share this function with it, are worn-out languages, on the way to complete dissolution.
- Are there other languages spoken in Spain besides Castilian?
- It can be said that in Spain only the Castilian language is spoken, since apart from this there is only Basque, which, as the sole language, is only used in some Basque villages and was reduced to dialect functions due to its linguistic and philological poverty.

---

[8] *El rasgo más totalitario fue la inconsecuencia y la arbitrariedad como métodos de terror de Estado: la imprevisibilidad de la censura se fundaba a menudo en las prohibiciones ejemplarizantes y en la exhibición de su carácter discrecional. Las contradicciones de sus dictámenes, el aparente carácter caprichoso de sus decisiones, la diversidad de censores pudieron aparentar una permisividad que no fue tal.*

- And what are the main dialects spoken in Spain?
- There are four main dialects spoken in Spain: Catalan, Valencian, Mallorcan and Galician.[9] (Solé i Sabaté and Villarroya 1995: 86)

The imperial fantasy is on display: French and English are completely worn-out languages, since they are spoken by the degenerated Allied powers, and Spanish is destined to be the language of the future civilization. The other Romance languages of the country are reduced to mere dialects, vulgar variations of Castilian—a strategy that would become a standard procedure during most of the dictatorship. Basque, on the other hand, may be a language, but it is not exactly *spoken*, since it is only used in some Basque farmhouses. The vernacularization of languages that only three years earlier had enjoyed full legal status in their respective regions had begun.

As we shall see, the totalitarian grip loosened after World War II was over, and Spain had to clean up its image by distancing itself from the ideology of the Axis powers. By the end of the 1940s, the first books in Catalan were published, though still under strict censorial control. After all, literature had a limited influence on the masses, much more important was the control over radio, film, theater and, later, television. A major shift occurred in 1959, both for the languages and, more generally, for oppositional culture. The Franco regime was close to bankruptcy and, for the first time since the war, social unrest was growing among students and workers. In order to survive in power, Franco purged the last Falangists from the government and turned toward a neo-capitalist, less ideological, and less autarkic policy. The reshuffle led to the employment of a class of technocrats, well-educated professionals belonging, almost without exception, to the secular Catholic order Opus Dei (Hooper 1995: 17). The technocrats courted rather than crushed the regional languages, and were led by the modern and dynamic minister of Tourism and Information, Manuel Fraga Iribarne. The Press Law had not been revised since the wartime

---

[9] – ¿Por qué decís que la lengua castellana será la lengua de la civilización del futuro?
 – La lengua castellana será la lengua de la civilización del futuro porque el inglés y el francés, que con ella pudieran compartir esta función, son lenguas gastadas, que van camino de una disolución completa.
 – ¿Se habla en España otras lenguas más que la lengua castellana?
 – Puede decirse que en España se habla sólo la lengua castellana, pues aparte de ésta tan sólo se habla el vascuence, que, como lengua única, sólo se emplea en algunos caseríos vascos y quedó reducido a funciones de dialecto por su pobreza lingüística y filológica.
 – ¿Y cuáles son los dialectos principales que se hablan en España?
 – Los dialectos principales que se hablan en España son cuatro: el catalán, el valenciano, el mallorquín y el gallego.

orders referenced above, and Fraga's *Ley de Prensa e Imprenta* (Law of Press and Printing) of 1966 was seen as a significant progressive step and an attunement to more democratic times (Torrealdai 2019: 26). The major change was that the prior authorization was canceled and substituted with a voluntary *consulta previa* ("prior check") but, in reality, not much was different: the State still reserved the right to control all publishing, and, according to Abellán, "there were in actuality more governmental interventions against publication of objectionable material than in preceding years" (in Ugarte 2005: 13).

In a country where the Catholic Church had been intertwined with political power, more substantial protection for the languages came from a somewhat unexpected direction. The Second Vatican Council of 1962 explicitly stated that Mass should be given in the vernacular, and in the language most understood by the people. Sections of the Spanish Catholic Church, especially in the bilingual regions, were dissatisfied with the way the local languages were treated by the monolingual regime (and with their role in the distribution of power, where they sometimes felt like mere alibis to the military dictatorship), and seized the opportunity granted to them by Vatican II to use the regional languages in sermons.

In the 1970s, near the end of the dictatorship, there were some drastic changes in the attitudes towards the languages, as we shall see. But let us first look at the different modes of vernacular resistance, without which those changes would never have been made.

Catalunya: Collaboration and cooption

Catalonia was (and is) the richest and most populous of the bilingual regions, with solid cultural traditions, a powerful and Catalan-speaking bourgeoisie, a broad and successful manufacturing industry, and a strong national identity. A Statute of Autonomy was approved in 1932, which, among other things, led to the creation of the Catalan Parliament and the Court of Justice, giving the region far-reaching autonomous rights. Due to the industrial economy and heavy influx of immigrants from other parts of Spain, Catalonia and its undeniable hub, Barcelona, were also the scenes of radical political activity, for both Anarchists and Socialists, which often led to street fights and violent clashes with the authorities. Even though the political class and the bourgeoisie were often conservative and Catholic, Catalonia therefore came to represent all that

Franco and the insurgents resented: leftism, separatism, and atheism, bundled together in the neologism *rojo-separatista* (*red-separatist*), despite the fact that many separatists were not leftists nor, certainly, were all leftists separatists.[10]

When the Civil War was over, the idea of Catalonia as the quintessential enemy of the Spanish nation—a recurring image over the centuries that has served Spanish nationalists well both in 1898 and in 2017—led to harsh state repression. Catalan was banned from all official use, including street signs, tombstone inscriptions, and first names; thousands of university professors, schoolteachers, and clergymen were fired and replaced with Castilian-speaking Franco loyalists; and all publishing of books, journals, newspapers, as well as films, musical acts, and theater plays in the language were prohibited. Catalan was in effect vernacularized: after a few years of official use during the Republic, the language was relegated to familiar and private life. Josep Benet, author of the pioneering *Catalunya sota el règim franquista* (Catalonia under the Franco regime), a thorough examination of the cultural and linguistic repression in Catalonia published anonymously in Paris in 1973,[11] states that the aims of the Franco regime were clear: the "persecution of the language and culture was the inexorable fulfillment of one of the essential objectives of Francoism, winner of the war of Spain: the disappearance of Catalonia as a national minority in the Spanish state, with the destruction of its linguistic and cultural personality and the reduction of its language to the condition of patois" (Benet 1973: 10).[12]

During the first post-war years, the repression was so broad and severe that Benet talks about an attempt at "cultural genocide."[13] As already mentioned, even Franco's Minister of Propaganda, Dionisio Ridruejo, a poet and a devoted Fascist

---

[10] According to Vilanova i Vila-Abadal (1998: 140–41), the term was invented by Maximiano García Venero at some point before January 1937.

[11] Benet's book (just as the later *La censura de Franco y el tema vasco* (Torrealdai 1998) in the Basque case) responds precisely to the lack of historical memory: if linguistic and cultural repression was only de facto and not de iure, then the only way to prove this repression was to document how it was carried out in practice, painstakingly enumerating the evidence. The first edition was published by the *Institut català d'estudis polítics i socials*, a "scientific institution that operates clandestinely in Barcelona." The prologue "regrets that the Francoist repression still faced by the Catalan Countries of Spain does not allow for the names of this report to be made public. Its authors, according to the legislation of the Francoist Spain, risk sentences as high as thirty years of imprisonment" (14). Later editions, published after the death of Franco, have Benet as the author.

[12] *La persecució contra la llengua i la cultura catalanes era el compliment inexorable d'un dels objectius essencials del franquisme, vencedor de la guerra de Espanya: la desaparició de Catalunya com a minoria nacional dins l'Estat espanyol, amb la destrucció de la seva personalitat lingüística i cultural, i la reducció del seu idioma a la condició de patois.*

[13] For a long discussion on the possibility of cultural genocide in Catalonia, see Vilanova's "Did Catalonia Endure a (Cultural) Genocide?" (2016).

(in contrast to Franco) expressed disappointment and nausea when the insurgent troops entered Barcelona and destroyed truckloads of propaganda leaflets, well aligned with the Francoists' political line, because they were written in Catalan (Abellán 1984: 160–61). In these dark years, which Gallén calls the "grau zero de la cultura catalana" (zero degree of Catalan culture) (1987: 213), Catalan intellectuals were left with few alternatives. Some writers, especially the more conservative ones, aligned with the regime and switched their working language from Catalan to Castilian; others preferred to continue publishing clandestinely in Catalan. The most radical choice was to move into exile, normally via Nazi-occupied France to the Spanish-speaking countries in the Americas. All of these choices had their obvious limitations, but they nonetheless lay the ground for a more significant cultural resistance once World War II was over and the regime somewhat loosened its grip.

However brutal the cultural repression during the first years of the dictatorship, it was fairly limited in time. After the Allied victory, when the Franco regime needed to distance itself from European Fascism, a period of minimal tolerance began in Catalonia. Some cultural manifestations in Catalan were now permitted: a few classical works were reprinted, theatrical plays were staged, and, notably, the Orfeó Català—a choir with huge symbolic importance, due to Catalonia's long-standing choral traditions—was allowed to perform again. These were minor steps in the recovery of Catalan culture, but, nevertheless, they represented an opening in State-enforced monolingualism, where "every niche of freedom was exploited by the cultural activists" (Conversi 1997: 115). From here on, clandestine classes in Catalan language and history were organized, new literary prizes appeared, the Institut d'Estudis Catalans slowly started to recover, and the publishing house Selecta, which would later be very important, was founded. The first major publication was a reprint of the complete works of Jacint Verdaguer, a Renaixença poet of great symbolic importance, which sold 100,000 copies within a year (Dowling 2018: 375). The regime underscored his Spanishness and that he wrote "in the Spanish language of Catalan," as one religious critic pointed out (375), but only allowed the publication language in its non-standardized form, prior to Pompeu Fabra's normative reforms in the 1910s, as a way to *dialectalize* the language and downplay its unity (Conversi 1997: 116). The number of books published rose steadily—from twelve books in 1946 to ninety-six in 1954—though, at least in the first years, they were mainly translations of works not already published in Spanish, poetry and folkloric and religious texts, while bilingual congresses and other intellectual, "para-official" collaborations began to flourish (Samsó 1999b: 223). Without the support of the literary system—criticism, publicity, and literary prizes, as well as bookshops and distributors—the task for the editors was to reach the literary audience. Sales went from public to individual, with distribution by subscription and home deliveries (Samsó 1999a: 235).

During the first two decades of the dictatorship, the Francoist approach to Catalan culture went from repression over tolerance toward a growing co-option. The permissiveness of the latter part of the 1940s was not only due to a shift in European politics but also included "the intention to de-victimize and normalize the Catalan peculiarity" (Samsó 1999b: 221).[14] State officials realized that all intents to suffocate Catalan culture would be in vain, so they shifted their strategy in order to assimilate Catalan heterogeneity as a natural part of the larger Spanish nation, while intent on not giving Catalan nationalists at home and abroad any reasons for martyrdom. At the same time, the defeat in the Civil War and the ensuing repression ignited a soul search on behalf of Catalan intellectuals, particularly Jaume Vicens Vives and Josep Ferrater Mora: in contrast to conservative, autarkic, enclosed, and reactionary Spain, Catalonia would be open, pluralistic, modern, and reflective.

In 1959, the regime laid out the Plan for Economic Stabilization, which brought about a major shift in the policy of the dictatorship. The new direction of the country was to be neo-capitalist[15] and Europeanist, as a response to the growing power of the financial oligarchy and the new industrial bourgeoisie. The Franco regime—at this point more interested in its own survival than in ideology—realized that the country needed economic reform, modernization, and a moderate opening to the outside world, and it had to deal with growing political opposition among students, workers, and cultural activists. New cultural organizations were created, such as the Òmnium Cultural in 1961, and even though it was temporarily banned by the increasingly erratic regime, it was highly influential in creating a new, more organized opposition.[16] The

---

[14] *La intenció de desvictimitzar i de normalitzar la peculiaritat catalana.*

[15] As with other Fascist movements in Europe at the time, the Falange was strongly anti-capitalist. Ramón Serrano Súñer, chief ideologue of the party after the death of José Antonio Primo de Rivera in 1936 and the architect of the Francoist Estado Nuevo (New State), made his position clear: "We know perfectly well that we cannot demand from the workers a love of the country, as long as that country is not something vital to them. But the working population of Catalonia will soon understand that we have not undertaken the task of war to defend a capitalist position" (Benet 1973: 229–30).

[16] Òmnium Cultural was also one of the leading actors behind the Catalan referendum for independence in 2017. As of 2021, two of its leaders are still imprisoned, convicted for sedition.

cultural resistance, with the strategy of "move, countermove, adjustment and negotiation" (Dowling 2018: 385), organized a flurry of activities, from semi-official to grassroots levels. Somewhat paradoxically, given the political symbiosis between the Catholic Church and the Franco regime and the fact that merely 15 percent of Barcelonans considered themselves Catholic in 1963 (Conversi 1997: 126), the local clergy took a leading role in the defense of Catalan language and culture. With the unexpected support of Vatican II and its vindication of vernacular languages, Catalan bishops and priests used their legitimacy to work for moderate language and cultural reforms. In 1947, the Benedictine abbey of Montserrat held mass in Catalan (and flew an enormous Catalan flag on top of a mountain), and in the 1960s, their publishing house "engaged in the publication of books and magazines that no private publishing house would dare to print" (127). Chairs of Catalan language and literature were created at the University of Barcelona in 1966 and at the Autonomous University of Barcelona in 1969, although courses on Catalan language and literature had first entered the university during the Republic (Subirana 2018: 219). Students, professors, and intellectuals organized in a common union, and a broad coalition of Leftist parties organized street protests and roundtables. The political apparatus of Catalanism offered a mode of organized resistance to disenchanted activists along the whole political spectrum, particularly on the Left, just as in the case of the *Indignados* movement in Catalonia that started on May 15, 2011. Perhaps most interesting of all was the everyday resistance organized by grassroots movements: through Scout organizations, hiking groups, soccer supporters, dance companies, and even mushroom excursions, a strong bond was created between the people and territory, tradition, folklore, and nation, hinged on the community-building of nineteenth-century Catalonia (Conversi 1997: 135). As Conversi points out, "this brought about a diffused sense of optimism, showing the unique value of cultural resistance—and cultural nationalism—shaping a country's identity without needing to resort to violent strategies" (135). As we shall see, the non-violent strategies, patent, too, in the independence activism of the 2010s, are in stark contrast to the case of the Basque Country.

In the face of such overwhelming activity at all levels of society, the Franco regime chose co-option before repression. Catalan culture was declared part and parcel of the Spanishness that was at the base of Francoism, even though it was expressed in the vernacular. In fact, by sleight of hand, vernacular heterogeneity was now seen as the core of Spanish grandeur. It is not difficult to see that the initial repression of all things Catalan in the end had the opposite effect of strengthening a culture at the brink of extinction, with lasting political consequences both in the transition to democracy and in today's national politics. The heavy-handed and blunt Francoist repression—hateful and bigoted in the beginning, inconsequential and morally confused toward the end—also gave Catalan nationalists a sense of "inner moral superiority" (Conversi 1997: 140) that, to some extent, has lasted to this day.

Euskadi: Ikastolas and violence

The Basque Country suffered repression similar to that in Catalonia. Although the region surrendered to insurgents in 1937 and was home to the ultra-Catholic and conservative (albeit also Basque Nationalist) Carlists that Franco used as ideological alibis, it nevertheless endured unprecedented state terror in the first postwar years. *Lehendakari* José Antonio Aguirre, the exiled President of the Basque government, who tirelessly travelled the world in support of the Basque cause, issued a statement to UNESCO in 1952, at the time Spain was applying for membership, in which he denounced a wholesale attack on Basque language and culture: universities and social and cultural associations had been closed, books written in Basque publicly burned, all public use of Basque prohibited, Basque names forbidden, and—once again that eschatological zeal—Basque inscriptions on tombstones had to be erased (Conversi 1997: 81). As in the case of Catalan, Basque itself was associated with separatism and thus needed to be eradicated from public use and relegated to the private sphere.

The first literary work in Basque published after the Civil War, Telesforo Monzón's significantly titled *Urrundik* (*From Afar*), came out in Mexico in 1945, initiating a rich and important trans-Atlantic interchange between the silenced Motherland and the uprooted exile community, particularly in Mexico, Chile, and the River Plate region. The first publication in the Basque Country proper, the Franciscan friar Salbatore Mitxelena's poetry collection *Arantzazu: Euskal sinismearen poema* (*Arantzazu: Poem of the Basque Faith*), saw the light of day in 1949. The book centers on the oral tradition of the Gipuzkoan monastery of Arantzazu, shrewdly telling a story of resistance and defiance through religious allegory, and served as a call for action among an array of intellectual Franciscans and artists to the defense and renovation of the Basque language (Juaristi 1987: 106). Publication of books in Basque was still heavily regulated by the regime, but religious and folkloric texts often passed censorship. The center of Basque intellectual and literary debate was still elsewhere; for example, the literary journal *Euzko Gogoa* was published in Guatemala and distributed to diasporic communities in twenty-six countries all through the 1950s (Gabilondo 2016: 226).

One of the Franciscans to heed the call of Arantzazu was Joan Mari Torrealdai, who later became the foremost scholar on Francoist censorship in the Basque Country. During the first two decades of the dictatorship, the censorship was, at the same time, extremely rigorous and subject to individual judgments and personal favors (such as in the semi-official system of *padrinos*, according to which a person with ties to the regime could recommend personally the publication of certain books). In general, the censors prohibited the publication of anything that smacked of opposition to the regime and its policies, to the extent that opposing theories could not even be mentioned in order to be refuted or by way of fictional characters. In the case of books in Basque, things became even more complicated. Since almost no censors read Basque, books in this language had to go directly to the provincial delegation in San Sebastian, where one reader had all the power to stop a work or let it pass. In giving their verdict, censors had to adhere to a centrally designed form with the following guidelines:

> Does it attack Dogma or Morals?
> The institutions of the Regime?
> Does it have literary or documentary value?
> Circumstantial reasons that advise one or the other decision.[17]
>
> (Torrealdai 1998: 24)

Consequently, there was a certain margin for subjective interpretation; not only did the censors have to judge whether a work followed Francoist principles (and here, even the *lack* of satisfactory Spanish national sentiment could be sanctioned) but also if the text in question had any literary value. Censors were not just bureaucrats but also more or less qualified readers (more so in the beginning of the dictatorship, when the ranks were still filled with Falangists) that often saw the censorship report as an opportunity to exercise literary criticism.

1959 was a watershed year in Spain in general and much more so in the Basque Country. The Plan for Economic Reform turned the tables with respect

---

[17] *¿Ataca al Dogma o a la Moral?*
¿A las instituciones del Régimen?
¿Tiene valor literario o documental?
Razones circunstanciales que aconsejen una u otra decisión.

to cultural politics and vernacular resistance throughout Spain, sparking myriad more-or-less significant semi-official and grassroots activities. It was also the year of the creation of *Euskadi ta Askatasuna* (ETA), the armed separatist guerrilla group that would be a major factor in Spanish and Basque political and social life until the final, unilateral ceasefire in 2011. These two struggles—cultural and military—have the same origins and run parallel over decades, although they underwent radically different developments.

In the beginning of the 1950s, a group of students, too young to have participated in the Civil War, became disenchanted with the main Basque opposition party, Partido Nacionalista Vasco (PNV). As mentioned before, the PNV's leader, the *lehendakari* Aguirre, had fought for the Basque cause ever since the end of the war, but when the United States came to see Franco more as a strategically located anti-Communist ally than a Fascist enemy, the students started to look elsewhere for ideological inspiration. In secret study groups, they discovered the radical roots of Basque nationalism and realized the need not just to save and preserve Basque culture and language but also to reformulate it according to the modern world. They were generally referred to as the *Ekin* [To Act or to Insist] group, after their clandestine literary journal. Their intellectual leader was the writer José Luis Alvarez Enparantza, who wrote under the nom de plume *Txillardegi* and whose literature and political thought were tinged by the existentialism of Albert Camus and Jean-Paul Sartre (Gabilondo 2016: 226). Indeed, Sartre would later voice his explicit support for ETA during the infamous Burgos trial in 1970 (Conversi 1997: 89). By the beginning of the 1960s, however, ETA was still a cultural movement, mainly concerned with the protection and cultivation of Basque language and culture. The shift toward the armed struggle came with the influence of another intellectual, Federico Krutwig, son of a German industrialist and adult learner of Basque, and the publication of his long book *Vasconia* (1963). Krutwig was heavily influenced by Franz Fanon's anti-colonialism and the revolutions in Algeria and Cuba, and he advocated for armed struggle against what he saw as the colonial occupation by Spain; his thinking was also decidedly anti-clerical and anti-racist, as opposed to the Catholic and racist leanings of the founding father of Basque nationalism, Sabino Arana. By straying away from the old ideas of blood and race, Basque nationalism could appeal to the newly immigrated masses of industrial workers from other parts of Spain and thus integrate a class perspective to the national struggle. From here on, and with the influence of Mao Tse-tung and Ho Chi Minh, ETA became a Marxist Nationalist movement, embarking on the deadly path of revolutionary war. Police repression was severe, which resulted in several controversial trials and executions as well as scores of ETA militants in exile, and internal strife estranged the moderates and gave way for militant hardliners. By the time ETA reached its peak of popular support, inside and outside the Basque Country, which coincided with the spectacular assassination of Franco's successor, the admiral Luis Carrero Blanco in 1973, the organization had abandoned theoretical discussions and cultural activity in favor of relentless guerrilla warfare.

The main grassroots movement during the dictatorship, which would have a lasting impact on Basque language, culture, and society, was the movement that resulted in the groundbreaking work of the *ikastolas*—schools with Basque as the language of instruction. Often conflated due to their supposedly separatist intentions (and strong industrial economies), the Basque Country was in most respects quite different from Catalonia. Where the latter had a well-developed literary system, a large publishing industry, and a broad, urban, Catalan-speaking bourgeoisie, the former had a very rich oral literature but scant book publications, no public universities (the only university in the region until the 1950s was the Jesuit-run University of Deusto, founded in the 1880s), and a middle class that almost exclusively spoke Castilian—and, as in the cases of highly prominent intellectuals such as Miguel de Unamuno and Ramón de Maeztu, even resented the use of Basque and declared it a moribund language.[18] Basque was widely spoken in the countryside, but by a fairly small population,

---

[18] See, for example, Unamuno's speech to Congress on September 18, 1931:
 And about thirty years ago, there, in my native land, I gave a speech that caused a great commotion, a speech in which I told my countrymen that Basque was dying, that we had no choice but to pick it up and bury it with filial mercy, embalmed in science ... Today that continues, that agony continues; it is a sad thing, but a fact is a fact, and just as it would seem to me a true impiety to try to awaken someone who is dying, the dying mother, it seems so impious to inject drugs to extend a fictitious life, because drugs are the works that are carried out today to make a cultured Language and a Language that, in the sense that is ordinarily given to this word, cannot become so.
 (*Y hace cosa de treinta años, allí, en mi nativa tierra, pronuncié un discurso que produjo una gran conmoción, un discurso en el que les dije a mis paisanos que el vascuence estaba agonizando, que no nos quedaba más que recogerlo y enterrarlo con piedad filial, embalsamado en ciencia ... Hoy continúa eso, sigue esa agonía; es cosa triste, pero el hecho es un hecho, y así como me parecería una verdadera impiedad el que se pretendiera despenar a alguien que está muriendo, a la madre moribunda, me parece tan impío inocularle drogas para alargarle una vida ficticia, porque drogas son los trabajos que hoy se realizan para hacer una Lengua culta y una Lengua que, en el sentido que se da ordinariamente a esta palabra, no puede llegar a serlo.*)
 However, he had not always had that somber view of Basque. In 1888, he participated in the *oposiciones* to the first chair in Basque at the Instituto de Bilbao, along with the founding father of Basque nationalism, Sabino Arana. The chair went to another 24-year-old, the priest Resurrección María de Azkue.

and with that plus a very large influx of Castilian-speaking industrial workers and a weak institutional status, the Franco repression meant a severe, even life-threatening blow for the language. The *ikastola* movement started with the semi-clandestine, collective homeschooling of the *casas-escuelas* in the 1950s, as a way of creating a community around Basque-language teaching that harkened back to the interrupted labor of the Basque-language schools of the Republic. Astutely tiptoeing the limit between private and public—or, if you will, between the vernacular and the national—the pioneer Elbira Zipitria and the *maestras* following in her footsteps provided the children of nationalist families with a primary education at least partly in Basque (Iza and Ikastolak 2011: 28).

The next step, the creation of more formal Basque-language schools, was made possible by fundraising campaigns throughout the Basque-speaking areas—even those belonging to France—and a genuinely popular mobilization. Even though a loose network was created, the schools grew organically, independently, and, again, semi-clandestinely, each one according to the work of teachers and parents and to their abilities to circumvent regime control. Through contacts with Catalan activists, with experience from schooling in Catalan during the Republic, they realized the potential of a school free from both State and Church influence. Once the first *ikastola* had opened in Bilbao in 1957, followed by another one in San Sebastian in 1961, there was a snowball effect, and in 1977, there were as many as 40,000 students attending 185 schools (Conversi 1997: 104). The first years were marred with obstructions and legal difficulties, where schoolteachers were imprisoned or given hefty fines. In 1965, the Franco regime introduced the *cartilla de escolaridad* (school card), which was necessary when a student wished to transfer to another school or access secondary education. Even though the *ikastolas* could not issue these cards as pedagogical institutions, they ingeniously managed to circumvent the rules, either by registering the schools as cultural or mercantile societies, or, as an act of solidarity, by teachers in public schools issuing the cards for *ikastola* students (Iza and Ikastolak 2011: 58). The *ikastolas*—still highly active, pedagogically advanced, and cooperatively owned—are a prime example of a genuinely grassroots vernacular resistance in the face of an aggressively monolingual dictatorial regime.

After 1959, there was also "a virtual explosion of culture in Basque" (De Pablo 2009: 55). Book publication increased significantly, music with lyrics in Basque became popular (in parallel to the Catalan *Nova Cançó*), poetry readings were held, and literacy campaigns for adults were initiated. The lively oral Basque culture, traditionally related to couplets, ballads, lyric songs, tales, proverbs, carnival productions, and Christmas plays (Etxeberria 2012), had its outstanding representation in the popular *bertsolaritza*, "a rhetorical genre of an epidictic, oral, sung, and improvised character" (Garzia 2012: 46). The *bertsolaritza* shows, unique to Basque culture on the Iberian Peninsula (and very rare even on a European scale), became acts of resistance, celebrations of vernacular and popular culture that excluded everyone without a thorough grasp of Basque, and reinforced the bonds of the community. Equally important was the standardization of the Basque language, finalized with the creation of *euskera batua* (unified Basque) in 1968, which brought together the myriad dialects and paved the way for a developed literary language. This cultural activity was a boost for a new generation of writers, especially Ramon Saizarbitoria and Bernardo Atxaga, who renewed Basque literature and made it part of the cosmopolitan circuits of world literature.[19]

Although a very different region, the vernacular resistance in the Basque Country partly mirrored the development in Catalonia: broad grassroots movements that took advantage of every opening and ambiguity in the regime control in order to foster and advance local culture and language. The major difference, of course, is that while Catalans favored non-violent action, part of the Basque resistance found that, due to the severe repression of an already weak linguistic culture, armed struggle was the only way to reverse the situation.

Galiza: The importance of the diaspora

Unlike Basque-language letters, Galician literature has a long and prestigious pedigree. The school of Galician poetry behind the important *Cancioneiros* was established in 1196 (Rodríguez Alonso 2004: 310). Galician-Portuguese was the language of poetry, both in Galicia and in the court of Castile, throughout the Middle Ages, until it was finally pushed aside by the expanding Castilian. Literature in Galician led a life in the shadows until the publication of the first poetry collection in the modern era, Rosalía de Castro's *Cantares gallegos* (1863), which sparked the *Rexurdimento*, the renaissance of Galician culture and language. Just as in the case of the Catalan *Renaixença*, this cultural movement was part of a general national awakening in Europe, both in nation-states and

---

[19] Atxaga is mostly known for his *Obabakoak* (1988), translated into 27 languages—all preserving the original Basque title.

in sub-state nations, where a people's efforts to distance itself from the Other frequently entailed a search for medieval roots. In nations without states, this endeavor was often seen as a struggle for cultural survival in the face of urbanization, industrialization, modernity, and the growing, homogenizing power of the modern nation-state. Its first decades saw a flurry of cultural activities, especially through the *Irmandades da Fala* (The Brotherhoods of Language), which strived not only for the use of Galician as a literary and cultivated language, but also for its implementation at all levels of society. The Statute of Autonomy was ratified in a referendum in June of 1936—no less than 99 percent of Galicians voted in favor (Rodríguez Alonso 2004: 315)—but, since the Civil War broke out the following month, it never came into effect. As in the cases of Catalonia and the Basque Country, the Statute declared that Galicia was to be bilingual at all official levels.

However, Galicia differed politically, economically, socially, culturally, and geographically from the other two bilingual regions. It had virtually no industry and was therefore a region of emigration, both to other parts of Spain and to the Americas, rather than immigration. Even though it was "fundamentally Republican" (Fernández Prieto 2011: 38) at the outbreak of the war, it was already within Francoist territory, and political refugees had nowhere to escape once the military crackdowns started. The region did not have the symbolic position of Catalonia or the Basque Country, but the strong support for the Republic made Francoist repression as severe here as in the other bilingual regions, including prohibitions of all official use of the vernacular language. The Caudillo himself was Galician, born and raised in the naval town of Ferrol, but he never spoke Galician publicly. Both the repression and neglect only confirmed a long history of marginalization: "the repressive policy of the Franco regime against Galician was not an absolute novelty but meant a qualitative leap in a long trajectory of the marginalization of Galician and subjugation of the people who spoke it: the culmination, in a particularly violent, extremist and subjugating way, of an age-old history."[20] *Dialect* or *vernacular* were regularly used to belittle the Galician language, framed in opposition to the universal Spanish. This rhetoric was even part of well-meaning efforts, as when the poet and editor Ramón González Alegre tried to convince the Galician poet Manuel María to write in Castilian: "Don't do

---

[20] *a política represiva do franquismo contra o galego non constituía unha novidade absoluta, senón que significaba un salto cualitativo nunha longa traxectoria de marxinación do galego e de asoballamento das persoas que o falaban: a culminación, por unha vía particularmente violenta, extremista e asoballante, dunha historia secular* (Monteagudo 2021).

it in Galician for God's sake. Don't humiliate yourself for no reason. Seek universality, seek transcendence" (María 1995: 28–9 in Monteagudo 2021).[21]

The linguistic situation was similar to that of the Basque Country: in the countryside, people spoke almost exclusively Galician, but the economic and intellectual elites of the urban centers tended to speak Castilian. In 1935, a mere thirteen books were published in Galician, among them a translation of Federico García Lorca (Alonso Montero 1991: 103). Between 1936 and 1946, due to the political climate, there were virtually no books published in the local language. As in other regions, publication in Galician was not officially banned; even though significant scholarly efforts have been made, no government documents stating formal prohibition of publications in other languages than Spanish have been found. As Alonso Montero states, this operating procedure, more insidious that an outright ban, cleared the Franco regime of possible international criticism—and also makes it possible for right-wing, present-day apologists to question that language repression during the Franco dictatorship ever existed.[22] Instead, the prohibition was informal—political rather than legal—and exercised by the police and local authorities, through oral threats, firings, closings of theaters, schools, and journals:

> For the Franco regime it is more important (effective) to create an atmosphere of fear, a climate of wariness, a thick fabric of suspicion, so that writing in Galician, which is not formally prohibited, feels like an obvious risk. It was also not forbidden to give lectures in our language, but no one, in that web of precautions, fears and threats, did so until ten years after the end of the Civil War.[23]
>
> (Alonso Montero 1991: 105)

Considering Galician literature's rather weak situation during the Republic, not to mention the immediate post-war years, things changed quite drastically in the beginning of the 1950s, mainly due to two important factors: the Galician diaspora in America and the creation of the publishing house Galaxia. Between 1850 and 1960, almost two million Galicians—roughly three-quarters of today's population and over half of the Spanish emigration in general—emigrated to America; even today, especially in the River Plate region, a *gallego* metonymically

---

[21] *No lo haga en gallego por Dios. No se humille sin motivo. Busque universalidad, busque trascendencia.*

[22] See, for example, Pío Moa's "Franco y las lenguas regionales" (2011) and Pedro Insúa's "La mentira del franquismo y las lenguas" (2017).

[23] *Para o franquismo é máis importante (eficaz) crear unha atmósfera de medo, un clima de recelos, un mesto tecido de sospeitas, de tal xeito que escribir en galego, que non está formalmente prohibido, se sinta como un risco evidente. Tampouco estaba prohibido pronunciar conferencias na nosa lingua pero ninguén, naquel entramado de cautelas, medos e ameazas, o fixo ata dez anos despois de terminada a Guerra Civil.*

refers to an *español* in general. This enormous diaspora—Buenos Aires was its unrivalled capital, with a Galician-speaking population five times larger than that of the biggest cities back home—became crucial for Galician literature throughout the dictatorship. In the 1940s, the darkest years of Francoist repression, the Centro Galego of Buenos Aires—"the most important entity of Galician emigration of all time" (Monteagudo 2021)—was a hub for all kinds of cultural activity, managed by the important figures of the artist Luis Seoane and writer Eduardo Blanco-Amor. The former was also the editor of the most important literary journal of the diaspora, *Galicia*, for the better part of the 1940s and 1950s and was succeeded in this role by the latter. Galician exiles from the Spanish Civil War could thus enjoy an ebullient cultural and literary life in Galician: publications, cultural and political celebrations, courses, and lectures on Galician language and literature; invitations of prominent intellectuals to the Xornadas Patrióticas/Galegas, conferences celebrated yearly from 1947 to 1980 (although they became infiltrated by Francoist intellectuals and lost some of the initial radicalism); economic support to institutions (especially the Real Academia Galega) and publishing houses in Galicia; literary prizes for poetry, fiction, essays, and scholarship, particularly on language and culture; and, importantly, denunciations of Francoist repression and solidarity campaigns, support of political prisoners, and boycotts of Spanish institutions.

The most publicized (and effective) of these denunciations is known as *a batalla de Montevideo*. When Spain entered UNESCO in 1953 and the seventh General Assembly was to be held in 1954 in Montevideo, across the River Plate from the very heart of the Galician diaspora, the exiled intellectuals were well prepared. They presented a manifesto called *Denuncia diante a UNESCO da perseguizón do idioma galego pol-o Estado Hespañol* (Denunciation before UNESCO of the persecution of the Galician language by the Spanish State) translated into English and French, where they drew attention to the persecution of language and culture not only in Galician but the other vernacular languages of Spain:

1. The prohibition to publish newspapers or cultural journals in Galician, as well as in Catalan and Basque, and the prohibition to use these languages in lectures and cultural events.
2. The prohibition to publish translations into these languages; for example, Heidegger's *The Essence of Truth* was translated to Galician before Spanish, but its publication was denied.
3. The prohibition to use Galician or other non-Castilian languages in school, universities, and churches.

Franco officials (among them the aforementioned Manuel Fraga, a Galician who would be a crucial part of the modernization process in the 1960s and was a senator for Galicia until 2011) explained that Galician was not legally forbidden, which was technically true, but he still made a few concessions after his return to Spain: a chair for Galician language and literature was opened at the Universidad Central of Madrid, a special issue of a prestigious literary review was dedicated to poetry in Galician—and Heidegger's *Da esencia da verdade* was published in 1956.

Like many other important books in Galician to appear during the dictatorship, the Heidegger translation was published by Galaxia, founded in 1950. This publishing house was not only meant to assure the continuity of the *Rexurdimento* and the generation Nós of the first decades of the century, interrupted by the Civil War and the dictatorship, but also to act as the cultural front of political resistance. Galaxia, under the auspices of the foremost Galician intellectual of the period, Ramón Piñeiro, had great ambitions for its cultural work: among them, to further Galician as a cultivated and literary language and put it on the same level as Spanish and Portuguese language literature; to promote fiction and essay writing in Galician (at this time, only poetry and folkloric texts were granted publishing permits by the government); to modernize and standardize Galician; and to foment historical and etymological studies of Galician language and literature. It was thus important not only to find a place in the Spanish literary system but also to relate, in the first instance, to Lusophone letters—through the language and its physical proximity, Galicia has always had a close relationship to Portugal—and, thereby, to the World Republic of Letters. Even though publication was made difficult and Galician literature dismissed, vilified, ridiculed, and censored,[24] Galaxia managed to carve out a space, thanks

---

[24] When Juan Aparicio, a Falangist hardliner and editor of the regime's mouthpiece *Pueblo*, learned about the Heidegger translation, he wrote a fuming open letter to Raimundo Fernández Cuesta, the Minister of Justice:

> In Galicia, some pedant translates German philosophy with the rhythm of a bagpipe, as with the Bernat Metge foundation, the Greco-Latin classics were translated into a jargon that was more like a French "patois" … The writer who writes in the "Grial Collection" from Editorial Galaxia de Vigo or writes verses in the ancient langue d'Oc or in more archaic Basque, because Spanish seems crude, unfaithful and inexpressive to him, is a writer who has spelling mistakes in his pen and in his soul, being ashamed that his private parts should be seen in the nude. Dear and respected Raimundo, they should be cured by a psychoanalyst or brought to Madrid by hook or by crook, so that they can tone their moral and nervous systems. (Alonso Montero 1991: 151)

Here, the contempt for the vernacular languages is not so much related to separatism as to aesthetics and the perceived superiority of Castilian. Condescendingly, Aparicio refers to the use of bagpipes in Galicia, a residue of the Celtic past.

to the efforts of the *galeguistas* and the support of the exile community. When the repression was eased in the 1960s, through Vatican II and the change of guard in the Franco government, Galaxia had paved the way for the robust recovery of Galician letters, the publishing boom, and the highly sophisticated *nova narrativa galega*, inspired by the French *nouveau roman*.

In a country with political prisoners, prisons may be used for political purposes. When Piñeiro was sentenced to prison for anti-fascist activities in 1946, he came to share a cell with Koldo Mitxelena, who later would be the creator of the unified Basque language, *euskera batua*. Books on philosophy, which most interested Piñeiro, were often considered subversive and difficult to get in prison, so he read Mitxelena's books on linguistics. The conversations between the two intellectuals made Piñeiro realize that a small and subjugated language like Galician needed to be standardized in order to thrive. The *Normas ortográficas e morfolóxicas do idioma galego* (Orthographic and morphological norms of the Galician language) was not published until 1970, but Galaxia had already set the standard for a unified Galician during its two decades of publishing (González González 1993: 145).

From brutal repression to legal protection

Although the repression of vernacular culture and language is similar in the different regions, it also becomes clear that the vernacularities differ among themselves. The strong position of Catalan—a broad, Catalan-speaking bourgeoisie, a well-developed intellectual and literary system, a long tradition, a unified language, and a far-reaching autonomy before the war—made it very resilient in the face of brutal and widespread repression. Despite the odds, books were soon published again after the war, every breach in the dictatorial machinery was used for cultural resistance, and once the monolithic wall had begun to crumble, there was no way to stop the counter-offensive of Catalan culture. In the second half of the dictatorship, after the reshufflings of 1959, Francoist authorities found that it would be more efficient to coopt Catalan culture than to combat it; Catalans, on the other hand, realized that sly and steady endurance and the strength of the vernacular culture, rather than direct confrontation, would break down the opposition. In contrast, Basque culture, with a much more precarious social and institutional status, suffered more from the Francoist stranglehold and could not afford the same passive resistance.

Once the spark of militant, confrontational nationalism was lit, fueled by its "Third World" anti-Colonialist struggles elsewhere, a realization of cultural specificity in the face of extinction, and a merciless and violent response from the authorities, there was no way to avoid the fire: what started as cultural resistance and study groups ended in a forty-year armed conflict that would deeply affect Spanish politics and traumatize Basque society. Especially in the later decades, the ETA conflict was as much a Basque civil war as a war against the Spanish state. Simultaneously, grassroots activists—or agents of the vernacular—initiated an assault on the institutions of the state, beginning with its foremost ideological apparatus: the school. The *ikastola* movement boosted Basque as a language of instruction and gave thousands of students the opportunity to study in the regional language, thereby strengthening their ties and loyalty to vernacular culture and specificity. Finally, Galicia benefited from the support of the very large groups of exiled Galicians in Spanish-speaking America, both in terms of economy and politics as well as cultural infrastructure and intellectual mobilization. Galicia had the most widely spoken vernacular of the three regions but the weakest nationalist sentiments; however, the persistent efforts of a fairly small group of intellectuals—just as during the Rexurdimento—made literature and culture in Galician not just survive, but flourish and spread in a hitherto unseen expansion.

Lastly, it is also illuminating to see how the regime's attitude vis-à-vis the vernacular languages changed through the decades. From the book burnings and violent repression in the immediate post-war years, through the growing but arbitrary permissiveness in the 1950s and the pragmatism of the 1960s, into the last years of the dictatorship, the regime even came to declare the vernacular cultures, with their specific languages, part of the greatness of the Spanish nation. In one of the last decrees to be issued in Franco's lifetime, published only five days before his death on November 20, 1975, the vernacular languages are conceded a status unthinkable at the beginning of his reign:

> Article One. — The regional languages are the cultural heritage of the Spanish Nation and all of them are considered national languages. The knowledge and use of them will be supported and protected by the action of the State and other Public Law Entities and Corporations.
>
> Article Two. — Regional languages may be used by all spoken or written mass media, and especially in acts and meetings of cultural nature.
>
> Article Three. — Spanish, as the official language of the Nation, and the vehicle of communication for all Spaniards, will be used in all actions of the High Bodies

of the State, Public Administration, Administration of Justice, Local Entities and other Corporations Public Law.

Article Four. — No Spaniard shall be subject to discrimination for not knowing or not using a regional language.[25]

(Decreto 2929/1975)

This might seem like a complete u-turn: the state had gone from a genocidal approach, stamping out all official use of the vernacular languages, to giving them protection throughout the entire State apparatus, not just making possible their use in all written and oral media but also especially in cultural gatherings. A less benevolent but more realistic reading is that the decree merely recognized a *fait accompli*—the vernacular languages were already widely used and the aggressively Spanish-nationalist rhetoric was doomed—and that it ultimately, especially in view of an imminent transition to democracy, served to safeguard the official status of Spanish and to convey the message that the vernaculars would not get further than this. Besides, what does it really entail to say that the knowledge and use of the vernaculars will be supported and protected? The wording more or less survived in the Constitution of 1978; the languages are a cultural patrimony that "will be the object of special respect and protection," and remains notoriously vague: not only are the vernacular languages not named, but neither is it specified what the respect and protection will actually look like. It was not until the beginning of the 1980s, with the reform of the Autonomous Communities and the bilingual reforms, that the vernacular languages were granted official status and thus real legal protection.

However, in Franco's decree the vernaculars are granted the status of national languages, which in fact makes this decree, still issued under the dictatorship, *more* progressive than the democratic Constitution of 1978. The constitutional text goes to great lengths precisely to avoid any identification of the bilingual regions as nations: the languages are called "different linguistic modalities" and "other Spanish languages," and the vernacular groups are labeled with the neologism *nacionalidades*. The government decree of November 1975, issued

---

[25] *Artículo primero.—Las lenguas regionales son patrimonio cultural de la Nación española y todas ellas tienen la consideración de lenguas nacionales. Su conocimiento y uso será amparado y protegido por la acción del Estado y demás Entidades y Corporaciones de Derecho Público. Artículo segundo.—Las lenguas regionales podrán ser utilizadas por todos los medios de difusión de la palabra oral y escrita, y especialmente en los actos y reuniones de carácter cultural. Artículo tercero.—El castellano, como idioma oficial de la Nación, y vehículo de comunicación de todos los españoles, será el usado en todas las actuaciones de los Altos Organos del Estado, Administración Pública, Administración de Justicia, Entidades Locales y demás Corporaciones de Derecho Público. Artículo cuarto.—Ningún español podrá ser objeto de discriminación por ro conocer o no utilizar una lengua regional.*

at the end of an almost forty-year-long dictatorship that emphasized the use of Castilian as the basis of citizenship, goes as far as to state that no Spaniard should suffer discrimination for not knowing or using a regional language. The history of the change in attitude from 1939 to 1975, reflecting the declining strength of the regime and the rise of the vernaculars, could not have had a more striking conclusion.

References

Abellán, M. L. (1984), "Literatura, censura y moral en el primer franquismo," *Papers: Revista de sociologia*, 21: 153–72.

Alonso Montero, X. (1991), *Informe(s) sobre a lingua galega (presente y pasado)*, Vilaboa: Edicións do Cumio.

Álvarez Junco, J. (2001), *Mater dolorosa: La idea de España en el siglo XIX*, Barcelona: Taurus.

Beecroft, A. (2015), *An Ecology of World Literature: From Antiquity to the Present Day*, London: Verso.

Benet, J. (1973), *Catalunya sota el règim franquista: Informe sobre la persecució de la llengua i la cultura de Catalunya pel règim del general Franco*, Paris: Edicions Catalanes de París.

Conversi, D. (1997), *The Basques, the Catalans and Spain: Alternative Routes to Nationalist Mobilisation*, London: Hurst & Company.

De Blas, J. A. (1999), "El libro y la censura durante el franquismo: Un estado de la cuestión y otras consideraciones," *Espacio, Tiempo y Forma, Serie V, Historia Contemporánea*: 281–301.

De Pablo, S. (2009), "Lengua e identidad nacional en el País Vasco: Del franquismo a la democracia," in Christian Lagarde (ed.), *Le discours sur les "langues d'Espagne" (1978–2008)*, 53–64, Perpignan: Presses universitaires de Perpignan.

Dowling, A. (2018), "Prohibition, Tolerance, Co-option: Cultural Appropriation and Francoism in Catalonia, 1939–75," *Contemporary European History*, 27: 370–86.

Etxeberria, I. (2012), "Basque Oral Literature," in Mari José Olaziregi (ed.), *Basque Literary History*, 25–42, Reno, NV: Center for Basque Studies.

Fernández Prieto, L. (2011), "Interpreting Galician History: The Recent Construction of an Unknown Past," in Kirsty Hooper and Manuel Puga Moruxa (eds), *Contemporary Galician Studies: Between the Local and the Global*, 24–39, New York: The Modern Language Association.

Gabilondo, J. (2016), *Before Babel: A History of Basque Literatures*, Lansing, MI: Barbarouak.

Gallén, E. (1987), "La literatura sota el franquisme: de l'ostracisme a la represa pública," in Joaquim Molas (ed.), *Història de la literatura catalana*, 205–20, Barcelona: Ariel.

Garzia, J. (2012), "The History of *Bertsolaritza*," in Mari José Olaziregi (ed.), *Basque Literary History*, 43–68, Reno, NV: Center for Basque Studies.

González González, M. (1993), "El proceso de normativización de la lengua gallega," *Revista de Lenguas y Literaturas Catalana Gallega y Vasca*, 3: 143–9.

Gracia, J. and D. Ródenas (2011), *Historia de la literatura española. 7. Derrota y restitución de la modernidad 1939–2010*, Barcelona: Crítica.

Herreras, J. C. (2010), "Políticas de normalización lingüística en la España democrática," *Nuevos caminos del hispanismo...: actas del XVI Congreso de la Asociación Internacional de Hispanistas*, 2.

Hooper, J. (1995), *The New Spaniards*, London: Penguin.

Insúa, P. (2017), "La mentira del franquismo y las lenguas," *El mundo*, December 13.

Iza, I. and E. H. Ikastolak (2011), *El movimiento de las ikastolas: Un pueblo en marcha. El modelo Ikastola 1960–2010*, Bilbao: Euskaltzaindia.

Juaristi, J. (1987), *Literatura vasca*, Madrid: Taurus.

Labanyi, J. (2013), *Spanish Literature: A Very Short Introduction*, Oxford: Oxford University Press.

María, M. (1995), "Lembranza de Alba," in Luis Alonso Girgado (ed.), *Alba. Hojas de poesía / Follas de poesía. Edición facsímile*, 17–32, Santiago: Xunta de Galicia.

Moa, P. (2010), "Franco y las lenguas regionales," *Libertad Digital*, May 3.

Monteagudo, H. (2021), *Da resistencia á normalización: Ideas e combates polo idioma (1950–1975)*, Vigo: Galaxia.

Moreno Fernández, F. (2005), *Historia social de las lenguas de España*, Barcelona: Ariel.

Perriam, C., M. Thompson, S. Frenk, and V. Knights (2000), *A New History of Spanish Writing: 1930s to the 1990s*, Oxford: Oxford University Press.

Rodríguez Alonso, M. (2004), "Lengua y literatura gallegas," in *Introducción a las lenguas y literaturas catalana, gallega y vasca*, 309–558. Madrid: Universidad Nacional de Educación a Distancia.

Samsó, J. (1999a), "Editorials i públic," in Glòria Bordons and Jaume Subirana (eds), *Literatura catalana contemporària*, 234–8, Barcelona: Proa.

Samsó, J. (1999b), "La represa literària," in Glòria Bordons and Jaume Subirana (eds), *Literatura catalana contemporària*, 219–27, Barcelona: Proa.

Sinova, J. (1989), *La censura de prensa durante el franquismo: (1936–1951)*, Madrid: Espasa Calpe.

Solé i Sabaté, J. M. and J. Villarroya (1995), *El catalán, una lengua asediada*, Barcelona: Columna.

Subirana, J. (2018), *Construir con palabras: Escritores, literatura e identidad en Cataluña (1859–2019)*, Barcelona: Cátedra.

Sueiro Seoane, S. (2009), "La configuración del nuevo Estado franquista en las imágenes publicitarias," *Espacio, Tiempo y Forma, Serie V, Historia Contemporánea*: 169–89.

Torrealdai, J. M. (1998), *La censura de Franco y el tema vasco*, San Sebastián: Fundación Kutxa.

Torrealdai, J. M. (2019), *De la hoguera al lápiz rojo: La Censura franquista en el País Vasco*, Donostia: Txertoa.

Ugarte, M. (2005), "The Literature of Franco Spain, 1939–1975," in David T. Gies (ed.), *The Cambridge History of Spanish Literature*, 611–27, Cambridge: Cambridge University Press.

Veres, L. (2010), "Lenguaje y censura literaria y periodística en el Franquismo," *Amnis: Revue de civilisation contemporaine Europes/Amériques*, 9.

Vilanova, F. (2016), "Did Catalonia Endure a (Cultural) Genocide?" *Journal of Catalan Intellectual History*, 1: 15–32.

Vilanova i Vila-Abadal, F. (1998), "Imagen y represión del 'rojoseparatista'. Algunos ejemplos de la izquierda catalana en 1939," *Espacio, Tiempo y Forma*: 139–57.

Weber, E. (1976), *Peasants into Frenchmen: The Modernization of Rural France, 1870–1914*, Stanford, CA: Stanford University Press.

3

The modern adventures of Kanian Poongundranar, classical Tamil poet: Reflections on literatures of the world, vernacularly speaking

S. Shankar

If the vernacular—understood as more than simply language, as also rooted in sensibility and practice—is that which in its very rootedness resists traveling globally, how is one to study it outside its particular sphere of operation? How are texts written in languages termed vernacular or texts exhibiting vernacular sensibilities to be comprehended outside their vernacular contexts? Given the qualities of the vernacular, what tools do we have available for a respectful and self-critical worldwide conversation about literatures and literary traditions in all their variety?

In this chapter, I reflect on questions such as these by way of an exploration of modern readings of "Yaathum Oorey, Yaavarum Kelir" (யாதும் ஊரே; யாவரும் கேளிர்), an ancient poem/song (henceforth simply "Yaathum Oorey") from the Sangam Age of classical Tamil literature. The Sangam Age is generally dated to the first couple of centuries of the Christian era, though this dating is by no means undisputed. An overview of the controversies is provided by David Shulman in *Tamil: A Biography* (2016), where he notes that Tieken locates the literary collections from which the name Sangam is taken as late as the eighth century, while the "regnant view ... places the poems in the first two or three centuries A.D." (67–82). P. T. Srinivasa Iyengar in *History of the Tamils: From the Earliest Times to 600 A.D.* (1929 [2001]) follows the regnant view in dating the earliest specimens of Tamil poetry (i.e. Sangam poetry) to the "beginning of the Christian era" (152), as does A. K. Ramanujan, whose translation of "Yaathum Oorey" appears below.[1] George Hart, whose co-translation of "Yaathum Oorey"

---

[1] See, e.g., p. xiii in *The Interior Landscape*; and p. 197 in "Form in Classical Tamil Poetry," in *The Collected Essays of A. K. Ramanujar* (1999).

is also provided below, dates the poem "between the first and third centuries" (1993: xv). In brief, there is much debate about the precise dates of the Sangam anthologies and, thus, about the historical period to which they have lent their name. I have chosen to be conservative in following the regnant view in assigning the period to the first couple of centuries. It is worth noting that a difference of even centuries in the dating of the Sangam collections does not affect the substance of the argument here, which is about the *modern* reception of an undoubtedly ancient poem/song.

That poem/song of whatever antiquity, and especially the first line "Yaathum Oorey, Yaavarum Kelir," which I translate as "Everywhere is my home, everyone my kin," has had an astounding revival in the last hundred years. In what follows, I track this revival by way of multiple readings. Through these readings, I intend not so much a definitive interpretation but rather to suggest how each reading in its own way and to a different degree illustrates the exigencies of the vernacular. To be sure, in one sense, it is oxymoronic to regard the same text as both *vernacular* and *classical*, because of the commonly perceived opposition between the two terms. However, as I have argued at length in *Flesh and Fish Blood*, in another sense *vernacular* is opposed to *transnational* rather than *classical* (2016: 131–2). In contradistinction to *transnational*, *vernacular* signifies rootedness and narrow geographical demarcation. As I also argue in that book, in yet another sense Tamil is a transnational language (found in Singapore, Sri Lanka, and Malaysia, in addition to India) rather than a vernacular one. It would be good to keep in mind here what I underscore there, that "[a]s a term of cultural critique, *vernacular* finds its greatest resonance in a relational mode that operates along many and sometimes contradictory trajectories" (147). In a literary context, the *vernacular* (as a term for the rooted and the spatially and temporally circumscribed) and the *transnational* (as a term for the traveling and the spatially and temporally expansive) are purely relational terms; that is, meaningful only in the context of the world literary system as historically produced (and as manifested in the idea of world literature). Of course, the conundrums of the vernacular for the world literary system are nonetheless real. Accordingly, this chapter draws on this relational signification of *vernacular* to explore the place of the literary in the contemporary.

Ultimately, my purpose is to underscore the methodological felicities of the formulation *literatures of the world*, a term I have advocated elsewhere (2016: 1405–13; 2013: 135–7); to expand here on those discussions; and to reflect further on a mode of apprehending the relationship between *literature* and *world* that is looser, theoretically more capacious, than the more common world literature (a term that in all its forms remains hegemonizing). In contrast to world literature, I propose "literatures of the world" as a formulation that resists an overarching universal definition of literature. Rather, my formulation maintains a strong sense of the multiple traditions of thinking aesthetically about the written or spoken word without neglecting their relationship to the world. In what follows, I begin with a review of translation issues in relation to the vernacular. Thence, I move to readings of "Yaathum Oorey." Where the review underscores the insurmountable challenges translation poses to the construction of a world literature, the readings illustrate the need for a specific kind of comparative method. Building on these translation challenges and provocations to comparatism, the conclusion presents the promised reflections regarding *literatures of the world*.

Translation, the vernacular, and "Yaathum Oorey" in English

How does translation relate to the vernacular in the context of a global literary landscape? Translation, in its narrowest construal, presumes (1) difference as well as (2) commonality on the terrain of (3) the linguistic.

Difference is constitutive of translation. To state the obvious, without difference—the difference of one natural language (as linguists term it) from another—there would be no need for translation. It is true that some philosophers of language—for example, Jacques Derrida—have such an extreme view of difference in relation to language that they consider the translative as constitutive of language itself.[2] In their view, all language acts are acts of translation, that is, negotiations over difference. This proposition may very well be true—whether it is, and if so to what extent, is part of the history of literary theory in the past half century—but it is equally true that there can be difference among differences. In other words, the difference that is constitutive of all language as such is not the same as the difference between natural languages.

So much for the difference of and in translation. What about commonality? As is well known, Walter Benjamin referred to the linguistic condition of

---

[2] For example in "Des Tours de Babel" (1995), Jacques Derrida writes, "The structure of the original is marked by the requirement to be translated" (184), thus suggesting the presence of the translative in an "original" text prior to what Roman Jakobson regarded, Derrida notes, as the "proper" act of translation (173).

commonality that makes translation possible, even as it is prior to or outside of translation, as "pure language" (257). From a prelapsarian realm of pure language there came (it would seem) a fall into translation, though his reference to "pure language" need not be understood temporally—it need not be that "pure language" existed before translation in any historical sense. Rather, it would seem from Benjamin's argument that pure language is immanent in all language. This is surely the implication of his well-known metaphor of the echo cast back from the forest—translation as the echo of pure language in natural language (258–9). Benjamin's elegant if cryptic recourse to the idea of "pure language" names the commonality that makes translation possible. Translation must presume not only difference but also commonality, for without the ground of commonality where is the bridge of translation to rest? If difference makes translation necessary, commonality makes translation possible, a banal enough observation, though the banality should not blind us to the observation's fraught nature, that is, the many ethical and political issues that attend the negotiation of difference and commonality.

I have written elsewhere that the vernacular is that which both invites translation and resists it (Shankar 2013: 148). What I mean by this is that the dance between commonality and difference staged by translation, and as choreographed by a skilled translator, is provoked by the latter and enabled by the former. The difference of the vernacular from the global, the standard, and the supralocal provokes the choreography of translation; and the common and shared, even if only apprehended in a shadowy and inconclusive manner, enables a realization of the choreography.

In translation narrowly construed this choreography of difference and commonality is performed on the stage of the linguistic. English translations of Kanian Poongundranar's Tamil poem/song—to come back to the subject of this chapter—offer an easy illustration of this point. Below are, first, the original in Tamil, and then two of the most well-known translations of the text—if you will, realizations of the choreography of difference and commonality between Tamil and English, two languages as well as literary/cultural traditions.

First, the Tamil:

யாதும் ஊரே; யாவரும் கேளிர் ;
தீதும் நன்றும் பிறர்தர வாரா ;
நோதலும் தணிதலும் அவற்றோ ரன்ன ;
சாதலும் புதுவது அன்றே ; வாழ்தல்
இனிதுஎன மகிழ்ந்தன்றும் இலமே; முனிவின்,

இன்னா தென்றலும் இலமே; 'மின்னொடு
வானம் தண்துளி தலைஇ, ஆனாது
கல்பொருது இரங்கும் மல்லல் பேர்யாற்று
நீர்வழிப் படூஉம் புணைபோல, ஆருயிர்
முறைவழிப் படூஉம்' என்பது திறவோர்
காட்சியின் தெளிந்தனம் ஆகலின், மாட்சியின்
பெரியோரை வியத்தலும் இலமே;
சிறியோரை இகழ்தல் அதனினும் இலமே.³

Next, the translation by George Hart and Hank Heifetz:

Every city is your city. Everyone is your kin.
Failure and prosperity do not come to you because others
have sent them! Nor do suffering and the end of suffering.
There is nothing new in death. Thinking that living
is sweet, we do not rejoice in it. Even less do we say,
if something unwanted happens, that to live is miserable!
Through the vision of those who have understood we know
that a life, with its hardship, makes its way like a raft
riding the water of a huge and powerful river roaring
without pause as it breaks against rocks because the clouds
crowded with bolts of lightning pour down their cold
drops of the rain, and so we are not amazed
at those who are great and even less do we despise the weak! (1993: 122)

And now the translation by A. K. Ramanujan:

Every town our home town,
every man a kinsman.

Good and evil do not come
from others.
Pain and relief of pain
come of themselves.
Dying is nothing new.
We do not rejoice
that life is sweet
nor in anger
call it bitter.

---

³ A convenient online source for the Tamil text is to be found in the archive of the Tamil Virtual Academy: http://www.tamilvu.org/library/l1280/html/l12806y6.htm (accessed March 14, 2021).

Our lives, however dear,
follow their own course,

>rafts drifting
>in the rapids of a great river
>sounding and dashing over rocks
>after a downpour
>from skies slashed by lightnings—

we know this
from the vision
of men who see.

So,
We are not amazed by the great,
and we do not scorn the little. (1985: 162)

My purpose in sharing these versions is not to adjudicate between them, that is, to suggest which of the choreographies is better. Rather, I offer them to show how consequential what I call the dance of difference and commonality can be in the transference of a text from one (vernacular) language to another (global).

To illustrate my point, I will focus on the first line of the poem/song. Here is my own variant of this first line ("Yaathum Oore, Yaavarum Kelir"), this most famous of lines from the poem/song about which I will have much to say below. I translate this line as "Everywhere is my home, everyone my kin," in comparison to Hart/Heifetz ("Every city is your city. Everyone is your kin") and Ramanujan ("Every town our home town,/every man a kinsman"). All three variants try to reproduce in English the line's form, that is, its alliterative and parallel syntactical structure, which conveys so much of the semantics of that first line by forcing a consideration of the relationship between *oorey* (home/home town/city) and *kelir* (kin/kinsman). They differ in rendering the former, and only two agree on the latter (Ramanujan inexplicably and unnecessarily genders *kelir*). I prefer *home* to render *oorey* because it conforms better with the spirit of universality in the poem/song. While *home* in English has as its main meaning a private residence, it can also indicate a larger space to which one belongs or owes allegiance (as in "she made her home in India"). In this sense, the word nets all space (not just town and city) within its meaning. However, both *town* and *city* are certainly possible cognates for *oorey*, in some senses even better ones because they are closer to the common use of *ooru* to designate a collective human settlement. Suffice it to say a direct cognate for *oorey* is lacking in English. However, various approximations offer semantic bridges, which are further strengthened by commentary such as the one I am currently engaging in.

I hope this brief detour into possible translations of the first line of "Yaathum Oorey" suggests sufficiently the charged complexities of the translative dance. Translation in all its guises—whether understood as a narrow kind of semantic transfer between natural languages (the translation of a poem/song from Tamil to English) or as a broader kind of semantic transfer focused not on the generation of an analogous text but on the conveyance of implied and associated values (a version of cultural translation)—is an interpretive act. While this interpretive act is always a complex dance of difference and commonality, because of distinctions of power the dance is especially complicated—difficult if you like—when it involves a language positioned as vernacular (Tamil) in the world literary system in comparison to a language positioned as transnational (English).

The text at the heart of my argument—"Yaathum Oorey"—is poem/song #192 of an ancient anthology in Tamil called the *Puranaanuru*. The anthology, part of the Sangam literature referred to above, is generally dated to the first couple of centuries of the Christian era. Sangam literature is so called because of three grand literary assemblies or sangams that were held during this period (or in many accounts before it). These sangams might very well have been mythic in nature; nevertheless, they have lent their name to a historical period and a literary canon. Over time, much has been written about Sangam literature—how it was largely lost to literary memory over the centuries until being "rediscovered" by U. V. Swaminatha Iyer (1855–1942), who painstakingly recovered and commented on the lost poems in the late nineteenth century. This story of loss and recovery too is quite possibly mythic, as A. R. Venkatachalapathy among others has suggested (2006; Ramajunan 1999: 184–96). What is incontestable is that beginning with U. V. Swaminatha Iyer, Sangam literature increasingly attains a central position in the culture and politics of Tamils as a canon of great thematic and aesthetic sophistication. As Venkatachalapathy argues, Iyer's monumental work in the late nineteenth century "marks the moment of the unmaking of an old canon and the construction of one anew" (2006: 96). In this celebrated new literary canon Kanian Poongundranar's much translated poem/song is one of the most celebrated.

The readings

I offer five readings below based on discussions, (re)citations, and allusions to "Yaathum Oorey" within the Tamil cultural sphere. Rather than an exhaustive enumeration, these readings are meant to illustrate the wide range of readings—some dominant and well established, others more obscure and nascent—available to Tamil audiences (and not quite so easily available to English-speaking ones).

The philosophical

In the preface to his commentary on *Puranaanooru*, P. K. Sundaram declares "The telling text of Kanian Punkunranar ... 'Every place is ours; all are our kin' is the crowning motto of the *Purananuru* culture" (1979: vii). Following this declaration regarding the most famous fragment of "Yaathum Oorey," Sundaram offers multiple readings of the poem consistent with his interpretation of the whole of the anthology *Purananuru* as moral commentary on life and living. It may be tempting to take his readings as "traditional" in comparison to the readings to follow but, to be sure, such a "traditional" reading is itself a modern phenomenon and should not be taken to be older or more authentic than the other readings.

In Sundaram's reading, "Yaadhum Oorey" is a philosophical meditation on life's tribulations. "The intention of the poet-philosophers of the *Puram*," Sundaram avers, "was to focus the attention of the people, set them reflecting on the basic puzzles and problems of life, and make them seek the enduring realities and values that underlie the passing phenomena" (42). And what are the enduring realities and values? Sundaram draws on the striking image in the poem/song of a boat swept along by a torrent over rapids to note, "Punkunranar bemoans the inexorability of fate. He likens the hapless soul operated by destiny to a tiny boat in a mighty current which rolls away huge rocks" (55). Sundaram's understanding of this image depends on rendering the word *muraivazhi* as "destiny," a lead followed neither by Hart/Heifetz nor Ramanujan who render the word "way" and "course," respectively. Destiny may not appear an unreasonable rendering given the image of a boat driven by a stream; but translating *muraivazhi* thus glosses over the complexity of the word, which is capable of suggesting a right course of action to be followed intentionally rather than simply a predetermined outcome. *Muraivazhi* as a recommended but chosen path of conduct is much more in keeping with the second and third lines of the poem/song ("Failure and prosperity do not come to you because others have sent them! / Nor do suffering and the end of suffering," in the Hart/Heifetz translation). These lines, however, do not fit quite so well with a rendering of *muraivazhi* as destiny.

In his interpretation, Sundaram discovers a feeling of equanimity within the poem/song. After all, "Yaathum Oorey" seems to exhort a kind of stoicism to its readers/listeners: "There is nothing new in death. Thinking that living / is sweet, we do not rejoice in it. Even less do we say, / if something unwanted happens, that to live is miserable " (Hart/Heifetz). Life is unpredictable, capable of being overtaken by a sudden and dangerous downpour of unforeseen and unforeseeable events. The speaker of the poem/song recommends remaining unperturbed in the face of these events, past or yet-to-come. In the last two lines, the poem/song extends this equanimity to social class distinctions—confronted by the socially great or small, the speaker remains unmoved, unimpressed. All of it—all of life, whether social or natural—is viewed serenely.

Commentators on Sangam literature have noted the distinction made in it between an inner (*aham*) and outer (*puram*) world (Ramanujan 1967: 99, 101; Sundaram 1979: 37, 112). This distinction is evident in the organization of Sangam literature into anthologies of the inner and outer worlds. The *Puranaanooru*, as the name indicates, is an anthology of poems focused on the outer world (*puram*). These outer-world poems concern war, public life, communal values. In contrast, the anthologies concerned with the inner world explore affective life (mainly, romantic love and happiness). But "Yaathum Oorey" makes clear the difficulty of the distinction between inner and outer. The apparent stoicism recommended by the poem/song might have the status of a (outer) public value but the purpose is to generate an understanding of life conducive to (inner) happiness.

Readers of "Yaathum Oorey" have also commonly noted the occurrence of the word *kaatchi* (காட்சி) rendered in both the translations I have provided above as "vision" and glossed by Sundaram as "revelation of objective truth" (104). The content of this *kaatchi*, this vision, is the image of a raft dashing against the rapids of a river swollen by rain. In the poem/song, this vision—that life is nothing but a frail boat—is framed as a quotation from an authoritative source, that is, knowledge given to us by great seers with the capacity, perhaps mystic, to fathom the mysteries of life. Sangam literature invests a great deal in the wisdom of these seers, philosopher-poets, among whom Kanian Poongundranar himself might have belonged. In the philosophical reading of the text of "Yaathum Oorey," this *kaatchi* as well as the associated appeal to authority acquire tremendous significance.

Language nationalism

Language nationalism has played a central role in the constitution of modern Tamil identity. Sumathi Ramaswamy's *Passions of the Tongue* (1997) is a thorough study of the political force of Tamil people's attachment to their language. Throughout the twentieth century the Tamil language has proven a rallying cry for Tamil identity. The most well-known of the various mobilizations centered on the Tamil language is probably the anti-Hindi agitations of the middle of the twentieth century. In these agitations, large swathes of Tamil society were organized in opposition to the attempt by the postcolonial central government to make north Indian Hindi the national language of India. More generally, though, language nationalism in the Tamil context presents itself as pride in the ancient and unrivalled distinction (or so the language nationalist believes) of Tamil. This language nationalism's link to the idea of a Dravidian Tamil identity, that is, a South Indian identity premised on a distinct cultural and/or racial sphere known as Dravidian in contrast to the North Indian Aryan, is also wellknown. The importance of this language nationalism and its links to Dravidian mobilizations cannot be overstated. Tamil politics to this day—dominated by Dravidian parties—continues to be an inheritor of this nationalism and mobilizations around it.

An example of the ideological as well as emotive force of this language nationalism is to be found in the celebrated film song "Thamizhukum Amudhendru Per" (தமிழுக்கும் அமுதென்று பேர்). The title may be translated as "Nectar Is One of the Names for Tamil." The first three lines of the song are as follows:

> Nectar is one of the names for Tamil
> This Tamil—this loving Tamil—
> To us is equal to our very life! (my translation)

The lyrics for the song were composed by the well-known poet Bharathidasan (1891–1974), who was closely associated with the Dravidian movement. The song, which should be viewed on YouTube to understand its full affective force, appeared in the 1965 film *Panchavarna Kili*, directed by A. C. Trilogchander. Twentieth-century texts such as this song convey not only the deep-seated emotional attachment to the Tamil language but the political uses to which this attachment is put. I offer the song as a prime example of language nationalism, and as such as a guide to the less readily visible language nationalist connotations of "Yaathum Oorey."

While "Yaathum Oorey" makes no reference to the Tamil language, the narrative of rediscovery within which it is located in literary history is part and parcel of language nationalism. Within the Tamil context, as I have argued, the literary and the linguistic are unavoidably linked in certain dominant ideas of literary aesthetics (Shankar 2016). Literary greatness is the manifestation of language greatness, understood both as greatness intrinsic to the language and as the willed expression of the writer; but the converse is also true—literary greatness confers greatness on a language. Sangam literature, ancient and widely celebrated, is invaluable to language nationalism in demonstrating a literary greatness that then confers greatness on the language.

"Yaathum Oorey" is one of the pre-eminent texts of the Sangam canon. This status of the poem/song explains the wide use of it in language-nationalist contexts. Thus, the line made a prominent appearance in the theme song composed by Tamil icon A. R. Rahman (primarily associated outside India with the Oscar-winning music for the film *Slumdog Millionaire*) for the 2010 edition of the World Tamil Conference held in Tamil Nadu in India. The lyrics for this song, entitled "Semmozhiyaana Thamizh Mozhiyaam" (செம்மொழியான தமிழ் மொழியாம்) were penned by none other than Dravidianist Chief Minister of Tamil Nadu M. Karunanidhi, a writer of some note himself. "Semmozhiyaana Thamizh Mozhiyaam," which may be translated as "The Tamil Language Is a Classical/Refined/Exalted Language," suggests the directness of the link to language nationalism here.

"Yaathum Oorey" played a role again in the tenth edition of the same conference in 2019, but now the entire poem/song rather than just the first line was invoked, becoming the anthem for the conference. In contrast to 2010, the use of the poem/song in 2019 is less easily identified with language nationalism as practiced within Tamil Nadu and as manifested in the Dravidian parties. Nevertheless, here too the poem/song remains exemplary of the language.[4]

Anti-caste politics

The Dravidian movements mentioned above were simultaneously Tamil nationalist and anti-caste, which is to say they proposed both a deep commitment to a geographical and linguistic identity (Tamil) as well as a social and political

---

[4] Both songs are available for viewing on YouTube.

critique (anti-caste politics). Though they were led largely by "middle" castes (rather than the "lowest"), in their most radical articulations they advanced a thoroughgoing critique of the system of caste—or "the varna-jati complex"—as a whole.[5] Since this anti-caste Dravidian politics is well-known, I will not review it in detail here, focusing instead on the ways in which Sangam literature in general, as well as "Yaathum Oorey" in particular, function in such anti-caste contexts.

Bernard Bate has shown that the Dravidianist movement drew upon a conception of the Sangam period, largely based on its literature, as a pre-Aryan realm (2009: 56). What this conception entails—its politically charged nature—may need elucidation. To be sure, the precise nature of the Sangam Era Tamil world remains a matter of debate. George Hart believed that caste formations were to be found in Sangam society (1993: xxi–xxii). However, others have argued that the Sangam period and the poems proper to it portray a pre-caste society. As long ago as 1929, P. T. Srinivasa Iyengar wrote that the "Tamils of those days [of the Sangam period] were not divided into rigid castes," explaining away the existence of references to caste in the Sangam anthologies as later interpolations (154–5). It is in this context, where the Sangam age itself was proffered as external to a caste society and thus came to be harnessed for the articulation of anti-caste ideas, that "Everywhere is my home, everyone my kin" must be read as a powerful anti-caste slogan.

Caste is nothing if not a tyrannical policing of space and kinship. Anyone with experience of a caste society will therefore understand why and how "Everywhere is my home, everyone my kin" can become a powerful anti-caste slogan. Considered in the context of a caste society, the line is a profound critique of tyranny. This is not to say that such an anti-caste reading is incontestable. It might be asked: How can a poem originating in a pre-caste society be read as being about or marked by caste? But the very posing of this question is a misunderstanding of the nature of the rhetorical work the line does in a modern, undoubtedly caste-marked, society. In this context, rather than simply performing a marvelous ancient expression of philosophical forbearing, the line harnesses in the interest of a full-throated critique an idealization of a time before the fall of Tamil society into the depravity of caste. No doubt, it is these multiple

---

[5] The social system simply rendered "caste" in English is better understood as a complex, articulated system of two related but distinct Indian social categories known as *varna* and *jati*. "Varna-jati complex" is a formulation of V. Geetha and S. V. Rajadurai (1998: xiii).

resonances—invocation of a golden pre-caste period as well as pointed critique of the tyrannical spatial and kinship arrangements of caste—that made the line beloved to C. V. Annadurai and M. Karunanidhi, both powerful if controversial Dravidianist leaders who rose to become Chief Ministers of Tamil Nadu.

Ecocriticism

The notion of the Sangam world as pre-Aryan has also been harnessed to render "Yaathum Oorey" ecocritical. Vital to this effort is the *tinai* philosophy expressed in the Sangam poems. Tinai is most often taken to refer simply to the landscapes portrayed in the poems—for example, mountain, seashore, desert, pastoral, and riverine—and associated themes and emotions. In this view, tinai is an elaborate aesthetic system, a way of organizing literary expression around certain land-based tropes. A. K. Ramanujan's Afterword to *The Interior Landscape* (1967), his celebrated translations of aham-oriented Sangam poems, is perhaps the most well-known expression of this view.

However, in stronger forms, as seen in contemporary critics like Nirmal Selvamony, *tinai* has been raised to an entire philosophy that is ecological in nature. In contrast to Ramanujan, in *Persona in Tolkappiyam*, an extended essay on a grammatical work belonging to (or prior to) the Sangam period, Selvamony considers tinai "one of the most formidable terms that a student encounters ... [A]t first glance, one may find that the term tinai is used to mean (a) grammatical class of being ..., (b) a poetic convention that has two components, namely, akam and puram ..., (c) one of the seven kinds of poetic convention ... and (d) conduct" (1998: 119).

Selvamony proceeds to focus, as the title of his work announces, on personae in Sangam poetry. This focus may itself be seen as a response to Ramanujan's assertion in his Afterword that "little need be said" about personae (1967: 98). In Selvamony's view, usages of the word *tinai* move from grammatical being (that is, ontological manifestation through language rules), through conventions of poetry, to the very behavior of the personae (loosely, characters) appearing in the poems. "[T]inai may be understood as what the personae speak and show by means of posture," Selvamony writes. "In short, tinai is the conduct—speech and attitude—of the personae" (1998: 125). Thus, tinai is seen to be at the heart of an extensive ethical code of conduct.

In *Persona in Tolkappiyam*, Selvamony emphasizes the foundational role of the various landscapes, indeed land itself, in the uses of *tinai* in the works of Sangam literature. He further explicates his thesis regarding the foundational role of land in the essay "Tinai in Primal and Stratified Society"; he notes, "Tinai is a land-based society which includes all organisms including the humans" (2008: 41). He argues that the idea of tinai properly understood reveals a profound consciousness and desire to live in harmony with natural surroundings. Tinai society is an exemplary pre-state pre-industrial non-stratified primal society in which human communities lived, and were exhorted to live, in close harmony with nature. The sacred was crucial to such a society, as was diversity.

In this view, the Sangam poems become instantiations of the ecological philosophy of *tinai* society. Thus, the word *kelir* in the first line of "Yaathum Oorey," translated as *kin* in most cases, expands to include all beings (trees, shrubs, animals great and small). And the striking comparison of a life to a boat making a dangerous journey over rocks in a rain-swollen river becomes a lesson about human puniness in the face of nature. This reading locates the poem/song within the general values of tinai society, including the sacred, and recommends a harmonization of the human with the non-human world. Accordingly, the other values of the poem—equanimity, refusal to be awed by the great or to look down upon the weak—are not erased but rather derived from this primary invocation of a harmonious and sacred relationship with the ecological environment.

Cosmopolitanism

Three examples will serve to open up one last reading of the poem/song, or at least of the first line. In the 1979 Tamil film *Ninaithaale Inikum*, the first line "Yaathum Oore, Yaavarum Kelir" is appropriated to be the first line of a song. This song is picturized—following the by now globally known Indian popular cinema form of the song-dance sequence—in Singapore, to which the hero and the heroine of the film have traveled from India. In the sequence, the hero and heroine appear at various sites and sights surrounded by Singaporeans of different races, no doubt to convey the glamorous world travel of the hero and the heroine. "Yaathum Oorey, Yaavarum Kelir" was also quoted by former President of India A. P. J. Abdul Kalam in his 1997 address to the European Union. Abdul Kalam translated the line in his address as "I am a world citizen, every citizen is my own kith and kin."[6] And these same words were quoted by Prime Minister of India Narendra Modi at the United Nations in 2019 to similarly invoke a

---

[6] https://www.youtube.com/watch?v=AXW5oi0_epg (accessed March 26, 2021).

worldwide community.⁷ These three examples suffice to indicate the wide use of the first line of the poem/song to convey a very worldly and perhaps modern sentiment: cosmopolitanism.

Cosmopolitanism is often defined as a form of worldliness commensurate with a commitment to universal humanity. This common notion of cosmopolitanism is articulated in Martha Nussbaum's widely referenced essay "Patriotism and Cosmopolitanism" (2002). This is not the place to review the limitations of Nussbaum's essay. Rather, I offer it simply as a cogent formulation of a widely held view of cosmopolitanism. In it, Nussbaum vigorously affirms the values of what she terms a "worldwide community of human beings" (4). She proposes that cosmopolitanism should be a call for the creation of "a citizen of the world" (15). She advances enthusiastically the virtues of cosmopolitanism in opposition to patriotism.

The resonances between the three "quotations" of "Yaathum Oorey, Yaavarum Kelir" proffered at the beginning of this subsection (whatever the actual values of the speakers or the texts) and Nussbaum should be readily evident. The sense of a human community of planetary scope; the idea of a citizenship that extends to the whole globe: both find expression in Nussbaum as well as the quotations. The three quotations largely isolate the first sentence and read it in the most global way possible. *Yaathum* and *yaavarum*, everywhere and everyone: these words become the alibi for a cosmopolitan interpretation of the poem/song. Where the song–dance sequence from *Ninaithale Inikum* presents this cosmopolitanism as a lifestyle choice of travel and glamor, Abdul Kalam, a Tamil himself, invokes it for a political statement in an international context, in the process echoing a phrase that appears prominently in Nussbaum's essay (citizen of the world). Thus, we arrive at the end of a series of readings of "Yaathum Oorey" within the Tamil vernacular sphere at a cosmopolitanism that attests to non-vernacular Tamil imagination, that is, the articulation of the non-vernacular within that which is deemed vernacular.

Conclusion

If I have offered five readings without evaluating their merits, it is because my interest here is not in adjudicating among them, that is, deciding the *correct* interpretation. Rather, I aim to illustrate and now, in this conclusion, make

---

⁷ https://www.youtube.com/watch?v=mg8RtOzQZIw (accessed March 26, 2021).

an argument regarding the challenges this record of varying treatments of the poem/song within the Tamil vernacular sphere in the last one hundred years presents to the idea of a world literature.

In one sense, the accession of the works of Sangam literature, including "Yaathum Oorey," to a canon of world literature is easily understandable. David Shulman writes in *Tamil: A Biography*:

> Since the publication of these great texts [of Sangam literature] and the appearance of partial translations of the anthologies into English, notably by the outstanding poet-translator A. K. Ramanujan, scholarship, sometimes intemperate, on the Sangam works has become a veritable cottage industry; what is more, these poems have to no small degree displaced attention within the Tamil world from the monumental literary works of the past thousand years or so to these more ancient, hence suddenly prestigious, poems.
>
> (2016: 28–9)

The prestige achieved by the Sangam literature within the Tamil vernacular intellectual sphere surely facilitated its integration into the canon of world literature; and, conversely, this very integration drove even further this literature's prestige within the Tamil vernacular sphere.

In the preceding section, we have reviewed what might be called the modern vernacular record of reading "Yaathum Oorey," that is, the record of how the poem/song has been read within the Tamil vernacular public sphere. What we have uncovered in pursuing this record is the ability of reading practices to approach a text in a diversity of ways, sometimes basing themselves on the poem/song as a whole and then again having recourse to one part of the poem/song over another. Certainly, sometimes the interpretation produced by one reading practice is in conflict with another. Reading the text as ecocritical, for example, is in tension with a cosmopolitan reading of it. Ecocriticism as articulated through the classical Tamil idea of tinai elevates, or at least values, a regionalism in a manner that is difficult to reconcile with cosmopolitanism. Unlike the ecocritical, and like the first "philosophical," a cosmopolitan reading of the poem/song is perhaps more easily available to readers not familiar with the vernacular cultural context I am laying out in this chapter.

The diversity of readings sketched out above is not unique either to "Yaathum Oorey" or to Tamil literature. Neither the poem/song nor the Tamil vernacular sphere is unique in generating and sustaining a diversity of readings. It is in the nature of literature—indeed, textuality in general—to generate a variety of interpretations, especially over long historical periods (after all, "Yaathum Oorey" is two thousand years old). Thus, Shakespeare's *The Tempest*, to pluck a text from the heart of the anglophone canon, has been read as a metafictional farewell by a great playwright, a meditation on political legitimacy, a fable of colonial ambition, a covertly anticolonial text, a key text in the invention of the human, and more. In this regard "Yaathum Oorey" is no different than *The Tempest*.

Rather than textuality as such, though, my argument is about the aesthetic and political valences of the critical approaches we adopt when confronted by the diversity of literary traditions. It is out of diverse literary traditions that the world literature canon is constructed. But how and to what end? And is it the only, or even best, possible response to the global diversity of literary traditions? Both of the two most widely used multivolume textbooks of world literature in the US—the Longman Anthology and the Norton Anthology—have included Sangam poetry (at least until recently). The examples included, however, are placed within Tamil literature and culture in only the most cursory of ways. The Longman Anthology gives a brief account of the "rediscovery" of Sangam poetry toward the end of the nineteenth century (Damrosch and Pike 2009), while earlier editions of the Norton Anthology leave out even this brief account and proffer them simply as aesthetic objects (Lawall and Mack 2002). The point of course is that these anthologies reveal—make inordinately visible as highly coded objects—the literary assumptions appended to world literature.[8]

Lost in the integration of these poems/songs into a global literary culture via the notion of world literature, then, is the rich intellectual history surrounding the poems/songs. Comparing the framing and presentation of these poems/songs in the anthologies with the readings of them above should be enough to illustrate that their integration into world literature exalts aesthetics over history— that is, an aesthetically reconstructed text over a political and intellectually contested one. Aesthetics is harnessed to produce a seamless global text out of a vernacular text that is fractured and jagged. Furthermore, this is done by imposing a predetermined (Eurocentric) idea of what the aesthetic is. I have written elsewhere about the ways in which ideas of the literary differ between Tamil and Western aesthetic traditions (Shankar 2016). In this context, not only does the absorption of Sangam poems/songs into world literature excise history and politics in the interest of rendering the poems/songs aesthetic objects, but

---

[8] For my related discussion of anthologies of "world literature," see *Flesh and Fish Blood* (2016: 128–36). As I show there, I am aware that there is some diversity among critics advocating a World Literature (such as Damrosch and Moretti); however, I am arguing that the very recourse to and desire for a world literature—in all its forms—is problematic.

it does so in ways that do not recognize constructions of the aesthetic within Tamil traditions. Insult is added to injury; the reduction, the diminishment, is multifold.

The relevant question for us as students of "literature" is as follows: Is the idea of world literature necessary and/or sufficient to study, to explore, global literary traditions? The answer must be: no, it is neither necessary nor sufficient. It is not necessary because the relationship of "literature" to "world" can be studied more powerfully in other ways. This relationship can and should be studied comparatively by the juxtaposition of multiple *but limited* linguistic textual traditions—multiple so as to allow comparison, limited so as to allow depth of engagement. The argument in this chapter, drilling deep into one example, is meant to illustrate the problems with *not* adopting such an approach. Rather than a form of comparatism based on a grand and universalistic orientation toward the World as a whole as a planetary object, the comparatism I intend would have a historical view of the world as the accumulation of human activities, never available to us in its entirety. To put it concisely: such a study would abandon the World for the world. Viewed this way, it is—or at least should be—evident that attempting to capture all the diverse "literary" activities of diverse human communities across the globe is a fool's—or else a colonialist's—errand. What will remain on the agenda, nevertheless, is an ever-evolving and ever-accumulating insight into human modes of existence in the world. In the kind of comparative study I have in mind, the variety and richness of the relationship of the world to linguistic textual traditions is revealed with depth, in contrast to the superficiality resulting from the canonizing function of the idea of world literature. Indeed, in this light, in addition to not being necessary, the idea of world literature is revealed as not even sufficient for a proper study of the literary in relationship to the world.

A proper understanding of both the vernacular and translation is useful for the approach I am calling "literatures of the world." The vernacular is one of a handful of terms that resist the blandishments of the global by insisting on the relevance of alternative epistemologies of situatedness. As such, an attention to the vernacular is a disruptive force with regard to world literature. As illustrated in the aforegoing readings of the modern adventures of the classical Tamil poet Kanian Poongundranar, the vernacular fosters deep and contextual literary explorations not only impossible but actively discouraged under the rubric of world literature. Similarly, an acute sense of translation—after all, exploring the literary in a global context is impossible without translation, especially when it comes to teaching in a classroom—as a dance of difference and commonality interrupts the facile reification of a text within world literature. This is not simply a matter of doing things better, more carefully, under the rubric of world literature; it is a fundamental reorientation for which the label world literature can never be adequate. Carefully approached, both the vernacular and translation disrupt the hegemony of world literature in productive ways, thus creating space for the articulation of a study of the literary in a global context as "literatures of the world." As a text of a literature of the world rather than world literature, "Yaadhum Oorey" can be examined with sufficient attention to its own intellectual context (however one construes that) and simultaneously also regarded comparatively alongside other texts from other traditions and languages in the interests of comprehending some of the dynamics at work in the constitution of what comes to be called the literary in the modern period. This is seemingly a far more modest endeavor than the grand gesture that is world literature, but in the end it might be the more consequential.

Note: I am grateful to Nirmal Selvamony for his careful and useful feedback on this chapter.

References

Bate, B. (2009), *Tamil Oratory and the Dravidian Aesthetic: Democratic Practice in South India*, New York: Columbia University Press.

Benjamin, W. (1996), "The Task of the Translator," trans. Harry Zohn, in M. Bullock and M. W. Jennings (eds), *Walter Benjamin: Selected Writings*, 253–4, Cambridge MA: Harvard University Press.

Damrosch, D. (2003), *What Is World Literature?* Princeton, NJ: Princeton University Press.

Damrosch, D. and D. L. Pike, eds (2009), *The Longman Anthology of World Literature*, 2nd ed. Vols. A–F, New York: Longman.

Derrida, J. (1995), "Des Tours de Babel," trans. J. F. Graham in J. F. Graham (ed.), *Difference in Translation*, 165–207, Ithaca: Cornell University

The Four Hundred Songs of War and Wisdom (1993), trans. and ed. G. Hart and H. Heifetz, New York: Columbia University Press.

Geetha, V. and S. V. Rajadurai (1998), *Towards a Non-Brahmin Millennium*, Calcutta (Kolkata): Samya.

Hart, G. (1993), "Introduction," in G. Hart and H. Heifetz (eds), *The Four Hundred Songs of War and Wisdom*, xv–xxxvii, New York: Columbia University Press.

Kalam, A. P. J. Abdul. Speech to the European Union. https://www.youtube.com/watch?v=AXW5oi0_epg (accessed March 26, 2021).

Lawall, S. and M. Mack, eds (2002), *The Norton Anthology of World Literature*, 2nd ed. Vols. A–F, New York: Norton.

Modi, Narendra. Speech to the United Nations. https://www.youtube.com/watch?v=mg8RtOzQZIw (accessed March 26, 2021).

Moretti, F. (2000), "Conjectures on World Literature," *New Left Review*, 1 (January–February): 54–68.

Nussbaum, M. (2002), "Patriotism and Cosmopolitanism," in J. Cohen (ed.), *For Love of Country?*, 3–17, New York: Beacon.

Poongundranar, K. "Yaathum Oorey, Yaavarum Kelir." http://www.tamilvu.org/library/l1280/html/l12806y6.htm (accessed March 14, 2021).

Ramanujan, A. K. (1967), *The Interior Landscape: Classical Tamil Love Poems*, New York: NYRB Books.

Ramanujan, A. K. (1985), *Poems of Love and War: From the Eight Anthologies and the Ten Long Poems of Classical Tamil*, New York: Columbia University Press.

Ramanujan, A. K. (1999), *The Collected Essays of A. K. Ramanujan*, Oxford: Oxford University Press.

Ramaswamy, S. (1997), *Passions of the Tongue: Language Devotion in Tamil India, 1891–1970*, Los Angeles: University of California Press.

Selvamony, N. (1998), *Persona in Tolkāppiyam*, Chennai: International Institute of Tamil Studies.

Selvamony, N. (2008), "Tinai in Primal and Stratified Society," *Indian Journal of Ecocriticism*, 1: 38–48.

Shankar, S. (2013), *Flesh and Fish Blood: Postcolonialism, Translation, and the Vernacular*, Los Angeles: University of California Press.

Shankar, S. (2016), "Literatures of the World: An Inquiry," *PMLA*, 131 (5): 1405–13.

Shulman, D. (2016), *Tamil: A Biography*, Cambridge MA: Harvard University Press.

Srinivasa Iyengar, P.T. (2001 [1929]), *History of the Tamils: From the Earliest Times to 600 A.D.*, Chennai: Asian Educational Services.

Sundaram, P. K. (1979), *Some Philosophical Concepts in Purananuru*, Chennai: Dr. S. Radhakrishnan Institute for Advanced Study in Philosophy-University of Madras.

Venkatachalapathy, A. R. (2006), "The Making of a Canon: Literature in Colonial Tamilnadu," *In Those Days There Was No Coffee: Writings in Cultural History*, by A. R. Venkatachalapathy, 89–113, New Delhi: Yoda Press.

"Yaathum Oorey, Yaavarum Kelir," Tamil Virtual Academy, http://www.tamilvu.org/library/l1280/html/l12806y6.htm (accessed March 14, 2021).

4

Vernacular soundings: Poetry from the Lesser Antilles in the aftermaths of hurricanes Irma and Maria

Christina Kullberg

The noise my leaves make is my language

Derek Walcott (2005)

Hurricane is a word derived from an extinct vernacular Caribbean language, Taino. This natural phenomenon is indeed quintessentially Caribbean. Most early modern European travelers to the region tell about storms so forceful and unimaginable that though they had plenty of models in literature for describing tempests, they needed local knowledge and words to make sense of them. In one anonymous French pirate's account from 1620, *hurákan* is even mistaken for a toponym, as if the islands were one with the storms that ravaged their shores (Moreau 2002: 116). The native Caribs noted changes in the cycle of hurricanes after over a hundred years of European intrusion: the number of hurricanes increased. Two old Carib men presumably explained this to a Monsieur Montel, according to Charles de Rochefort, a protestant travelling in the Caribbean in the middle of the seventeenth century (1658: 380). Interestingly, the Caribs, who might, of course, be fictive, linked the change in natural forces with a process of cultural transmission: as the Natives assimilated European practices, nature changed, too.

These Carib voices, even if they have a slight European tenor, give a rare early indigenous perspective on something that we might call climate change; they express a consciousness of an impending ecological crisis. Today, hurricanes hit the region harder than ever in a locally felt consequence of global warming, attributed to centuries of what Rob Nixon described as a "slow violence" that the rich inflict upon the poor through colonization and global capitalism

(Nixon 2013; Watts 1987). In the wake of the 2010 earthquake that hit Haiti, and hurricanes Irma and Maria, both category five, that devastated the islands in 2017, Caribbean poets in particular have engaged directly with the hard-felt effects of slow violence. To name a few, James Noël (Haiti) responded to the earthquake in *La Migration des murs* (2012) and through his editorial work with the journal *Intranqu'illités*, and Ana Portnoy Brimmer (Puerto Rico/New York) has written and performed several poems about hurricane Maria (Bonilla and LeBrón 2019). From the Lesser Antilles Richard Georges (Tortola) published *Epiphaneia* (2019), Lasana M. Sekou (St. Martin) came out with *Hurricane Protocol* (2019), and Celia A. Sorhaindo (Dominica) with *Guabancex* (2020). These works testify to a vibrant creativity in contemporary Caribbean poetry, which has not gone unnoticed in the global field of literature. Yet, in this context, that creativity tends to be leveled out through generalizing categorizations such as "hurricane poets." The label no doubt shows the force of what Elena Machado (2015) has described as a "market aesthetics," which extend to poets from peripheral places who publish with local and/or independent publishing houses.

Such labeling captures a dilemma in the theorization of world literature. On the one hand, we are complicit in reducing literature from small marginalized places to recognizable categories. From distant readings and systemic approaches to attention to circuits of translation and reception, the conceptualization of the literatures of the world is dictated by (Western) centers. On the other, an important conversation within world literature is precisely about rethinking it from peripheral spaces (Müller and Siskind 2019: 16). As Elizabeth DeLoughrey puts it, thinking about global phenomena, be it literature or environment, would gain from being "*grounded* by engaging specific places such as postcolonial islands" (2019: 2; emphasis in original). However, the question remains of how to read and incorporate literature from an archipelagic region such as the Lesser Antilles into world literature without absorbing it into the center–periphery divide that determines so much of the critical discussion within the field.

In this chapter, I will use an ecocritical approach, not necessarily to resolve this dilemma but at least to explore how we can think about global effects of literature. Following Chris Campbell and Michael Niblett's suggestion that we need to think through "Caribbean ecology from the perspective of aesthetic practice" (2017: 11), I will investigate on a textual level how three poets from the Lesser Antilles—Georges, Sekou, and Sorhaindo—mobilize vernacular sensibilities by working with sound and resonance in poems that have emerged out of natural catastrophes.[1] Indeed, the massive cultural response in recent years to natural catastrophes would call for a pan-Caribbean and intermedial approach to works from all of the languages and art-forms in the larger creole cultural region. Likewise, insisting on the fact that hurricanes start on the sea, DeLoughrey suggests that they convey a transoceanic imaginary (2018: 9). Yet, the limited space of this chapter prompts me to focus my analysis on these three anglophone poets from Dominica, St. Martin, and the Virgin Islands. And the choice is not entirely contingent on the economy of the chapter. There are reasons to focus on the archipelago and the small islands of the Antilles as a singular space in this larger hemispheric and oceanic continuum.[2] More than other creole contexts, proximity between the islands has historically increased processes of mixing between languages, cultures, and ecologies. The islands have been subject to radical transformations due to the transplantation of crops, plants, and animals as well as landscaping, from the establishment of plantations in the seventeenth century to today's destruction of mangroves and coral reefs for the tourist industry. In a way the Lesser Antilles are like laboratories proving Timothy Morton's now classic point that nature and culture are inseparable (2009). In these precarious spaces culture/nature is never strictly local but points to other places and times across the planet.

What is particularly interesting from an ecocritical and world literary perspective is the ways in which the poets operate through the globally dominating English language, not to convey the "untranslatability" (Apter 2013) of local experience but, rather, I argue, to make a different kind of sense by creating a world of soundscapes. As Eric Doumerc points out in his review of *Guabancex*, language becomes the ultimate "resource to address the trauma and shock" (2021). In this regard, it is noticeable that Georges, Sekou, and Sorhaindo include very few direct instances of vernaculars, at least not in the

---

[1] I discovered these collections of poetry thanks to a discussion between Georges, Sekou, and Sorhaindo organized by the Bocas Lit Fest 2020. The discussion was entitled "The Strength of Islands" and was moderated by Naila Folami Imoja. https://www.youtube.com/watch?v=IT6Q5Udg3Mg (accessed May 24, 2021).

[2] The contextual differences between the larger islands and the Lesser Antilles are significant. Most smaller islands became independent well after the Second World War or remained in some kind of dependent relationship to colonial powers (Guadeloupe and Martinique being French overseas departments, for example) even if there are signs today of coming change. At the same time, they are not, like Puerto Rico, part of an empire, or, like Cuba, an important player in international politics, or like Haiti, dependent on international aid. Comparisons between these different contexts would be fruitful but falls beyond the scope of this study.

poems studied here.[3] We are, in other words, far from a prose saturated with vernaculars that we can find in Jamaican Marlon James's *A Brief History of Seven Killings* (see Chapter 8 in this volume for an analysis of James). Yet while they are not exploring vernacular language *per se*, they do forge vernacular sensibilities in English. This particular aesthetics of language can be read through the lens of Kamau Brathwaite's famous talk about "nation language." He situated the Caribbean poet's aesthetics in a postcolonial double bind position of having been taught an English that does not correspond with the reality of the archipelago. The problem is not vocabulary or even language but form and style: "we haven't got the syllables, the syllabic intelligence, to describe the hurricane, which is our own experience whereas we can describe the imported alien experience of snowfall" (1984: 8). "The hurricane," Brathwaite said, "does not roar in pentameters. And that's the problem: how do you get a rhythm which approximates the *natural* experience, the *environmental* experience?" (1984: 10). At the basis of nation language lies the idea that poetry mediates the way we live the environment. Drawing on this insight, Brathwaite argues for the necessity of creating a "nation language" within another language by altering the language's rhythm, timbre, and sound. In similar terms, Édouard Glissant—quoted in Brathwaite's talk—speaks about Martinican cultural expressions as "forced poetics" that emerged out of a situation where one's language is not able to express the surrounding world. "Forced poetics," Glissant writes, "exist where a need for expression confronts an inability to achieve expression" (1989: 120). For Glissant, coherent meaning has become impossible in situations of extreme inequality, which permeate Caribbean societies. Nevertheless, expressive possibilities remain entrenched in noises, screams, and pitches that camouflage the process of making meaning into "one impenetrable block of sound" (1989: 124). Sound then is meaningful as effect or affect rather than of signification or representation. Meaning is created indirectly, hidden in folds and layers, in noise and rhythm, which Glissant ultimately reads as a form of counter-poetics. It is an active way to eschew understandability while actively seeking to express the world.

My approach also takes its cue from recent attempts by Sarah Phillips Casteel (2020), Eric Hayot (2016), Pheng Chea (2016), and others who look at

---

[3] The linguistic context of the region is complicated. On most islands a (colonial) language is used for official purposes. This dominating language exists alongside other languages, often spoken, used in the daily life of people: either Creoles or Papiamento (characterized as languages), or *patois* (dialect). Particularly in the Lesser Antilles colonial languages tend to be fluid: on St. Martin English, Dutch, and French have dominated alternatively; St. Lucia is highly influenced by French, and so on. These linguistic contact zones have historical and geographical explanations, and the different languages continue to influence one another (Michaelis et al. 2013).

texts in terms of world-making in order to shift the attention from circulation of literature as a commodity to exploring how literature actively intervenes in the world. Following these scholars, I propose that the sonic fabric of the poems can mediate other relationships between world and work, relationships that often escape world literary debates. I will consider how Georges, Sekou, and Sorhaindo use the vernacular in terms of sound grounded in layers of local geography, history, cultures, and literatures in order to create what we may call a sound-world of hurricanes. Such soundscapes emerge from a locality (be it a place or the speaking body) but are not fixed to it. Rather they seek to explore an uncertain spatiality, an unstable way of being in the world that recalls Wai Chee Dimock's claim that the sonic fabric of a text releases a temporal instability, especially when displaced and read elsewhere (1997: 1060). Dimock argued that the aural dimensions of a text can be read in terms of frequencies, which have a shifting quality, "moving farther and farther from their points of origin, causing unexpected vibrations in unexpected places" (1997: 1061). There is arguably something about paying attention to sound that, as suggested by Shuangyi Li, can help us rethink not only comparative modes of reading, but also the relationship between text and world (2020: 400). This is what we see in the poems by Georges, Sekou, and Sorhaindo. The sonic fabric appears as a means to search the ravaged island space and this sensory exploration turns into an uncertain world-making that reaches beyond the archipelago. My contention here is that whether these poems are characterized as world literature or not does not necessarily have to do with determining to what extent they circulate in the world. Their "worldliness" can be captured by analyzing the ways in which they produce echoes of sensory experience that re-sound in other places. I will start by discussing the intersections between world literature and eco-criticism, and place the Caribbean within these conjectures. From there I will move to the readings of the poems, looking first at how the play with sound and naming channels an intimate experience of the hurricane. Finally, I will examine how the poems use the sonic fabric to create a poetics of resonance to make sense of an unstable world.

Vernacular sounds between ecocriticism and world literature

World literature, with its attention to global movements, has contributed to rethinking ecocriticism in terms of what Ursula Heise calls "environmental cosmopolitanism" (2008). Her discussion of how texts "negotiate the juncture between ecological globalism and localism" makes it clear that ecocriticism shares many of the stakes and challenges raised by world literature (2004: 126; 2013). Yet even if Heise refers to a global ecological imaginary or consciousness that does not restrict itself to a eulogy of place, the idea of "environmental cosmopolitanism" has different connotations in 2020 than when her *Sense of Place and Sense of the Planet* was published in 2008. During the past decade, we have witnessed the rise of a grassroots movement promoting radical measures to save the planet initiated by young upper-middle-class Europeans and picked up by adolescents across the globe. We have also seen an increasing commitment to environmentalism from the liberal uber-rich: celebrities fly on private jets to conventions organized by Google to raise climate awareness; multinational companies like Amazon showcase investments made in sustainable resources while they, at the same time, own large shares in the oil industry. Indeed, it is difficult not to be cynical today when evoking "environmental cosmopolitanism." Heise is of course aware of the problem of a mainly Western and white perspective on environmentalism as she quotes postcolonial researchers' astute reservations about the good will of those engaging with the humanitarian and natural concerns of remote places (2013). A type of global environmental consciousness may be well-intentioned but it implies a particular vision of global connectedness and a particular relationship to place and to the world, which should not be taken as universal. As underscored by Graham Huggan and Helen Tiffin (2015), following Ramachandra Guha and Joan Martínez Alier (2013), the full-bellied and the empty bellied environmentalisms do not necessarily have the same perspectives on or the same solutions to the current crisis (Hunt and Roos 2012).

As a backdrop to these postcolonial warnings about the predicament of environmental thinking, Heise seeks to "model forms of cultural imagination and understanding that reach beyond the nation and around the globe," as well as to investigate "the question of how we might be able to develop cultural forms of identity and belonging that are commensurate with the rapid growth in political, economic, and social interconnectedness that has characterized the last few decades" (2008: 6). These challenges are not new to the Caribbean, which might explain why the region is important, not only for Heise, who turns to notions such as hybridity and mixing, intrinsic to the Caribbean context, to connect to place without lauding it, but also for other ecocritics. If the current ecological crisis is symbiotic with the capitalist world system, the Caribbean with its long history of colonization, extraction, and human displacements becomes a crucial site for thinking about both the politics and the aesthetics of ecocriticism as Campbell and Niblett (2017, Niblett 2012) have argued. There are several examples of this. Lawrence Buell (2005) along with Huggan and Tiffin (2015) cite Derek Walcott's writing as an example of a "global sense of place." Nixon finds in the Black Atlantic a good starting point for examining his notion of slow violence (2013). Similar to the idea of "slow violence," Mark D. Anderson argues in *Disaster Writing* that catastrophe is part of everyday life in Caribbean and South American societies and not lived as a new consequence of the Anthropocene: disasters are the "culmination of historical processes that have resulted in certain populations living in a state of heightened vulnerability" (2011: 21). Similarly, Niblett argues that natural violence is part of the Caribbean cultural identity (2009: 62). DeLoughrey too, underscores that from the perspective of marginalized and precarious places such as islands, the Anthropocene is not conceptualized in terms of newness but, rather, as in continuity with a long history of exploitation, which changes not only the way it is lived but also how the Anthropocene is conceptualized (2019). Drawing from Caribbean thinkers, DeLoughrey further points out that the history of slavery and colonization entails a dispossessed relationship to land. Consequently, the way Caribbean literature conveys a sense of place does not replicate the regionalism or anxiety with regionalism that can be seen in the United States, Canada, or Europe. Writing nature/culture takes complex manifestations in Caribbean literary history and is constantly being revisited and reactualized.[4] Often used by authors as a means to explore the silenced past of slavery, it is linked to aesthetic experimentation and to rethinking local identity in relation to the world (DeLoughrey, Gosson, and Handley 2005; Casteel 2007; Deckard 2017).

There is an interesting contradiction in the ways in which Caribbean thinking is included in the conjunction between world literature and ecocriticism.

---

[4] On the French islands, for instance literary movements' struggle to preserve local languages (Creole) has turned into green activism. The disclosure in 1993 of the uses of chlordyne on banana plantations in Martinique prompted writers to call for sustainable biodynamic agricultural practices. The devastation of the island after hurricane Dean in 2007 further propelled an ecocritical approach. Glissant and Chamoiseau published co-authored manifestos in *La Tribune des Antilles* and on the website *Potomitan*, and appeared on television to argue for an ecofriendly way of being in the world. Interestingly, these initiatives come from on the one hand a reflection on literary language in its relation to place and, on the other hand, from a reflection on an alternative globalization, what Glissant and Chamoiseau call a "alter-mondialiste" movement, which had been theorized by Glissant notably in *Traité du Tout-monde* from 1997. In this regard, they forward an ecocritical argument that Martinique should enter into global relations and not only interact with or through France: "Le monde, et non pas seulement la France, est à notre horizon," writes Chamoiseau in a text called "Manifeste pour un projet global" (2000). See Ferdinand (2017).

Whereas a number of household poets—Brathwaite, Glissant, and Walcott—are quoted in works on world literature and ecocriticism, questions of form and aesthetics are often sidelined in favor of a focus on theme and on the form of the novel, perhaps as a result of its centrality in world literary studies. Disaster writing in particular has mainly been theorized in relation to the novel and in extension of questions around nation formations (Anderson 2011; Deckard 2017) or apocalyptic revelations (Munro 2015). This seems to have led to a kind of critical engagement that opts for a straightforwardly political reading of the novels and appears driven by a desire to define a sub-genre that taps into other literary discourses around ecocriticism and chimes in with theories of the "global novel." Mads Rosendahl Thomsen, for instance, classifies natural catastrophe as a world literary theme (2008: 103). The tendency can also be found in Heise's analysis of the "environmental epic" (2012), Huggan's idea of postcolonial rewriting of Romantic nature writing (2009), or in DeLoughrey's examination of allegorizations of nature writing in the Caribbean (2019). Such emphasis on narratives is no doubt accurate, especially concerning storms. Sharae Deckard, among others, has shed light on the long literary history of hurricanes in the region, where these natural phenomena have been used as symbols of societal upheavals and have served as the backbone of narratives of nation and cultural identity in various constellations (2017: 26, 40). In the case of world literature, however, storms are no longer symbols for particular nation or group formation. Quite on the contrary, they become "universal": if natural catastrophes are a "world literary theme" it is because they spur that sense of solidarity, which is at the basis of environmental cosmopolitanism. After all, an earthquake such as the one that hit Haiti in 2010 is a "planetary event. It belongs to everyone," as Haitian author and seism survivor Dany Laferrière states and ironically predicts a "race to write the great earthquake novel or the major essay about reconstruction" (2013: 139). Such a novel would give Haiti a spot in the contemporary literary world market. Only this form does not necessarily adhere to Haitian life since the novel "demands a minimum of comfort that Port-au-Prince can't offer; it's an art form that flourishes in industrialized nations" (2013: 139).[5]

---

[5] The seism that struck the island in 2010 confronted Haitian authors with the issue of how to account for the earthquake at the same time as images of the devastation spread internationally, propelling NGOs and Hollywood celebrities to rush to the scene. Incidentally, this also became a world literary event. That second week of January 2010, Port-au-Prince hosted a global literary festival called *Étonnants voyageurs* (the initiators of this ambulant festival coined the term *littérature-monde en français*, a French version of or response to world literature). The catastrophe thus imposed world literary responses that exposed complicated questions of the role of literature in the world and of belongings. Laferrière's notes, taken just moments after the earthquake struck, were quickly published in major newspapers across the globe and ultimately turned into a book.

While recognizing the global response to the earthquake, Laferrière points to the inevitable fact that suffering triggered by natural disaster exposes global inequities, which poses serious questions about the idea of the natural catastrophe as a globally shared experience in a basic, almost banal way: how a catastrophe is lived cannot be mediated directly through language. What kind of representation does a natural disaster require then? Is it not a most local experience that would resist both world market circulation and political allegorization? After all, most of the immediate artistic expressions following hurricanes and earthquakes do not enter into for example art institutions or print-culture but take the form of street art painted on vehicles and walls, and story-telling and performances at church or at home, in schools or in community buildings. It seems to me that in the wake of the catastrophes of recent years the poems by Georges, Sekou, and Sorhaindo seek alliances with these kinds of direct responses and turn away from transforming the hurricanes into political symbolism and from appealing to environmental cosmopolitanism.[6] Sekou writes that he explicitly wants to block out both international and local news after the hurricanes because they politicize the event, wiping out that sense of intimacy that the poems seek to restore. It is as if turning a deaf ear to news reports is necessary to respond to the hurricane. And if there is any epiphany in Georges' poems it is the absence of revelatory meanings or dramatic endings: "No useful predictions. The prophets / are all mealy-mouthed and impotent. There is only this ball, / madly spiraling through space–and that is the most reassuring thing" (34). It is here that an attention to aesthetics in terms of expressions of a sensible experience of the world may open up for rethinking the connection between ecocriticism and literatures of the world. The point is that locally felt events are expressed in ways that escape coherent narratives in general and world literature in particular. So, while the poems might draw world literary ecocritical attention, they also remind us of the limitation of that understanding. Sorhaindo, for instance, explicitly refuses to narrate the disaster as she opens her poems by addressing the expectations of an (un)implied reader:

> im not going to sit here and paint a heavy hurricane picture for you to
> visualize in pretty clever metaphor words will never carry you to what

---

[6] The dilemma of how to escape turning writing of the hurricane into an idealization of catastrophe was discussed by the poets at the Boca Lit Fest.

its like actually lets just leave it like that words cannot ever take you
there at all ...
go out and experience it for your self
metaphor the world however you want

The address goes to an outsider, presumably a North American or European reader (like myself), who here is both implied and excluded. The speaker of these lines knows that there will be readers from the outside as she explicitly states that she does not write for them. In so doing she takes control of what she knows too well: the centers for world literature in Europe and North America assume to have the privilege of interpretation and categorization. The refusal to metaphorize and narrativize "a hurricane picture for you" can be read as a resistance to being romanticized, pitied, or neatly categorized as a "hurricane poet." She questions the ocular interpretative bias, which has and still holds primacy in European and North American cultures (Dimock 1997: 1061), and calls for another sensible way of understanding the poems. Instead of using words that pretend to take the reader "there," her poetics recalls Gilles Deleuze and Félix Guattari's conceptualization of minor literatures in which "language stops being representative in order to now move toward its extremities or limits" (1986: 23). It is a scripture that moves from visual intelligibility towards a sensory way of representing where the auditive plays a crucial role, as we shall see in the readings.

This is a strategy of writing that transforms into a different kind of global environmental connectedness that, I suggest, singles out these three poets from the Lesser Antilles. They break not only with a visual tradition in poetry and literature studies, but also with the politically charged symbolism of storms, which has dominated South American and Caribbean writing (Anderson 2011; Deckard 2017; Fonseca 2021). In so doing they inscribe the hurricanes in a different Caribbean literary continuum that foregrounds sound and rhythm as representative mediums. We see it in Sorhaindo's address to the reader as she sketches out an aesthetic of the un-representable that works with language to sound out rather than visualize a turbulent world. I would call this poetic investigation a search for resonance in two senses of the term. First, Dimock's idea of literary resonance, according to which paying attention to the sonic textures of literature opens for alternative modes of reading comparatively, although, in the case of Sorhaindo, and also Georges and Sekou, auditive dimensions appear as ways to look for entangled temporal continuity in relation to a particular landscape as will be shown in my readings. Second, moving from visual intelligibility toward an auditory way of making sense is a strategy to express an intensely local, sensible experience of the hurricane and the ravaged landscape it leaves behind. This leads me to turn to a sociologist understanding of resonance as a way to make sense of the world: natural catastrophes challenge our being in the world, our "ontological security" that the ground upon which we walk will hold us, as Hartmut Rosa suggests (2019: 47). In Rosa's theorization, the modern idea of resonance is very much a search for harmony. However, Georges, Sekou, and Sorhaindo do not search for resonance to make the world speak and confirm the subject. They display a more investigative approach in their poems in which sounds create vibrations and evoke responses; the world is not there to be revealed, the poems relationally vibrate with the surroundings. Nevertheless, Rosa's theory is useful for conceptualizing how the poems seek to transfer the turbulent experience and the transformed landscape into living sound, delineating a new soundscape in the aftermaths of the hurricanes, rather than to work through representation.

As in Rosa's theory, voice plays a crucial role here as a way to respond to the hurricane. In the aftermath of Maria, the killing of metaphor evoked by Sorhaindo corresponds to a materialization of words into sounds. Simultaneously, it is a resistance to letting writing turn the hurricane into a symbol. "Words are all we have left," she writes. Words are like debris and not like *metaphora*; they are not a means of transport for the reader. Literature, then, Sorhaindo states over and over again, cannot substitute for lived experience, particularly not in a situation of unequal power relations and racisms: "in a billion years i dont / want some reader to come here think / this world of words was literal think / this blank ink represents black feeling / or that this white page feels any thing" (1). Yet, even if words cannot render the experience of natural disaster, they do seem to hold the promise of relationality: "let's just leave it like that words cannot ever take you there at all although to be fair Mum is always saying kannót is a boat" (1). The vernacular homonym *kannót*, a creole word derived from Taino (English: canoe), seems to open a crack where the words do something else than what they say. Cannot/*kannót* is at once a refusal to speak and an opening up towards other shores. Together with the bodily sensibility of voice and hearing, it produces a "literary frequency," in Dimock's words (1997: 1061), which is at once directly related to the moment and place of experience yet also to other undefined and undecided places and bodies of reception. What does this imply in regard to ecocriticism and world literature? In the following sections, I propose that reading sound and noise as modes of the vernacular in the poetry of Georges,

Sekou, and Sorhaindo will enable us to trace how the poets work through the ecological crisis created by the hurricanes. What is fascinating is that they try to respond to the natural forces, put them in relation to history, place, and lived experience. In this work they reimagine the conditions for their poetry in the world, forcing the reader to relate to the experiences of the hurricanes without relying on prefixed forms and meanings.

Naming and intimacy

In his notes from the 2010 earthquake, Laferrière remarks that the challenge for literature is to restore a certain "intimacy" that got lost in the global clamor around the tragedy (2013: 140). The emphasis on the intimate is striking in light of the amount of criticism focusing on the larger political dimensions of writing in the wake of disasters. Laferrière is not alone. In an essay written shortly after the seism, Edwidge Danticat detects a similar search for intimacy and lets it emerge in the act of naming the catastrophe (2011: 161). The people she meets ascribe agency to the earthquake and seek ways to talk about it by naming it. Should you have no name to give it, you would simply call it *bagay la*, "the thing," in Haitian Creole. Her relatives draw from their own life stories: one uncle calls the earthquake Ti Roro after a boy who used to bully him at school; another calls it Ti Rasta for the same reason (Danticat 2011: 168). Laferrière too cannot name it, yet he knows its effects are insidious, affecting both mind and body: "You can't have experienced it and go your way as if nothing had happened. It'll catch up to you one day. Why do you say 'it'? Because 'it' doesn't have a name yet" (2013: 39). After a few days the earthquake enters into culture and language: "'Goudougoudou,' the sound the earth made as it trembled … What does Goudougoudou want?" (2013: 135). The name is a sound that calls for interpellation rather than explanation. This is why "the thing" has not one name but many, drawn from Haitian Creole (*bagay la*), onomatopoeia (*Goudougoudou*), and personal experience (the names of boys who were bullies at school). Creating a juncture between an exterior world of turmoil and the personal and collective intimate experience of the disaster, the play with sound makes it possible to relate to the names given to the earthquake without ascribing a fixed meaning to the event.

These are not performative acts of naming to impose power, as is the case usually in places marked by colonial history. Instead, naming is here deeply immersed in the life of the individual and the community. Naming has a particular function in the cultures of the African diaspora in terms of identitarian reappropriation (Bousquet 2013), meaning that the trope of naming orients the reading of natural catastrophe toward intimacy. Instead of ascribing symbolic meaning to the event, both Laferrière and Danticat use the sonic fabric of orality to seek out vernacular experiences that call into question attempts to universalize the earthquake. We could call this work an aesthetic strategy where naming turns into a performance of resonance, not to make the world fit neatly into language but rather to release complicated histories. This is precisely what we see in poetry from the Lesser Antilles about the hurricanes of 2017. Celia Sorhaindo's title *Guabancex* invokes the name of the native Caribbean word for the supreme female deity associated with all natural destructive forces. Richard Georges's *Epiphanea* could be placed within Derek Walcott's tradition of the Caribbean as a New World Mediterranean. The title comes from ancient Greek and refers to "a glorious manifestation of the gods, and especially of their advent to help," as the epigraph states. Here as in Sorhaindo's work, the hurricane is supra-human but also, through the evocation of ancient words, connected to gods. The use of Greek plunges the poems into the historical deep time of the Caribbean by working through the European components that have determined the islands. With his choice of words and soothing sounds, Georges softly takes the devastating experience of the hurricane and links it to centuries of violence and exploitation. He evokes villages stoically standing, even after the hurricane, where one still feels, "the centuries of molasses still thick in the nose" (41). Saving objects from the hurricane reverberates with a long history of oppression but also with resilience: "We said our prayers with tongues swollen with language, / gripping our lies like lines, that our bodies were still not bodies / that every part does not speak its own corrugated talk / that navigates the brutal architecture of light and still sound" (41). In line with what Sharae Deckard (2017: 29) observes in Brathwaite's poetry, a consciousness of the multiple temporalities of the Caribbean emerges out of the storm in Georges' poem. The Greek name of the title finds anchor on the islands, sounds out to Africa and the Mediterranean and then connects to personal, detailed observations of the hurricane aftermaths.

The title of Lasana M. Sekou's poems points in the opposite direction from the divine presence in Sorhaindo and Georges. These are not poems; they are "protocols" that record and take note of the hurricane. Yet he too turns to the longer history of the region as if to inscribe the personal in a broader shared experience. The poems are accompanied with drawings copied from the Maya

Codex as a tribute to the native languages and cultures that gave the word to denote tropical storms. Sekou, known for his politically committed writing, testifies in the preface that the hurricane forced him into another kind of writing. He calls the poems "sketches" made with resistance. Facing a completely reshaped island space, he says his writing became "personal," conveying intimate experiences that he was in fact reluctant to write. Naming is part of this movement toward the personal. In one of the poems, Sekou lingers on naming as a practice of grounding that is, at the same time, shifting.

> before it name irma   there was grand case
>   there was rio grande
> before it call maria   there was barbuda
>   there was la habana,
>   ayay was there before
>   yabucoa was there, before
> the road town and the valley,
> *lontan avan ou té vinn konnèt lapwent,*
> *antes de punta cana,*
> and before the mayaimi too once,
> there was huracan to name it
> so that though it came first,
>   movingallovertheplace,
>   it had to have a name
>   to be known for what it is. (27)

Naming can activate the geographical and environmental dimensions of a text by grounding it in the local. Here the grounding is itself a palimpsest, not only because of the diasporatic vernacular sensibilities unleashed by names in the colonial context of the Lesser Antilles, but because the hurricanes force a rethinking of grounding. The poem establishes horizontal relationships between islands embodied in the typography and in the languages present in the writing, recalling what Anna Reckin (2003) defines as Brathwaite's "sound-scape": it reverses the power dynamics inherent in naming and releases its relationality. Colonial and indigenous toponomies are juxtaposed with French Creole and Spanish. The English is incomplete or open (*before it name* ...), or merging as if the syllables recreated the intensity of the hurricane (*movingallovertheplace*). Naming is linked to history, but rather than reaching across the Atlantic and to the Mediterranean as in Georges's poems, Sekou's poem works within the multiple histories of the Antillean islands. The archipelago's diversity can be seen in languages and names, but whereas the Christian names given to the 2017 hurricanes appear as sequences in history, there is an eternal resonance in the name *huracan*. In an ultimate act of defiance of colonial practices of possession, the storm seems to name itself. Ultimately, the poem renegotiates the meaning of the hurricane by trying out names that resonate with the intimate experience and with the place after it passed.

A similar exploration of horizontal relationships appears in one of Sorhaindo's poems, suggesting a kind of weaving between the outside world and an intimate sphere of experience. The only time the name Guabancex appears in her collection is in relation to a mad homeless woman:

> There is a toothless guabancex-grinning woman
> called Mad Maria, living under a bus shelter in a
> now bare-bone village. She spins
> out skeletal arms and cackles
> when they still tease, call her name,
> relentlessly.
> I gifted my daughter the family name
> Maria. She struck on her 13th birthday.
> She sang hauntingly with eyes closed the
> whole crashing night till dawn. I did not know
> her words but metronomed with shak-shak
> teeth and knocking knees. (2020: 17)

Social injustice, place, mental illness, motherhood, coming of age—the intimate and the social merge with the force of the hurricane through names. The toothless mouth of the woman named Maria grinning opens up the abyss of history. Her answer to the scorn to which she is subject is simply to make noise. Through the sound and the name Maria, this woman is intimately linked to a young woman, a daughter, who entered into maturity when the hurricane hit. Her answer to the winds is to sing. The rhythm of the sound she makes while singing rejoins vernacular instruments (shak-shak) with the body: "guabancex-grinning" Maria's skeleton arms join the young Maria's "teeth and knocking knees."

Interestingly, in these poems naming appears as a way to make the hurricanes resonate; it is a calling out to the world. By working on temporal and spatial scales simultaneously, naming here becomes an exploratory practice that does not reify the world but shifts and changes, seeking without necessarily finding the right words and sounds. As a means to face a turbulent world that cannot be but needs to be expressed, it can be read in terms of a Glissantian forced poetics that opens up relationality (Glissant 1997). And it is here that intimacy is restored: the uncertain investigation which relates the outside world to the personal unfolds layers of history and sounds out the devastated landscape.[7]

Turbulent soundscapes

Naming as an intimate sound that unfolds and connects to a collectivity, to the past, and to the shock of the event and the disaster-struck landscape, stands in stark contrast to a concern with silence expressed by all three poets. While international news spread about the hurricanes, the local experience was that of isolation from the rest of the world. Power was out. No internet was working, making it impossible to reach loved ones at home and abroad. Another world of sounds occurs and the poems listen to the silence after the catastrophe. Sorhaindo calls it a "brutal wake-up silence, this downsidetippedup / outsidenowin we are deciphering" (7). The world is smashed to pieces, and as the landscape is brutally affected by the hurricane, so is the soundscape. Sorhaindo writes, "we hear nighttime noises we don't recognise / we don't hear tree frogs we don't hear crickets we hear generators" (25). The silence of nature seems frightening, as if it materializes the idea that people will now exist differently in the world.

One of Georges' poems is called "A Mixtape for Tortola," linking the storm directly to music (notably dub and hip-hop). Time is intensified and the turbulence creates "bodiless voices," "gutted, gaping houses," and "still bleeding wounds" (51). The poem evokes helicopters cutting through the sky and the spinning of the cyclones. Yet the collective voice in the poem cannot make sense of the noise of devastation. They listen but can only hear silence. Listening appears as a theme in Georges's poetry. His lines are inhabited by an explorative uncertain *I* who turns his ear both outside and inside. The difference between human and material, nature and culture, seem blurred. In one poem, entitled "Listening," the lyrical "I" turns inward while relating to deep-time:

---

[7] The idea of unfolding names is, of course, indebted to Roland Barthes's famous analysis of proper names in Proust. However, in Georges, Sekou, and Sorhaindo, names are much more slippery, and the tonal qualities of their sounds are linked to a history of violence as to aesthetics. Moreover, they are actively naming; it is a practice of subjectivation to relate to the outside world, not subjugate it under language.

What could I have known of the easeful ways
of sliding through this world? A dew drop
descending the petal's sloping splendor;

this same moon that rose over giant beasts
and effervescing pools now rises
over your back's prickling flesh and—

there is only so much matter, bodies
with obligations to other bodies.
For instance, death need not be

Such a final, final thing. The days
heave along at a lazy pace.
If there were still leaves in this naked place

they would be still too, or at least listening
for the sighing tides of the Atlantic
for the shuddering clouds' fearsome report,

for the cyclic storms of trauma tracing
the exhausted courses of our ancestors,
for the chanting sky's low hollow sound. (2019: 42)

Time is leveled out, as are differences between species, all belonging to one world. The waters produced by the hurricane resonate with the water in our bodies: "there is only so much water within us, / yet we are all pooling through our bodies, / pretending to be solid masses" (42). In this altered land- and soundscape, bodies and water merge, as matter relating to matter. The poem then shifts perspectives and depicts nature in the process of listening. It plays with the anthropocentric perspective in giving agency to leaves: like humans they listen, or they would listen had they been there. The voices they listen to belong to the oceans and the sky. Working to inscribe the singular event into a continuum of Caribbean aesthetics and experience, Georges again alludes to a long traumatic, cyclic history of soundings, linked to the un-representable. The "sighing tides" recall the Middle Passage, as the hurricane approaches from the Atlantic, thus speaking to an oceanic imaginary that draws from Brathwaitian "tidalectics" (DeLoughrey 2018). Brathwaite famously defined tidalectics as a kind of Caribbean dialectics modeled after the constant turbulent movements of the ocean, proposing a chaotic yet unified notion of time and space: "instead of the notion of one-two-three, Hegelian, I am now more interested in the movement of the water backwards and forwards as a kind of cyclic, I suppose, motion, rather than linear" (Brathwaite in Mackey 1995: 14). In Georges' poems too we find temporal discontinuity and tidal movements as if the oceans continued on these islands. Here the absent leaves listening creates a trembling moment, a stasis containing spatial orientations. While working through the violent history connecting nature and culture, the poem conveys the softness of sound and rhythm. Thus, we are far from the realm of hurricane roaring evoked by Brathwaite. Georges' nation language can rather be described as a kind of nature language that seeks out signs and signals beyond hegemonic language use. There is language and agency in listening, too, he seems to suggest, a hearing through upheaved times and spaces.

Rather than insisting on the hurricane as an eradicating force, Georges' poems explore how the turbulences have moved or blurred frontiers. They urge us to rethink space, time, and language. He lets his poems "linger in doorways" (2019: 35) and search the in-between spaces in nature, culture, and languages, spaces created by the uproar of the hurricane. What lies in front of the people after the hurricane is a lesson in continuity: "I've begun to learn that *devastated* does not mean *dead*, / that ruin can be resplendent, / that what has been emptied can be filled" (34). The poems search an in-between situation of destruction but where life prevails and it is this in-between world that demands other types of resonance. One poem, "The Transmutation of Grief" (45), depicts a bored boy who takes to drumming to make time pass. His beating on hollow tree trunks fills the valley, and it responds to him. Hope imbues the poem in the sense that the boy makes the hurricane-ravaged valley resonate anew. The silence abounds with sound. There is no revelatory meaning in the communication between the boy and the valley. Instead, a relationship has been established through the drum, allowing for resonance to begin.

Many poems by Sorhaindo and by Sekou evoke a similar process of seeking resonance. It is clear that Sorhaindo's poetry is very much about finding oneself after Maria in a flooded landscape. People sing while holding a door to resist the water, but it ignores all frontiers and slips into the most sealed spaces. They push and chant, as if looking for ways to make the water resonate: "There are endless loud cracks, crashes—I see myself / lifted, flung, flying across the room, landing head first / into bookshelves; imagine this hysterical poetic ending" (2020: 6). The subject in the poem listens to the hurricane and hears sounds that make her imagine an ending. In the midst of the traumatic turbulence she seeks her own "resonating words" to resist the forces unleashed by the winds: "So now I push and push, chant and chant, over and over. / Ajai Alai ... Aganjae Alaykhae,

Ajai Alai … Aganjae Alaykhae" (6). The chanting is a way to resist but also relate to the force of the hurricane. It is not the meaning of the words that matters but the cadences echoing in the trembling bodies of the people living through the hurricane. Much like the daughter Maria in the poem quoted earlier, the *I* experiences noises of the hurricane at first and then uses her own voice to address her inner fears as well as the flooding waters.

The movement between intimacy and the outside world is also a tension between individual and collectivity, a personal and a shared sounding that must remain differentiated. The poem that ends the book is like a long litany built around contradictions.

> we sing out loud loud we beat our drums play our jing ping instruments
> we play our shakshaks   we cannot
> we lose our voices   we cannot speak   we do not want to speak
> (2020: 30)

Again, instead of the translation of a hurricane experience that would appeal to the sentimental reader is this "Hurricane PraXis (Xorcising Maria Xperience)" as the poem is entitled. Natural catastrophes symbolize nothing, Sorhaindo seems to suggest. They call for action, practice, as a mode of survival and rebuilding. Within the communitarian "we," a number of voices resonate and emerge in contradictions. They are torn between things they do then cannot do, feel and do not feel, and so on. The poem's rhythm is in these morphing tensions that in their repetition create a sense of waves, rocking you but sometimes crashing, throwing you around. Creole rhythms come through in lines where the same word, often an adjective or an adverb, is repeated, as in "loud loud," enhancing movement and sound. Voices respond to each other, expressing the hurricane experience in dialogue and polyphony. It is a song sung by one single body containing many individual bodies, a choir in which voices sing in harmony, addressing one another. The singing and playing are themselves answers, reactions, but they become restrained. To have a voice is not guaranteed. It can be lost; it is lost. But then the loss of voice turns into a choice: "we do not want to speak." The refusal to speak is not to stop resonating; it is to find another type of resonance in the silence and devastation. The blank spaces, inscribing the silence in the poem between lines and words, create an auditive effect in the visual act of reading.

The importance of sound and noise clearly affirms Deckard's suggestion that the hurricane takes on a "material representation" (2017: 42). On the middle spread of Sorhaindo's book, a poem entitled "Invoked" covers both pages and reads vertically, like strong winds coming in from the side. The words become rain falling on the page, using the blank spaces between the words in a double sense: to invoke silence and to create a rhythm. It is the voice of the hurricane speaking:

When I leave,   for all I know,   for all I   care,
you will seek   to solve   my riddle in rubble,   ask why—
my mayhem will be a   lunatic's   mystery,
pressure popping hurricane tied roofs   but fluttering over nailed tin on
                                                                    shack;
crushing crystal   caressing   calabash. (2020: 15)

The scattered words on the page produce on a graphic level the soundscape of the hurricane—the debris left, the rain crushing down, the objects the hurricane draws with her. The four final alliterative words capture both destruction and tenderness, a contrast mimicked in their sounds, both harsh (*k*) and soft (*s* and *sh*). The ellipses visually create the sounds evoked in the poem; it becomes spatialized on the page.

In Sekou's poems, sounding out works differently. Instead of a tension between inner and outer worlds, it is language that turns into an in-between space, as if the hurricane revitalized the multiplicity or the polyphony of the Caribbean language-scape. The generic categorization of Sekou's poems as protocols has an interesting effect here: the notion of protocol would suggest that what we read is a registration of behavior and events or the conduct in which markers of orality would reflect direct discourse. However, placed within the domain of dub poetry, the vernaculars become signposts of writing even if it is in contingence with orality. Sekou works with graphs, punctuation, and spacing on the page and creates a border space within the poems. He carves out a liminal zone that recalls Georges' thresholds and ripped-off roofs, by working through sound: "iiiiiiiiiiiiiiiiiiiiir / malonglongsong / ahlingehlongahsong / ahsirensingsingahgolonglong / song" (2019: 22). Here language is condensed. It is both just noise and also meaning. Words fuse into one another, repeat themselves and are separated yet connected by the lines in the poem. It is a performative poem, singing out the song that is its subject.

Sekou is the only one among the three poets here who inscribes the vernaculars of St. Martin into his poems. What is interesting is that the function of multilingualism is not first and foremost to denote a linguistic situation; it has a spatializing function. We can see this in "Hurricane Protocol 9.12.17":

the wind-scald hillsides
gone to dusk

the mangroves, mauled, and things
that had brazen up and flush down to wetlands
float and sink
and currentless posts are lumbering well after
their lifeless veins, entangled alone and along
the roadside
> *dans la rue*
>   *in het steegje*
>   *à l'impasse*
we are a world.unwired. (10)

The poem suggests a devastated landscape with trees swiped off the hillsides, mangroves turned upside down, and wetlands spreading out. Modernity, too, has been destroyed and, in the process, negatively animated, wires hang like "lifeless veins." The lines in French and Dutch perform a type of localization. The English says on the roadside, the French, on the street and in the cul de sac, and the Dutch, in the alley. The poem thus sounds off the changing landscape by means of other languages breaking through the English-language poem. Voice and space often converge in Sekou's poetry: "as i turned, without a sound; / to see the confusion, the catastrophe, / the clearing on the path / the path became a voice too. / it turned into me.it spoke" (23). Rosa says at one point that projecting voice into a "nature" separated from "culture" is an expression of late modernity's objectification of nature (2019: 270). Here we have a subject who tries not to master but to navigate in the world after the catastrophe. There is human activity—clearing on the path—though the people involved are absent; only the activity remains. The subject in the poem merges with the path, which, in turn, addresses him. The difference between the subject and the landscape is not erased, but they are closely linked. The movement of the poem suggests a search. From the first line where voice is negatively evoked to the last two lines where the path addresses the subject, a process of resonance has taken place.

In their poems, Georges, Sekou, and Sorhaindo emphasize vernacular responses and experiences of natural catastrophes by working with sound, noise, and rhythm. It is this aesthetic practice, rather than a "disaster genre" or allegory of social upheaval, that marks their inscription in the Caribbean continuum. The question is, what does this tell us? How can such writing, which frankly does not seem to care about global consecration or the circulation scene at all, be read as world literature? Should it even be read as such? What would such an approach bring? Coming to the end of this chapter, I would like to consider a different perspective. These texts contribute to rethinking world literature not because they are about hurricanes with the world literary system at the horizon but because they seek, in different ways, to make the devastated island space resonate beyond its borders. Sound, Anna Reckin writes in her analysis of Brathwaite, is concerned with "a sense of relation that is expressed in terms of connecting lines, back and forth, not only across the surface of the ocean [...] but also in the form of airwaves and 'bridges of sound' (radio broadcasts and sound recordings for example) that connect colony to colony and colony with metropole, often enacting tidalectic echoes" (2003). By actualizing sound rather than meaning as a way to make sense of the world, the poets investigate a relational approach both inwards (intimacy, collectivity) and outwards (the world). The reason sound, noise, and rhythm are central to Caribbean aesthetics is, according to Glissant, because these modalities form a counter-poetics in that their meaning is "camouflaged" so that the Master could not understand it (Glissant 1989: 124; Munro 2010: 12). If the Anthropocene is a consequence of the capitalist world system, it finds its roots in plantation economy and colonial system thinking, which were the basis for Glissant's analysis of counter-poetics. It seems, in fact, that Sekou, Georges, and Sorhaindo in these poems relate to world literature in a similar way. They are acutely aware of the economic and cultural capital of the literary centers but choose aesthetic strategies that speak to the archipelagic region they inhabit. Following Glissant, such strategies do not imply isolation, but the forms of relating to the texts will differ depending on the reader. The radical proposal here is that we can read into the poems and their world-making without claiming to understand them. We do not have to reduce them under a universalizing system of thought or of economic exchanges in order for them to resonate in the world. According to this line of thinking, the world literary reach of "nation language" or "forced poetics" is not about enhancing a specific vernacular as an embodiment of the local, but a way of operating in and through language with noise, rhythm, and sound. It is on these premises, not as an ecological "world literary theme," that the poetry of Sorhaindo, Georges, and Sekou make noise (sense) elsewhere.

Note: I would like to thank Paula Henrikson and Paul Tenngart for their insightful readings of this chapter. My gratitude also goes to Christian Claesson, Katarina Leppänen, Shuangyi Li, Lena Rydholm, and David Watson for their helpful comments and encouragement.

References

Anderson, M. (2011), *Disaster Writing: The Cultural Politics of Catastrophe in Latin America*, Charlottesville: University of Virginia Press.

Apter, E. (2013), *Against World Literature: On the Politics of Untranslatability*, New York: Verso.

Bonilla, Y. and M. LeBrón, eds (2019), *Aftershocks of Disaster: Puerto Rico Before and After the Storm*, Chicago, IL: Haymarket Books.

Bousquet, D. (2013), "'Dis Poem Shall Call Names Names': Naming in Reggae Culture, the Example of Dub Poetry," *Commonwealth: Essays and Studies*, 36 (1): 45–55.

Brathwaite, K. (1984), *History of the Voice: The Development of Nation Language in the Anglophone Caribbean*, London: New Beacon Books.

Buell, L. (2005), *The Future of Environmental Criticism: Environmental Crisis and the Literary Imagination*, Hoboken, NJ: Wiley-Blackwell.

Campbell, C. and M. Niblett, eds (2017), *The Caribbean: Aesthetics, World-Ecology, Politics*, Liverpool: Liverpool University Press.

Casteel, S. (2007), *Second Arrivals: Landscape and Belonging in Contemporary Writing of the Americas*, Charlottesville: University of Virginia Press.

Casteel, S. (2020), "The Caribbean," in S. Helgesson, G. Rippl, and B. Neumann (eds), *Handbook of Anglophone World Literatures*, 395–414, Berlin: De Gruyter Press.

Chea, Ph. (2016), *What Is a World? On Postcolonial Literature as World Literature*, Durham, NC: Duke University Press.

Danticat E. (2011), *Create Dangerously: The Immigrant Artist at Work*, New York: Vintage.

Deckard, S. (2017), "The Political Ecology of Storms in Caribbean Literature," in C. Campbell and M. Niblett (eds), *The Caribbean: Aesthetics, World-Ecology, Politics*, 25–45, Liverpool: Liverpool University Press.

Deleuze, G. and F. Guattari (1986), *Kafka: Toward a Minor Literature*, trans. Dana Polan, Minneapolis: University of Minnesota Press.

DeLoughrey, E. (2018), "Revisiting Tidalectics: Irma/José/Maria," in S. Hessler (ed.), *Tidalectics: Imagining an Oceanic Worldview through Art and Science*, 93–101, Boston: MIT Press.

DeLoughrey, E. (2019), *Allegories of the Anthropocene*, Durham, NC: Duke University Press.

DeLoughrey, E., R. Gosson, and G. Handley, eds (2005), *Caribbean Literature and the Environment: Between Nature and Culture*, Charlottesville: University of Virginia Press.

De Rochefort, C. (1658), *Histoire naturelle et morale des Isles Antilles de l'Amérique*, Rotterdam: Arnauld Leers.

Dimock, W. (1997), "A Theory of Resonance," *PMLA*, 112 (5): 1060–71.

Doumerc, E. (2021), "Celia A Sorhaindo, *Guabancex*," *Miranda* 22, https://doi.org/10.4000/miranda.38241.

Ferdinand, M. (2017), "Ecology, Identity, and Colonialism in Martinique: The Discourse of an Environmental NGO (1980–2011)," in C. Campbell and M. Niblett (eds), *The Caribbean: Aesthetics, World-Ecology, Politics*, 174–88, Liverpool: Liverpool University Press.

Fonseca, C. (2021), *The Literature of Catastrophe: Nature, Disaster and Revolution in Latin America*, London: Bloomsbury.

Georges, R. (2019), *Epiphaneia*, London: Outspoken Press.

Glissant, É. (1989), *Caribbean Discourse*, trans. M. Dash, Charlottesville: University of Virginia Press.

Glissant, É. (1997), *Poetics of Relation*, trans. B. Wings, Ann Arbor: University of Michigan Press.

Guha, R. and J. Alier, eds (2013), *Varieties of Environmentalism: Essays North and South*, New York: Routledge.

Hayot, E. (2016), *On Literary Worlds*, Oxford: Oxford University Press.

Heise, U. (2004), "Local Rock and Global Plastic: World Ecology and the Experience of Place," *Comparative Literature Studies*, 41 (1): 126–52.

Heise, U. (2008), *Sense of Place and Sense of the Planet: The Environmental Imagination of the Global*, Oxford: Oxford University Press.

Heise, U. (2012), "World Literature and the Environment," in T. D'Haen, D. Damrosch, and D. Kadir (eds), *The Routledge Companion to World Literature*, 404–12, New York: Routledge.

Heise, U. (2013), "Globality, Difference, and the International Turn in Ecocriticism," *PMLA*, 128 (3): 636–43.

Huggan, G. (2009), "Postcolonial Ecocriticism and the Limits of Green Romanticism," *Journal of Postcolonial Writing*, 45 (1): 3–14.

Huggan, G. and H. Tiffin (2015), *Postcolonial Ecocriticism: Literature, Animals, Environment*, New York: Routledge.

Hunt, A. and B. Roos, eds (2012), *Postcolonial Green: Environmental Politics and World Narratives*, Charlottesville: University of Virginia Press.

Laferrière, D. (2013), *The World Is Moving Around Me: A Memoire of the Haiti Earthquake*, trans. D. Homel, New York: Arsenal Pulp Press.

Li, Sh. (2020), "Introduction," *Canadian Review of Comparative Literature*, 47 (4): 399–406.

Machado Sáez, E. (2015), *Market Aesthetics: The Purchase of the Past in Caribbean Diasporic Fiction*, Charlottesville: University of Virginia Press.

Mackey, N. (1995), "An Interview with Kamau Brathwaite," in S. Brown (ed.), *The Art of Kamau Brathwaite*, 13–32, Wales: Seren.

Michaelis, S. M., P. Maurer, M. Haspelmath, and M. Huber, eds (2013), *The Survey of Pidgin and Creole Languages*, Oxford: Oxford University Press.

Moreau, J.-P. ed (2002), *Un flibustier français dans la mer des Antilles*, Paris: Payot.

Morton, T. (2009), *Ecology without Nature: Rethinking Environmental Aesthetics*, Cambridge, MA: Harvard University Press.

Munro, M. (2010), *Different Drummers: Rhythm and Race in the Americas*, Los Angeles: University of California Press.

Munro, M. (2015), *Tropical Apocalypse: Haiti and Caribbean End Times*, Liverpool: Liverpool University Press.

Müller, G. and M. Siskind, eds (2019), *World Literature, Cosmopolitanism, Globality: Beyond, Against, Post, Otherwise*, Berlin: Walter de Gruyter.

Niblett, M. (2009), "The Arc of the 'Other America'," in M. Niblett and K. Oloff (eds), *Perspectives on the Other America Comparative Approaches to Caribbean and Latin American Culture*, 51–72, Amsterdam: Rodopi.

Niblett, M. (2012), "World Economy, World Ecology, World-Literature," *Green Letters*, 16 (1): 15–30.

Nixon, R. (2013), *Slow Violence and the Environmentalism of the Poor*, Cambridge, MA: Harvard University Press.

Reckin, A. (2003), "Tidalectic Lectures: Kamau Brathwaite's Prose/Poetry as Sound-Space," *Anthurium: A Caribbean Studies Journal*, 1 (1): 5, http://doi.org/10.33596/anth.4

Rosa, H. (2019), *Resonance: A Sociology of Our Relationship to the World*, trans. J. Wagner, Cambridge: Polity Press.

Rosendahl Thomsen, M. (2008), *Mapping World Literature: International Canonization and Transnational Literatures*, London: Continuum.

Sekou, L. (2019), *Hurricane Protocol*. Philipsburg: House of Nehesi Publishers.

Sorhaindo, C. (2020), *Guabancex*, London and Roseau: Papillote Press.

"The Strength of Islands," https://www.youtube.com/watch?v=IT€Q5Udg3Mg (accessed May 24, 2021).

Walcott, D. (2005), "Isla Incognita," in *Caribbean Literature and the Environment: Between Nature and Culture*, 51–7, E. DeLoughrey, R. Gosson, and G. Handley (eds), Charlottesville: University of Virginia Press.

Watts, D. (1987), *The West Indies: Patterns of Development, Culture and Environmental Change since 1492*, Cambridge: Cambridge University Press.

From *Fesiten* to *Fesibuku*: Shifting priorities in the Saamaka vernacular

Richard Price and Sally Price

How does vernacular culture shift when people living beyond the reach of Western literacy move out of their traditional villages and into more cosmopolitan settings? Focusing on the Saamaka Maroons of Suriname, we address this question by exploring changes we have been following since the mid-1960s. Specifically, we trace a shift from a distinctive, largely secret historical discourse passed on from generation to generation for most of Saamakas' three-century history to new forms of vernacular communication. As Saamakas have been moving increasingly out of their rainforest villages and into the multi-ethnic, cosmopolitan setting of coastal Suriname and Guyane (French Guiana), the careful preservation of specific historical knowledge has gradually diminished, and forms of discourse better suited to life in more cosmopolitan settings have been creatively adopted. In addition, we follow Saamakas' fascination with the idea (and power) of literacy from their earliest history to their participation in settings where their children are in school and much of their social interactions are thumbed into the keyboards of their ubiquitous cellphones.

Creolization in Saamaka

In the middle of the seventeenth century, Suriname formed part of a vast forested area that stretched from the Atlantic to the Andes, the home of countless indigenous peoples who lived by hunting, fishing, and gardening. The first European settlers were Englishmen from Barbados who arrived with their African slaves in 1651, but in 1667 they ceded the colony to the Dutch in return for Manhattan, and it soon became one of the most profitable slave plantation societies in the Americas. By the end of the century, some 8,000 African slaves were laboring for 800 Europeans. Most of the indigenous population had simply retreated into the hinterlands.

The ancestors of today's Saamaka Maroons hailed from a large number of West and Central African societies, situated primarily in the Bight of Benin, in West-Central Africa, and, to a lesser extent, in the Gold Coast.[1] These people spoke a large variety of languages and came from scores of different states and polities, many of them at war with one another. Once landed in Suriname, each shipload of captives was further dispersed by the planters, who chose their purchases with the intent of separating people who might have known each other or spoken the same language. Combined with a firm policy of keeping slave families together when plantations were sold, the slaves' primary identity rapidly shifted from their African origins to their plantation community, where they now had family and comrades, and where they had already begun to bury their dead.

Within the earliest decades of the African presence in Suriname, the enslaved Africans had developed the core of a new social identity, a new religion, and much else. The new creole language for many of them was Sranantongo, but on the largely Jewish-owned Suriname River plantations, whence the ancestors of the Saamakas fled, it was the closely related Dyutongo, lexically influenced by Portuguese. These languages became the vehicles of everyday communication. The striking "non-Europeanness" of this early cultural synthesis, when compared to developments in other parts of the Americas, can be explained in part by the unusually high ratio of Africans to Europeans in the colony—more than 25:1 for much of the eighteenth century, with figures ranging up to 65:1 in the plantation districts. On Suriname plantations, it was in large part the recently arrived Africans (rather than Europeans) who effected the process of creolization, building a new culture and society. There, creolization was built on a diversity of African heritages, with far smaller inputs from European and Amerindian sources. By the time the ancestors of the Saamakas escaped into the forest during the late seventeenth and early eighteenth centuries, they carried with them the seeds of a new cultural system as well as a new language.

The great bulk of the people who became known as Saamakas escaped from Suriname's plantations between 1690 and 1712. With rare exceptions, they had

---

[1] See, for the numbers from each region, R. Price 2008: 291–3.

been born in Africa and had spent little time in slavery, more often months than years. Most were men still in their teens or twenties. By the time of their escapes, however, most of them spoke Dyutongo, which they then quickly developed into their own distinctive creole language, Saamakatongo. As they faced the challenge of building political, social, and religious institutions while waging war and trying to survive in an unfamiliar environment, they drew on the immense riches of their African pasts, though their relative youth meant that much of the esoteric and specialized knowledge of their homelands was not available to them. Leadership drew authority not only from personal charisma and knowledge but also from various forms of divination, which encouraged the communal negotiation of developing institutions. The runaways, fighting for their individual and collective survival, had strong incentives for rapid nation-building.

By the end of the seventeenth century, significant numbers of enslaved Africans had escaped into the surrounding rainforest. The colonists fought back, sending countless militias in pursuit, and handing out gruesome punishments for those they recaptured—hamstringing, amputation of limbs, and a variety of deaths by torture. But by the late 1740s, the colonists were finding the expense overwhelming and recognizing that the expeditions themselves (which included enslaved men as guides) were contributing to further marronage by making known to the enslaved both the escape routes from the plantations and the locations of Saamaka villages.

The colonists saw that the increasingly costly warfare was not achieving its goal and decided, during the late 1740s, to sue their former slaves for permanent peace. After several great battles between Saamakas and colonial armies during the 1750s, a peace was at last negotiated. On September 19, 1762, several hundred Saamaka men met with representatives of the Dutch colonial government, and a peace treaty was sealed.[2]

Our first outsiders' view of Saamaka life (including language) dates from the middle of the eighteenth century, thanks to the detailed diaries of the German Moravian (Herrnhuter) missionaries who were sent out to live in Saamaka villages right after the 1762 peace treaty and to the excellent Saamakatongo-German dictionary compiled by one of the missionaries (Schumann 1914). What we learn is that by this time, Saamakas had created a society and culture

---

[2] The Okanisi Maroons had signed a similar treaty with the Dutch in 1760, and the Matawai concluded their own in 1767.

that was at once new and dynamic. African in overall tone and feeling, it was nonetheless unlike any particular African society. The governing process had been a rapid and pervasive inter-African syncretism, carried out in the new environment of the South American rainforest.

Indeed, Saamaka culture, including language and religion, was already in its main lines very similar to its twentieth-century form, and included frequent spirit possession and other forms of divination, a strong ancestor cult, institutionalized cults for the Apuku and Vodu gods encountered in the forest, and a variety of gods of war. But even the great Saamaka war *obia*s (magical powers), including those with names that point to a particular African people or place such as Komanti, were in fact radical blends of several African traditions, largely developed in Suriname via processes of communal divination. By the time Saamakas had signed their peace treaty with the Dutch crown, there were few African-born Saamakas still alive and Saamaka culture already represented an integrated, highly developed African-American synthesis whose main processual motor had been inter-African syncretism.

Take language, for example. The lexicon of standard (everyday) Saamakatongo is derived roughly 35 percent from English, 25 percent from Portuguese, 5 percent from Amerindian, Dutch, or French, and 35 percent from one or another African language. If, however, we include esoteric (largely ritual) languages, we find that the African contribution is closer to 50 percent.

Saamakas have a number of esoteric languages, known only to those (almost all men) who learn and practice the particular spiritual cults associated with them. They include Apuku (forest-spirit language), Dungulali (an *obia* language), Komanti (the major *obia* language, associated with warrior-gods), Luango (associated with the Langu clan), Papa (used only during funeral rites), Pumbu (associated with the Langu clan), Papagadu (snake [boa constrictor]-spirit language, sometimes called Vodu), Tone (river-god language), Watawenu (anaconda-spirit language), Wenti (sea-god language), as well as others. Saamakas, like other Maroons, also have a well-developed drum language, known as Apintii, which is used in various rituals and for political events.[3] Much of the lexicons of these esoteric languages draw on a variety of African languages but they also use words from other Maroon languages as part of their practices of disguise and play. For example, the speech of Saamaka Komanti mediums is heavily infused

---

[3] Hundreds of examples from the lexicons of these languages as well as hundreds of songs, proverbs, and drum rhythms performed in them are available (R. Price 2008: 309–89).

with borrowings from the Okanisi Maroons of eastern Suriname, and Okanisi Kumanti mediums incorporate words from Saamakatongo in their speech.[4]

First-Time in the Saamaka vernacular

Our first two years of anthropological fieldwork with the Saamaka people were predicated on our obeying two taboos, spelled out publicly by gods and oracles when we first arrived in 1966 and often reiterated by village officials after that: Sally would have to go to the menstrual hut upon the first sign of blood each month and obey rules designed to contain the ritual dangers of her contaminated state; Rich would have to avoid ever discussing anything about *fesiten* ("First-Time," seventeenth- and eighteenth-century history). Nor were we to walk on the path that led by the shrine to the Old-Time People (those who shed their blood for freedom), or travel upriver to the creek where the Saamakas' ancestors had lived during the wars of liberation. Anthropology was allowed, history strictly forbidden.

But Saamakas and their gods had not fully considered the extent to which their coveted early history, the stories of their formative years fighting the whites, animated their everyday lives. The near daily prayers at the local ancestor shrine, at which we were welcome as part of our participation in village life, called upon a myriad of First-Time people, whose feats and foibles were evoked; references to First-Time permeated the proverbs and sacred songs that we recorded; sicknesses and other afflictions were mitigated by rituals intended to placate the offended First-Time people who were causing them. Indeed, because early history was never far from the surface of day-to-day interactions, it was simply not something that we could ignore. By the time we left at the end of 1968, Rich knew that someday he would be returning to work more directly on the secret history that he already understood lay at the heart of Saamaka identity.

A decade later, after several shorter-term stints of fieldwork in Saamaka, we spent a year at the Netherlands Institute for Advanced Study, a pleasant bicycle ride away from the Algemeen Rijksarchief in The Hague, where Rich worked very much as a traditional historian, copying out court proceedings, materials written by colonial administrators or soldiers who had led expeditions against

---

[4] Until the early twentieth century, the Okanisi people were referred to in the literature as Ndyuka (or Djuka).

the Saamakas, and other eighteenth-century documents. By our return to Saamaka in 1978, he was in possession of what was to become a precious gift for the men who held the secrets of Saamaka history—important new materials about their own early past, always exchanged with the greatest discretion.[5] Fortunately, the growth of his historical knowledge that work in the archives had produced coincided with a realization by some Saamaka elders that their sons and nephews were losing interest in preserving historical details and that if knowledge of First-Time (at least the nonritual parts of it) was not written down it could be lost forever. In 1978, at a meeting in the paramount chief's council house, they made a formal request to Rich to be their chronicler. This official approval, which contrasted so strikingly with the explicit prohibitions of the 1960s, encouraged him to forge ahead and begin working with the (mostly elderly) men who had painstakingly built up stores of First-Time knowledge, serving as the guardians of Saamaka history. He recognized that although they were unschooled in Western terms—that is, they could neither read nor write—they were historians in the fullest sense of the term.[6]

In the 1970s and 1980s, many traditional Western historians vehemently denied that oral history that recounted events of the seventeenth or eighteenth centuries could be considered anything other than "myth" or "legend." Human memory, they argued, was simply too fallible, too susceptible to dilution and distortion over the course of repeated tellings. But Rich, along with historians of Africa and Oceania working during the same period, was able to demonstrate that Western historians had grossly underestimated the capacity of humans in non-literate societies around the world to transmit knowledge over the centuries and to help open up oral history to the same degree of historiographical attention that had traditionally been given to the written word.[7]

For the Saamakas in the 1960s–1980s, First-Time—the era of the Old-Time People—differed most sharply from the recent past in its overwhelming inherent power.[8] Stretching roughly up to 1800, First-Time was not more "mythologized"

---

[5] For detailed discussion of these exchanges with Saamaka elders, see R. Price 1983: 14–30.
[6] Calling these men "historians" (rather than "informants") was at the time quite radical, as was publishing their photos with accompanying brief biographies (R. Price 1983: 32–7).
[7] Two of the best examples from that period are Cohen 1977 and Dening 1980. In addition to *First-Time* and *Travels with Tooy*, Rich's contributions include *Alabi's World* (1990) and *The Convict and the Colonel* (1998).
[8] The following paragraphs reprise observations that appeared in *First-Time*, where many detailed examples are offered. The use of the present tense—the ethnographic present in this case—stretches from the period of our initial fieldwork until the Suriname civil war that began in 1986, after which much changed.

or less accurately recalled than the more recent past, but knowledge of it was singularly circumscribed, restricted, and guarded. It formed the fountainhead of collective identity; it contained the true root of what it meant to be Saamaka. The imminent danger of First-Time resides, in part, in its specialized uses in social action. The recent past (roughly the last hundred and fifty years) that intrudes on everyday life tends to affect only individuals, domestic groups, and occasionally, whole village units In contrast, First-Time relates to larger and older collectivities, most often the "clans" that trace their ancestry matrilineally back to an original group of rebel slaves. It most often comes alive in the restricted but highly charged arena of interclan politics. It was the migratory movements of the First-Time people that established land rights for posterity; it is the details of how they held political office that provide the model on which modern succession is based; and it is the particular alliances and rivalries among the wartime clans that shape the quality of their descendants' interactions today. Any dispute between clans—whether over land, political office, or ritual possessions—immediately brings knowledge of First-Time to the fore. In these settings, when corporate property and prestige are at stake, such knowledge becomes highly perspectival; the point of knowing about a First-Time event is to be able to use it in support of one's clan.

First-Time also provides the "charter" for the most powerful ritual possessions of each clan, many of which date back to that formative period. It is to these powers, and the First-Time ancestors associated with them, that knowledgeable Saamakas appeal in times of real crisis. Learning the details of their history provides an unmatched degree of personal security, for one need thereafter never be alone: the Old-Time People and their enormous powers will be standing by one's side. Such specialized knowledge of the past, then, means power in a very direct sense; it permits some measure of control over the vagaries of the unpredictable present.

Saamaka collective identity is predicated on a single opposition: freedom versus slavery. The central role of First-Time in Saamaka life is ideological; preservation of its knowledge is their way of saying "Never again." As Rich overheard one man reminding another, "If we forget the deeds of our ancestors, how can we hope to avoid being returned to Whitefolks' slavery?"[9] Or, in the memorable words of Peleiki—a middle-aged Matyau clan man then being groomed as a possible successor to Paramount Chief Agbago Aboikoni—"This

---

[9] *Ee u lasi fa dee gaansembe du a fesi, dee bakaa o toona buta u a katibo?*

Figure 5.1 1707 painting by Dirk Valkenburg of a "play" on the Suriname River plantations of Palmeneribo-Surimombo, from which the ancestors of the Saamaka Dombi clan escaped soon thereafter. Such drum/dance/ritual performances were a central part of vernacular expression for enslaved Africans on Suriname plantations. (Photo: Danish Royal Museum of Fine Arts, Copenhagen.)

is the one thing Maroons really believe. It's stronger than anything else ... This is the greatest fear of all Maroons: that those times [slavery and the struggle for freedom] shall come again."[10]

[10] *Hen da di soni businenge abi moo taanga! ... De taki, 'Di ten de o toona ko baka.'* Saamaka proverbs and folktales are filled with morals about not trusting other people, and self-defensive posturing and manipulation permeate interpersonal relations—see, for examples, Price and Price 1991.

It may be useful to outline the ways that Saamaka men of knowledge become historians. (We continue to write in the present tense but are thinking of the period that lasted until the mid-1980s.) The pursuit of First-Time knowledge is a strictly solitary endeavor, and in any clan the number of older men considered to really "know things" can be counted on a single hand. (Women and youths, with few exceptions, are prohibited from entering into the world of First-Time knowledge.) Within any clan, each expert's knowledge is idiosyncratic, learned from a unique network of older kinsmen and reflecting that individual's particular strengths as a historian. Over the course of his adult lifetime, each interested man must construct his own convictions and support for his claims about "what really happened" two and three centuries earlier, based on bits and pieces of relevant songs and rites, disputes, and celebrations that he makes it his business to attend to, as well as on the supplementary narratives he is able to wheedle out of his often-reluctant older kinsmen. The Saamaka historian-in-training hoes a very long row; those that take it on as a vocation, like the finest Western historians, seem positively driven by an inner need to make sense of the past, quite apart from the prestige that may incidentally accrue from their special mastery. Question-asking about First-Time was traditionally prohibited. As Peleiki explained, "[a]sking about things in detail simply did not occur. The old folks would tell you things. You just sat there without a sound, listening. And that was all." Several of the most knowledgeable Saamaka historians explicitly credit their accumulation of special knowledge to their own natural curiosity and "shameless" insistence in pressing their elders. Such learning requires tact, strategy, and patience, the skills of a master elicitor.

The research procedures of the apprentice Saamaka historian (like those of his Western counterpart) include a good deal of plain sitting (often after having traveled a considerable distance for the privilege). "First-Time things," Peleiki once mused, "don't have only one head … Your ears must truly grow tired of the thing before you will really know it." Likewise, Asipei, a Watambii clan elder in his late sixties, stressed the need for patience when he used to go to be instructed by his mother's brother: "You can't get up from your stool quickly if you really want to hear things!" Certainly, the necessity to sit passively for long periods is one reason why the pursuit of First-Time knowledge is not for everyone. Cock's crow, with an older man speaking softly to a younger kinsman: this is the classic Saamaka setting for the formal transmission of First-Time knowledge. (Cock's crow is the hour or two that precedes dawn, when most villagers are still asleep in their hammocks.) Although the bulk of any man's First-Time knowledge is in fact pieced together from more informal settings—from overheard proverbs and epithets, from songs and discussions of land tenure—discreetly prearranged cock's crow discussions are, conceptually, the epitome of First-Time learning. It is at such times that a captain is supposed to instruct a potential successor, a grandfather his grandson, or a mother's brother his sister's son. Indeed, the standard phrase with which a Saamaka denies knowledge of First-Time is: "I never sat down with the oldfolks at cock's crow."

The nuggets of historical knowledge transmitted at cock's crow are deliberately incomplete, masked by a style that is at once elliptical and obscure. It is a paradoxical but accepted fact that any Saamaka narrative (including those told at cock's crow with the ostensible intent of communicating knowledge) will leave out most of what the teller knows about the incident in question. A person's knowledge is supposed to grow only in very small increments, and in any aspect of life people are deliberately told only a little bit more than the speaker thinks they already know.

Clearly, the elders that a man knows, and the reputation of these teachers, have much to do with establishing the worth of his own historical knowledge. Even when a person is denigrating his own knowledge in comparison to another's, he uses this idiom. Rich once overheard the 91-year-old paramount chief say, "Tebini ... he saw the very oldest generation. He knew them all! Unlike me, who lived with my father's people [the Fandaaki], whose knowledge really doesn't go back very far." Constant allusions to authority, a repeated shoring up of one's bona fides, pervade every discussion of First-Time. One of the most salient features of cock's crow discourse is its recurrent, pervasive historiographical "digressions." Indeed, well over half of cock's crow speech consists of what a Western historian would consider "footnote material"—detailed discussion of sources and prior authorities. Our calling them "interruptions," "digressions," or "footnote material" is not intended to diminish their import; in this nonliterate society, they are a central datum for the Saamaka listener, a crucial part of his critical apparatus. They are the single leitmotif running through all cock's crow instruction.

In any Saamaka narration, the citation of specific sources complements these more general appeals to authority: "My 'great grandfather,' Kositan, heard this from his own father, Adoboiti, who was a [member of the clan called] Abaisa"; or "[the late] Captain Maaku used to tell us boys this." Such specific citations often include copious details about the travel arrangements to set up the meeting, who was sitting where, what they were wearing, and so on—all lending a sense of veracity and immediacy to the account. And Saamaka historians "criticize" such sources in much the same way as their Western counterparts: [Tebini, skeptically, to Rich:] "Where did he say he heard that story?" [Rich supplies the information.] "That's a no-good place! [an unreliable source] Of course it isn't true!" Similarly, Rich has witnessed accusations of "false footnoting"—of the citation of spurious sources—by one man criticizing (behind his back) the words of another. As in our own system, a person's scholarly integrity in this regard can be his most valuable possession, and any such accusation is taken very seriously.

During our stays in Saamaka, from the 1960s into the 1980s, "First-Time" knowledge remained the core of Saamaka morality. For Saamakas, it held the essential lessons of the universe.

Toward a new, cosmopolitan vernacular

While the transmission of First-Time knowledge has always taken place through a vernacular of sparse, heavily guarded nuggets of historical details, virtually limited to senior men, the vernacular of daily verbal interactions runs along very different lines, practiced by every member of the community, bursting with virtuosity, and constituting one of the signal pleasures of social life.

Indeed, one of the central pleasures of such interactions is creative play with words. For example, a person talking about a watch may call it a "back-of-the-wrist motor" and a Haitian may be referred to as a "Back-of-seven," since the Saamaka pronunciation of *Haiti* sounds like the Saamaka word for "eight" (*aiti*). There is no set lexicon of such terms; they're something that individuals have fun coming up with spontaneously in the course of conversations. The names given to items of material culture imported from coastal stores, such as cloth patterns or enamel dishes or styles of machetes, are similarly treated as fodder for linguistic play, drawing on the objects' physical attributes, the history of their arrival in the villages, their association with local scandals, or other considerations that enhance the pleasure of talking about them.

During the second half of the twentieth century, women sewed men's shoulder capes in colorful patchwork, using pieces of the cloth that their husbands brought back from coastal stores, and assigning names to each cloth pattern based on anything from local scandals, current events, or visual properties. For example: *Kankan fatu* ("blackbird fat," for a cloth as vividly orange as the fat of a blackbird), *Ameika go a gadu* ("Americans go to heaven," just after the 1969 moon landing), *Agbago singi a mote* ("Agbago sank with a motor," referring to Chief Agbago's

Figure 5.2 Patchwork shoulder cape (*aseisente*) that belonged to Captain Kala of Dangogo, sewn mid-twentieth century. (R. and S. Price Collection, Schomburg Center for Research in Black Culture, New York; photo S. Price.)

first ride from Paramaribo in a motorboat, which sank in a rapids), *Silaliko opo lagima* ("Suralco raised up the poor man," commemorating increased job opportunities with the Suriname Aluminum Company in the 1960s, during the construction of the hydroelectric project), *Silo a bedi* ("Sloth in the bed," a name made up by a woman after her husband replaced her cowife's hammock with a bed imported from the coast), or *Mangumuyee booko Daume* ("Mangumuyee ruined Daume," after a woman in the village of Daume was accused of neglecting menstrual prohibitions).[11]

The kind of joy that Maroons take in playing with such names is well documented for societies throughout the Black Atlantic. Take this example from Ghana, reported at the moment when flared trousers were in fashion:

---

[11] For a list of forty-four cloth names, see Price and Price 1980: 82–3.

> "Perhaps you feel shy" ("*Gyama wo fere*") refers to a type of Afro trousers with [only] moderately flared bases ... "Gun and bullet" ("*Tunabo*") is a teasing title for a pair of trousers without a flared base. The trouser leg represents the gun and the leg, the bullet. "*Po*," the sound made by a gun shot, is the same as "*Tunabo*." "*Po*" was introduced after people were beaten up for shouting "*Tunabo*." At times the "critics" don't say anything, but rather run past and fall down in front of the person indicating that he has shot the "critic" dead with the "*tunabo*."
>
> (Warren and Andrews 1977: 14–15)

And playful naming of items of material culture can be found in countless other societies around the world; see, for example, the discussion of the role of humor in assigning names such as "ant droppings" or "drunken pattern" to the designs on cloth among the Iban of Southeast Asia (Gavin 2003: 170).

The motifs that Saamaka men include in their famous art of woodcarving (Saamakatongo *tembe*) are also given names, generally based on their physical form ("gun-mouth" for a circle, "monkey tail" for a small spiral, or "turtle penis" for a small band ending in an arrow-like point).[12] Names like this have fed easily into stereotypes of Maroon artistry, as outsiders, misunderstanding them to be a lexicon of closely guarded meanings, have worked them into an all-too-familiar Western stereotype about the often-secret symbolic essence of artistic production among "primitive" peoples.

Partly because most Maroon woodcarvings are made by men for women, outsiders have long cherished the idea that Maroon art functions as a symbolic language between male woodcarvers and the women for whom their carvings are intended as gifts of affection. Each named motif, the idea goes, carries a specific meaning, and the various motifs on a given carving work together to transmit a discursive message. As a (non-Maroon) forestry worker who compiled a dictionary of Maroon symbols put it,

> The motifs can be considered like words ... By assigning the right meanings to these motifs and reading them correctly, just like letters and words, it is possible to bring out the maker's intent. Exactly the way a comma can change the sense of a sentence, the presence of a particular motif next to another one alters its meaning.
>
> (Muntslag 1979: 31)

This misconception of an esoteric "language" of Maroon art, which extends even to claims of grammatical structure, has been widely perpetrated at least since the

---

[12] The names of hairdos and cicatrization patterns follow the same principle.

late nineteenth century, producing whole dictionaries of symbols designed for tourists and other outsiders. Saamaka artists have consistently tried their best to debunk these interpretations, explaining that their art is made for aesthetic pleasure and that names, which reflect formal attributes of design elements, are simply descriptives (S. Price 2018).

Until the civil war between Maroons and the government (1986 to 1992), Maroons in Suriname lived largely in their traditional territories in the interior, almost as states-within-a-state. But after the civil war, when the government began an active program of integrating Maroons into the larger society (in part with the aim of emptying out the interior of the country to free it up for mineral and timber extraction by foreign multinationals), large numbers of Maroons moved to the coast, in Suriname or Guyane, becoming part of the urban underclass. Today, many traditional villages are barely inhabited and something over half of all Maroons live outside of traditional territories.

A Dutch colony until it gained independence in 1975, Suriname often boasts of being the most multiethnic country in South America. Today, its ethnic groups, in descending order of size, are Hindustanis (East Indians), Maroons (descendants of self-liberated African slaves), Creoles (non-Maroon, largely urban Afro-Surinamers), Javanese, Brazilians, Chinese, Amerindians, and others.[13] The national language remains Dutch, which is used in schools, by the government, and on TV and radio. But the first language of each group is distinct and the first language of most Creoles, which is used by everyone for communication across ethnic lines, is an English-based creole called Sranantongo ("Suriname language"). Two of the six Maroon peoples (the Saamaka and Matawai, who live in the central part of the interior) speak a variant of Saamakatongo (a Portuguese-, English-, and African-based creole) while the other four (the Okanisi, Pamaka, and Aluku, who live in the eastern part of the country, as well as the tiny group of Kwinti) speak varieties of Okanisi/Ndyuka (an English-based creole related to Sranantongo). Chinese, Brazilians, and Amerindians speak their own languages among themselves.[14]

In neighboring Guyane, which is politically a distant outpost of Europe, the ethnic mix is equally diverse. Although French law does not permit ethnic

---

[13] According to the latest (2012) census (modified by our own investigations—see R. Price 2018), the total population of 542,000 is composed of 27% Hindustanis, 26% Maroons, 14% Creoles, and 13% Javanese, with the remaining 20% divided among Brazilians, Chinese, Amerindians, and miscellaneous others (including Dutch). In addition, there are something like 400,000 people of Surinamese descent living abroad, mostly in the Netherlands.

[14] For further information on the linguistic situation in Suriname, see Carlin and Arends 1992.

enumeration in the census, estimates suggest that the population of about 280,000 people includes 36 percent Maroons, 28 percent Creoles (non-Maroon Afro-Guyanais), 14 percent Brazilians, and 11 percent Haitians, plus smaller numbers of metropolitan French, Chinese, Hmong, Peruvians, and diverse others. The official language is of course French, with a French-based creole as the lingua franca except in western Guyane, where Okanisi serves as the lingua franca.[15]

Under the new post-civil war cosmopolitan circumstances, Maroon languages and language use, as well as the meaning of Maroon identity, are rapidly changing. There are now some 100,000 people in the world whose first language is Saamakatongo.[16] That language (like all languages) is in constant flux, and it now includes lexical items and ways of speaking adopted during the twentieth and twenty-first centuries from external sources such as Sranan, Okanisi, French, Dutch, and more recently Brazilian, Chinese, and Russian—the latter because of the new Soyuz base in Guyane, where a small number of Saamakas are employed. But even beyond that, and their array of ritual languages already mentioned, Saamakas master, to variable extents, generation-specific play languages that add to the intellectual and aesthetic pleasure of language use (Price and Price 1976).

In today's urban environments of Suriname's capital, Paramaribo, and the coastal towns of Guyane, Maroons confront identitarian issues of a new kind. In St. Laurent-du-Maroni, on the Guyane side of the border river with Suriname, for example, the population of 60,000 includes at least 46,000 Ndyuka, Saamaka, Aluku, and Pamaka Maroons who interact with one another as well as with Guyanese Creoles, Chinese, Haitians, Hmong, French, and others—in schools, hospitals, administrative offices, and so forth. Ethnic stereotypes remain strong, multilingualism is the order of the day, and questions of nationality matter a great deal. Since 1986, when the civil war broke out, Saamaka life (like that of other Maroons) has experienced a veritable sea change. By the end of the war (1992), Saamaka territory—once relatively sovereign and closed to outsiders—had been opened up to the world outside. Soon, government schools and police, churches of many denominations, the U.S. Peace Corps, large numbers of tourist lodges (and mostly Dutch tourists), Chinese grocery stores, electricity, ubiquitous cell

---

[15] For further information on the linguistic situation in Guyane, see Renault-Lescure and Goury 2011 and Migge and Léglise 2013.

[16] For Saamaka children born in the Netherlands or the United States, Saamaka is often a second or third language. Saamaka parents in Rotterdam, for example, have sponsored Saturday morning classes in Saamakatongo designed to discourage their children from abandoning the language.

phones and towers, women now covering their breasts and men now wearing blue jeans rather than loincloths, and much else had arrived. Transportation to the capital, even from the most remote villages, soon became a matter of hours rather than days. And interest in (and transmission of) First-Time knowledge, particularly among the younger generations, greatly diminished. Once men were having relations on a daily basis with people of many different ethnicities, including the Whitefolks who had been sworn and eternal enemies, First-Time was almost on the way to becoming folklorized.

Since the civil war, one third of Saamakas have been living in Guyane, where children attend French schools, become literate, and learn to operate in this cosmopolitan setting. In several notable cases they have even gone on to university educations in France. One young woman whose parents remain non-literate and do not speak French has become an epidemiologist; several others are getting their M.A. at Sciences Po in Paris; and many other Saamakas have gone on to attend French universities. Because they have grown up in a South American outpost of France, the relevance of the First-Time exploits of their ancestors in Suriname is severely diminished, becoming a mainly identitarian one, rather than one to be evoked in everyday matters.

Young Saamakas in Guyane grow up in a world of TVs, schools, commercial clothing, electricity, and indoor plumbing, not to mention ethnic diversity and other "Western" aspects of daily life. And when they visit their families' villages in the rainforest (for example, during summer vacation), they arrive on paved roads, travel between villages by motorboat, speak on cell phones, and have access to outhouses for bathrooms. So, in our more recent writings, we have tried to help them picture the life their parents had left behind by recounting the world we knew in the 1960s and 1970s.

But we have found that explaining to young Saamakas the once-pervasive uses of history in everyday life—the grave spiritual dangers that surrounded the transmission of (or simply the speaking about) First-Time knowledge—has proved much more challenging than alluding to the physical details of life in the villages. For example, the idea that many of the Saamakas we knew in the 1960s were genuinely frightened of Whitefolks is more or less difficult to be persuasive about, depending on the sophistication, age, and life experience of today's Saamaka reader. At the same time, Saamakas in urban Suriname and Guyane still continue to identify strongly as Saamaka, taking pride in their culture and struggling to maintain their cultural identity even in the face of tremendous pressures from national political and cultural forces. During the early twenty-first century, traditional Saamaka political leaders fought a last-ditch effort to maintain their people's sovereignty, in the face of incursions by the national government. And in 2007, they won a signal victory.

In that year, with our participation as expert witnesses, the Interamerican Court for Human Rights heard the case of *Saramaka People v. Suriname*, in which the Saamakas, whose traditional territory was in the process of being despoiled (with Suriname government approval) by Chinese and other multinational logging companies, won their case.[17] The Court ruled that the government of Suriname must respect Saamaka territory and sovereignty, and that the ruling extended to other Maroons throughout the Americas, who would henceforth be treated as equivalent to Indigenous Peoples in international law.[18] Unfortunately, more than a decade later, the national government has carried out almost none of the court's orders, and Saamakas are increasingly being integrated into the world that they once considered sharply alien. Indeed, by the time the official organization of the Saamaka People asked us to translate *First-Time* into their own language, and then bought 3,000 copies to distribute in their schools (where youths, traditionally barred from hearing about "First-Time," would read it), it was clear that this knowledge was undergoing a radical shift in meaning and social importance. Traditional authorities (the paramount chief, village captains, and their assistants) were losing much of their power and influence; disputes about clan land ownership were becoming less frequent and relevant; Whitefolks, who had been the prototypical enemy, were now visiting villages as paying tourists; the capital city, once a place of danger and alienation, was now an attractive residence option; and more.

Toward the end of his life, our friend Tooy (a learned and respected Saamaka captain) told us, in a tone of sardonic pessimism: "We once could have confidence in our First-Time *obia*s, But nowadays, who knows how much of their powers are left? Let's say someone comes running at you with an axe and you have to choose whether to see if your *obia*s are still worth something or to make your escape. Which makes more sense? I'd say, Run for it!" (R. Price 2003: 226–8). And then

---

[17] See for example, http://goldmanprize.org/2009/southcentralamerica. This website includes a five-minute video about the Saamakas' legal victory, narrated by Robert Redford.
[18] Richard Price's *Rainforest Warriors: Human Rights on Trial* (2011) tells the story of the lengthy Saamaka legal battle against the government of Suriname, with much of the testimony that swayed the justices based on First-Time knowledge.

he giggled. There was a real sense of a world on the wane. Today it seems ever clearer that Saamaka collective memory of First-Time—their knowledge of their heroic beginnings as a people—is fading, along with the core of their identity as one of the most remarkable peoples in the African diaspora.

Speech into text: The *Fesibuku* era

Although until recently Suriname Maroon languages have been almost exclusively oral, Maroons have always been well aware of the power that literacy represents, and they maintain a strong interest in the idea of the written word. As early as the 1760s, immediately following their peace treaty with the colonists, they pleaded (largely in vain) with the Whitefolks for schools that would allow them to harness some of that power. The plot of a Saamaka folktale turns on a magical book that grants every wish to the person who opens its pages.[19] And Maroons have always been intrigued by the abstract idea of systems of graphic signs.[20] In Saamaka, woodcarvings and engraved calabashes often carry small marks, sending simple messages or identifying the object's owner. An X, for example, is said to thank the person who complements the object's beauty and curse the person who criticizes it. Eastern Maroons have always been even more intrigued than Saamakas by the idea that graphic signs might communicate meaning; in 1908, an Okanisi man literally "dreamed up" a whole script.[21]

Attempts by outsiders to develop an orthography for the Saamaka language began soon after the 1762 peace treaty with the Dutch Crown, when German Moravian missionaries first arrived in Saamaka territory. From 1765 until 1813, thirty-seven Moravian men and women attempted to bring their pietist brand of Christianity to the Saamaka,[22] writing biblical texts in the Saamaka language and producing the remarkable Saamakatongo–German dictionary mentioned above. Since that time, there have been others—by the Dutch linguist Jan

---

[19] For the folktale, see Price and Price 1991: 315–46, 409–10. Other African American versions of "The Talking Book" can be found in Gates 1988: 127–69.

[20] This is in spite of their rejection of the idea promoted by outsiders that their graphic arts communicate messages.

[21] See Dubelaar and Pakosie 1999. No more than a dozen men ever learned this so-called Afaka script, though it has been reinvigorated as a symbol of Okanisi identity by contemporary artist Marcel Pinas—see Chaia 2011.

[22] See R. Price 1990, which explores the relationship between Saamakas and missionaries during the second half of the eighteenth century.

Voorhoeve and the R. C. priest Antoon Donicie in the 1960s, by the SIL field linguists Catherine Rountree and Naomi Glock in the 1970s and 80s, and by amateur linguists in French Guiana during the past decade.[23]

Most recently, Saamaka linguist Vinije Haabo developed a new orthography and compiled an extensive Saamakatongo–Dutch dictionary. And we have written two books using that orthography with the hope that Saamakas will learn to use it—*Fesiten* (2013) and *Boo Go a Kontukonde* (2016).[24]

Today, in spite of increased literacy and the omnipresence of social-media devices, middle-aged Saamakas tend to use WhatsApp for voice communication more than they text. A Saamaka woman who lives in her husband's village now calls her mother, who lives two days away by paddle canoe, on her cellphone to find out how she's doing rather than visiting her, as before. But younger people, who have been to school in French or Dutch, also spend hours on social-media texting and reading, often in Saamakatongo. With little concern for orthographic conventions, they express themselves according to their sense of how the language sounds orally, eschewing regularity across texts, but easily making themselves understood by anyone who knows the (verbally expressed) language. Writing, in this context, is a directly communicative tool.

In Guyane, the current situation of Maroons provides an interesting window onto the malleability of Maroon identitarian discourses and ideas about language in the context of rapid assimilation. As Guyane has moved from a sleepy little colony with a population in the tens of thousands at mid-twentieth century to the booming home of the European space center and a population fast approaching the 300,000 mark, France has implemented a program of *francisation* which is designed to bring Guyane more into line in terms of French language, education, values, and lifestyle.

This assimilationist politics has had a profound impact on (among other things) the Maroon art of woodcarving, known in the various Maroon languages as *tembe*. The idea that *tembe* constitutes a secret language, which has always been promoted by enthusiastic but misinformed outsiders, has been elaborated in new directions over the past several decades, especially in Guyane. There, the cooperatives that have been popping up with ever-increasing frequency—often with (literate)

---

[23] See, e.g., Donicie and Voorhoeve 1963; Rountree, Asodanoe, and Glock 2000 (http://suriname-languages.sil.org/Saramaccan/English/SaramEngDictIndex.html); and Lienga 2013.

[24] The orthography, which does not use diacritical marks (as earlier proposed orthographies of this tonal language do), mimics the way Saamakas write on their smartphones. (For speakers of the language, it turns out that diacritics are not necessary either for reading or writing the language.)

European directors and (less literate) Maroon artists—are in a privileged position to define, develop, and promote not only the art itself, but also the interpretation of its meanings. And as Maroons move into an ever-more-integrated role within the larger society, that means refitting both forms and interpretive discourses for a market economy, something that the European members of the cooperatives are particularly well equipped to oversee. In the process, widespread/longstanding popular stereotypes about Maroons—most notably the view of *tembe* as a language of graphic signs—are called into service for promotional purposes, and the idea of a vernacular system of coded messages has become omnipresent in books, magazines, exhibit brochures, websites, and media outlets such as radio and television. One of the many coffee-table books put out by one cooperative, for example, asserts: "The symbolic figures ... constitute a kind of lexicon that is transmitted from generation to generation ... Each sign is there both for the way its form contributes to the overall composition and for its meaning. The message can be romantic, moral, humorous, or even insolent" (Doat, Schneegans, and Schneegans 1999).

Claims of this sort have appeared periodically throughout Maroon history, but recently there have been some new twists in the discourse. A coloring book for children called *Colorie Tes Tableaux Tembé!* by a talented Aluku artist named Franky Amete, in a section entitled "A Secret Code," explains that *"art tembé"* can be studied like a language, with colors playing a significant part in the themes to be expressed. Red, it asserts, represents man and blood, white is woman and beauty, black is earth (soil), blue is the earth (planet), and so on (S. Price 2007). A follow-up volume contains even more extensive claims, placing the origin of *tembe* symbols in the prehistory of Maroon societies:

> The art of *tembé* was used as a means of communication among plantation slaves, comparable to secret messages in code. After the slaves escaped their servitude and established themselves on the banks of the river ... it became the written language of a community that had until then been based on an oral tradition.
>
> (Maïs n.d.)

Local cooperatives were making similar claims, taking readers back to the era of slavery to recount the birth of Maroon *tembe*:

> Knowledge of escape, charged with vigilance, calling each day on a new creativity. And at the beginning, communication ... The marks of secrecy, the marks of combat ...[A] few lines furtively scratched in the soil. The mark of the Maroon

in full power preparing his flight in complicity ... The trace, the sign, the mark ... Coded messages, discrete, secret, and ritualized ... So many powerful images in these marks for those who knew to find them, to recognize them, to read them, to accept them, to follow them. Once peace came and freedom was won, the Tembe was transformed into an artform.

(Association Mama Bobi 2004, 2015)

This depiction of slave-era origins for *tembe* was a serious eyebrow-raiser, given the decades-long, multi-sited research that had placed the beginnings of Maroon woodcarving in the early- to mid-nineteenth century.

Another coloring book repeated Amete's claim of color symbolism, and went on to assert that Africans fresh off the boats from Africa (the *beaux-sales*) invented a writing system for communication on the plantations that they then used to record the genealogy of each family as well as information on "customs, traditions, culture, and other kinds of information that was indispensable for the transmission of their history and identity" (Maïs n.d.: 2).

Part of the problem with the claim that *tembe* is a communicative language capable of sending messages from men to women can be traced to gender relations in the encounters between outsiders and Maroons. If, indeed, the motifs carry meanings by which the man who makes the carving sends a message to the woman who receives the carving, one would hope that the woman could make out the message from her lover. Because almost all the descriptions of *tembe* in the literature come from male outsiders talking with male Maroons, the question of to what extent women can interpret the symbols has rarely come up. But when women *are* asked about how they read *tembe* designs, the response is universally negative.[25]

Saamakas in present-day Guyane have in no way allowed outsider interpretations of their artistic life to get in the way of the ongoing creativity that has always characterized vernacular aspects of their life. Take, for example, women's textile arts, in which recent developments have depended on changes in gender roles that came about precisely because of the women's move into the more Westernized/commoditized lifestyle of coastal settings. Although

---

[25] Our own efforts over the past half century to get women to "read" trays, combs, stools, and so forth have resulted in the identification of lots of names for motifs, but no symbolic meanings for them and no messages in the way they were combined. None whatsoever. Nor have the efforts of the Brazilian anthropologist Olívia da Cunha, who has interviewed Okanisi women explicitly about this.

innovation in sewing techniques and designs were always an aspect of women's lives in the villages of the rainforest, the need to adapt to a very different social/economic situation in Guyane gave them increased independence together with increased financial responsibilities. No longer dependent on the cloth and other products bought with the money that men of an earlier generation earned via wage labor, they had both the need to take on more responsibility for their own material life, and the resources that allowed them to do so, most notably through welfare checks, but also stands in the local markets, participation in cooperatives, and other money-earning possibilities that had not been available back in the villages.

In the 1980s and 1990s, Saamaka women in Guyane were inventing new styles and techniques of sewing very much the way their mothers and grandmothers had done back home, (for example, developing a new art of curvilinear designs realized in "reverse appliqué" (S. Price 2003). But by the second decade of the twenty-first century, the experimentation had taken on a new dimension, as women bought sophisticated sewing machines and multi-thread sergers, exploited the technical options that these devices allowed to invent entirely new forms, and began participating in a market aimed at both fellow Maroons and non-Maroon outsiders (S. Price 2020).

For the first time they were turning their creative energy to the elaboration of their own outfits, literally flipping the long-standing Saamaka understanding that decorative sewing was exclusively for men's garments, a thank-you for the goods and services men provided to wives and female relatives. (This of course coincided with a drop in the frequency with which men were donning "Maroon-style" garments such as loincloths and shoulder capes.[26])

Unlike the ethnographic techniques we had used to explore Maroon arts for over a half century (in "the field," as well as in libraries, museum collections, and archives), our investigation of twenty-first-century textile arts began taking place to a great extent on Sally's laptop. A several-week-long 2018 visit with women in Guyane opened up the subject, as women introduced her to basic techniques, terms, and ethnic associations (mainly Okanisi vs. Saamaka), but emails and Facebook pages then took over the elaboration of the trend. Questions posed in the Saamaka language on Facebook messaging sites were answered in

---

[26] For special occasions (funerals, holiday festivals, etc.), men often slip a shoulder cape over their Western clothing and sometimes even don a loincloth or a pair of decorative calfbands, but their day-to-day dress is shirts and pants.

From Fesiten *to* Fesibuku: *Shifting Priorities in the Saamaka Vernacular* 149

Figure 5.3 Maroon women showing off the latest fashion, wrap-skirts sewn in cross-stitch embroidery. (Photo posted on Facebook in 2015 by Steven Alfaisi.)

Saamakatongo, based on the responder's own often-impromptu spelling. Daily postings of people posing for the camera constituted a rich scrapbook of new styles and novel kinds of garments that could then be followed up by emailed questions. And Google searches for "Maroon clothing" led to lively YouTube videos and sites devoted to Maroon cultural events and beauty contests.[27] It became clear that Western promoters upped the sensationalist nature of some of the showmanship, but the embroidery designs and techniques were the women's own.

A few traditional items of Maroon dress disappeared in this new fashion world; for example, the frontal aprons that all teenage girls once wore as their sole garment became obsolete except in rites of passage. But other items were retained and newly elaborated. For example, the white calfbands with red/black/yellow stripes in the middle that men, women, and children wore on an occasional basis in the rainforest villages (especially at funeral celebrations) were doubled in size, incorporating lavish multicolor designs and becoming a ubiquitous element of high fashion as well as an art object suitable for display on

---

[27] See, for example, "Sociaal Culturele Vereniging Kifoko" and "Kula Skoro."

a shelf over the television in an urban apartment. And the plain folded squares of cloth that Saamaka women always used to belt their wrapskirts became canvases for elaborate embroidery, often supplemented by written aphorisms.

The role of Saamaka vernacular expression, and the aspects of life in which it plays a part, reflect the changing physical, cultural, social, economic, and political situation of the society itself. The maintenance of a detailed memory of Saamakas' seventeenth- and eighteenth-century ancestors' heroic struggle for independence depended on vernacular forms that fit with the social, political, and cultural life of upriver villages, where there was strong pride in Saamaka identity, strong gender roles that governed the maintenance of that identity's formation, and strong reliance on verbal forms of communication. Once Saamakas moved beyond life in those villages, they entered a whole new universe where their self-image was no longer so fully anchored in a heroic past of self-liberation, where their physical, social, and cultural surroundings were suddenly multi-ethnic, and where they finally had access to the gift of literacy that their earliest ancestors had only dreamed of. It was in this new setting that the novel vernacular forms that we describe were able to emerge.

References

Association Mama Bobi (2004), *Tembe: Repères essentiels*, Matoury: 4è Biennale du Marronnage.
Association Mama Bobi (2015), *Ferfi Tembe: Un visuel pour l'émancipation*, Guyane: Association Mama Bobi.
Carlin, E. B. and J. Arends, eds (1992), *Atlas of the Languages of Suriname*, Leiden: KITLV.
Cohen, D. W. (1977), *Womunafu's Bunafu: A Study of Authority in a Nineteenth-Century African Community*, Princeton, NJ: Princeton University Press.
Dening, G. (1980), *Islands and Beaches. Discourse on a Silent Land: Marquesas 1774–1880*, Honolulu: University Press of Hawaii.
Doat, P., D. Schneegans, and G. Schneegans (1999), *Guyane: L'art Businengé*, Grenoble: CRATerre Editions.
Donicie, A. and J. Voorhoeve (1963), *De Saramakaanse Woordenschat*, Paramaribo: Bureau voor Taalonderzoek in Suriname van de Universiteit van Amsterdam.
Gates, H. L. (1988), *The Signifying Monkey*, New York: Oxford University Press.
Gavin, T. (2003), *Iban Ritual Textiles*, Leiden: KITLV Press.
Lienga, R. (2013), "Le saamakatöngö et 'gdi saamakatöngö alifabëti' dans le contexte multilinguistique de la Guyane," paper presented at the Colloque pluridisciplinaire "Les marronnages et leurs productions sociales, culturelles dans les Guyanes et le

bassin caribéen du XVIIème au XXème siècle: bilans et perspectives de recherche," Saint-Laurent du Maroni, Guyane.

Maïs, J.-L. (n.d.), *Mon tembe magique (L'enfant du fleuve vol. 1)*, Guyane: self-published.

Migge, B. and I. Léglise (2013), *Exploring Language in a Multilingual Context: Variation, Interaction and Ideology in Language Documentation*, Cambridge: Cambridge University Press.

Muntslag, F. H. J. (1979), *Paw a paw dindoe: Surinaamse houtsnijkunst*, Amsterdam: Prins Bernard Fonds.

Nouh Chaia, M., ed. (2011), *Marcel Pinas, Artist, More than an Artist*, Heijningen: Jap Sam Books.

Price, R. (1983), *First-Time*, Baltimore: Johns Hopkins University Press.

Price, R. (1990), *Alabi's World*, Baltimore: Johns Hopkins University Press.

Price, R. (1998), *The Convict and the Colonel*, Boston: Beacon Press.

Price, R. (2008), *Travels with Tooy*, Chicago, IL: University of Chicago Press.

Price, R. (2011), *Rainforest Warriors: Human Rights on Trial*, Philadelphia: University of Pennsylvania Press.

Price, R. (2018), "Maroons in Guyane: Getting the Numbers Right," *New West Indian Guide*, 92: 275–83.

Price, R. and S. Price (1976), "Secret Play Languages in Saramaka: Linguistic Disguise in a Caribbean Creole," in B. Kirshenblatt-Gimblett (ed.), *Speech Play*, 37–50, Philadelphia: University of Pennsylvania Press.

Price, R. and S. Price (1991), *Two Evenings in Saamaka*, Chicago, IL: University of Chicago Press.

Price, S. (2003), "Always Something New: Changing Fashions in a 'Traditional' Culture," in E. Bartra (ed.), *Crafting Gender: Women and Folk Art in Latin America and the Caribbean*, 17–34, Durham, NC: Duke University Press.

Price, S. (2007), "Into the Mainstream: Shifting Authenticities in Art," *American Ethnologist*, 34: 603–20.

Price, S. (2018), "Maroon Art in Guyane: New Forms, New Discourses," in S. Wood and C. MacLeod (eds), *Locating Guyane*, 168–82, Liverpool: Liverpool University Press.

Price, S. (2020), "Maroon Fashion History: An Update," *New West Indian Guide*, 94: 1–38.

Price, S. and R. Price (1980), *Afro-American Arts of the Suriname Rain Forest*, Berkeley: University of California Press.

Renault-Lescure, O. and L. Goury (2011), *Langues de Guyane*, La Roque d'Anthéron: Vents d'ailleurs.

Rountree, C. S., J. Asodanoe, and N. Glock (2000), "Saramaccan–English Word List," Paramaribo: Summer Institute of Linguistics, http://suriname-languages.sil.org/Saramaccan/English/SaramEngDictIndex.html.

Schumann, C. L. (1914), "Saramaccanisch Deutsches Wörter-Buch (1778)," in H. Schuchard (ed.), *Die Sprache der Saramakkaneger in Surinam*, 46–116,

Verhandelingen der Koninklijke Akademie van Wetenschappen te Amsterdam 14 (6), Amsterdam: Johannes Müller.

Warren, D. M. and J. K. Andrews (1977), *An Ethnoscientific Approach to Akan Arts and Aesthetics*, Philadelphia, PA: I.S.H.I.

6

Cosmopolitan and vernacular dynamics in modern Chinese fiction and Lao She's satirical novel *Cat Country*

Lena Rydholm

This chapter contributes to the discussion about theorizing the vernacular through a study of cosmopolitan–vernacular dynamics in modern Chinese fiction in the early twentieth century. With his studies of vernacularization in southern Asia, Sheldon Pollock showed that "[t]he very idea of vernacularization depends upon understanding something of the world against which it defines itself" (1998: 6). Following Pollock's example, I have applied an expanded timeframe to include cosmopolitan–vernacular dynamics in Chinese literary culture in pre-modern times before considering this dynamic in modern times, and in the analyses of modern literary works. Of course, the Western concepts of cosmopolitan and vernacular were not used to discuss literature in pre-modern China. However, applying these concepts to Chinese literature in both pre-modern and modern times generates results that may be relevant for theorizing the vernacular in world literary studies. I apply Pollock's definition of the terms: "*Cosmopolitan* and *vernacular* can be taken as modes of literary (and intellectual, and political) communication directed toward two different audiences, whom lay actors know full well to be different," written in "a language that travels far and one that travels little" (2000: 593).

The first and second sections of this chapter deal with cosmopolitanism and vernacularization in pre-modern Chinese literature. However, including all genres and literary works that may be relevant to discuss in this context during the past 3000 years in Chinese literary culture is well beyond the scope of this study. I provide examples from only a few genres, mainly prose fiction, that I find relevant for the discussion of a cosmopolitan–vernacular dynamic in pre-modern times, and how these relate to this dynamic in modern times. I also compare my conclusions with Pollock's in his studies of the Sanskrit cosmopolis and the vernacularization in reaction to it that took place in South Asia (1998; 2000). The third and fourth sections of this chapter, before my conclusion, deal with the vernacularization in China in the early twentieth century, and is based on analyses of two literary works. Section three deals with a kind of "cosmopolitan vernacular" of the new elite, based on the results of my study of Lu Xun's "A Madman's Diary" (1970 [1918]), which is included in volume 3 of this series (Rydholm 2022) and briefly summarized here. The fourth section contains the main focus of my study, an analysis of the vernacular in Lao She's *Cat Country* (1933). I will also show how Lao She's multiglossic vernacular differs from Lu Xun's, being much closer to oral literature, spoken language, and dialect. This chapter shows that we cannot leave oral literature out of the picture when theorizing the written vernacular in China, as opposed to the case in Pollock's study of vernaculars in South Asia (2000: 606), since it has played an important role in the vernacularization of Chinese literature in pre-modern as well as modern times.

Widening the timeframe: The development of a "cosmopolitan" *wenyan*

The vernacular movement in China in the early twentieth century was not a reaction against any of the foreign imperialist languages. It was a response to the Chinese classical literary language, *wenyan* 文言 (embellished words), the major vehicle for traditional culture and Confucianism. This literary language was the written language used in the imperial administration and in high literature, history, philosophy, poetry, and non-fictional prose in China, and it was a "cosmopolitan" language in East Asia for almost two millennia.

Wenyan had developed and gained its position to a large extent through its alliance with imperial rule. The First Emperor of the Qin dynasty (221–206 BCE), ordered the unification of the script system for use in the imperial administration to cope with dialectal diversity and to facilitate the ruling of the empire (Rydholm 2014; 2021). During the subsequent Han dynasty (206 BCE–220 CE), Confucianism became state ideology. The anonymous preface (allegedly by one of Confucius' disciples, but probably written during the Han dynasty) of the ancient poetry collection *The Book of Poetry Shijing* 诗经, became the doctrine for a "didactic view" of poetry as "moral instruction and social comment," that regarded poetry as being vital for the rule of the empire (see Liu

1962: 65–6). This view, which became a paradigm in mainstream literary theory, was summed up in neo-Confucian Zhou Dunyi's 周敦颐 (1017–1073) famous words: *Wen yi zai Dao* 文以载道 (Literature is the vehicle of the [Confucian] Way). To gain office in the imperial administration, men of means studied the Confucian Classics for the civil service examination, which also secured the position of *wenyan* as the standardized written language used for official, scholarly, and literary purposes, even while most of the population was illiterate (Rydholm 2014; 2021).

The standardized lexical and grammatical rules of *wenyan*, which developed during the Qin and Han dynasties, were based on the written language in prose works from the latter part of the spring and autumn period (770–476 BCE) up to the end of the Han dynasty (Norman 1988: 83). It was based on the written language of philosophical and historical works, such as *The Analects of Confucius, Mencius, Mr Zuo's Commentary*, and *Records of the Grand Historian* (Norman 1988: 83). According to Jerry Norman, the languages in these works were not uniform and "almost certainly based on the vernacular language of the period which it was produced in' (1988: 83). However, after the Han dynasty, if not earlier, *wenyan* diverged more and more from the contemporary spoken languages (Ge 2001: 10). This division of speech and writing was facilitated by the Chinese logographic script. Ping Chen points out that "the lack of direct association between sound and graphic forms in the Chinese writing system gave *wenyan*, as a written language encoded by such a writing system, a degree of accessibility across times and space" (1999: 68). Literary Chinese texts could be pronounced in local languages and dialects; *wenyan* became, to use Wiebke Denecke's and Longxi Zhang's term, the *scripta franca* of East Asia (Denecke and Zhang 2015: vii–viii).

For almost two millennia, *wenyan* was the written medium of communication between the elites of Japan, Vietnam, and Korea, who adopted the Chinese script and literary language for scholarship, law, administration, high literature, and other important communication (Denecke and Zhang 2015: VII). Literary Chinese became the main vehicle for what has been called cosmopolitan Confucianism, under the patronage of the Manchu emperors of the Qing dynasty (1644–1911/12 CE):

> Eighteenth-century Confucians ... saw themselves as citizens of a world-encompassing empire. This is because the only way their principles could be validated was for them to be universally valid, leaving little room for discourse

on localism. Mid-Qing Chinese Confucians were servants of a multilingual, multiconfessional and multiethnic empire.

(Guy 2016: 51)

The cosmopolitan political-literary formation in China shares certain similarities with what Pollock calls the Sanskrit cosmopolis that developed in South Asia during the first millennium (Pollock 1998; 2000). Pollock studied Sanskrit inscriptions commissioned by royal courts and how Sanskrit became "a vehicle of political expression" with a standardized grammar (1998: 14). Sanskrit inscriptional culture spread to Thailand, Myanmar, Malaysia, Indonesia, Cambodia, Vietnam, and Laos (Pollock 1998: 11).

Wenyan, as a vehicle for political will and with a standardized script and grammar, became a kind of "cosmopolitan" language in East Asia, so in that sense we may call it the *wenyan* cosmopolis, with reference to Pollock's Sanskrit cosmopolis. Pollock remarked on similarities in the literary cultures using Latin and Sanskrit: writers learned standardized rules of writing, emulated the literary canons and "masterworks of systematic thought," and "both Sanskrit and Latin were written to be readable across space and through time" (2000: 600). This description fits with *wenyan*, a highly standardized written language readable across time and space, the vehicle of a Confucian value system. In his comparison between *Latinitas* and the Sanskrit cosmopolis in the first millennium, Pollock states,

> Two vast, historically influential supraregional cultures and their associated conceptions of power—*imperium sine fine* (power without limit) and *diganta rajya* (power to the horizons)—came into existence at either end of Eurasia. They were discursively embodied … in a new literature that … was composed in a language that traveled everywhere.

(2000: 614–15)

The corresponding concept of power in the Chinese imperial context is *tianxia* 天下, which literally means "all under heaven," that is to say, all of the world under Chinese imperial rule by an emperor ruling by the mandate of Heaven. Pollock argued for the existence of a kind of "empire-model" with "imperial cultural politics" in pre-modern times, the corresponding equivalent of the national language and nation-building in modern times (1998: 13–14). The creation of a standardized written language that became a vehicle of cosmopolitan Confucianism, which spread and became a kind of "*wenyan* cosmopolis" in East Asia for two millennia, may be said to be linked to empire-building. However, this requires further study and consideration of the literary cultures and languages in East Asia affected by *wenyan* in pre-modern times, such as Japan, Korea, and Vietnam. Different Chinese dynasties cannot be treated as one singular imperial formation either. The first emperor of the Qin tried to erase Confucianism, and Confucianism itself was never "pure" and static but developed over time, assimilating traits from other philosophies and religions. The Yuan dynasty Mongol rulers put a temporary stop to civil service examinations and *wenyan*'s elevated position. There was no single, coherent imperial-cultural strategy promoted by the Chinese rulers of all dynasties that persisted for two millennia.

The *wenyan* cosmopolis and Confucianism had a profound influence in East Asia on Japan, Korea, and Vietnam. However, the Sanskrit cosmopolis and Buddhism also influenced Chinese literature in pre-modern times. Literary cultures and languages in Asia interacted through trade along the Silk Road, China's tributary system, wars, migrations, and missionaries. Buddhist missionary monks came to China in the first century CE (Schmidt-Glintzer and Mair 2001: 160), and the Buddhist canon was translated into Chinese. The prestigious form of Tang dynasty Recent-style verse, included in the civil service examination and greatly appreciated and imitated by elites in East Asia, owed much of its defining features, its sophisticated tonal prosody, to Sanskrit (Mair and Tsu-lin Mei 1991).

Within the Sanskrit cosmopolis there was, according to Pollock, a "division of linguistic labor": Sanskrit was used for "the public literary expression of political will"; vernaculars were limited to practical functions (1998: 11). In China, we also find "division of labor," or what Ferguson calls diglossia. Ferguson's description of "High language" fits with *wenyan*, in being a "highly codified ... superposed variety, the vehicle of a large and respected body of written literature ... which is learned largely by formal education and is used for most written and formal spoken purposes but is not used ... for ordinary conversation" (Ferguson 1964: 435; Norman 1988: 250).

The Low language in China was the written vernacular, *baihua*, used, for example, in prose fiction, in novels during the Ming and Qing dynasties, with roots in oral storytelling. However, neither *wenyan* nor *baihua* were pure or static but were according to Gang Zhou mutually influenced: "many texts in Classical Chinese display the clear influence of the contemporary vernacular: ... it is impossible to find a pure vernacular literary work. Vernacular texts are usually permeated with elements of classical Chinese" (2011: 18). Still, as Zhou points out, "every language choice made by a language user is a socially bounded act, reflecting his or her understanding of the rules as well as the social context" (2011: 10), and "men of letters were certainly aware of the distinction between classical Chinese and the vernacular, and they used these two language varieties for different purposes" (2011: 18). The official attitude among the cultural elite towards the vernacular was that of disdain: "*wenyan* was considered refined and elegant ... ideal for high-culture functions ... *baihua* was despised as coarse and vulgar, suitable only for low culture functions" (Chen 1999: 69). Up to the May Fourth Movement in 1919, according to Norman, *baihua* "was considered fit only to be a vehicle of popular entertainment, and totally unsuited for the expression of elevated and serious thought" (1988: 246). It was not a vehicle for *Wen yi zai Dao* (the Confucian Way), the criteria for high literature. The cultural elite still enjoyed reading and writing vernacular prose fiction, as I will discuss in the next section, but the status of *baihua* remained low until the 1920s.

A widened timeframe: The rise of traditional vernacular, *baihua*

Several early narrative genres, such as *zhiguai* 志怪 (supernatural stories) of the Six Dynasties (317–589 CE), were written in *wenyan* and modeled on historiography. *Soushen ji* 搜神记 (*In Search of Spirits*), a collection of supernatural stories, often regarded as the beginning of Chinese fiction (Rydholm 2014), was compiled by Han dynasty court historian Gan Bao 干宝 (d.336). However, fiction *xiaoshuo* 小说 (small talk), a form of entertainment and not the main vehicle for the Confucian Way, had a very low status. Ban Gu's 班固 (32–92 CE) famous statement on *xiaoshuo* is usually summed up as *jietan xiangyan* 街谈巷语 (street talk and gossip of the alleys). Hence editors would often claim that the collected supernatural stories were true (and thus history or biography) and based on oral or written material as Gan Bao did (see Rydholm 2014).

Supernatural stories merged with Buddhist tales on miracles and karma (Schmidt-Glintzer and Mair 2001: 170–1). In the Eastern Han dynasty, vernacular elements appeared in written texts, in translations of Buddhist writings (Chen 1999: 68). Many translators did not master *wenyan*; they included oral expressions in their writings, which were often used in public performances (Ge 2001: 18). Buddhist monks preaching in public and using semi-vernacular prosimetric narratives, *bianwen* 变文 (transformation texts), for relating events such as Buddhist miracles and Buddha's reincarnations through oral performances, influenced the development of vernacular fiction and drama in China (Schmidt-Glintzer and Mair 2001: 161–7). The alternating between prose and verse in *bianwen* is seen in several performative genres and later vernacular fiction (Ge 2001: 22), and these genres were also influenced by Buddhism.

By the late Tang dynasty (618–907 CE), a new kind of written, vernacular language had emerged called *baihua* 白话 ("unadorned [plain] speech"), with vocabulary and grammar close to contemporary spoken language (Chen 1999: 68). Chen calls this "traditional *baihua*," to distinguish it from "new-style *baihua*" of the early twentieth century. Traditional *baihua* was used in popular culture, scripts for stage performances, storytellers' tales, Buddhist teachings, and the like (Chen 1999: 69). Famous novels of the Ming and Qing dynasties were written in traditional *baihua*, of which several include karmic retribution and Buddhist imagery, such as *Journey to the West* (Schmidt-Glintzer and Mair 2001: 168). In spite of the low status of popular genres, novels in traditional *baihua* were incredibly popular and read by "emperors and school children alike" (Chen 1999: 69).

Liangyan Ge claims the development of the written vernacular to be the result of an "interaction" between oral and written culture, through public entertainment, popular drama, and storytelling since the Tang dynasty (2001: 20). As Ge points out, although vernacular prose was not "equivalent to written colloquialism … in its early stage, the written vernacular must always develop in close contact with living orality, typically appearing in either a notation of or a composition for an oral performance" (2001: 21). Ge claims that vernacular prose mainly developed from the Southern Song (1127–1279 CE) up to the Ming dynasty (1368–1644 CE) (2001: 32). By then, the written vernacular, traditional *baihua*, had become a "full-fledged literary language" and a genre convention in fiction, with famous novels such as *Shuihu zhuan* (*Water Margin*), *Sanguo yanyi* (*Romance of the Three Kingdoms*), *Xiyou ji* (*Journey to the West*), and *Jin Ping Mei* (*The Golden Lotus*) (Ge 2001: 2). This period, according to Ge, coincides with the "textualization" of the most crucial novel in this regard, *Shuihu zhuan* 水浒传 (*Water Margin*) (1540 CE), China's "earliest full-length fictional narrative in the true vernacular prose" (2001: 3). The heroes of Mount Liang in *Water Margin* appeared in story-cycles at least as early as the Southern Song dynasty and were re-used in performance arts and storytelling through the ages (Ge 2001: 6). In his book *Out of the Margins*, Ge shows *Water Margin* to be the long-term, cumulative result of interplay between orality and writing. He uses the term "textualization" for the "long process punctuated with successive written versions, both notational and compositional, each representing a certain point on the axis of transition from voice to print," and of writing not "in" but "toward" a mature, written vernacular prose (Ge 2001: 7).

In China, *wenyan* continued to dominate until it was replaced by the modern vernacular in the 1920s. However, Ge claims that "in narrative literature that revolutionary change had started a few centuries earlier" (2001: 2) and we may speak of a "vernacularization movement" in China since the Yuan dynasty (2001: 27). The status of *wenyan* learning suffered during the Mongol-ruled Yuan dynasty (1206–1368), when civil service examinations were stopped. Men of letters had to seek a livelihood writing fiction and plays in the quarters of oral performance and theater, so popular at the time (Zhou 2011: 20). In the subsequent Chinese-ruled Ming dynasty, civil service examinations were resumed and *wenyan* gained value. Still, educated men who failed the examination turned to popular entertainment and vernacular fiction-writing, which offered commercial possibilities as the printing industry developed, literacy increased, and a "middle-brow readership" emerged (Ge 2001: 8).

According to Ge, *Water Margin* was textualized first because men of letters identified with the fate of the "rebels" on Mount Liang and voiced their own grievance through them. Many of the rebels in the story were government officials or army officers, unjustly treated and forced to become outcasts, fighting for just causes or revenge, still deeply loyal to the emperor (Ge 2001: 167–78). *Water Margin* was a work in the tradition of *fafen zhushu* 发愤著书 (venting indignation in writing) (Ge 2001: 174). Socio-political circumstances and social protest played a part in the development of vernacular prose fiction. According to Ge, "the frustrated men of letters revolted against the craft literacy in the *wenyan* tradition" with a "defiant spirit of rebellion" (2001: 8). Ge further stresses the narratological difference between prose fiction in *wenyan* and traditional *baihua*. *Wenyan* tends to "level" dialects, individual voices, and speech among different social groups (Ge 2001: 184–6). *Water Margin*, on the contrary, according to Ge, "took over from the oral tradition the manner of dramatizing speaking voices, which became a convention in vernacular fiction" (2001: 197). Storytellers would strive to attune the character's speech to "portray a character's unique ideology in his or her own discourse. That is precisely what Chinese vernacular fiction inherited from its oral antecedents" (Ge 2001: 187). According to Ge, *Water Margin*'s life-like characters were created through the dramatization of their speech, through "linguistic mimesis," citing Gérard Genette's statement that "mimesis in words" actually is "mimesis of words" (1980: 164).

In southern Asia, according to Pollock, "starting around 1000, but in most places by 1500, writers turned to the use of local languages for literary expression in preference to the translocal language that had dominated literary expression for the previous thousand years" (1998: 6). Today when we talk about vernacularization in China, most scholars refer to the vernacular movement in the twentieth century and the new-style *baihua*. A broadened timeframe reveals that "traditional *baihua*" developed in China during the second millennium, just as the vernacular did in Europe and southern Asia, and culminated in the mature written vernacular we find in such works as the 1540 CE edition of *Water Margin*. However, at the time China was still an empire in East Asia. The vernacular movement was not initiated to achieve independence from a foreign cosmopolitan imperial order and establish local geo-political entities or nations. It developed in response to different socio-economic circumstances than those in Europe and southern Asia. It was, as Ge showed in his study (2001), partly a social protest: neglected "men of letters" created a literary space to vent frustrations, but they were still loyal to the emperor. The situation would change with the semi-colonization of China by Western imperialists starting in the mid-nineteenth century with the Opium Wars, which led to demands for political and cultural reforms and the development of new-style *baihua* in the early twentieth century. This was a vernacular movement that started with the late-Qing reformists, at a time when traditional vernacular fiction thrived due to the increasing readership of popular literature in the wake of growth of areas such as urban culture, the print industry, and the public media (see Wang 1997). The subsequent New Culture Movement's influential manifestos calling for vernacularization and the May Fourth writers' literary practice finally raised the status of the vernacular. This process, and my conclusions regarding cosmopolitan and vernacular dynamics in Lu Xun's "A Madman's Diary," from volume 3 of this series (Rydholm 2022), is briefly summarized in the next section.

The development of new-style *baihua* and Lu Xun's "A Madman's Diary"

After defeats in the Opium Wars and in the Sino-Japanese War (1894–1895 CE), and after the 1911 revolution, the Qing dynasty fell, along with the Manchu government criticized for being weak and unable to withstand foreign aggression. A "national salvation" discourse had developed among intellectuals, many whom had studied abroad (Rydholm 2022). They demanded reforms to build a strong, modern nation able to resist foreign imperialists and based on "Western learning" in areas such as science, technology, and democracy. Many Late-Qing reformists were inspired by the vernacular movement in Japan's Meiji period (1868–1912 CE). In Japan, the traditional written language had been largely divorced from speech, as was the case with *wenyan*, and the replacement by a written language based on the vernacular had resulted in increased literacy and facilitated political reforms and modernization (Chen 1999: 70). In 1898, Qiu Tingliang wrote that "there is no more effective tool than *wenyan* for keeping the whole population in ignorance, and there is no more effective tool than *baihua* for making it wise" (Chen 1999: 70). In 1902, Liang Qichao published a manifesto promoting fiction as the best means to influence and educate people, along with the use of *suyu* 俗语 (vulgar [vernacular] language).[1] The vernacular movement also entailed raising the status of prose fiction as a vehicle for political expression, not simply popular entertainment (Rydholm 2014). The journal *Xin qingian* 新青年 (*New Youth*), started in 1915, published the New Culture Movement's manifestos, such as the chief editor Chen Duxiu's attacks on the *wenyan* of the traditional scholarly elite and demands for a simple, written vernacular for the people (see Rydholm 2018b). The New Culture Movement viewed the abolition of Confucianism, traditional culture, and *wenyan* as a pre-requisite for modernization (Rydholm 2018b). Nation-building required a national language in the vernacular, a language for Western learning and political reforms (Rydholm 2022). Hu Shi's 胡適 (1891–1962) 1918 manifesto in *New Youth* forged a slogan that became popular during the May Fourth Movement of 1919: 國語的文學, 文學的國語 (A literature in our national language; A national language for literature). According to Hu, *huowenxue* 活文學 (a living literature) cannot be created when using *siwenzi* 死文字 (a dead written language), by which he refers to *wenyan* and

> If China wants to have a living literature, we must use the vernacular [*baihua*], we must use our national language, we must create a literature in our national language
>
> 中國若想有活文學, 必須用白話, 必須用國語, 必須做國語的文學
>
> (Hu 1970 [1918]: 347).

---

[1] Translations of quotations in Chinese into English in this chapter are my own unless otherwise stated. For a short summary of reformist discourses on language and literature in Late Qing and the New Culture Movement, see Rydholm (2018b).

The New Culture Movement's struggle against *wenyan* was also a battle between the worldviews and value systems (Rydholm 2018b; 2021). As Ping Chen points out, "*wenyan* was taken to be synonymous with traditional Chinese values," but by the time of the May Fourth Movement in 1919, "*baihua* was assumed to be the only appropriate linguistic vehicle for the whole set of new, mostly imported Western concepts subsumed under democracy and science" (1999: 79).

Wenyan took a first major blow when the civil service examination system was abolished in 1905, and after the May Fourth Movement, in the 1920s, it was replaced by the vernacular in official areas such as education and administration. However, establishing a national language was not so easy; there was no standard for the written vernacular at the time and no consensus as to what such a standard would look like among writers.[2] Several types of writing were in use. There was "traditional *wenyan*" of pre-modern texts and "modern *wenyan*," with some colloquial expressions and foreign loan words (Chen 1999: 76). There was also "traditional *baihua*" of the famous vernacular novels from the Ming and Qing dynasties, discussed above. But these novels were written in different times and regions, with differences in vocabulary, grammar, amounts of words in *wenyan*, and dialect (Chen 1999: 76). The fourth type, the May Fourth style *baihua* or "new-style *baihua*," was "a general name that referred to the various types of the new style that reformist writers were experimenting with at the time" (Chen 1999: 76). May Fourth writers and other reformists were often trained in *wenyan* but had studied abroad and engaged in translation, from Japanese, English, German, French, or Russian into written Chinese (Rydholm 2022). Their written vernacular often included foreign loan words and neologisms, phonetic transcriptions of foreign names and terminology, and Europeanized grammar and syntax, in addition to remnants of *wenyan* and their own dialect, resulting in "an awkward mixture of styles" (Chen 1999: 78). The May Fourth writers aimed to create a written vernacular close to the spoken language, but their 1920s new-style *baihua* was "still quite removed from the actual speech of any group of speakers" (Chen 1999: 77) and the product of a foreign educated elite. According to Shu-Mei Shih, a May Fourth writer was: "a *double translator*, translating Chinese vernacular into a more scientific and 'modern' language, while translating Western and Japanese languages into Chinese. His or her

---

[2] Several reformists advocated changing to an alphabetic writing system to increase literacy; see Norman 1988: 257–63.

heavily Europeanized and Japanized (translated) vernacular might in effect be as alien to the ordinary reader as *wenyan*" (2001: 71).

The May Fourth writers have been variously praised and criticized through the years. They have been criticized as Westernized elitists who destroyed traditional culture and, more recently, for having internalized orientalism (Rydholm 2022). They have also been criticized for having repressed Chinese modernities. (Wang 1997). However, according to Zhou, the May Fourth writers worked in "uncertainty" and their "*proper abode* was extremely *shaky* and *precarious*," for which Zhou coined the term "Shaky House" experience (2011: 77). May Fourth literature belongs, in Zhou's view, to "the specific kind of vernacular literature produced at certain historical junctures of linguistic upheaval, whose writing begins with a revolutionary language choice, and whose literary medium manifests dramatic language change and is replete with linguistic tension and precariousness" (2011: 97). This Shaky House situation also opened up for linguistic experimentation and creativity. Some of the most influential works in modern Chinese fiction were created at the time. This was the case for Lu Xun's 鲁迅 (1881–1936 CE) *Kuangren riji* 狂人日记 ("A Madman's Diary"). It was published in *New Youth* in 1918 and is regarded as the first instance of modern Chinese fiction in the vernacular. In his efforts to promote reforms and the written vernacular, Lu Xun turned fiction into an arena for the battle between languages and ideas (see Rydholm 2018b; 2021). The narrative structure in "A Madman's Diary" is constructed as a "diglossic battle" between the preface and diary (Rydholm 2022). The preface, by the fictional narrator and friend of the madman, is written in traditional *wenyan*. The diary is written by the madman in the new-style *baihua*, the vehicle of national-language and nation-building discourse of Hu Shi (Rydholm 2022). Through their allegiances to competing worldviews and ideologies, Chinese and Western, *wenyan* and *baihua* are the main contestants, and what Zhou calls "a deadly language war" broke out (2011: 85). As I have shown elsewhere, the binary opposition between the preface and the diary is undermined, ideologically and linguistically, by a third contestant, by what Lydia Liu calls Western "translated modernity" and "translingual practice" (1995), turning the story into a skillfully constructed, multiglossic hybrid that implicitly supports the Madman's call for change, for the modernization of culture and society (Rydholm 2022).

As Pollock has pointed out, culture and power are often linked, and "vernacular literary cultures were initiated by the conscious decisions of writers," and "using a new language for communicating literarily to a community of readers and listeners can consolidate if not create that very community, as both a socio-textual and a political formation" (2000: 592). Lu Xun chose to write in the vernacular, and he chose the genre of prose fiction, which Liang Qichao had already pronounced to be the best vehicle for influencing people and changing their minds (see Rydholm 2014; 2018b). Vernacular prose fiction turned from being a vehicle of popular entertainment into a medium for social criticism and political will that continued the tradition of ascribing a didactic purpose to literature, *Wen yi zai Dao* (literature as the vehicle for the Way) (Rydholm 2014). However, the Way no longer referred to the Confucian Way, but to the enlightenment discourses of the New Culture Movement, and vernacular prose fiction was elevated to the status of high literature (Rydholm 2014). The new-style vernacular did not appropriate the grammar, syntax, and rhetoric of *wenyan* to elevate its status, in the way the vernaculars had adopted those of Sanskrit in southern Asia (Pollock 1998). However, new-style *baihua* still relied heavily on the paradigm *Wen yi zai Dao* in literary tradition to reach its new and elevated status.

In China, the vernacular, as we have seen, had a historically low status. The vernacular movement Liangyan Ge described in his study (2001) did not aim to overthrow the empire or *wenyan*; writers sought their livelihood, an outlet for their creativity, and a place to vent their grief in vernacular fiction and drama. The semi-colonization of China by foreign imperialists in the nineteenth and early twentieth century, by contrast, sparked a "national salvation" discourse and demands for vernacularization. The vernacular movement in the twentieth century "was carried out by Chinese intellectuals as part of their modernity and nation-building enterprise, following the lead of foreign nations" (Zhou 2011: 5). However, in the sociolinguistic situation of diglossia in China, the support for *baihua* was not a reaction against English, Japanese, or any language of the imperialists; it was a reaction against the traditional *wenyan*. Late Qing reformists were inspired by the Japanese vernacular movement, while May Fourth reformists, such as Hu Shi, emulated the European Renaissance (Zhou 2011: 131). In addition, in *Translingual Practice* (1995), Lydia Liu shows how Western "translated modernity" was mediated via Japanese, a language with deep roots in Chinese script, and Western terms could, for example, first be translated into Japanese using *kanji*, Chinese characters, and then assimilated into modern Chinese. Benedict Anderson's model of vernacular movements and nationalism in *Imagined Communities* cannot account for the complexity of the vernacularization process in non-European countries (Zhou 2011), and presumes as well a rather passive reception of unmediated Western influence, affording too little agency to Chinese writers in this process (Liu 1995: 22). This was evident in my analysis of diglossia and multiglossia in Lu Xu's "A Madman's Diary (Rydholm 2022)" and it is also evident in my analysis of Lao She's multiglossic *Cat Country*.

The vernacular in Lao She's *Cat Country* and the ridicule of everything

Lao She 老舍, pen name for Shu Qingchun 舒庆春 (1899–1966 CE), is one of the most beloved writers of modern Chinese fiction. He grew up in poverty in the run-down neighborhoods of Beijing and often depicted the lives and hardships of the poor and working class, as seen in his most famous novel *Luotuo Xiangzi* 骆驼祥子 (*Camel Xiangzi*) about a rickshaw puller. Growing up, he spent much of his free time in the local teahouse, listening to storytellers. In his literary works, the written vernacular is interspersed with colloquial expressions and Beijing dialect to paint a vivid picture of the city of Beijing, its inhabitants, and the local customs. A strong influence of the storyteller's art is evidenced in his works, and he has been called "China's master storyteller." He received a traditional education in the Confucian classics, sponsored by a Buddhist relative, and became a teacher. He then studied English at the Christian Church in Beijing and moved to England, where he taught Chinese at the University of London's School of Oriental Studies for five years, during which he read novels by Charles Dickens, James Joyce, Jonathan Swift, and Joseph Conrad and also started to write his own. Returning to China in 1930, he worked as a teacher in Jinan, a city that had experienced a massacre in 1928 followed by Japanese occupation until 1929 (Vohra 1974: 60), and in 1931 Japan invaded Manchuria.

Lao She was deeply influenced by what he learnt about the 1928 Jinan Incident and he became an advocate for writers' resistance against Japanese imperialism. In the novel *Cat Country*, according to Ranbir Vohra, the foreign soldiers invading Cat country refer to the Japanese (1974: 63). *Cat Country* (*Maocheng ji* 猫城记; literally "Notes on Cat City"), first serialized in the journal *Les Contemporains Xiandai* (in vol. 1 [4–6] and vol. 2 [1–6] 1932-33) (Słupski 1966: 106), is a hybrid novel, with features of both Chinese and Western fiction. It has roots in storytelling and traditional vernacular novels in China. However, it is also one of China's earliest science fiction novels, inspired by H. G. Wells' *The First Men in the Moon* (Lao She 2013 [1935]: 187). The novel is a dystopian satire, according to Vohra, "a vitriolic satire of China, and gives an unrelieved and a totally pessimistic picture of a nation in the throes of a death struggle" (1974: 61). In the novel we also find the farcical element from Lao She's earlier novels and mimicry of grotesque and greedy characters, inspired by Dickens's but in animal form (Wang 1992: 136). The novel is also clearly inspired by Swift's *Gulliver's Travels*, particularly Gulliver's visit to the Yahoos (Wang 1992: 136). In *Cat Country*, a spacecraft crashes on the planet Mars. The surviving Chinese man encounters the Cat people, learns their language, and starts to study them, taking notes and commenting on their civilization in an orderly manner. Like Swift, Lao She also creates a fictional language, Felinese. Cat country has huge socio-economic and political problems and is on the verge of being invaded by foreigners. Lao She claimed it was "disappointment in the state of the nation, military and diplomatic failures," that made him write the novel (Lao She 2013 [1935]: 185). At the time, China was under threat from both Western and Japanese imperialism. In my view, Lao She, as well as Lu Xun (see my discussion about Lu Xun, in Rydholm 2022), were working within the "national salvation" paradigm, and in addition, heavily influenced by the Social Darwinist discourse of the time. Many intellectuals regarded Social Darwinism as the main justification used by foreign imperialists for invading China, thus reformists were pushing Chinese people to change their culture and society, and build a strong, "modern" nation. However, due to his portrayal of the Cat people's deficiencies, Lao She has been criticized for internalizing Orientalism. *Cat Country* ends with foreign invasion and extermination of the Cat people, and the traveler cries out:

> This was the punishment for the Cat people not strengthening themselves.
>
> 这是猫人不自强的惩罚
>
> (Lao She 2013 [1933]: 287)

Lao She was accused of encouraging pessimism with this novel at the time instead of offering solutions, a critique Lao She addressed in an essay in 1935:

> It is undeniable that the Cat people are terrible. But it is also undeniable that I exposed their evils out of my love for them. I am sorry I could not think of a solution for them, thus I am equally terrible!.
>
> 猫人的糟糕是无可否认的。我之揭露他们的坏处原是出于爱他们也是无可否认的。可惜我没给他们想出办法来。我也糟糕！
>
> (Lao She 2013 [1935]: 187)

The mockery of young Communists in the novel was politically sensitive. After 1949 it was criticized for "serious political mistakes," among other failings (Sheng 2010: 381–5). In a later preface to the novel, Lao She claimed it to be simply "a nightmare" he had "due to indigestion" and that "the Cat people had nothing to do with the Chinese" (Lao She 2013 [n.d.]: 141). In 1951, Lao She stopped further publication (Sheng 2010: 382).

Lao She was among the first to write full-length novels in the vernacular in the late 1920s. He is considered "a master of language" and a distinguished writer of fiction in the Beijing dialect, his maternal language (Cui 2015: 67). In a quantitative study, Cui Yan 催燕 distinguished eight linguistic styles that deviate from the standard vocabulary or syntax in the modern Chinese language developing at the time, and she finds the occurrences of these eight styles in ten of Lao She's novels written between 1925 and 1962 (Cui 2015). Cui's study suggests that Lao She for the most part adhered to standard modern Chinese, which is perhaps not surprising, considering he was a teacher of Chinese. However, Cui also shows that Lao She's literary language is a *hunhe yuyan* 混合语言 (hybrid language). Beijing dialect is frequently used in the ten novels according to the study (Cui 2015: 192–3). Few writers within the cultural elite at the time were willing to use dialectal words used in daily speech by housewives and people with no education (Cui 2015: 71). Lao She reported on some initial difficulties in finding written characters to represent colloquial and dialectal words (Lao She 1981 [1945]: 235), a problem not uncommon to authors of vernacular fiction in earlier periods (Ge 2001: 339).

The result in Cui's study shows that in *Cat Country*, formal, written language is the most common of the eight linguistic styles, followed by colloquial language, and Beijing dialect.³ *Cat Country* has the lowest proportion of Beijing dialect of all the ten novels in the study (Cui 2015: 196), perhaps not surprising for a novel set on Mars, though it is still used. Not having counted each word, as Cui did, my impression is that the Chinese traveler uses most of the words in Beijing dialect, hence he is likely from Beijing (as is the author). He often uses Beijing dialect when making bitter comments about the Cat people. However, in a monologue in which an angry Cat widow pours her heart out, she uses some dialectal words

---

³ *Cat Country* (ca. 95,000 characters), contains the following occurrences of the eight linguistic styles: formal written language (*wenyan* words that remained in modern Chinese in writing but not in speech) 1,686; colloquial language 1,350; Beijing dialect 551; *wenyan* 23; Southern dialect 15; rare or self-made words 112; Europeanized syntax 55; deviations from standard syntax 58 (Cui 2015: 194–6).

and expressions (Lao She 2013 [1933]: 209–14). This recalls language used by women in Beijing in Lao She's *Camel Xiangzi* (Rydholm 2018a) and, as stated above, housewives were expected to use dialect. My conclusion is that the Beijing dialect in *Cat Country* is not intended to add a "Beijing flavor." It is rather to add vividness to outbursts of emotion by the narrator and some characters, outbursts often of moral rage; thus Beijing dialect becomes the language for the ostensibly objective, normative evaluation of morals in *Cat Country*.

Cui found 112 "self-made" words in *Cat Country*, thus being the novel with the largest proportion of such words of the ten novels included in the study (Cui 2015: 196). However, Cui does not explain the reason for this and does not mention Cat speech. In my view *Maoyu* 猫语 (Felinese) is the most interesting language in this multiglossic novel. Words in the fictional language Felinese are "translated" into Chinese by the traveler in his notes, sometimes using semantic translation (of meaning), thus creating new words in Chinese, such as *miye* 迷叶 (magic leaves), the national food in Cat country, addictive leaves initially brought by foreigners (a metaphor for opium). Some words in Felinese, supposedly adopted from other languages on Mars, are translated by the traveler into Chinese characters using phonetic transcription, in the same way Cat people supposedly transliterated foreign terms into Felinese, as discussed below. Felinese turns out to be a caricature of the Chinese language, used by Lao She to mock both *wenyan* culture and the new-style *baihua*, and which is described by the traveler as "childish":

> Four or five hundred words changed back and forth could say everything. Naturally, many phenomena and principals could not be clearly explained, but the Cat people had a way of dealing with this: not talking about it … Just memorizing a few nouns is enough to have a conversation, most verbs are expressed through gestures.
>
> 四五百字来回颠倒便可以讲说一切。自然许多事与道理是不能就这么讲明白的，猫人有办法：不讲。……其实只记住些名词便够谈话的了，动词是多半可以用手势帮忙的。
>
> (Lao She 2013 [1933]: 162)

The traveler gives an example of a sentence in Felinese through the question he asks his friend Big Scorpion:

> "In that case, why do you still plant magic trees?" I used Cat speech—according to correct Felinese, the sentence goes like this: A twist of the neck (to signify "in that case"), pointing my finger (you), rolling my eyes twice (why) tree (verb) tree? There is no word for "still".

> "那么,你为什么还种树呢?"我用猫语问——按着真正猫语的形式,这句话应当是:脖子一扭(表示"那么"),用手一指(你),眼球转两转(为什么),种(动词)树?"还"字没法表示。

(Lao She 2013 [1933]: 163)

This description of how the question in Felinese is communicated gives a comic image of the person talking and gesturing. Lao She's dramatization of the character's speech shows inspiration from storytelling and performative genres. The traveler also gives a description of the Felinese script:

> They also have a script that looks like small towers or pagodas, very difficult to distinguish; most of the Cat people can only remember ten or so of these.
>
> 他们也有文字,一些小楼小塔似的东西,很不好认; 普通的猫人至多只能记得十来个。

(Lao She 2013 [1933]: 162)

Here, Lao She is ridiculing the Chinese logographic script, criticized by many reformists for being difficult to learn and contributing to low literacy at the time.

In *Cat Country*, the traveler meets with three groups of scholars and students in Cat country, distinguished in their speech through linguistic stratification (Lao She 2013 [1933]: 233–9 and 268–70). First, he meets the older generation of traditional scholars. The astronomer proudly announces he is able to study the stars with his own eyes without having to use "gadgets and mirrors" like the foreigners. He is also able to divine good and bad fortune by the stars, another deficiency in foreign astronomers. The historian studies ancient forms of torture and advises the government in such matters. The philologist claims philology holds the answers to all questions. However, their proud and dignified appearance is soon shattered when they start arguing over who is the foremost scholar. They curse at each other in the crudest street slang, calling each other "bastard" and other obscenities (Lao She 2013 [1933]: 236). The philologist threatens to "screw the head off the neck" of the historian, who owes him magic leaves. The historian, unimpressed by this threat, gives in only once the philologist threatens to delete his family name from his *Record of Ancient Family Names*. The historian is still only able to repay half his debt, so the philologist threatens to steal his wife. Then everyone becomes upset about the fact that scholars are only allowed one wife each; they need at least three. United in common interest, they stop arguing, and the philologist produces an argument to support their claim:

Just judging by the character itself, in ancient times when the character was created it included several women radicals [referring to a semantic part of the characters in Chinese logographic script], which indicates that one should have several wives.

就以字体说吧，古时造字多是女字旁的，可见老婆应该是多数的。

(Lao She 2013 [1933]: 237)

In this passage, Lao She mercilessly mocks some traditional Chinese scholars of the time, averse to science and technology, and seeking answers to contemporary problems in ancient history, philology, and cosmology. The wives-joke is based on the Chinese logographic script, as word games often feature prominently in performance arts. The traditional Cat scholars seem to be mainly concerned with status, money, and women. When they start cursing each other in the crudest street slang, their true characters are revealed: they completely lack the Confucian virtue and morality that traditional scholars in China should embody.

Next, the traveler in the novel meets the young scholars of Cat country. They utter strange sounds, presumably phonetic transcriptions of foreign words from languages on Mars, and the traveler complains:

I did not understand a word! … I only heard some sounds: Gulu-baji, didong-didong, huala-fusiji .. what kind of word game was this?

我是一字不懂！……我只听到一些声音：咕噜吧唧，地冬地冬，花拉夫司基……什么玩艺呢？

(Lao She 2013 [1933]: 239)

The traveler asks his other friend, Little Scorpion, what they said, and he replies:

"Huala-fusiji"? There is also everything-fusiji … There are so many! They just string together a couple of nouns in a foreign language and speak, no one understands them, and they don't understand these words themselves, but it sounds exciting. Those who can talk like this are considered to be modern scholars.

"花拉夫司基"？还有通通夫司基呢……多了！他们只把一些外国名词联到一处讲话，别人不懂，他们自己也不懂，只是听着热闹。会这么说话的便是新式学者。

(Lao She 2013 [1933]: 239)

Through these statements about the vocabulary of the young scholars of Cat country, Lao She is ridiculing young scholars and writers of the May Fourth era, educated abroad, and their new-style *baihua* (Vohra 1974: 66), which was interspersed by phonetic transcriptions of foreign names and in-vogue Western terms. As Ping Chen stated, some May Fourth writers used a "Europeanized style, producing texts that read like literal translations from a foreign language" (1999: 78). It is through Lao She's highly satirical linguistic stratification and dramatization of their speech that this group's ignorance and superficiality is revealed.

Finally, the traveler meets a group of young students, kneeling down in front of a big stone in worship of Mazu Daxian 马祖大仙 (Father Marx the Great) and debating his *shenyan* 神言 (sacred words). Many Cat people support a foreign, revolutionary political ideology called *Dajia-fusiji* 大家夫司基 (Everybodyovskyism).[4] This ideology was summarized by Little Scorpion for the traveler, earlier in the novel:

> Society is a big machine and everybody is a worker in that big machine, a happy and safely working little nail or gear wheel.
>
> 社会是一个大机器，人人是这个大机器的一个工作者，快乐的安全的工作着的小钉子或小齿轮。
>
> (Lao She 2013 [1933]: 247)

"*Dajia-fusiji*" is, according to Vohra, intended by the author to mock both Socialism and Communism (1974: 68). Kneeling by the holy stone in the novel, a student leader shouts to the group:

> Long live Father Marx-ism! Long live Everybodyovskyism! ... We will overthrow our fathers, overthrow our teachers ... We will overthrow the emperor and implement Everybodyovskyism ... We will capture the emperor, then we will kill our fathers and teachers, kill them all! Once we've killed them, we'll have all the magic leaves, all the women, and all the people will be our slaves! ... Father Marx the Great said: Puluo-pulou-pulapu is didong-didong of the yaya's upper class and lower class hua-lala! Let's go to the palace!
>
> "马祖主义万岁！大家夫司基万岁！" …… "我们要打倒家长，打倒教员…… 我们要打到皇上，实行大家夫司基！……捉到了皇上， 然后把家长教员 杀尽， 杀尽！ 杀尽他们，迷叶全是我们的，女子都是我们的，人民也都是我

---

[4] "*Dajia*" 大家 in Chinese means "everybody." "*Fusiji*" is an ending (also used by the young scholars) indicating that it is a phonetic transcription from a foreign language on Mars. This ending is identical in sound to the Chinese characters pronounced "*fusiji*" 夫斯基, often used in transcriptions of the Russian ending "вский" into Chinese (in English "-vsky," e.g. Dostoevsky). Vohra translates "*Dajia-fusiji*" as "Everybodyovskyism" (1974: 68).

们的，作我们的奴隶 ……马祖大仙说过：扑罗普落扑拉扑是地冬地冬的呀呀者的上层下层花拉拉！我们现在就到皇宫去！"

(Lao She 2013 [1933]: 269)

In this farcical scene, Lao She clearly mocks some young Communists at the time for what he saw as preaching Marxism without having a clue about it, treating it as a religion, aiming to use Marxism only to gain power and wealth for themselves. The Cat students, just as the young Cat scholars, shout slogans with foreign transliterated words they do not understand. Again, it is through linguistic stratification and dramatization of their speech that the students' ignorance and self-interest are revealed.

It is interesting to compare *Cat Country* with Lu Xun's "A Madman's Diary" with regard to the ideological conflicts that play out in these works, but even more so because the battles between ideologies in both works are carried out through specific language varieties in these authors' multiglossic, literary worlds.[5] Both made use of the linguistic and ideological tensions of the time. Choosing a language could be seen as a statement, with different language varieties "aligned" with certain worldviews and ideologies, and in opposition to each other. Lu Xun launched an ideological and linguistic battle between the traditional scholars' Confucian worldview and the May Fourth reformists' modernization project, through pitting the preface in *wenyan* against the diary written in *baihua* (Rydholm 2018b; 2021). Lu Xun's story favors the New Culture Movement and the new-style *baihua* promoted in *New Youth*. Lao She attacks *both* traditional Confucian scholars and the modern, Westernized May Fourth elite in addition to some young Communists, using the fictional Felinese to ridicule them all. The former group is critiqued for seeking answers to China's problems in the Classics; the latter two for adopting foreign concepts and ideologies without understanding them. Lao She was highly skeptical of the prospect of "Western learning" saving China (see Rydholm 2018a). In *Cat Country*, foreigners and foreign learning only brought misery to the Cat people of Cat country. *Cat Country* is linguistically more complex than Lu Xun's story, including at least eight linguistic styles. In addition, Lao She created the fictional Felinese language, a language for the ridicule of everything and everyone,

---

5   For all the criticism of tradition, several of Lao She's literary works, as well as Lu Xun's, still display an inclination towards some Confucian core values, such as the importance of moral education and of "benevolence" (or humanity) ren 仁 (Sheng 2017: 136; Davies 2013: 233).

which he used to launch into battle with both traditional *wenyan* culture and Westernized, new-style *baihua*.

In these examples from the novel, each of the three groups of scholars and students spoke in a certain linguistic style, reflecting their socio-economic status, age, and education as well as their worldview and morals. The traditional scholars used vulgar street slang, revealing their morals. The invented, phonetic transcriptions from foreign languages and nonsense words used by young scholars and students betray their ignorance and superficiality. It is not just *what* they say, but *how* they say it that reveals their true character and makes them appear ridiculous. In an essay on "Language and Style," Lao She stressed the importance of letting the characters speak in their own voice in order not to sound like the author himself:

> In the dialogues one must use the language of everyday life ... We must know our fictional characters very well, what they say must suit the occasion and how they say it must be in line with their personality.
>
> 对话必须用日常生活中的语言……我们应当与小说中的人物十分熟识，要说什么必与时机相合，怎样说必与人格相合。
>
> (Lao She 2013 [1936]: 231)

The dialogues should be vivid, include gestures and responses by the listeners, and "make people feel like they're truly listening to two people talking to each other" (Lao She 2013 [1936]: 231). For creating dramatic effects and speedy action, he also advocated the use of short sentences (one action per sentence), and alternating speech and action. He found just one novel to be successful in this regard, *Water Margin* (Lao She ([1936] 2013: 229–30). Lao She drew inspiration from the dramatization of characters' speech and actions in *Water Margin* and from performative genres, and later he wrote several plays.

In terms of the Western analytical tools used in this study, with regard to substance and form, Lu Xun's new-style *baihua* was the vehicle of cosmopolitan ideas and translated modernity, supporting Western learning. His writing has been labeled a "cosmopolitan vernacular" by Wang Hui and others (see Davies 2013: 250). Lu Xun's vernacular was distinct from *wenyan*, but it was still a vernacular from above, written by and for an educated elite. Although they both wrote in the vernacular, Lao She chose to base his on the talk of the streets and the local dialect, rooted in oral storytelling and traditional vernacular prose novels. It is a vernacular from below and does not fit the label "cosmopolitan vernacular," used for Lu Xun's work. Although Lao She was a foreign-educated and well-traveled writer, he still wrote from the margins. In so many of his novels, most evidently in *Camel Xiangzi*, he wrote from the perspective of the non-elite. In *Cat Country*, he wrote against Western learning in China, as opposed to Lu Xun's stance. Angela Taraborrelli uses the concept of "cultural cosmopolitanism from below," in which "authors who occupy a wide range of positions" write "*pars destruens* and a *pars construens*" (2015: 91). The former refers to writers who:

> make several criticisms of contemporary cosmopolitanism such as that being contaminated by abstract universalism, of expressing western values and ideals—including an idea of progress and unilateral and one-dimensional modernity—of ignoring relations of social and political power that this presupposes and the new forms of exclusion that it produces, as well, finally, as of being elitist.
>
> (Taraborrelli 2015: 91)

Lao She's "cosmopolitanism" is that from below, written much in the same sense as Taraborrelli's *par destruens*, against the Westernized cosmopolitanism in China at the time; we may perhaps regard it as a kind of "vernacular, cultural cosmopolitanism from below."

Cosmopolitan and vernacular dynamics in Chinese literature and theorizing the vernacular

In this study, I used the Western concepts of cosmopolitan and vernacular as analytical tools in the analysis of Chinese literature in order to contribute to the discussions of theorizing the vernacular in world literary studies. This study confirms the need to apply an expanded timeframe, as Pollock in his study of vernaculars in southern Asia, to gain a better understanding of vernacularization in China during the twentieth century. Vernacularization in China was not simply a case of passive reception of Western languages and modes of literary-political communication, which awards too little agency to the writers in this process, as pointed out by Liu (1995). Lao She's vernacular, as opposed to Lu Xun's, was grounded in the talk of the streets and his local dialect. Lao She developed a vernacular from below and a cosmopolitanism in opposition to Western languages and "Western learning" in China, a cosmopolitanism from below and from the margin, which we may call a kind of "vernacular, cultural cosmopolitanism from below," in contrast to Lu Xun's "cosmopolitan vernacular from above."

As the study shows, neither cosmopolitanisms nor vernaculars as modes of literary-intellectual or political communication can be discussed in the singular, and with regard to both substance and form, they are rarely, if ever, pure, and static. As Ge pointed out, "No work in the entire history of Chinese literature is in a 'pure' vernacular, a 'pure' type of *wenyan* is equally nonexistent. What we have instead is a whole spectrum of different mixtures of *wenyan* and *baihua* ingredients" (2001: 17). *Wenyan* and *baihua* interacted and developed over time, and, in addition, assimilated influence from other languages, literary cultures as well as worldviews and ideologies, such as the influence of Sanskrit in pre-modern times and Japanese and Western languages in modern times. Lydia Liu rightly stated, "to draw a clear line between the indigenous Chinese and the exogeneous Western in the late twentieth century is almost an epistemological impossibility" (1995: 29). This study shows how, in the multiglossic literary worlds of Lu Xun and Lao She, several language varieties, real and fictional, evoking Chinese or foreign authorities, are skillfully manipulated and launched into the linguistic-ideological battles of their time.

In theorizing the vernacular, I consider both the cosmopolitan and the vernacular, since they are mutually constitutive, as Western analytical tools. They are both modes of literary-political communication in translocal or local languages, languages that travel far or travel little, in Pollock's words. They are defined by both substance and form, content and language. From the point of substance and based on my limited study, I would say that it is possible that any language variety could become the vehicle of "cosmopolitan consciousness" or "nationalist discourses" if power claims it. From the point of language, what distinguishes the vernacular *baihua* from *wenyan* is a much closer relationship to the spoken language and dialect, as a conscious language choice made by the author. Lu Xun's ambition was to contribute to the creation of a language for the masses (Davies 2013), even though his new-style *baihua* was a vernacular from above, perhaps as "alien" to people as *wenyan*, as stated by Shih (2001: 71). Lao She's vernacular, by contrast, was a complex, hybrid language. Lao She chose to write in a vernacular from below, including the talk from the streets, the colloquial as well as the dialectal, and additionally incorporates features from oral storytelling and traditional vernacular prose fiction. This contributed to his successful portrayal of characters in the novels, and gained him the epitaph "The people's writer." Like Lu Xun, Lao She chose to write in the vernacular as opposed to in *wenyan*, and both contributed to the development of modern vernacular prose fiction in China. Both of their works display hybridity and multiglossia to various degrees, each one experimented with language and style in the contemporary vernacular and thrived in the Shaky House situation. This shows the huge capacity of the vernacular to easily assimilate different language varieties, including fictional ones, and translations from foreign languages as well as the colloquial and dialectal. *Wenyan* is less flexible in this regard.

The vernacular is never a finished product; it is always in a state of change and development, in *statu nascendi*, as Kullberg and Watson discuss in the Introduction to this volume. Chinese vernacular prose fiction in pre-modern times as well as in modern times, as seen in Lao She's novels, developed and thrived much through its close relationship to and interaction with spoken language, performative genres, and storytelling. Thus, these factors are also relevant to consider when theorizing the vernacular.

References

Chen, Ping (1999), *Modern Chinese. History and Sociolinguistics*, Cambridge: Cambridge University Press.

Cui Yan 催燕 (2015), *Lao She de wenxue yuyan fengge yu fazhan—Cong xiaoshuo cihui yunyong kan bada fengge tedian* 老舍的文学语言风格与发展—从小说词汇运用看八大风格特点 [Lao She's Literary Language Style and its Development—Distinguishing Eight Major Styles through his Use of Vocabulary in the Novels], Shanghai: Fudan daxue chubanshe.

Davies, G. (2013), *Lu Xun's Revolution: Writing in a Time of Violence*, Cambridge, MA: Harvard University Press.

Denecke, W. and Longxi Zhang (2015), "Series Editors' Foreword: *East Asian Comparative Literature and Culture*," in J. Fogel (ed.), *The Emergence of the Modern Sino-Japanese Lexicon*, vii–ix, Leiden and Boston: Brill.

Ge, Liangyan (2001), *Out of the Margins: The Rise of Chinese Vernacular Fiction*, Honolulu: University of Hawai'i Press.

Genette, G. (1980), *Narrative Discourse: An Essay in Method*, trans. J. Lewin, Ithaca: Cornell University Press.

Guy, R. K. (2016), "Quotidian Cosmopolitanism in Qing Provincial Government," in M. Hu and J. Elverskog (eds), *Cosmopolitanism in China, 1600–1950*, 51–87, Amherst, NY: Cambria Press.

Hu Shi 胡適 ([1918] 1970), "Jianshe de wenxue geming lun" 建設的文學革命論 [On the Construction of Literary Revolution], *Xin qingnian* 新青年 [*New Youth*], 4 (4), [Photocopy], Dongjing: Jigu shuyuan, vol. 4: 343–60.

Lao She 老舍 ([1933] 2013), *Maocheng ji* 猫城记 [*Cat Country*], in *Lao She quanji* 老舍全集 [The Collected Works of Lao She], vol. 2: 139–288, Beijing: Renmin wenxue chubanshe.

Lao She 老舍 ([1939] 2013), *Luotuo Xiangzi* 骆驼祥子 [*Camel Xiangzi*], in *Lao She quanji* 老舍全集 [The Collected Works of Lao She], vol. 3: 1–215, Beijing: Renmin wenxue chubanshe.

Lao She 老舍 ([1935] 2013), "Wo zenme xie *Maocheng ji*" 我怎么写猫城记 [How I Came to Write *Cat Country*], in *Lao She quanji* 老舍全集 [The Collected Works of Lao She], vol. 16: 184–7, Beijing: Renmin wenxue chubanshe.

Lao She 老舍 ([1936] 2013), "Yuyan yu fengge" 语言与风格 [Language and Style], in *Lao She quanji* 老舍全集 [The Collected Works of Lao She], vol. 16: 227–32, Beijing: Renmin wenxue chubanshe.

Lao She 老舍 ([1945] 1981), "How I Came to Write the Novel *Camel Xiangzi*," trans. Xiaojing Shi in *Camel Xiangzi* 231–6, Beijing: Foreign Languages Press.

Lao She 老舍 ([n.d.] 2013), "Zixu" 自序 [Preface to *Cat Country*], in *Lao She quanji* 老舍全集 [The Collected Works of Lao She], vol. 2: 141, Beijing: Renmin wenxue chubanshe.

Liu, J. J. Y. (1962), *The Art of Chinese Poetry*, Chicago, IL: The University of Chicago Press.

Liu, L. H. (1995), *Translingual Practice: Literature, National Culture, and Translated Modernity—China, 1900–1937*, Stanford, CA: Stanford University Press.

Lu Xun 鲁迅 ([1918] 1970), "Kuangren riji" 狂人日記 [A Madman's Diary], *Xin qingnian* 新青年 [*New Youth*], 4 (5), [Photocopy], Dongjing: *Jigu shuyuan*, vol. 4: 483–93.

Mair, V. H. and Tsu-lin M. (1991), "The Sanskrit Origins of Recent Style Prosody," *Harvard Journal of Asiatic Studies*, 51 (2): 375–470.

Norman, J. (1988), *Chinese*, Cambridge: Cambridge University Press.

Pollock, S. (1998), "The Cosmopolitan Vernacular," *Journal of Asian Studies*, 57 (1): 6–37.

Pollock, S. (2000), "Cosmopolitan and Vernacular in History," *Public Culture*, 12 (3): 591–625.

Rydholm, L. (2014), "Chinese Theories and Concepts of Fiction and the Issue of Transcultural Theories and Concepts of Fiction," in A. Cullhed and L. Rydholm (eds), *True Lies Worldwide: Fictionality in Global Contexts*, 3–29, Berlin and Boston: Walter de Gruyter.

Rydholm, L. (2018a), "Lao She's Fiction and *Camel Xiangzi*," in Ming Dong Gu (ed.), *Routledge Handbook of Modern Chinese Literature*, 59–71, London and New York: Routledge.

Rydholm, L. (2018b), "Reformist Discourses: Classical Literary Language Versus Modern Written Vernacular in Lu Xun's Short Story 'A Madman's Diary,'" in S. Helgesson, A. Mörte-Alling, Y. Lindqvist, and H. Wulff (eds), *World Literatures: Exploring the Cosmopolitan–Vernacular Exchange*, 70–88, Stockholm: Stockholm University Press.

Rydholm, L. (2022), "The Worlds of Multiglossia in Modern Chinese Fiction: Lu Xun's 'A Madman's Diary' and the 'Shaky House,'" in S. Helgesson, H. Bodin, and A. Mörte-Alling (eds), *Literature and the Making of the World: Cosmopolitan Texts, Vernacular Practices*, New York: Bloomsbury.

Schmidt-Glintzer, H. and V. H. Mair (2001), "Buddhist Literature," in V. H. Mair (ed.), *The Columbia History of Chinese Literature*, 160–72, New York: Columbia University Press.

Sheng, Anfeng (2010), "A Cultural Critique in the Age of Darkness: Reinterpreting Lao She's Allegorical Novel *Cat Country*," *Neohelicon*, 37: 373–90.

Sheng, Anfeng (2017), "Exploring the Cosmopolitan Elements in Lao She's Works," *Comparative Literature Studies*, 54 (1): 125–40.

Shih, Shu-mei (2001), *The Lure of the Modern: Writing Modernism in Semicolonial China, 1917–1937*, Berkeley, CA: University of California Press.

Słupski, Z. (1966), *The Evolution of a Modern Chinese Writer: An Analysis of Lao She's Fiction with Biographical and Bibliographical Appendices*, Prague: Publishing House of the Czechoslovak Academy of Science.

Taraborrelli, A. (2015), *Contemporary Cosmopolitanism*, trans. I. McGilvray, London, New Delhi, New York and Sydney: Bloomsbury.

Wang, D. D. (1992), *Fictional Realism in Twentieth-Century China: Mao Dun, Lao She, Shen Congwen*, New York: Columbia University Press.

Wang, D. D. (1997), *Fin-de-siècle Splendor: Repressed Modernities of Late Qing Fiction 1849–1911*, Stanford, CA: Stanford University Press.

Vohra, R. (1974), *Lao She and the Chinese Revolution*, Cambridge, MA: Harvard University Press.

Zhou, Gang (2011), *Placing the Modern Chinese Vernacular in Transnational Literature*, New York: Palgrave Macmillan.

7

Worldly themes and vernacular literature: Aino Kallas on gender, ethnicity, and class

Katarina Leppänen

This chapter explores the work of the Finnish-Estonian author Aino Kallas (1878–1956, née Krohn) in the early twentieth century, particularly her literary thematization of Estonian traditions and culture as part of a national awakening. The aim is to highlight instances where she uses vernacular tales as something more than expressions of the local. I argue that her work should be understood as taking part in the creation of a legitimate foundation for a sovereign people. Kallas did not understand the vernacular as isolated from the cosmopolitan; instead, the vernacular for her was a blend of local and foreign elements, even when it was dedicated to furthering national interests.[1] In this chapter the term *vernacular* refers not only to language but also traditions, rites, practices and material culture, and literature, which were central means of creating local and vernacular forms of belonging to, and affiliation with, a place. In accordance with this wider definition, the vernacular is seen as communicating a sense of commonly shared history and identity as well as familiarity with the local, which could be used in opposition to imperial and cosmopolitan masters.

Historically and geopolitically, the Gulf of Finland, with Finland to the north, Russia to the east and Estonia to the south, has been a region not only of wars but also of vibrant cultural exchanges and negotiations. My approach is methodologically inspired by Shu-Mei Shih's "relational comparison," which regards text and context as closely connected and interdependent (2013). Finland gained independence from imperial Russia in 1917, and Estonia became independent in 1918. Both countries had previously been part of the Swedish

---

[1] As the focus will be on Kallas's works, the political discussion of nation-making will not be further explored here. For political and literary developments and general historical comparisons between the two nations, see Koistinen 1999; Stråth and Sørensen 1997; Kaljundi 2015b; Branch 1999.

Empire, and Estonia had further historical experiences of German, Polish, and Danish rule. Aino Kallas's life and texts will be used as a prism for my investigation, as she is often seen as a hybrid figure that manages to represent both nations (Olesk 2011; Leppänen 2013, 2017). Throughout her life, she continued writing in Finnish while exploring mainly Estonian themes. Aino Kallas was involved in societal movements for national awakening in both countries and participated in the literary scenes on each side of the Gulf of Finland, as did many others in the relatively small intellectual circles. This was made possible because of the similarity between the Finnish and Estonian languages, and it was strengthened by similar conditions under Russian rule and censorship. I therefore write about Finland and Estonia, not as mutually distinctive in their processes of nation-building but, rather, as acknowledging the fundamental relationality of their literary and cultural histories.

In her writing, Kallas reworks historical narratives and emphasizes vernacular details, engaging implicitly and explicitly with political and nationalist themes in a great number of fictional and autobiographical texts, which have been explored by literary scholars (Laitinen 1973, 1995; Leskelä-Kärki 2006; Melkas 2006; Kurvet Käosaar and Rojola 2011a). Kallas's husband Oskar Kallas, her father, and her brother were all folklorists while her sisters were engaged in literary and educational endeavors, and she was deeply aware of the process of uncovering and inventing the vernacular as a foundation for new nations. Her brother Kaarle Krohn had assigned her a role as literary author, viewing this as an important task for the Fennoman (Finnish-minded) movement. Kallas's works reflect the complexities of nation-making and the vernacular while critically commenting on injustices based on class, gender, sexuality, and ethnicity—themes that will be further explored in this chapter. Her novels and short stories are filled with strangers, liminal figures, and outcasts, who, despite the insignificance of their power historically, were instrumental in founding a nation (Leskelä-Kärki and Melkas 2009). Without a legitimate people, there could be no legitimacy for an independent nation state, as Anthony Smith has argued (1999).

In this chapter, I will analyze two short stories, "Ingel" (1904) and "Häät" (1905), translated in the collection *The White Ship* as "Ingel" and "The Wedding" (1924), and the novel *Barbara von Tiesenhusen: Liivinmaalainen tarina* (1923), translated as *Barbara von Tiesenhusen: A Livonian Tale in Three Novels* (1975). I start by foregrounding some aspects of theory in world literature in order to discuss the implicit methodological globalism that is evident in parts of the scholarly field. The theoretical positioning is followed by a short historical background to give the reader a rudimentary geopolitical context to my readings. My subsequent analysis focuses on three of Kallas's texts, highlighting especially how power and conflicts are addressed in her narratives. The chapter ends with a discussion on how this case study of Kallas's work can contribute to a more complex and nuanced understanding of world literary relations from a historical and regional perspective.

Theoretical perspectives

Terms such as *cosmopolitanism* and *world literature* draw our immediate attention to phenomena that transcend place. A cosmopolitan person is one that belongs nowhere and everywhere at the same time; she is "at home in any place; free from local attachments or prejudices," a world citizen. Similarly, world literature can be identified as that which "gains in translation" and circulates in a global world system, due to form, style, or genre (Apter 2013; Damrosch 2003; Walkowitz 2015). Terms like the *vernacular*, *minority*, or *national literatures* have quite the opposite connotations, often referencing local and place-bound peoples, languages, and cultures, and therefore signalling limited circulation and interest (Pollock 2000: 596). If the vernacular and the cosmopolitan are understood as mutually exclusive, literary history is left with several unsolvable problems. As the Introduction to this volume shows, new perspectives on world literature can be gained by more closely analyzing the interplay between binary concepts such as vernacular/cosmopolitan and local/global, rather than viewing them as mutually exclusive opposites.

Instead of the biases of a methodological nationalism, duly recognized and widely discussed for the last decades in the humanities and especially in the social sciences, we now seem to face its opposite, a methodological globalism.[2] The concept of methodological globalism aims to capture the idea that the only phenomena that merit serious scholarly interest and can contribute to understanding our modern or postmodern world societies must circulate

---

[2] A number of sociological and political theories, from Marxist to conservative, have warned against methodological nationalism. See, e.g., Luhmann 2012; Wallerstein 2004; Wimmer and Glick Schiller 2002.

globally. Yet, studying small literatures and languages, it becomes evident that that which does not circulate globally can still be part of a global development, a study of the local can contribute to understanding the global. Only in a naive sense is the influence of the local, the vernacular, or even the national restricted to only one place—these are truly global phenomena. Further, much of world literature theory builds on the premise of a presumed dynamic between center and periphery, which emphasizes differences in cultural and economic power that are rooted in relations based on domination and colonialism (WReC 2015). Colonial relations are clearly present in the geographical area studied here, but the Russian Empire did not impose its culture and institutional standards to the same extent as the British and French Empires did. The connection of the center and periphery in both economic and cultural terms reflects a different dynamic (Annus 2014; Thompson 2000). For example, the Russian language never achieved the status of a learned, or even administrative, language in either Finland or Estonia, as it did not replace formerly dominant languages, such as Swedish and German, nor local languages or dialects. Russian was never cosmopolitan in the same sense as, for example, English, French, or Spanish was. Of course, I am not suggesting that the postcolonial and world literary studies are in any way unimportant or outdated; these fields have had a decisive impact on how we understand world literature. However, when viewed from the Northeastern European perspective, these disciplines offer too limited an understanding of the dynamics of world literatures, and as many have pointed out, they risk furthering Eurocentrism or Westernism at the cost of transnational dynamics between the vernacular and the cosmopolitan. Thus, this chapter investigates whether the vernacular can be theorized, in time, in space, and in literary history, in a manner that interacts with and contributes to questions in world literature theory, without relying on the premises of methodological globalism.

My exploration of vernacular/cosmopolitan dynamics draws on both Sheldon Pollock's and Alexander Beecroft's works. Especially appealing is Pollock's emphasis on active language choice as culturally and politically motivated actions and practices, rather than as mere ideals expressed in declarations or propositions. The importance of the distinction between action and declaration lies in the fact that actions bring about change in the world, and this perspective emphasizes that literary languages are purposefully constructed by actors who have cultural and political aims. For the purpose of this chapter, I thus understand the writing of literature as an activity and Kallas's writing as an intervention in the cultural and political arena. The vernacularization of literary and political discourses bring geocultural and political entitlements, and a corpus of literature was essential, as Pollock writes, in creating a vision of interdependence between political power and culture. Beecroft makes similar arguments regarding the vernacular by shifting focus to literature's role in creating self-reflective communities when he claims that a "language is a dialect with a literature" (2015: 6). Beecroft's and Pollock's literary examples differ greatly from those of the Baltic region in the beginning of the twentieth century, both in terms of scale as well as the historical and geographic specificities. However, both Pollock and Beecroft offer tools for reconfiguring literary history in other contexts (Pollock 2000: 592, 612).

According to Shu-mei Shih's definition, world literature is comprised of "texts from different parts of the world [that] are related to each other through their partaking and representation of world historical events" that make a transversal exchange possible (2016: 141). She is interested in horizontal and vertical interconnections that mutually enrich cultures, aspects that she points to as often lacking in world literature studies and transnational studies (Shih 2015: 432; Lionnet and Shih 2005: 2, 4). In many contexts references to historical roots (and sometimes even imaginary early nations) are important for emerging cultures to prove that they share and build on "a common faith within a relatively coherent territory," and therefore qualify as having a history of relevance to the nation (Hroch 1999: 98). Interestingly, the history of the people and their literatures in Finland and Estonia very much rely on deep connections to the same oral literatures and myths, as they base their respective literary cultures in the same *ur*-stories that were collected and literarized by Elias Lönnrot's in the national epic *Kalevala* (Koistinen 1999: 35).

When Jacques Rancière argues that literature "makes visible what was invisible, it makes audible as speaking beings those who were previously heard only as noisy animals" (2011: 4, 13), his characterization could just as easily apply to Lönnrot as to the French modernists he was interested in. The hierarchical manner of distinguishing between matters worthy of literary representation and matters unworthy of such acknowledgment, as theorized by Rancière, gives legitimate space for representing lives that have previously been unrepresented. When it comes to understanding how vernacular experiences and lives are communicated in literature, Rancière offers valuable inspiration.

Pollock's insistence on the importance of literarization as an activity, Rancière's emphasis on literature as an essential stage for voices that challenge exclusion, and Shih's focus on understanding literary history in close interplay with world history all guide my analysis of how Aino Kallas's work addresses class, gender, and ethnicity at a time when such issues were widely prevalent in the public discourse.

From the periphery

It is evident that many of the characteristics of vernacularization, often identified as recurring step-by-step over a long period in established nations, appear to be condensed in emerging nations. In a 1918 survey of the Young Estonia movement Aino Kallas describes this as an extraordinary cultural acceleration (see Hinrikus 2020). Pascale Casanova, for example, describes the development in Italy where Dante's fourteenth-century proclamation of the superiority of the vernacular language did not gain political form until the nineteenth-century unification of Italy. Casanova further writes about a process of "depoliticization" as literature freed itself from the political and national authorities it had helped to establish, and describes the process as happening "little by little" (2004: 37, 56).

The development of the Finnish and Estonian written languages commenced during the Reformation, which introduced vernacular liturgies and translations of Luther's *Little Catechism*, and the publication of the first *ABC* books in Finland in 1543 and in Estonia in 1575. People were encouraged to learn to read in order to further Protestant Christianity. However, as the Fenno-Ugrist Cornelius Hasselblatt argues, the Counter Reformation also produced vernacular versions of the *Catechismus Catholicorum* in 1585 (Hasselblatt 2006: 106, 109, 125). These first steps in the sixteenth century, though significant for later developments, were not politically charged, and literary culture in the vernacular started developing as late as the mid-nineteenth century. The timeframe from the publishing of the epic *Kalevala* (1835) and the first Finnish language novel, Aleksis Kivi's *Seven Brothers* in 1870, to the independent state in 1917 is exceptionally short compared to the political and cultural development of many other European countries. In this situation national narratives played an important role, as the nation relied on pre-national folk traditions and fantasies of a pre-modern community as its source of origins, with customs and songs understood as traces of a culture predating foreign dominations (Annus 2014). It was clear that a nation required its people and its own language, and that folklore in the form of songs and folktales should be gathered in order to consolidate a state (Nisbeth

1999: 80–1). Vernacular languages were engaged and activated by elites who communicate in old languages (in this case Swedish and German), but had "full awareness of the significance of their decision" in using vernaculars "as modes of literary (and intellectual, and political) communication," to borrow Pollock's description (2000: 592–3). States emerging in the beginning of the twentieth century had a set template to emulate: they aspired to achieve status as modern European states with strong national cultures and literatures, just like other modern states around them, although they could be seen as lacking in genuinely authentic cultural history of any greater quality (see, for example, Leerssen 2006; Berger and Lorenz 2011).

Johan Vilhelm Snellman (1806–1881), academic, politician, and Finnish-minded publicist, asserted that without its own language and literature, Finland could not constitute a nation-state—the Finnish people would die unless they had a national awakening. Thus the Swedish-speaking elite, to which Snellman belonged, needed to re-educate themselves and learn Finnish (Savolainen 2019: 354). The Finnish speakers, on the other hand, needed to raise their level of education to meet the needs of a new national culture. It was of utmost importance that local authors, whether they wrote in Finnish or Swedish, promoted the national cause. Aesthetic judgments were thereafter based on how well literature lived up to nationalist political aims, a theme that has been thoroughly explored in joint projects by Finnish and Estonian researchers in the anthology *Kaksi tietä nykyisyyteen: Tutkimuksia kirjallisuuden, kansallisuuden ja kansallisten liikkeiden suhteista suomessa ja virossa* (Two Roads to the Present Day: Studies in Literature, Citizenship and the National Movements in Finland and Estonia; Koistinen 1999). This echoes the cultural relativism of Johann Gottfried Herder and the Romantics who promoted the idea of strong, unique, equal cultures that were grounded in artistic representations in the vernaculars, without which the feeling of national identity was impoverished (Honko 1999: 29). After the independence in 1917 and the civil war in Finland, it was even more important for the nation to create an identity of its own, to resist foreign influence, and to criticize the elite for its Europeanness. However, literary themes and inspiration were sought in European and Russian literary trends, and the rationale behind the discussions about the appropriate aesthetic style or the proper depiction of national subjects in literature were in essence international rather than national. Thus, in the Baltic region, too, national literatures were more international than their local *language* may at first sight convey (Sevänen and Häyrynen 2018: 18). In states without glorious pasts or long-established national symbols to fall back on, myths and imaginations were very important for creating a common territorially bound identity. Cultural consolidation was the main long-term strategy for strengthening the state, and there was a strong commitment to the national project from the majority of authors and artists (Sevänen 1999; Alapuro 1999: 112, 115).

Vernacular themes and style

The stories by Aino Kallas analyzed here activate vernacular historical material that could be used for the national political struggles of her time. The first set of material was partly collected from people Kallas met during her stays in the Estonian archipelago, which described peasant life of the mid-nineteenth century.

The second set of texts consisted of old chronicles such as Balthasar Russow's *Chronica der Prouintz Lyfflandt* (1578).[3] The chronicles are the first more comprehensive literary sources of Baltic history, and Russow described them as tales of how Livonia was first founded and christened, its rulers and knights, and what surprising and fantastic things had happened there. Even during Russow's lifetime the importance of these vernacular stories was noted, and in a second edition he added more tales depicting peasant rituals and religious traditions, such as weddings, christenings, and funerals. He also added more details to support his major theme, which was the nobility's abuse of power. Stories dealing with historical injustices, the settlement of scores with ruthless masters, the defense of the weak and oppressed, and descriptions of the ordinary people's sorrows and joys instilled a belief that twentieth-century Estonians were a community.

As historian Ann Rigney (2001) has argued, readers attribute representative value to works of historical fiction because the genre combines facts with

---

[3] The chronicles that Kallas relies on are mapped in Laitinen 1995: 84–7. The stories she rewrites are shortly mentioned in several publications: Russow was translated by Eduard Pabst from Low German to modern German in 1845; Johannes Renner (1525–1583), *Livländische Historien* (first published in 1876); Christian Kelch (1657–1710), *Liefländische Historia* (1695). A research article by A (August Alexander?) von Dehn in *Sitzungsbericht der gelehrten estnishen Gesellschaft* (1885) is the one closest to Kallas's adaptation and it introduces material from new sources, including Swedish archives. Russow's chronicles were published in Estonian translations by Kaarel Leetberg in two volumes (1920–21). The edition used here is Balthasar Russow, *Liivinmaan kronikka 1584*, translated by Timo Reko (2004).

invented elements. In the anthology *Novels, Histories, Novel Nations: Historical Fiction and Cultural Memory in Finland and Estonia* the contributions show, through Finnish and Estonian case studies, how a highly selective retelling of historical events was used in order to create cultural memories that could resist the dominant cultures of Swedes and Baltic Germans (Kaljundi, Laanes, and Pikkanen 2015: 11). But who is entrusted with writing historical novels? The answer is not free from power dynamics and genre conventions, especially in periods of intense nationalism. Kukku Melkas has written about how Kallas was, in fact, breaking genre conventions (Melkas 2006: 54–70). Taking inspiration from historical tales was not a nostalgic or Romantic gesture; rather it has been a foundational strategy in female authors' attempts to place themselves on the stage of world history. As Rita Felski has argued, "the meaning of history lay less in its past than in its as yet unrealized future" (1995: 31, 147–9). In Estonia, reactivating Russow's chronicles seems to have functioned as a way to own history and to create a modern Estonia out of available sources, and Kallas adopted this culturally acceptable practice. Rewrites of the chronicles were published regularly in the Estonian newspapers, and several of the basic storylines were thus widely known, but Kallas's perspective often shifted from male protagonists and heroes to the destinies of female characters. The literary scholar Kai Laitinen notes that such close reliance on existing stories would probably have raised questions of plagiarism had she published primarily for the Finnish market (1973: 136). However, for Kallas it was not only a question of finding inspirational themes in the chronicles; she further strived for a stylistic resemblance to "a Russowian rhythm" and generously used Latin as well as biblical language to create an archaic tone (Laitinen 1973: 75, 116). In an essay on aesthetic principles from 1912 by the esteemed Estonian author and translator Friedebert Tuglas (1886–1971), the importance of vernaculars, proverbs, riddles, and colloquialisms in modern literature are emphasized. He was a leading member of Noor Eesti (Young Estonia) a national, political, and literary movement, and the vernacularization carried specific political overtones. The Young Estonians, who counted Kallas as their only female member, experimented with style and were not interested in reviving the Estonian peasant language but, rather, sought to create a new Estonian literature according to international models of modernist and decadent intellectual discourse (Hinrikus 2015). Yet, it was important that a language had a history that gave it exotic and lyrical depth, as opposed to, for example, the new "Americanized language" that lacked both depth and history (Tuglas cited in Laitinen 1973: 76). Archaic or vernacular style was deemed especially suitable for artistic prose, and Kallas termed her style *proosaballadi* (prose ballad).

However, Kallas did not intend for her archaic style to be merely a way of making historical references, and her attempts to contribute to Estonian culture were discussed and criticized. When her friend, fellow literary author, and yet another Young Estonian Gustav Suits reviewed the novel *Ants Raudjalg* (1907) he thought that she failed to "deal with issues taken from our [Estonian] lives" and would always remain "a 'stranger' in our lives" (see also Leskelä-Kärki and Melkas 2009: 37). Her aim, Kallas answered Suits, was to unravel humanity's eternal and universal questions by exploring them within a national context, and, therefore, the Estonian setting was only one possible scene for this exploration (Kallas 1954: 60–3). Thirty years later, in 1935, the play *Imant ja hänen äitinsä* (Imant and His Mother) was banned because the Estonian Republic (and its all-the-more-openly fascist regime) vigilantly censored cultural expressions that could be interpreted as opposed to an intensified form of nationalism. The accusation was that Kallas's focus on the anguish of a mother who had lost her son, rather than on the original story's male heroism, was a serious distortion that amounted to treason.

Kallas's Estonian novels

In her novels and short stories, Kallas often explores power relations that highlight gender and class injustices in hierarchical and multiethnic societies. The protagonist's situation as subordinate is based on gender, class, and ethnicity, and the ability to resist domination and injustice is attributed to inner strengths and moral insight grounded in local, vernacular traditions. The evils, one could say, originate from the foreign cosmopolitan German crusaders in the twelfth century that started the oppression. The 700 years of oppression is used as a shorthand for the many masters that dominated the area, but most importantly it establishes a parenthesis in history. There has been a time *before* oppression and there will again be a time of freedom if the movement for national awakening that Kallas participated in succeeded. Connecting contemporary political struggles to the historically oppressed peoples was an important way to sidestep foreign influence in nation-building. What remains as sources of prehistory are local peoples, their traditions, rituals and artefacts, as well as their tales and words. All these are connected to the idea of a vernacular culture, original and local, which can overturn the foreign powers. What Kallas and the likes of the previously mentioned Tuglas and Suits do is to bring the vernacular into the modern literature of Estonia (again remembering that she wrote in Finnish) by combining inspiration from archaic language, Latin, the Bible, and the *Kalevala* mythology, with local folk tales. They combined world literary sources with the vernacular to create the foundations of a national literature that addressed contemporary concerns. Keeping in mind Kallas's and her family's understanding of literary writing as a complement to other folkloristic scholarly activities, her mixing of local material, historical chronicles, and biblical themes appear as sound methodological choices. For example, among folklorists in this newly established scientific discipline, a debate about the national epic *Kalevala* was raging. Some, among them Kallas's brother Kaarle Krohn, read *Kalevala* as evidence of the deep Christian morals of the Finns, even before their conversion to Christianity. Others, among them the female theosophist Maria Ramstedt, wanted to diversify readings of *Kalevala* by interpreting it in terms of an ancient Finnish cosmology, comparable to the Bible, the Bhagavad-Gita, and the Qur'an. As such, it could fertilize the contemporary nationalist movement (Harmainen 2013).

The following three stories exemplify how Kallas transforms the vernacular into a mode of resistance. In these stories, the idea of the vernacular is used to identify moments when that which is in opposition to dominant forces surfaces, be it through words, acts, clothes, or traditions. The short story "Ingel" tells the tale of a young peasant wet nurse. The narrative starts by locating her origins in the county of Sõrve, before describing the girl as strongly built, ample bosomed, and as having a sweet face that displayed the formation of the "*saariston ruotsalainen sekaveren muovailu*" (archipelagic Swedish mixed-bloodedness) in her features. She radiates an almost vegetative peacefulness while nursing the child of her German lords, while the Estonian energy drains from her body and flows into the "*vierasrotuiseen lapseen*" (child of a foreign race).[4] Suddenly, Ingel shivers at the memory of her own child, whom she has abandoned. She sends for the boy and finds him malnourished and bruised. She then dresses the two children in each other's clothes, trading rags for delicate laces, and sees that each child could easily be taken for the other. Their differences lie purely in the external markers

---

[4] English translations are my own. References to the stories in Finnish are consequently to Aino Kallas, *Valitut teokset* 2008 [1970: 382]. English translations are available in Aino Kallas, *Three Novels* (1975) and Aino Kallas, *The White Ship: Estonian Tales* (1924).

of wealth. She comes to fully realize the injustice and absurdity of her feeding the little baron, a new generation of masters. The lady of the mansion returns unexpectedly, but Ingel accepts the cost of transgressing social class; "The lady will beat me bloody and drive me out on the road. Let her beat me and drive me out. I will take my child and leave" (389).[5] The story ends with the understanding that Ingel will be on her own with the child because the father had set out to sea to avoid being drafted to the army. The exact year of the story's events is unclear, but the story most likely takes place after the full abandonment of serfdom in the mid-1800s since Ingel is actually free to leave.

In the second story, "The Wedding," the exploration of women's predicament in the power relations between peasants and Baltic Germans continues. It is set in the early nineteenth century and tells the story of a traditional wedding with detailed descriptions of rituals and ceremonies. The bride sits in the middle of the room as guests toss coins into her lap for good fortune. Events take an unexpected turn as an elderly man approaches, looking like he is going to a funeral rather than a wedding. It turns out that the lord of the mansion requests for the bride to go to the mansion for the night. Her parents and all the guests are horrified but ready to submit to the master's unquestionable power. The bride turns to the groom and asks if he could take her back after such a night, and he replies that he could, only it would not be the same. A strong instinct of wrongdoing is awakened in the bride, and they decide that she will stab the lord and that they are willing to take the punishment of forced labor in Siberia.

The third story that turns the vernacular into resistance is the novel, or prose ballad as Kallas chose to call it, *Barbara von Tiesenhusen* (1923). It is based on fragments from the previously mentioned sixteenth-century sources as well as nineteenth-century research articles. The narrator is the vicar of Rannu, Matthæus Jeremias Friesner, telling the tale of the young maiden Barbara of German nobility, who falls in love with the clerk Franz Bonnius, a German of lower class. Relationships between nobles and plebians were forbidden by the Pact of Pärnu and enforced by the Livonian Order of the Teutonic Knights, dictating that relationships transgressing class should be punished with death by starvation. Barbara refuses to follow the law, and a court is assembled, consisting of her brothers and brothers-in-law, including the wretched Friesener, who is rooting for Barbara and Franz. Franz escapes, but Barbara is left to the mercy of her brothers, who drive her out on the wintry Lake Võrts, cut a hole in the

---

[5] *Rouva pieksee verille ja ajaa maantielle. Antaa piestä ja antaa aja. Minä otan lapseni ja menen.*

ice and drown her. Franz turns out to be a strong and vindictive man who gathers a guerrilla army of men with similar faiths to take revenge on the entire Tiesenhusen clan.

Resistance: Gender and class

The three stories I have summarized differ greatly, in regards to elements such as time (spanning the fifteenth to nineteenth centuries) and genre (two short stories and a novel), and also because of Kallas's stylistic development as an author over fifteen years. However, Barbara's destiny bears a resemblance to Ingel's and the bride's situations. Although she belongs to the ruling class, Barbara is totally subordinate to her male relatives and the laws of the Teutonic order. The story hints repeatedly at her unwillingness to behave according to her class and gender. When Barbara is still a child, the narrator warns that her strong-headedness would surely cause problems. She rejects lavish dresses in gold her loving stepmother ordered for her. She is repelled by the excessive and Satanic eating and drinking not only of the knights, but also the burghers and the non-German local farmers. She is appalled by the customary bloody bear and dog fights. Her actions suggest that she rebels against the expectations of classed and gendered behavior. Gender is also integral in "Ingel" because of the intimate service she provides as a wet nurse. She is giving her body, which in a sense is her blood, to a stranger. The abandonment of her own child is a key sacrifice she has to make because of poverty. It is the double burden for lower-class women to shoulder the responsibility as domestic labor for the upper classes, as well as carry the responsibility of their own children. In this story, Barbara abandons hers to strangers, which causes her grief. Of course, there are also gendered differences within the classes. For example, the male serfs do work in the fields and gardens, rather than having the master's child feeding off their own bodies, and Ingel's husband/fiancé can leave while she is left behind. "The Wedding" raises significant questions of the relationship between power and sexuality. Notably, the protagonist not only challenges the power of the master; her will to self-determination goes against the norms of all the villagers. Her resistance thus reaches beyond personal liberation, as it disrupts the attitudes of a whole society.

All three women reach breaking points and dare to rebel, by both speaking and acting according to their own convictions and against institutional powers in the form of masters, landlords, brothers, and the law. The literary plots force them into processes of political subjectivation, and their rebellions from below question the ethnic and social hierarchies from gendered perspectives. One decisive class difference is that Ingel's and the bride's realization overcomes them: they are struck by sudden clarity when they understand that they can defy the social order. In the short stories, emotions take physical forms such as dizziness, sudden urges, and rushes of instincts, and insights. They are propelled to refuse their lot as women, as peasants, but this refusal is not politically rationalized. A related story by Kallas (1913) dealing with the 1905 peasant and workers' uprising in the Russian Empire tells the tale of the "Death of old Org," a man who cannot understand the anger of the mob of farmhands. Org is shocked that they burn down the mansion instead of putting out the fire. He never grasps the politics of his time (the mob is a socialist uprising) while Ingel, Barbara, and the bride come to understand their own place in the social hierarchy and their power to actually challenge authority. Contrary to Ingel and the bride, Barbara's actions are rationally thought through and executed. She seeks the vicar to have him not only read her the Teutonic Law but to discuss his learned interpretation of it. She even challenges him by questioning how the law can be reconciled with the Christian ideology of love and equality. Reason, rather than instinct or sudden emotions, leads to her defiance of society's gendered and classed order.

Regardless of their different paths to resistance, these female protagonists all share a stoic attitude toward being punished for their transgressions. None of them question the rightfulness of retribution and they take full responsibility for their actions. In the context of nation-building, their actions and responses show the political strength that can be won from the vernacular, that is to say, in the form of the people, their way of life, and traditions. They are not pure or untainted by foreign elements or lifestyles, but they have an alternative source of reasoning founded on vernacular, or traditional, thinking. Barbara finds strength in joining the local people's lives, the bride finds strength in a genuine love and sexuality that is in direct defiance of the masters' predatory sexuality, and Ingel awakens to her own historical role as a facilitator for the masters.

Belonging: Ethnicity and the vernacular

In the search for origins, the vernacular is and has been a central element. Whether the vernacular appears as language, as customs, or as a historical attachment to territory, it has been seen as a guarantee of authenticity, which, in turn, is a prerequisite in the logic of nation-states. Yet, most vernacular cultures have always been mixed, including Nordic and Baltic ones.

The characters in Kallas's stories come from different places, but she always assures the reader that they nevertheless belong in their local setting. Ideas of race and blood play a central role in her thinking, but they are not used in a simplified racist manner (Kurvet-Köösaar 2011; Hinrikus 2015). On the one hand, race and class interact in "Ingel," as her peasant mixed-bloodedness is commented on in a positive manner. On the other hand, there are "foreign races" such as Ingel's German masters. However, their negative characteristics are primarily products of their abuse of power rather than their Germanness. As Barbara's fate shows, the abuse of power can just as well be directed at a woman from one's own people. When it comes to distinguishing between those in power and those without, Kallas uses the term *epä-saksalainen*, un-German, to refer to the local inhabitants in order to divide peoples and languages into two groups. Defining people by what they are not allows Kallas to be inclusive regarding those who belong to a society. Considering that the Estonian state did not exist prior to the twentieth century and that modern Estonia consists of several counties, it would indeed have been historically incorrect to call the different peoples Estonians. Thus, Kallas does not present any "pure" Estonians as those who unveil and reject German power; instead the dilemma of mastery is expressed by women of what we today would identify as an ethnic minority of mixed race, a member of the peasantry who is willing to murder, and a lady of nobility who refuses to follow the law of her class. However, some of Kallas's Baltic German contemporaries viewed her as a dangerous agitator (Laitinen 1973: 86).

The sense of the ethnic authenticity of the people is further emphasized by sartorial markers such as Ingel's traditional Sõrve dress for women or Barbara's rejection of the extravagant dresses that would be suitable for a woman of her class. There is joy and innovation in the vernacular traditions, and some are made up just for fun. This is the case with Ingel's local hat, a "silly, playful headdress made up at some reckless, joyous moment" (382).[6] Of course, such attire was mostly worn on festive occasions, and it is most unlikely that everyday chores were carried out in colorful tassels, but the description gives Kallas the chance to firmly ground Ingel in the local tradition by having her wearing local attributes, a kind of sartorial performance of ethnic authenticity. The passage about the hat

---

[6] *hullunkurinen, veikistelevä päähine, keksitty jonakin ylimielisenä, ilosta pulppuavana hetkenä.*

signals two things: first, there is such a thing as vernacular dress, and, second, the vernacular can be fictitious and does not necessarily need to originate in anything deeply authentic. Naming exact locations and the natural world more generally signals the vernacular (Melkas 2011: 54). Kallas often names lakes and places, which strengthens the air of authenticity without there necessarily being any connection to a place in the chronicle she is creating.

In the novel *Barbara von Tiesenhusen*, the Barbaras, Ingels, and brides of the world come together. Friesner, the benevolent narrator, describes how Barbara seeks the company of the pagan peasants all the more frequently and how she seems to prefer them to the company of the knights and ladies of the castle. She learns their language and takes part in their storytelling and singing; she even writes their stories down, which could be a hint of the first woman to collect and transcribe oral stories. For Kallas she was perhaps something of a chronicler, like Russow, her mission similar to Kallas's own, to collect folklore. Barbara's extensive contact with the peasants in the novel is an aspect introduced by Kallas and does not, to my knowledge, appear in any of the sixteenth-century chronicles or in any of the nineteenth- and twentieth-century interpretations that were available to her. Reading these selected stories together suggests that women can create room for both resistance and reconciliation between hierarchical ethnic, class, and gender differences, but it is not easy. The resistance and reconciliation are evident when Barbara's brothers are about to drown her and the peasant men, who were ordered by her brothers to make a hole in the ice, refuse to sink her into the water because she has been good to their wives and children. The peasant men thus side with the noble woman, who had accepted their lives as equal, maybe even superior, to those in her own class. As Finnish literary historian Kukku Melkas has pointed out, Kallas has mainly been read in the framework of romance and women's passion. Instead, Melkas suggests a more contextual reading that acknowledges Kallas's genre-transgressions and her historical tales as ways of producing knowledge and power as a strategy for resistance and change (Melkas 2006: 19, 22, 36, 53–4).

Uses of the vernaculars: Toward a conclusion

Kallas's literarization of vernacular oral tales along with her way of representing rituals and traditions brought vernacular aspects of everyday life into Estonian literature. This was one of the modernist aesthetic-political purposes of the literary scene in Estonia, as well as in Finland, at the time of national awakening (Raun 2009: 120–3). The peasants' and serfs' lives, experiences, and material objects were dealt with as noteworthy in their own right. Kallas's archaic language and style can be seen as a way to combine vernacular literary themes with a cosmopolitan style. Expanding on Beecroft's argument that national literature is "marked by a rapture with the cosmopolitan past" and entails a "marginalization" of other local languages, Kallas's style rather emphasizes their simultaneity (Beecroft 2015: 200, 198, respectively). The archaic/cosmopolitan is then not in opposition to the local/vernacular; on the contrary, it enhances the historicity of the local. The vernacular was, Kallas's style and method suggests, already cosmopolitan. Thus, Kallas connects to the vertical historical repository of the chronicles, to borrow Shih's terminology, by exploring class-determined, bodily, and sexual subjectivities historically (Kurvet-Käosaar and Rojola 2011b: 8–11). Exploring oral tales, traditions, and the folkloric emphasizes the historical continuity of the peoples (Beecroft 2015: 228).

An analysis of the works of Aino Kallas can give some indications as to how vernacularization was put to work in a nation-making project, and how ambivalence and difference could be dealt with in literature. While literature can function as a medium to convey normative values and imaginations, it can also be "a medium of thought and imagination in which questions of what is valuable for us and how to understand the value of literature are articulated from new perspectives and addressed in an open process of exploration" (Meretoja 2015: 3). My reading of Kallas suggests she is writing in the spirit of exploration of national histories rather than in a normative manner. Perhaps the most important contribution that the study of small national literatures can offer to the field of world literature studies is complexity. As I have shown here in relation to Kallas's work, when the concept of the vernacular is applied as an analytical tool in relation to small literatures, the dynamic between the vernacular and the cosmopolitan appears more clearly. By intertwining the two, she shows that the cosmopolitan is always present in very local and vernacular stories. Smaller literatures call for renegotiations in world literature theory by bringing a variety of examples that require recontextualizing theories, in terms of similarities, differences, and the purported universality of their claims. The dialogue between major and minor literatures illuminates world literary theories because, of course, the scholarly field has its own power relations that include some and exclude others. To understand world literature as only already translated literature or literature that has traveled is to be seduced by the lure of methodological globalism. World literature can instead be understood as something that engages with world history, and as part of the nation-making processes in local languages as in this example from the northeastern periphery of Europe. Engaging with vernacular themes was most certainly part of shaping both literature and history. Such engagement always takes on local forms suitable for historical, political, cultural, and social contexts.

References

Alapuro, R. (1999), "Social Classes and Nationalism: The North-East Baltic," in M. Branch (ed.), *National History and Identity: Approaches to the Writing of National History in the North-East Baltic Region Nineteenth and Twentieth Centuries*, 111–21, Helsinki: Finnish Literature Society.

Annus, E. (2014), "Layers of Colonial Rule in the Baltics: Nation-building, the Soviet Rule and the Affectivity of a Nation," in D. Goettsche and A. Dunker (eds), *(Post) Colonialism Across Europe*, 359–84, Bielefeld: Aisthesis Verlag.

Apter, E. (2013), *Against World Literature: On the Politics of Untranslatability*, London: Verso.

Beecroft, A. (2015), *An Ecology of World Literature: From Antiquity to the Present Day*, London: Verso.

Berger, S. and C. Lorenz, eds (2011), *The Contested Nation: Ethnicity, Class, Religion and Gender in National Histories*, London: Palgrave Macmillan.

Branch, M. ed. (1999), *National History and Identity: Approaches to the Writing of National History in the North-East Baltic Region Nineteenth and Twentieth Centuries*, Helsinki: Finnish Literary Society.

Casanova, P. (2004), *The World Republic of Letters*, Cambridge, MA: Harvard University Press.

Damrosch, D. (2003), *What Is World Literature?* Princeton, NJ: Princeton University Press.

Felski, R. (1995), *The Gender of Modernity*, Cambridge, MA: Harvard University Press.

Harmainen, A. (2013), "Kansallinen historiakuva: Uskonto ja sukupuoli Maria Ramstedtin *Kalevalan sisäinen perinrö*-teoksessa," in M. Jalava, T. Kinnunen, and I. Sulkunen (eds), *Kirjoitettu kansakunta: Sukupuoli, uskonto ja kansallinen historia 1900-luvun alkupuolen suomalaisessa tietokirjallisuudessa*, 71–108, Helsinki: Suomalaisen Kirjallisuuden Seura.

Hasselblatt, C. (2006), *Geschichte der estnischen Literatur: Von den Anfängen bis zur Gegenwart*, Berlin and New York: Walter de Gruyter.

Hinrikus, M. (2015), "J. Randvere's 'Ruth' (1909) as an Example of Literary Decadence and the Quintessence of Young Estonia's (1905–1915) Modern Ideology," *Interliteraria*, 20 (2): 199–214.

Hinrikus, M. (2020), "Theoretically European and/or Upstart? Decadence in an Estonian Key," in P. Lyytikäinen, R. Rossi, V. Parente-Čapkov, and M. Hinrikus (eds), *Nordic Literature of Decadence*, 173–91, New York and London: Routledge.

Honko, L. (1999), "Traditions in the Construction of Cultural Identity," in M. Branch (ed.), *National History and Identity: Approaches to the Writing of National History in the North-East Baltic Region Nineteenth and Twentieth Centuries*, 19–33, Helsinki: Finnish Literature Society.

Hroch, M. (1999), "Historical Belles-Lettres as a Vehicle of the Image of National History," in M. Branch (ed.), *National History and Identity: Approaches to the Writing of National History in the North-East Baltic Region Nineteenth and Twentieth Centuries*, 97–108, Helsinki: Finnish Literature Society.

Kaljundi, L., E. Laanes, and I. Pikkanen (2015a), "Preface," in L. Kaljundi, E. Laanes, and I. Pikkanen (eds), *Novels, Histories, Novel Nations: Historical Fiction and Cultural Memory in Finland and Estonia*, 8–25, Helsinki: Finnish Literature Society.

Kaljundi, L., E. Laanes, and I. Pikkanen (2015b), "Historical Fiction, Cultural Memory and Nation Building in Finland and Estonia," in L. Kaljundi, E. Laanes, and I. Pikkanen (eds), *Novels, Histories, Novel Nations: Historical Fiction and Cultural Memory in Finland and Estonia*, 26–76, Helsinki: Finnish Literature Society.

Kallas, A. (1913), *Lähtevien laivojen kaupunki*, Helsinki: Otava.

Kallas, A. (1918), *Nuori viro: Muotokuvia ja suuntaviivoja*, Helsinki: Otava.

Kallas, A. (1924), *The White Ship: Estonian Tales*, trans. Alex Matson, London: Cape.

Kallas, A. (1954), *Päiväkirja vuosilta 1907–1915*, Helsinki: Otava.

Kallas, A. (1975), *Three Novels*, trans. Alex Matson, Helsinki: Otava.

Kallas, A. (2008 [1970]), *Valitut teokset*, 2nd edn, Helsinki: Otava.

Koistinen, T., P. Kruuspere, E. Sevänen, and R. Turunen, eds (1999), *Kaksi tietä nykyisyyteen: Tutkimuksia kirjallisuuden, kansallisuuden ja kansallisten liikkeiden suhteista Suomessa ja Virossa*, Helsinki: Suomalaisen Kirjallisuuden Seura.

Kurvet-Käosaar, L. (2011), "'The vitality of primeval peasant blood': The Hereditary Potential of Estonians in the Work of Aino Kallas," in L. Kurvet-Käosaar and L. Rojola (eds), *Aino Kallas: Negotiations with Modernity*, 94–113, Helsinki: Suomen kirjallisuuden seura.

Kurvet-Käosaar, L. and L. Rojola (2011a), *Aino Kallas: Negotiations with Modernity*, Helsinki: Suomen Kirjallisuuden Seura.

Kurvet-Käosaar, L. and L. Rojola (2011b), "Introduction," in L. Kurvet-Käosaar and L. Rojola (eds), *Aino Kallas: Negotiations with Modernity*, 7–15, Helsinki: Finnish Literature Society.

Laitinen, K. (1973), *Aino Kallas 1897–1921: Tutkimus hänen tuotantonsa päälinjoista ja taustasta*, Helsinki: Otava.

Laitinen, K. (1995), *Aino Kallaksen mestarivuodet: Tutkimus hänen tuotantonsa päälinjoista ja taustasta 1922–1956*, Helsinki: Otava.

Leerssen, J. (2006), *National Thought in Europe: A Cultural History*, Amsterdam: Amsterdam University Press.
Leppänen, K. (2013), "Political Dimensions in Aino Kallas's Texts," *Journal of Baltic Studies*, 44 (4): 527–39.
Leppänen, K. (2017), "Crossing Borders and Redefining Oneself: The Treacherous Life of Aino Kallas," in M. Andrén, T. Lindkvist, I. Söhrman, and K. Vajta (eds), *Cultural Borders of Europe: Narratives, Concepts and Practices in the Present and the Past*, 128–42, New York: Berghahn Books.
Leskelä-Kärki, M. (2006), *Kirjoittaen maailmassa: Krohnin sisaret ja kirjallinen elämä*, Helsinki: Suomalaisen Kirjallisuuden Seura.
Leskelä-Kärki, M. and K. Melkas (2009), "Oudot naiset," in M. Leskelä-Kärki, K. Melkas, and R. Hapuli (eds), *Aino Kallas: Tulkintoja elämästä ja tuotannosta*, Helsinki: BTJ.
Lionnet, F. and S. Shi (2005), *Minor Transnationalism*, Durham, NC: Duke University Press.
Luhmann, N. (2012), *Theory of Society vol. 1*, trans. Rhodes Barrett, Stanford, CA: Stanford University Press.
Melkas, K. (2006), *Historia, halu ja tiedon käärme Aino Kallaksen tuotannossa*, Helsinki: Suomalaisen Kirjallisuuden Seura.
Melkas, K. (2011), "From Apocalypse to New Paradise: Early Ecological Thinking and Aino Kallas' Work in the 1920s," in L. Kurvet-Käosaar and L. Rojola (eds), *Aino Kallas: Negotiations with Modernity*, 54–65, Helsinki: Finnish Literature Society.
Meretoja, H., S. Isomaa, P. Lyytikäinen, and K. Malmio (2015), *Values of Literature*, Leiden: Rodopi.
Nisbet, H. B. (1999), "Herder: The Nation in History," in M. Branch (ed.), *National History and Identity: Approaches to the Writing of National History in the North-East Baltic Region Nineteenth and Twentieth Centuries*, 78–96, Helsinki: Finnish Literature Society.
Olesk, S. (2011), "Aino Kallas and the Boundaries of Finland, Estonia and the World," in L. Kurvet-Käosaar and L. Rojola (eds), *Aino Kallas: Negotiations with Modernity*, 165–83, Helsinki: Finnish Literature Society.
Pollock, S. (2000), "Cosmopolitan and Vernacular in History," *Public Culture*, 12 (3): 591–625.
Rancière, J. (2011), *Politics of Literature*, trans. Julie Rose, Cambridge: Polity.
Raun, T. (2009), "The Estonian Engagement with Modernity: The Role of Young-Estonia in the Diversification of Political and Social Thought," *Tuna Past Ajalookultuuri Ajakiri*: 114–26.
Rigney, A. (2001), *Imperfect Histories: The Elusive Past and the Legacy of Romantic Historicism*, Ithaca, NY: Cornell University Press.
Russow, Balthasar (2004), *Liivinmaan kronikka 1584*, trans. Timo Reko, Helsinki: Suomalaisen Kirjallisuuden Seura.

Savolainen, R. (2019), *Med bildningens kraft: J.V. Snellmans liv*, Helsinki: Svenska litteratursällskapet i Finland.

Sevänen, E. (1999), "Nationalismi ja kansakuntien muodostuminen luokiteltavasta, vertailevasta ja historiallisesta näkökulmasta," in T. Koistinen, P. Kruuspere, E. Sevänen, and R. Turunen (eds), *Kaksi tietä nykyisyyteen: Tutkimuksia kirjallisuuden, kansallisuuden ja kansallisten liikkeiden suhteista Suomessa ja Virossa*, 394–406, Helsinki: Suomalaisen Kirjallisuuden Seura.

Sevänen, E. and S. Häyrynen (2018), "Varieties of National Cultural Politics and Art Worlds in an Era of Increasing Marketization and Globalization," in V. Alexander, S. Hägg, S. Häyrynen, and E. Sevänen (eds), *Art and the Challenge of Markets Volume 1: National Cultural Politics and the Challenges of Marketization and Globalization*, 3–42, London: Palgrave Macmillan.

Shih, Shu-mei (2013), "Comparison as Relation," in S. Friedman and R. Felski (eds), *Comparison: Theories, Approaches, Uses*, 79–98, Baltimore: Johns Hopkins University Press.

Shih, Shu-mei (2015), "World Studies and Relational Comparison," *PMLA Publications of the Modern Language Association of America*, 130 (2): 430–8.

Shih, Shu-mei (2016), "Race and Relation: The Global Sixties in the South of the South," *Comparative Literature*, 68 (2): 141–54.

Smith, A. (1999), "National Identity," in M. Branch (ed.), *National History and Identity: Approaches to the Writing of National History in the North-East Baltic Region Nineteenth and Twentieth Centuries*, 111–21, Helsinki: Finnish Literature Society.

Stråth, B. and Ø. Sørensen (1997), *The Cultural Construction of Norden*, Oslo: Scandinavian University Press.

Thompson, E. (2000), *Imperial Knowledge: Russian Literature and Colonialism*, Westport, CT: Greenwood Press.

Walkowitz, R. (2015), *Born Translated: The Contemporary Novel in an Age of World Literature*, New York: Colombia University Press.

Wallerstein, I. (2004), *World-systems Analysis: An Introduction*, Durham, NC: Duke University Press.

Wimmer, A. and N. Glick Schiller (2002), "Methodological Nationalism and the Study of Migration," *European Journal of Sociology*, 43 (2): 217–40.

WReC, Warwick Research Collective (2015), *Combined and Uneven Development: Towards a New Theory of World-Literature*, Liverpool: Liverpool University Press.

8

Specters of the vernacular: Neoliberalism, world literature, and Marlon James's *A Brief History of Seven Killings*

David Watson

To encounter people who can speak with one another in exactly that transformation of standard English which is patois, which is creole—the hundreds of different creole and semi-creole languages which cover the face of the Caribbean in one place or another—that these have become as it were the languages in which important things can be said, in which important aspirations and hopes can be formulated, in which an important grasp of the histories that have made these places can be written down, in which artists are willing for the first time, the first generation, to practise and so on, that is what I call a cultural revolution.

—Stuart Hall, "Negotiating Caribbean Identities" (1995)

At the announcement of the 2015 Man Booker Prize, Michael Wood, the chair of the judging committee, remarked that Marlon James, who would go on to win the prize for *A Brief History of Seven Killings* (2014), and the other shortlisted novelists "created new 'Englishes' that remade and reshaped the language" (Airey 2015). We may surmise that one of the things Wood had in mind was the relentless orality of James's novel. *A Brief History of Seven Killings* begins with an apostrophizing injunction to the reader—"*Listen*" (James 2014: 1)—before launching into a polyphonic narrative which consists of a dozen or so narrators speaking in vernacular languages that include Standard Jamaican English and Jamaican Creole, as well as Rastafarian Iyaric or Dread Talk, and an idiomatic American English saturated with colloquialisms from the 1970s. "Dead people never stop talking" (James 2014: 1) the novel tells us furthermore, and these specters speak in their own vernacular, a digressive, errant English punctuated and interrupted by howls and hisses, wails and moans (James 2014: 1).

This chapter is about the use of vernaculars—vernacular languages but also cultural expressive forms as I will go on to explain—in James's *Brief History*, a novel unimaginable without what Stuart Hall calls the "cultural revolution" (1995: 13) that made available for literary purposes the vernacular languages of the Caribbean. How do we make sense of the turn toward the vernacular in this counterfactual account of the 1976 attempted assassination of Bob Marley (the unnamed "Singer" in the novel), and retrospective narrativization of the neoliberal turn in the Caribbean, which saw the rise of illicit economies and extractive regimes, as well as the imposition of structural adjustment programs on nation-states throughout the hemisphere, including Jamaica? I contend that *Brief History* takes part in a renewed encounter with the vernacular within the anglophone global novel, a development that asks of us to reflect upon how American institutions such as creative writing programs modulate this genre. I then go on to argue that the vernacular plays a double role within the novel's retrospective account of the ascendance of neoliberalism. It gives expression to a kind of postcolonial melancholia, serving as a reminder of the decolonial and collective potentialities foreclosed upon by economic and political destabilizations in the Caribbean and Latin America. At the same time, *Brief History* raises the prospect that vernacular languages, writing, and music do not exist outside of neoliberalism and its cultural logic, but become incorporated within what Jodi Melamed calls "neoliberal multiculturalism" (2011: 138) as signs of racialized and classed differences endowed with aesthetic rather than political value.

For many readers of *Brief History*, its novelistic successes and failures can be summarized exactly by a single word, excess. Nadia Ellis, for instance, locates within the novel a "poetics of excess" comparing poorly to the "easier styles of earlier masters of Caribbean literary Creole" (2015: n.p.) such as that of Sam Selvon. In her rebuttal of Ellis's critique, Sheri-Marie Harrison argues that James's excesses are "thrilling" because his novelistic excess both articulates a "broad critique of (late) global multicultural capitalism and … eschews much of the dignifying, empowering and ostensibly liberating national politics that we may have come to expect from a novel written by a Jamaican" (2015: n.p.). Leaving to one side the question of how we may adjudicate the matter of James's relationship to a Caribbean or, more narrowly, Jamaican literary tradition, the point I wish to make is a simple one: James's excesses extend not only to matters of sex and violence, their imbrication, or to the density and length of the novel, but also to the vernacular languages and expressive cultural forms he employs and references during the narrative. The multivocal narrative of *Brief History*, its indebtedness to the vernacular modernism of William Faulkner, whose world is populated by "listeners, talkers, and tellers" (Waid 2011: 763) rather than readers and writers, the novel's redeployment of minor Latin American and Jamaican literary genres—*narcoliteratura, testimonio*, the maximalist total novel, yardie fiction about the urban poor (Deckard 2018: 171)—its allusions to reggae music, dancehall, and early rap music are all suggestive of a novel steeped in the vernacular languages and cultures of Jamaica as well as those of a hemispheric geography that includes Latin America and the United States.

What we may call the novel's dense vernacularity prompts Sharae Deckard to suggest that "James is like a dancehall emcee, sampling a whole repertoire of tunes from the past, rewriting and recalibrating familiar riffs and beats into new music, playing with a multitude of narratorial voices and genres in order to weave the texture of a new epic" (Deckard 2018: 171). As Deckard indirectly suggests, there is a citational quality to James's encounter with vernacular languages and forms. As he deploys them in *Brief History*, he is performing a type of memory work, excavating past vernacular forms without allowing any one of these to become identified tout court with the novel in its entirety. Moreover, following Deckard, it becomes possible to understand *Brief History* as a remediation of the musical idiom of dancehall: the form of the novel is used to imitate the characteristics and effects of a different medium. James is transformed into an emcee summoning his readers with the opening imperative "*Listen*" (James 2014: 1), while the novel assumes the qualities of a sound system playing different vernacular sounds for the reader, an implied reader performatively transformed into a listener via the force of James's opening address. We may wonder furthermore whether the novel is not also offering a remediated version of the musical form of dub reggae. Lee "Scratch" Perry has spoken of dub as "the ghost in me coming out" (Toop 1995: 129). With its name echoing the Jamaican patois term for a ghost or malevolent spirit, "duppy," the genre consists usually of remixed recordings from which vocal tracks have been removed—a reminder of the silent "Singer" around which *Brief History* revolves—the drum and bass parts have been emphasized, and echoes, reverbs, delays, and other vocal and instrumental musical snippets have been added. Characterized by a collage aesthetic and shot through with absences, dub both "reinserted the mystery and spookiness into reggae" and played a role in a "diasporic project of reclaiming an African heritage" (Veal 2007: 212) that took form in Jamaica in the 1970s. In *Brief History* the diasporic vector has shifted and now connects

Jamaica and the United States, yet it too remixes the vernacular languages and expressive forms it has inherited to recover an earlier historical moment—that of the neoliberal turn in the Caribbean—a moment infused with silences and populated by ghosts. Riddled with spectral voices—"Maybe I'm a ghost talking to you now" (James 2014: 644) one character ponders—the novel sets up a series of correspondences between the vernacular voices it reanimates and the voices of the dead. It furthermore invites comparisons between imaginative identification and ghostly possession. Bam-Bam, a teenager involved in the assassination attempt, says of Weeper the gang enforcer that "I just wanted to go inside him like a duppy, and move when he move and buck when he buck and wind when he wind and feel myself pull out little by little by little and ram back in hard then soft, fast then slow" (James 2014: 80). Bam-Bam's queer, libidinal identification with Weeper, enacted via the mediatory figure of the duppy or ghost, resembles overtly the readerly contract or promise of realist narratives—verisimilitude, identification with characters—and presumably echoes the desires of an author to get into the heads of characters. Whether or not we connect the novelistic form of *Brief History* with dub music, the novel's indebtedness to vernacular languages and expressive forms is clear. And this indebtedness raises questions about novelistic form, and whether the medium of the novel can be understood, in this instance, as replicating vernacular genres belonging to other media.

It would be incorrect, however, to assume that the relationship between *Brief History* and vernacular languages and expressive forms renders it a largely regional work. While there has long been an intimate connection between regional writing and vernacular languages, *Brief History* is a self-consciously hemispheric novel, as I intimated earlier, that not only pivots toward the United States, in contrast with Caribbean fiction concerned with the legacies of older forms of imperialism and colonialism, but also encompasses and references American vernacular languages (the purportedly cool slang of the 1970s) as well as expressive forms—rap, country and western music, gangster films, westerns, B-movie pulp fictions. In this sense, James's novel forms part of a growing number of works, often from the global South, that deploy the vernacular within anglophone writing concerned with international or global themes and concerns (Nadiminti 2018). A partial list of authors producing global writing inflected by the vernacular would include Kiran Desai, Junot Díaz, Tania James, Karan Mahajan, and Chigozie Obioma, a finalist for the 2015 Man Booker prize that James would go on to win. The anglophone global novel is shaped increasingly it seems by voices speaking in the vernacular. And, in a sense, authors such as

James appear to be making good on the promise of what the African American novelist Gayl Jones described earlier on as the "multicultural, multilingual, multi-vernacular" (1994: 508) global novel.

For some readers, however, the question of the vernacular, partially one about dialect writing, is increasingly a redundant topic in the face of the development of the world or global novel in the twenty-first century. This genre, to which *Brief History* belongs, is characterized by amongst others the use of multistranded narratives, an expansive geographical reach, and an interest in the ethics and politics of cosmopolitanism (Irr 2011: 660–1). One of its features is also an increased sensitivity to the opportunities and problems posed by multilingualism (Irr 2011: 661), perhaps most overtly those complexities for which the term translation serves as a shorthand. In *Du Bois's Telegram* (2018), her magisterial account of U.S. literature and the state, Juliana Spahr argues that the contemporary interest in multilingual writing and globality, in contrast to the often-regional preoccupations of vernacular literatures, renders dialect writing something of a residual formation within contemporary anglophone literary culture (19). Yet turning to contemporary fiction—Spahr is primarily interested in poetry—it appears her dismissal of vernacular writing is premature. Even so, this dismissal of the significance of the vernacular for globally oriented writing resonates with other attempts to cordon off the vernacular from the global and to reinscribe it within fading local or regional formations. Sheldon Pollock, for instance, warns that the globalization of English is resulting in a homogenization of language and culture, a "reduction of diversity in the cultural ecosystem" (2000: 567), that will bring about a demise of the vernacular. Alexander Beecroft, in his account of world literature, sounds a similar note: "when the era of the coexistence of cosmopolitan and vernacular came to an end, it was a specifically European ecology that was to take its place," he argues, "that of the national literature" (2015: 193), which subsumes the vernacular before giving way itself to global writing. In both cases, we are asked to imagine if not the demise of the vernacular, then certainly its transformation into a residual form of expression.

It may be the case that to think of vernacular languages as artifacts of the past is to misread the situation. Luisa Martín Rojo points out that multilingualism, at least, is an increasingly prized commodity: multilingual "skills are commodified, and constitute a key element in the process of *personal mastery* by which individuals make themselves competitive" (2018: 551; emphasis in original). While this situation alters very little concerning the dominance of English and other international languages of trade, it does suggest the persistence of a multilingual field which may hold consequences for the development and persistence of vernacular languages. Moreover, it is not clear to me that literary and language histories approaching the vernacular as a residual formation have much to say about a novel such as *Brief History* or, indeed, that of any writer opting to turn to vernacular languages and expressive forms, a turn that from this perspective would at best be a form of archival work, or be driven by a nostalgia for outdated modes of expression. Such a perspective would, among others, foreclose on a reading of contemporary vernaculars that would discover in them the same political potential Gavin Jones associates with earlier forms of vernacular writing, particularly dialect writing coming from the United States during the late nineteenth and early twentieth centuries, which saw an increase in the popularity of writing in vernacular languages. He argues that "dialect could encode the possibility of resistance, not just by undermining the integrity of a dominant standard, but by recording the subversive voices in which alternate versions of reality were engendered" (1999: 11). In other words, the vernacular was understood during this period as a potentially political tool for African American and migrant writers, among others.

Recently S. Shankar, in his *Flesh and Fish Blood* (2012), has attempted to restore to the vernacular some of its political valences. He argues, for instance, that the vernacular should be understood as a "critical term that does the theoretical work of locating cultural specificity as well as challenging overpowering models of globality" (2012: 109). Mobilizing the vernacular as an oppositional term setting itself off here against the transnational, Shankar is not straightforwardly associating it with the autochthonous qualities of local cultures, but framing it as a site for the production of "alternate versions of reality," to use Jones's phrase, subsisting within and challenging normative accounts of globality and globalization.

Perhaps the most rigorous and productive account of the vernacular and its present-day situation to my mind, however, appears in the cultural historian Michael Denning's *Noise Uprising: The Audiopolitics of a World Musical Revolution* (2015). *Noise Uprising* attempts to account for a global recording boom that began with advances in recording technology in 1925 and brought to an end by the financial depression of the 1930s, even though Denning is interested in this boom's reverberations and afterlife as well. Focusing on a series of recording sessions in predominantly colonial spaces—Havana, Honolulu, Cairo, Jakarta, Rio de Janeiro as well as New Orleans—Denning charts the contribution to the musical world made by commercial recording companies equipped with electric recording equipment and shellac discs, which enabled the global dissemination of vernacular musical idioms such as rumba, samba, tango, jazz, calypso, flamenco, and hula. As he puts it, this was a "vernacular music revolution … analogous to the tectonic shift from Latin to the European vernacular languages in the fifteenth and sixteenth centuries" (2015: 7). For Denning this musical, vernacular revolution had consequences far beyond the world of music:

> For these vernacular phonograph musics not only captured the timbres of decolonization; the emergence of these musics—hula, rumba, beguine, tango, jazz, samba, marabi, kroncong, ṭarab, chaabi—was decolonization. It was not simply a cultural activity that contributed to the political struggle; it was somatic decolonization, the decolorization of the ear and the dancing body. Decolonization, I will suggest, was a musical as well as political event. Moreover, this decolonization of the ear preceded and made possible the subsequent decolonization of legislatures and literatures, schools and armies. The global soundscape was decolonized by the guerrilla insurgency of these new musics before the global statescape was reshaped.
>
> (2015: 136)

Arguing for the interrelated histories of cultural and political decolonization, Denning understands vernacular music as initiating and underwriting the histories of anti-colonial struggle that would shape the twentieth century. While the financial depression of the 1930s brought an official end to this vernacular music revolution, Denning identifies its afterlife, what he terms its "remastering" (2015: 220), within two formations useful for our understanding of the contemporary situation of the vernacular. In the first instance, transformed into folk music the vernacular soundscape is linked both with the nation-state and with the cultural politics of emancipatory social movements (2015: 220). Remastered as "world music," however, vernacular music idioms are given a very different articulation from that associated with folk music: "if the remastering of them as world music is a form of commercial enclosure," Denning writes, "it has also figured the cultural recognition and sonic enfranchisement of a planet of slums" (2015: 220).

Different media have different histories, and it would be a mistake to collapse Denning's history of vernacular musical idioms into a generalized account of the vernacular during the course of the twentieth century, or an account that affords us immediate insight into James's *Brief History*, no matter how overwhelmingly the novel insists on homologies between it and vernacular musical idioms such as reggae, dancehall, and dub. It is unclear, after all, whether twentieth- or twenty-first century literature can be associated with the same revolutionary, decolonial force as Denning attributes to musical idioms during this time period. His account is instructive, however, for its insistence on the historicity of the vernacular, how it is shaped and transmutated within decolonial and national contexts, how it serves to give representation to both emancipatory movements and economically marginal surplus populations, and how it also becomes a form of capital circulating across borders, largely as a result of the International Monetary Fund and the World Bank pressuring postcolonial states to adopt "neoliberal trade and property regimes" (Denning 2015: 229), including ones pertaining to intellectual property rights and copyright control. In a dialectical move on Denning's part, the vernacular shapes and is shaped by this history of decolonization, nation-building, and neoliberalization. Remarkably similar to Sarah Brouillette's short, materialist summary of the post-World War II history of world literature—"from liberalism through decolonizing left-liberalism to neoliberalism" (2019: 2)—Denning's account helps us see that the vernacular is neither a static nor an *a*historical category. Implicitly it also calls on us to think through and stay with questions concerning how the vernacular shifts and transforms, rather than relegating it prematurely to the dustbins of history.

Turning to the situation of world literature, it seems to me we could usefully supplement Denning's history by attending to the type of questions recently raised by Kalyan Nadiminti. Arguing for the emergence of a form of vernacular realism within the global novel, Nadiminti suggests that this contemporary encounter with the vernacular needs to be understood in relation to a very different set of developments than the ones Denning is primarily interested in. Noting that it is increasingly the case that writers from the global South are educated at or work in universities in the United Sates, particularly their creative writing programs, he suggests that international authors are influenced by the emphasis given to voice, particularly the voice of the ethnic minority writer, within such programs. Rather than encouraging writers to adopt "metropolitan speak," global South writers are exhorted to deploy the "vernacular within anglophone realism" (Nadiminti 2018: 384). In doing so, the creative writing program creates "the global professional writer" (394) producing fiction in the vernacular for a "globalized elite, albeit now of the non-Western kind" (389), which is to say a global readership that identifies with the "tenets of American globalism" (384). In this account, it is the American university that produces vernacular literature for the international publishing market and literary institutions such as literary prizes, where writing in the vernacular is increasingly associated with literary prestige. Like Denning, Nadiminti is concerned with how the vernacular articulates with the contemporary global economy. The result of this confluence is the imbrication of the vernacular with the transnational circulation of commodities and capital, and with the life worlds of the people instantiating and accompanying these global flows.

Taken together, Denning and Nadiminti provide a complex set of coordinates to make sense of the dense vernacularity of *Brief History*, in particular its historicization of reggae music. During the 1970s, reggae provided the soundtrack to a singular moment in Jamaican history: Michael Manley and his People's National Party came to power with a purportedly democratic-socialist agenda that promised to redistribute wealth and power, address inequalities, and to acknowledge the nation's diasporic African heritage. The One Love Peace Concert of April 22, 1978, which features in *Brief History* as well, was intended as an intervention into the violent political situation in Jamaica, with Manley's government increasingly destabilized by U.S. interventions spurred along by concerns over Manley's democratic-socialism and pivot to Cuba. James includes in *Brief History* an extract from the speech made at the concert by Peter Tosh, the increasingly politicized former member of the Wailers (the reggae band led by Bob Marley):

> Is word sound and power that break down the barriers of oppression and drive away transgression and rule equality. Well right now you have a system or a shitstem wha' go on in this country fi a long ages and 'imes. Four hundred years and the same bucky massa business and black inferiority and brown superiority and white superiority rule this little black country here fi a long 'imes. Well I and I come with Earthquake Lightning and Thunder to break down these barriers of oppression, drive away transgression and rule equality between humble black people.
> (2014: 319)

Tosh's tripartite invocation, "*word sound and power*," evokes the Rastafari idea of "the convergence of mental, sonic, and spiritual forces of transformation, truth, and resistance" (Mathes 2010: 35), putting it to use, in an apocalyptic key, as a decolonial promise to put an end to centuries of imperialism and inequality—the "*shitstem*" in Jamaican patois. In citing Tosh's speech, James is also alluding to this association between reggae music and decolonial politics, the same type of conjuncture that Denning dates back to the early twentieth century. Yet, *Brief History* is sensitive to the conditions that render this connection untenable. Reggae is also associated with an individualistic, entrepreneurial sensibility—"go to a studio and cut a tune and sing hit songs and ride the riddim out of Copenhagen City," one character declares before pessimistically noting that outside of the Copenhagen City ghetto (James's version of the Tivoli Gardens ghetto in Kingston, Jamaica) waits the discovery that, in fact, the whole "world is a ghetto" (2014: 8). This reference to the American band War's 1972 funk hit song underlines indirectly the material stakes associated with reggae music as a commodity form. A different complication arises when we encounter in the novel an American doctor who proclaims his appreciation of Jamaican patois: "It's so musical, it's like listening to Burning Spear and drinking coconut juice" (2014: 631). A vernacular language, a roots reggae band, and coconut water come together in this evocation of a kind of postcolonial exoticism, betraying an anxiety that the global circulation of the vernacular languages and music emboldens and feeds upon a touristic sensibility geared toward the exotic.

James offers a complex, discrepant itinerary to make sense of the musical idiom of reggae, connecting it with a promise of decolonization yet also linking it with the burgeoning of an individualistic, entrepreneurial sensibility—the same ethos informing the characters in the novel directly involved in the narcotics trade for whom "politics don't mean shit ... Money mean something" (2014: 644)—as well as with the transnational circulation of exoticized commodities. In a striking moment in the novel a "big box marked Audio Equipment/Peace Concert" (2014: 415) is revealed to be filled with M16 rifles smuggled in from the United States, with this dissonant, ironic image figuring for the reader the destructive possibilities associated in the novel with the circulation of goods across borders. Yet, it is not just reggae, narcotics, or military equipment that are entangled with the transnational flows of goods and people. James received an MFA from Wilkes University and is currently Writer in Residence at Macalester College in Minnesota. Of Jamaica he remarked that "If you are a writer in Jamaica, maybe even in the Caribbean, there comes a point when you just have to go" (Talentino 2019: n.p.), and go he did by taking up an academic position in the United States. Indeed, his most recent novel, the fantasy *Black Leopard, Red Wolf* (2019), was nominated for the National Book Award in Fiction, a literary prize reserved for U.S. citizens. Whatever the motivations for James's itinerary, which is not my concern here, he participates in the same trajectories and institutions that Nadiminti identifies as formative of the renewed interest in vernacular writing within the global novel. More generally, his career has unfolded against a backdrop within which U.S. government agencies and private foundations such as the Ford Foundation have emphasized the multicultural, global characteristics of U.S. literature. In this situation, which Spahr aptly describes as constituted by the use of "state-sponsored multiculturalism as a tool of cultural diplomacy" (2018: n.p.), the international writer, whose multicultural identity is testified to via his or her language usage as much as anything else, inadvertently plays the role of underwriting an imaginary within which U.S. literary culture is associated with diversity, tolerance, and cosmopolitan hospitality.

From decolonization to a state-sanctioned rhetoric of multicultural and transnational inclusiveness, the multiple, contradictory valences of the vernacular in this account of James's *Brief History* ask for closer scrutiny. The novel articulates two moments in the history of the vernacular, or, more precisely, the vernacular languages and expressive forms of Jamaica: the moment of cultural revolution, which Denning prompts us to identify as an instance of decolonial rupture, as well as a series of interrelated retrenchments within which the vernacular is exoticized, commodified, and put to work within a hemispheric or transnational narrative of national inclusiveness. What takes place between these moments, which we can identify loosely with the early days of the Manley government and the time during which James wrote his novel respectively, is neoliberalism's economic, political, and cultural ascendance, what one character in the novel describes as the coming of "progress, markets, freedom. That's the free market, son" (2014: 412).

There is good reason, as Aihwa Ong (2007) and Jamie Peck (2010) have respectively argued, to think of neoliberalism as a set of discrepant processes and practices assuming different shapes when deployed within divergent spaces, a hybrid technology entering into alliances with disparate political, economic, and social formations wherever it is deployed. There is no pure, essential neoliberalism. However, there is a shared historical account underwriting its divergent projects which include the liberalization of the market since the 1970s, the rise of finance capital, and attendant processes of deregulation, privatization, and free trade playing out globally. It also includes narratives concerning the fragmentation of communal bonds, the rise of the *homo economicus* and the citizen-consumer, the waning of the welfare or social state, and the recoding of political and ethical values in market terms. If there is a shared logic linking these projects, it is that the political economic transformations and state restructuring associated with neoliberalism go hand in hand with the market-mediated transformation of the population, the citizen-subject, and culture. Accordingly, neoliberalism names something like the transformation of "every human domain and endeavour ... according to a specific image of the economic" (Brown 2015: 10).

For my purposes here I am interested in two interrelated narratives pertaining to neoliberalism and its ascendence in the Caribbean. The first concerns James's portrayal of how the United States attempted to contain the democratic socialism of the Manley government through indirect military force and neoliberal economic policies. Summarizing this series of events, Brian Meeks writes that

> When, however, the dominant hegemon entered the fray, particularly after the regime's principled support for Cuban intervention to help save Angola from South African invasion, violence grew, and middle-class support was lost, as the country appeared increasingly to be ungovernable. This was worsened by the economic contractions which accompanied both the crisis of the global economy, following the 1973 Oil Crisis, and the obvious attempt, to quote Richard Nixon in reference to the Allende regime in Chile, to "make the economy scream". The subsequent IMF agreement to purportedly return fiscal balance to the economy exacerbated the political pressure on the government and initiated policies that, some forty years later, are being questioned from the bottom up by the officers of the very IMF.

(2019: 356)

Significantly, in an interview James has clarified that he is not concerned with older colonial relations between Jamaica and the British imperial metropole; instead, he is interested in "how we were colonized mentally and economically by the U.S." (McKenzie 2015: n.p.).

The novel's narrative refracts the history of interventions by the U.S. in Jamaica: the use of CIA operatives to undermine Manley's government, their distribution of arms to militias, and the destabilization of the state as well as the economy in the wake of neoliberal structural adjustments, which, among others, stood in the way of the nationalization of the bauxite mining industry, which remains central to the Jamaican economy. Situating the assassination attempt, presented in the novel as instigated by the CIA, within this context, the narrative presents Jamaica as part of a series that includes Patrice Lumumba's Republic of the Congo and Salvador Allende's Chile—both leaders are referenced in *Brief History* (2014: 7)—where interventions by former and current imperial powers destabilized revolutionary decolonial movements. The reasons for the containment and destabilization of Manley's government were two-fold yet interrelated:

Enough of this government and this Michael Manley wanting to suck cash from the bauxite companies like they don't already do enough to help this country. Shit, Alcoa transformed this fucking backwater island, sure they didn't build the railway but they certainly put it to profitable use. And other things: schools, modern buildings, running water, toilets, it was a slap in the face really, demanding a levy on top of all we do for this country. And that slap in the face was the first shot heard around the world for Jamaica's entry into communism, mark my words. Nationalization is always the first step, how these fucking people voted the PNP back into office is a fucking mystery to me, babykins.

(2014: 282)

Anti-communist ideology and business interests coalesced to prompt the U.S. intervention in Jamaica, which resulted in the privatization of businesses, the propping up of the extractive mining economy, and the imposition of a debt regime on the nation which has resulted in three decades of mounting international debt and low growth in the country's GDP. In short, *Brief History* tracks the collapse of Jamaican history into what David Scott has described as the order of "ruined time," that is to say the aftermath of "the catastrophic collapse of revolutionary futures past and the re-hegemonization of the world by a cynical imperial and neoliberal agenda" (2014: 12, 28).

The second narrative regarding neoliberalism I am interested in is a perhaps less well known and commented upon one. As Patricia Stuelke has noted, it is a strange coincidence that it was during the early 1980s, when the Caribbean was becoming fully inducted into a neoliberal regime, that there was a growing sense of the Caribbean and the United States as relationally bound together by shared histories and cultures. Focusing on black feminists identifying the Caribbean as a "locus of a shared utopic past" (2014: 125) for African Americans, Stuelke argues that this retrospective focus both elides contemporaneous political and revolutionary concerns and, ultimately, resonates with claims made by then U.S. President Ronald Reagan, who proclaimed that "like America itself, the Caribbean Basin is an extraordinary mosaic of Hispanics, Africans, Asians, and Europeans as well as native Americans" (Stuelke 2014: 127). Stuelke draws our attention to what we may think of as a type of cultural repair work, with cultural archives—in this instance that of Zora Neale Hurston—and expressive forms being called upon to resolve political and economic tensions by substituting for a fraught and heteroclite political terrain a narrative of relationality and consanguinity. As a result, an account of interconnectedness and inclusiveness takes the place of a reckoning with fraught, antagonistic histories, an account that is tilted, moreover, in favour of the United States because of its economic and political predominance. Stuelke's account serves perhaps as a useful heuristic for making sense of the burgeoning interest in the Caribbean in American academia during the last few decades; more pertinently it sheds light on James's account of the funeral and legacy of the Singer.

Narrated by the ghost, or rather duppy, of the murdered politician Sir Arthur George Jennings, the chapter of *Brief History* based on the funeral of the "Singer," the unnamed Bob Marley, takes as its key concern the questions "How do you bury a man? Put him in the ground or stomp out his fire?" (2014: 599). With Jennings situating the "Singer's" funeral within a hemispheric context in which the neoliberal counter-revolution has proved to be successful and the trade in narcotics is booming and linking, "Colombia, Jamaica, Bahamas, Miami" (2014: 600), the chapter is concerned with tracking the containment and waning of a decolonial vernacular culture and its transformation into something else. Awarded posthumously the Commonwealth Order of Merit for distinguished military, scientific or cultural work, the "Singer" "joins the order of British Squires and Knights ... A fire that lights up Zimbabwe, Angola, Mozambique, and South Africa doused out by two letters, O and M" (2014: 600). The subsequent reference by Jennings to Marley's "Buffalo Soldier"—a song about a black U.S. cavalry regiment involved in the American Frontier Wars waged against indigenous people to secure the nineteenth-century settler colonial project—hints further at the implication of the "Singer" within the discursive project of an imperial power. In the song, after all, Marley overtly identifies with the figure of the Black American soldier, who is awarded the "Medal of Honor for killing a people and an idea" (2014: 600). Yet, the music of the "Singer" lives on. Circulating globally it inspires three girls in Kashmir to "sling on bass, guitar, and drums," and the music is "a balm to spread over broken countries" (2014: 601). Jennings tells us that

> in another city, another valley, another ghetto, another slum, another favela, another township, another intifada, another war, another birth, somebody is singing Redemption Song, as if the Singer wrote it for no other reason but for this sufferah to sing, shout, whisper, weep, bawl, and scream right here, right now.
>
> (2014: 601)

In this account of the afterlife of Marley's work, James approximates what Denning has described as the "sonic enfranchisement of a planet of slums" via the global circulation of vernacular musical idioms. The tone is elegiac, melancholic, yet hopeful too, looking forward to the music of the "Singer" being used to articulate and represent the emotions of disenfranchised and surplus populations across the globe. But Jennings's narration begins with an invocation of the "fire" of the "black revolutionary" (2014: 599) as a way of figuring the performative force of Marley and his music. Subtly the chapter intimates that a shift has taken place in the way Marley and his music are to be understood. An understanding of the vernacular idiom of reggae as a decolonial, revolutionary sound gives way to a depiction of it as a curative resource, a "balm" providing momentary relief for the sufferer (Marley's version of "Redemption Song" runs for three minutes and forty-seven seconds). The audience for the music is no longer a potentially revolutionary people, but the victims of dispossession and disenfranchisement. In other words, in this account vernacular culture is stripped of its decolonial potential, and reconfigured as a transnational resource for surplus populations, providing comfort. Whatever we may say about this association of affective work with vernacular expressive forms, what is clear is that the narrative here follows the same trajectory as the neoliberal one proposed by Stuelke, with anti-racist and anti-imperial expressive forms becoming incorporated within a different discursive project that also obscures from view the complex political histories that first shaped these vernacular articulations.

When Jennings's account of the Singer's funeral and legacy concludes with the image of "Redemption Song" being sung "right here, right now" the reader is necessarily reminded that this here and now also include the novel that we are reading. *Brief History*, as I have argued, provided the reader with resignifications, perhaps cover versions, of vernacular languages and expressive forms, including that of the unnamed Bob Marley. The complex history of vernacular idioms—the association of the vernacular with the decolonial, its neoliberal transformation into a transnational commodity signifying inclusiveness and the type of affective work I have discussed—also constitutes the frame within which we read and make sense of *Brief History*. In part, this is to say that the novel is intensely self-reflexive, knowing full well its historicization of the situation of vernacular languages and cultural forms is partially an account of its own situation within the global literary field. What James is doing, after all, is putting into circulation via the global novel vernacular languages and expressive forms, relocating them within a hemispheric framework where they articulate with other vernaculars, and rendering them accessible to a transnational readership. This business of circulation is allegorized for the reader in *Brief History* during a moment when Weeper narrates his prison experiences:

> Either way, in prison you always carrying something in your asshole, and all the battyholes behind bars add up to one trade route. Asshole in the east take goods to asshole in the west, destination: inmate in the south with money or other goods. Bag of cocaine, pack of Wrigley's, Hershey bar, Snickers, Milky Way, ganja, hashish, beeper, toothpaste, diet pill, Xanax, Percocet, sugar, aspirin, cigarette, lighter, tobacco, golf ball with tobacco or cocaine, rolling paper, matches, Lip Smackers, lubricant, syringe with eraser over the needle, fifteen lottery tickets.
>
> (2014: 447)

This triangulation of East, West, and South is suggestive of Cold War divisions of the globe, with South here standing in for the so-called Third World. Weeper's "trade route" runs between inmates in the carceral system yet it also provides a map of the Cold War geography within which we need to make sense of the imposition of neoliberalism on the Caribbean, and the global dissemination of its languages and musical idioms. But the North is absent in Weeper's account, the negative space created by its absence standing in by implication for something like freedom, or perhaps for the ones running this prison. We may also say that the North points toward both the United States and the direction of travel of the illicit narcotics economy the novel is concerned with. But if we understand *Brief History* as a self-reflexive account of the vernacular and its circulation then this passage intimates something about James's doubts and ambivalences regarding the routes through which the vernacular travels, the same flows within which his novel is implicated.

There is a scene toward the end of the novel that foregrounds such doubts and ambivalences. It involves the character of Nina Burgess, who adopts during the course of the novel the pseudonyms Kim Clarke, Dorcas Palmer, and Millicent Segree. A witness to the attempted assassination of the Singer, Nina is desperate to move to the United States and finds herself in the Bronx, New York toward the end of the novel. As Naomi Adam reminds us, James has declared Nina to be his mouthpiece in the novel (2020: 27). Perhaps unsurprisingly her language usage is marked by a high degree of style shifting, with her moving between the more prestigious Standard Jamaican English and Jamaican Creole with ease, and even adopting Rastafarian "Dread Talk" on one occasion (Adam 2020: 27). She is also reflecting on such shifts between different vernaculars, upbraiding her sister Kimmy at one point for "playing ghetto" (James 2014: 155) by adopting Jamaican Creole. In the final chapter of the novel, Nina is desperate to "have something Jamaican in my mouth" (2014: 682). After gorging herself on Jamaican cuisine, "fry chicken and rice and peas ... and some fry plantain and shredded salad" (2014: 682), Nina tells the reader:

> I make it through the door just before the vomit burst my lips open and splatters all over the sidewalk. Somebody across the street must be watching me hack fried chicken while my own belly is contracting the life out of me. Nobody is coming but I still left a mess right near his door. I'm trying to stand up straight but my stomach kicks itself again and I bowl over hacking but no vomit.
>
> (2014: 685)

Overtly Nina is expelling Jamaican cuisine, but the semantic drift suggested by "something Jamaican in my mouth" implies that the food also serves as a stand-in for language and song, among others. It is as if she is purging herself of an excessive amount of vernacular culture, with the novel—a narrative characterized by its own excesses—calling upon itself to purge its own excesses in its final pages. Too much food, too much of the vernacular, its languages and music, the narrative seems to be suggesting, with the novel concluding shortly after this scene with Nina calling her sister Kimmy, who is still living in Havendale, an affluent neighborhood in Kingston, Jamaica.

At this point, one may well ask whether vernacular languages and expressive forms, once uprooted from what is presented in the novel as their originary relation to a decolonial politics of anti-imperialism and anti-racism, constitute something like an excess in the narrative, a surplus of language and culture to be set in motion along various routes, but ultimately to be purged. It may be the case that the narrative is trying to distance itself from its imbrication in vernacular cultures and flows, both indulging in and, yet, suspicious of the transnational circulation and neoliberal resignifications of the vernacular. After all, it too is implicated in "playing ghetto." However we make sense of James's self-reflexive account of the vernacular and its complication it is certainly the case that *Brief History* offers the reader a set of coordinates by which to understand the complexities surrounding the vernacular today, its entanglement with histories of decolonization and neoliberalization, its shifting valences as both a mode of expression and representational form for the disenfranchised inhabiting a planet of slums, and a component of the genre of the global novel that finds its readership amongst globalized populations.

It is to the global novel and its renewed emphasis on the vernacular I want to turn in conclusion. I want to do so by invoking Cristina Beltrán's account of what constitutes a neoliberal aesthetics. In her account of representations of race in the United States, she argues that racial presence, that is to say the rendering visible of racial differences, has been conflated with the aesthetic category of the beautiful, and through this conflation has been understood "to signify not only racial progress but racial justice" (2014: 138). Much like Patricia Stuelke, Beltrán is concerned with what we can call category errors, with how accounts of inclusiveness and relationality in the cultural realm or judgments about what constitutes the beautiful substitute for the political, whether it be the politics of decolonization or of racial justice. With implications for how we approach the vernacular turn within the contemporary anglophone global novel, *Brief History* cautions ultimately against such misrecognitions and substitutions, even while not necessarily fully resisting participating in them. In other words, it resists a reading that would find in the vernacular—whether language or expressive form—a straightforward expression of transnational relationality or interconnectedness, a reading that would suture together the Caribbean and the United States without giving recognition to the hemispheric fault lines opened by counter-revolutionary and imperial histories. *Brief History* insists that the vernacular, throughout all of its permutations and transformations, is shadowed by the specter of histories of decolonization and neoliberalization, and that our reckoning with the vernacular cannot escape confronting these specters as well.

References

Adam, N. (2020), "'Playing Ghetto': Style Shifting to Jamaican Creole in Marlon James's *A Brief History of Seven Killings*," *The English Languages: History, Diaspora, Culture*, 6: 26–42.

Airey, J. (2015), "Jamaican Novelist Marlon James Makes History by Winning Man Booker Prize," *The Conversation*, October 14. Available online: https://theconversation.com/jamaican-novelist-marlon-james-makes-history-by-winning-man-booker-prize-49156 (accessed April 14, 2021).

Beecroft, A. (2015), *An Ecology of World Literature: From Antiquity to the Present Day*, New York: Verso.

Beltrán, C. (2014), "Racial Presence Versus Racial Justice: The Affective Power of an Aesthetic Condition," *Du Bois Review*, 11 (1): 137–58.

Brouillette, S. (2019), *UNESCO and the Fate of the Literary*, Stanford, CA: Stanford University Press.

Brown, W. (2015), *Undoing the Demos: Neoliberalism's Stealth Revolution*, Cambridge, MA: The MIT Press.

Deckard, S. (2018), "'Always Returning from It': Neoliberal Capitalism, Retrospect, and Marlon James's *A Brief History of Seven Killings*," *CounterText*, 4 (2): 169–91.

Denning, M. (2015), *Noise Uprising: The Audiopolitics of a World Musical Revolution*, London: Verso.

Ellis, N. (2015), "Marlon James's Savage Business," *Public Books*, March 1. Available online: https://www.publicbooks.org/marlon-jamess-savage-business/#fnref-1140-2 (accessed April 15, 2021).

Hall, S. (1995), "Negotiating Caribbean Identities," *New Left Review*, 209: 3–14.

Harrison, S. M. (2015), "Excess in *A Brief History of Seven Killings*," *Contemporaries*, 24 October. Available online: https://post45.org/2015/10/excess-in-a-brief-history-of-seven-killings/ (accessed April 15, 2021).

Irr, C. (2011), "Toward the World Novel: Genre Shifts in Twenty-First-Century Expatriate Fiction," *American Literary History*, 23 (3): 660–79.

James, M. (2014), *A Brief History of Seven Killings*, New York: Riverhead Books.

Jones, G. (1994), "From 'The Quest for Wholeness': Re-imagining the African-American Novel: An Essay on Third World Aesthetics," *Callaloo*, 17 (2): 507–18.

Jones, G. (1999), *Strange Talk: The Politics of Dialect Literature in Gilded Age America*, Berkeley: University of California Press.

Mathes, C. (2010), "Circuits of Political Prophecy: Martin Luther King Jr., Peter Tosh, and the Black Radical Imaginary," *Small Axe*, 14 (2): 17–41.

McKenzie, A. (2015), "A Conversation with Marlon James," *Jamaica Observer*, October 18. Available online: http://www.jamaicaobserver.com/news/A-Conversation-with-Marlon-James_19234263 (accessed May 5, 2021).

Meeks, B. (2019), "Roadblock on Hope Road: The End of Imagination and Capitalism's Late Afternoon," *Caribbean Quarterly*, 65 (3): 347–66.

Melamed, J. (2011), *Represent and Destroy: Rationalizing Violence in the New Racial Capitalism*, Minneapolis: University of Minnesota Press.

Nadiminti, K. (2018), "The Global Program Era: Contemporary International Fiction in the American Creative Economy," *Novel*, 51 (3): 375–98.

Ong, A. (2007), "Neoliberalism as Mobile Technology," *Transactions of the Institute of British Geographers*, 32 (1): 3–8.

Peck, J. (2010), *Constructions of Neoliberal Reason*, New York: Oxford University Press.

Pollock, S. (2000), "Cosmopolitan and Vernacular in History," *Public Culture*, 12 (3): 591–625.

Rojo, Luisa Martín (2018), "Neoliberalism and Linguistic Governmentality," in J. W. Tollefson and M. Pérez-Milans (eds), *The Oxford Handbook of Language Policy and Planning*, 545–64, Oxford: Oxford University Press.

Scott, D. (2014), *Omens of Adversity: Tragedy, Time, Memory, Justice*, Durham NC: Duke University Press.

Shankar, S. (2012), *Flesh and Fish Blood: Postcolonialism, Translation, and the Vernacular*, Berkeley: University of California Press.

Spahr, J. (2018), *Du Bois's Telegram: Literary Resistance and State Containment*, Cambridge, MA: Harvard University Press. KINDLE edition.

Stuelke, P. (2014), "'Time When Greater Disciplines Are Born': The Zora Neale Hurston Revival and the Neoliberal Transformation of the Caribbean," *American Literature*, 86 (1): 117–45.

Talentino, J. (2019), "Why Marlon James Decided to Write an African *Game of Thrones*," *The New Yorker*, January 28. Available online: https://www.newyorker.com/magazine/2019/01/28/why-marlon-james-decided-to-write-an-african-game-of-thrones (accessed May 2, 2021).

Toop, D. (1995), *Ocean of Sound: Aether Talk, Ambient Sound, and Imaginary Worlds*, London: Serpent's Tail.

Veal, M. (2007), *Dub: Soundscapes and Shattered Songs in Jamaican Reggae*, Middletown: Wesleyan University Press.

Wald, C. (2011), "Faulkner and the Southern Novel," in L. Cassuto (ed.), *The Cambridge History of the American Novel*, 750–66, Cambridge: Cambridge University Press.

9

Vernacular imagination and exophone reconfiguration in Francophone Chinese diasporic literature

Shuangyi Li

In the Introduction to this volume, Kullberg and Watson outline the multiple meanings and implications of the notion of the vernacular, which can be variously understood as a localized, indigenous language; a literature written in such a language; an aesthetic strategy; a mode of reading; a sensibility; a form of oral mediality, in addition to other meanings. Such wide-ranging notions of the vernacular demand a geopolitical, cultural, and critical contextualization to reify its theoretical relevance while helping to yield new insights into the epistemic reality as well as the creative potential of a particular context. This chapter sets out to explore the vernacular in francophone Chinese diasporic literature written by first-generation migrant writers, such as François Cheng (1929–), Dai Sijie (1954–), and Shan Sa (1972–). Franco-Chinese literature on the whole may still occupy a relatively marginal place in today's world literary scene, despite some of the texts' availability in multiple languages and the individual global commercial successes, such as Dai's *Balzac et la Petite Tailleuse chinoise* (Balzac and the Little Chinese Seamstress). However, it has been widely promoted in the francophone, and, to some extent, sinophone spaces of articulation, and it has enjoyed the highest French and Western institutional recognitions, from the *Prix Goncourt des Lycéens* (Shan), the *Prix Femina* (Cheng, Dai), and the *Grand Prix de la francophonie* (Cheng), to the Nobel Prize for Literature (Gao Xingjian).[1]

To some, my attempt may seem rather unorthodox, as this particular group of writers' works are often conceptualized as exophone literature, literature written

---

[1] For an in-depth discussion of the different external and internal factors that may have contributed to this varied promotion and reception of Franco-Chinese literature in the anglophone and francophone world, see Chirila 2012.

in languages other than the author's native one, as signaled by the prefix "exo-" meaning "outside." The notion of exophony first and foremost highlights these (originally) Chinese writers' non-nativeness to French, a(nother) cosmopolitan language, which has become their dominant language of literary creation. In addition, exophony may be seen as etymologically associated with exoticism, which, in those writers' works, is palpably expressed through a desire to revisit, thematically, aesthetically, and historically, their native land and culture through the fictional medium of literature.

Linguistically, exophone literature, which embodies a displaced articulation of cosmopolitanism through diasporic mobility, may appear to be the exact opposite of vernacular literature, which is often "willed" to be written in an indigenous language that is seemingly rooted in, and confined to, a relatively small, local culture and topography. Yet, this apparent opposition does not preclude the vernacular from featuring as a theme, manifesting as a variety of genres, and emerging as a sensibility in Franco-Chinese exophone novels.

To clear some epistemological ground, "vernacular" is the English word that is customarily employed to translate the word *baihua* 白话, "plain, unadorned language," in the Chinese context, referring to variable forms of *written* language that are close to the spoken form of Chinese, mainly in terms of vocabulary and grammatical structure, but not pronunciation. *Baihua* is contrasted with *wenyan* 文言, "literary language," also known as Classical Chinese, which is a highly codified—according to some ancient texts—written language that is largely divorced from speech. Historically, speakers can read both *baihua* and *wenyan* texts according to the pronunciation of their own spoken language variety. *Wenyan* enjoyed an unchallenged cultural prestige. As a written cosmopolitan language, *wenyan* became and stayed the *scripta franca* of the elites of East Asia up until the twentieth century and the vehicle of transnational education (Denecke and Zhang 2015: viii). It is worth stressing that both writing traditions, each assigned a distinctive set of social and political roles, coexisted in China for thousands of years. While most writings demonstrated varying degrees of mixtures between Classical and vernacular Chinese, each tradition historically followed its own path of evolution. Therefore, the difference between Classical and vernacular Chinese is "not just a matter of diachronic change, as between Old English and Modern English"; rather, it is "a distinction between two separately structured linguistic media" (Mair 1994: 708). Further, their working relationship may be best characterized as that of translation. The unification between the spoken and written forms of language then became *the* goal of the radical language reform during the New Culture Movement, from the mid-1910s to the 1920s, led by the

May Fourth intellectuals, which resulted in the creation of *modern* vernacular Chinese. Interestingly, as I will later demonstrate, some of the linguistic and cultural dilemmas and struggles faced by May Fourth intellectuals, as well as their stylistic and aesthetic inventions, are shared by the featured exophone writers. Subsequently, from 1949 to 1979, the drastic political movements following the establishment of the People's Republic of China led to another major transformation of the modern vernacular Chinese, decidedly marked by lexical, syntactical, and even semiotic differences from those employed in other regions of the sinophone world.

This development of modern vernacular Chinese is registered as a theme in exophone novels, such as in Cheng's *Le Dit de Tianyi* (1998) (*The River Below* [2000]) and Shan's *Les Quatre Vies du saule* (1999) (*The Willow's Four Lives*).[2] Meanwhile, Dai in *Balzac et la Petite Tailleuse chinoise* seeks to reenact the long-standing Chinese cultural ritual of vernacular storytelling. The author's vernacular imagination reaches its apotheosis in *Par une nuit où la lune ne s'est pas levée* (2007) (*Once on a Moonless Night* [2009]), as he fictionally elaborates on a lost, indigenous, mystical language that leads to the creation of a global linguistic network through the polyglottal protagonists' tortuous cosmopolitan journey.

In this chapter, I will first clarify the epistemic confusion when we employ the English word "vernacular" in the Chinese historical context to describe the variable forms of close-to-speech written language, and by extension, certain genres of literature thought to be closely associated with the "vernacular" language—genres that I seek to expand on conceptually in this chapter. Yet, this epistemic confusion and ambiguity becomes a source of inspiration for Franco-Chinese writers, exemplified through their exophone novelistic reconfigurations. It is precisely through such epistemic confusion that they are able to exercise their vernacular imagination across time and space, expressing a vernacular sensibility beyond the vernacular language(s).

Chinese vernaculars and vernacular literatures

There are generally two kinds of written Chinese "vernacular." The historical or old-style written vernacular has its roots in folksongs, early translations of Buddhist texts, and written supports for oral storytelling. However, it was

---

[2] Shan's text has not been made available in English, the translations of the passages from this text are mine.

later associated with a genre and/or function of fiction writing particularly popularized during the Ming (1368–1662) and the Qing (1644–1912) dynasties, commonly known as the "Chinese vernacular novel." Although this written vernacular Chinese is linguistically contrasted with the aforementioned *wenyan* or Classical Chinese, most *vernacular novels* demonstrate a varying mixture of the two or were written "in some intermediate language between Classical and vernacular"; their language was by no means straightforwardly "colloquial." Additionally, "the author's or editor's preface, if there is one, is always in Classical, even though it is addressed to the same reader" (Hanan 1981: 10). To complicate the matter, these novels are actually called "classical vernacular novels" 古典白话小说 or even just "classical novels" 古典小说 in China. These are "classical" not because they are written in Classical Chinese or *wenyan*, but because they exemplify an old literature in terms of language, style, and themes, in contrast to *modern* Chinese literature developed since the beginning of the twentieth century. These linguistic and cultural specificities indicate that the vernacular does not have a fixed and stable referent, and it needs to be understood as a relational term and used always in a contextualized manner. The vernacular can operate as a conceptual as much as *translational* matter on multiple fronts. It is noteworthy that the actual legitimate use of the written vernacular Chinese was generically confined to novels, plays, and songs, and socially limited, reserved, for instance for non-official purposes. It was never promoted to seriously challenge or replace Classical Chinese—not until the early twentieth century, when the modern or new-style vernacular Chinese was born.[3] Therefore, certain literary or cultural practices, especially those often seen as located outside the Western framework, are described as "vernacular" through translation for reasons that may well be different from its referents, connotations, and assumptions within Western traditions.[4]

Modern vernacular Chinese was the result of a radical language reform (or, indeed, revolution) violently pursued by May Fourth intellectuals during the

---

[3] Such cross-cultural terminological confusions caused by translation have led some scholars to advocate for the abolishment of the English designation "Chinese vernacular fiction," adopting directly the Chinese term *gudian xiaoshuo* instead (Tong 2014).

[4] Comparing the vastly heterogeneous notions of the vernacular across the European, African, Chinese, and Arabic contexts, Shaden M. Tageldin brilliantly tackles this problem by suggesting "a *minimal commensurability and maximal difference* between the *vernacular* and its non-Europhone translations, for their imagined equivalence often founders on broader epistemic grounds that transcend the strictly linguistic" (2018: 116; emphasis in original). However, such a commensurability and difference will be again readjusted in the Franco-Chinese novelistic articulations examined in this final chapter.

New Culture Movement at the beginning of the twentieth century. The political agenda behind this envisaged linguistic "modernity" or "modernization" is reflected in their resolution to unite the spoken and written forms of Chinese, so that this new national language-to-be could be better suited to accommodate and engage with the new scientific realities and global cultural orders, pioneered but also intrusively dominated by the West. In the meantime, May Fourth intellectuals were inspired by the recent Japanese language reform during the Meji period (1868–1912), which was part of the modernization and Westernization that had rapidly transformed Japan into a major international power. To this end, some core reformers, such as Hu Shi and Chen Duxiu, advocated for a total abolishment of Classical Chinese,[5] only to realize that the old-style written vernacular Chinese they were so set on elevating could hardly fulfill the reformative purposes without some drastic standardization, due to the varieties, and refinement, because of its profound entanglement with Classical Chinese. Against this backdrop, the translation of foreign works into vernacular Chinese (from Western languages as well as Japanese) became an indispensable way to raise the literary prestige of the new-style vernacular. Translation itself became a site of linguistic, aesthetic, and stylistic experimentation, which was epitomized in the use of what we now call "translationese" (or *fanyiti* in Chinese) that directly impacted those writers' making of modern vernacular Chinese.[6] The result was an "awkward mixture of styles" (Chen 1999: 78) that neither sounded nor appeared "vernacular," and the scholar Shu-mei Shih goes so far as to argue that this new "vernacular" language "might in effect be as alien to the ordinary reader as *wenyan*" (2001: 71). Lu Xun's "A Madman's Diary" (1918) may be regarded as the first instance of modern Chinese fiction written in this vernacular.

Thus, we may relate the process of modern Chinese vernacularization to Sheldon Pollock's formulation of the "cosmopolitan vernacular" that undoes "the local/global dualism," for the vernacular of an "indigenous" culture is "produced in the course of long-term translocal interactions by the very same processes

---

[5] In fact, some reformers, such as Qian Xuantong, even suggested abandoning the Chinese writing system altogether in favor of a Western-style phonetic script, several forms of which had already been invented and put into practice, particularly by earlier Western missionaries in China (Norman 1988: 257–65). One of the obvious advantages of a phonetic script was that it could help unify and standardize the pronunciation of this national language-to-be.

[6] "Translationese" designates the deliberate use of unidiomatic language in a translated text. As Laurence Venuti adds, "what is unidiomatic in one cultural formation can be aesthetically effective in another" (2008: 98).

that produce the global itself" (1998: 31).⁷ Accordingly, if we reverse this line of enquiry, we may see Franco-Chinese writers' exophone writings as linguistic, aesthetic, and stylistic attempts to express and embody a kind of "vernacular cosmopolitanism"; that is, the outright global and transcultural outlook of their literary works is both linguistically and diegetically mediated through the writers' vernacularizing as well as exoticizing imaginations.

Modern vernacular in Cheng's *Le Dit de Tianyi*

The protagonists in Cheng's *Le Dit de Tianyi* were born in the 1920s. By then, the New Culture Movement was technically approaching its end, and the protagonist Tianyi and his male poet companion Haolang represent a new generation of Chinese intellectuals who were yet to live through the profound consequences of and the changed critical reactions to, this movement, including its languages, literatures, and cultures in general. This generation was confronting new sociopolitical realities complicated by the Sino-Japanese War (1937 until 1945), the intermittent Chinese Civil War (1927 to 1949), and the ever-growing Soviet influence throughout these periods.

A few years Tianyi's senior, Haolang, who "knew both classical and modern Chinese literature" (Cheng 2000: 51),⁸ is portrayed as the protagonist's literary initiator. However, in the early stages of their friendship, Tianyi notices that Haolang's vocational interest was drastically shifting to Western literature, thanks to the substantial boost of translation activities following the New Culture Movement, as well as Lu Xun's strong advocacy for reading such literature:

> In the twenties, and all through the thirties, the Chinese had translated prodigiously, "right and left" so to speak, chaotically, and with mixed results, for many translators worked not from original texts, but from Japanese or English versions. All the same, a trend had begun. Hadn't Lu Xun, in 1925, with all the weight of his authority, advised a young reader to forge ahead and read "as few Chinese books as possible and as many foreign books as possible?" (Cheng 2000: 51–2)⁹

---

⁷ Note that Pollock's focus is on the vernacularization in pre-modern southern Asia. Nevertheless, his persistent calling for the local/global dualism to be "historicized out of existence" is still applicable here and should inform our theorization of the vernacular more generally in this volume.
⁸ *connaissait aussi bien la littérature chinoise classique que moderne* (Cheng 1998: 80).
⁹ *Dès les années vingt et tout au long des années trente, on avait énormément traduit, "à tour de bras" pour ainsi dire, dans un grand désordre, et de manière inégale; car beaucoup le faisaient non à partir de l'original mais de versions anglaises ou japonaise. Toutefois, le mouvement était lancé. En 1925, Lu Xun, avec tout le poids de son autorité, ne conseillait-il pas à un jeune lecteur de lire résolument "le moins possible de livres chinois et le plus possible de livres étrangers"* (Cheng 1998: 81).

Lu Xun is also famous for his literary experimentation with translationese (Wang 2013: 134–7), which epitomizes the Chinese vernacularizing process of the time. Tianyi describes his encounter with a contemporary translation of the Gospel of John in the following passage: "[I] soon find myself transported elsewhere, disoriented. Will I ever be able to figure out the message of this translation into an odd idiom, which is Chinese without being Chinese, a language with puzzling neologisms, a syntax at times wobbly, a rhythm that is jerky?" (Cheng 2000: 251–2).[10] Translation activities intensify even more later into the war period, as the presence of Western allies, particularly the British, Russian, and American, facilitate another introduction *en masse* of Western texts to China, as Tianyi remarks: "We pounced on everything that appeared, poetry and novels, plays, essays, without neglecting any author, including those from northern and central Europe" (Cheng 2000: 52).[11] While translation accelerates the process of vernacularization, Haolang is seen to be constantly preoccupied with the renewal of Chinese poetic language.[12] As a self-proclaimed disciple of Lu Xun, Haolang largely shares the preceding May Fourth intellectuals' radical discourses on Chinese language and culture, whose past must be torn asunder and whose present and future are to be salvaged and reborn through Westernization and modernization, as he resolutely asserts:

> I am strongly on the side of Lu Xun ... If we are to be reborn, we shall be reborn. If we are to disappear, let us accept becoming ashes; perhaps from them something else will be born of which we know nothing now. For the moment, salvation comes from elsewhere, from abroad. And first, from the West ... Yes, we must have this drastically different other, to shake us up, to tear out the degenerate, rotten part of our roots. Without the enrichment of new blood and new knowledge [*lumière nouvelle*], how do you expect us to recognize properly amid the great hodgepodge of our heritage the values that must be retained? Strangely enough, it is after reading all those Western works that I am beginning to see our own culture more clearly. (Cheng 2000: 62–3)[13]

---

[10] *je me trouve soudain déporté ailleurs, passablement désorienté. Parviendrai-je jamais à déceler un message au travers de cette traduction au langage étrange, qui est du chinois sans être du chinois, avec ses néologismes déroutants, sa syntaxe parfois bancale, son rythme qui heurte?* (Cheng 1998: 362)

[11] *Nous nous jetons sur tout ce qui paraissait, poésie et romans, pièces de théâtre et essais, sans négliger aucun auteur, y compris ceux de l'Europe du Nord et de l'Europe centrale* (Cheng 1998: 81–2).

[12] *le souci de renouveler le langage poétique* (Cheng 1998: 96).

[13] *Moi, je me range résolument du côté de Lu Xun ... Si nous devons renaître, nous renaîtrons. Si nous devons disparaître, acceptons de devenir cendres, d'où naîtra peut-être quelque chose d'autre que nous ignorons. Pour le moment, le salut vient d'ailleurs, de l'étranger. Et en premier lieu, de l'Occident ... Oui, il faut bien cet extrême autre pour nous secouer, pour nous arracher à la partie dégénérée, pourrie, de nos racines. Sans la fécondation de sang nouveau, de lumière nouvelle, comment veux-tu que nous accédions à l'authentique vie, qui seule en réalité nous permettra de repérer avec discernement, dans tout le fatras de notre héritage, les valeurs qu'il faut garder? Curieusement d'ailleurs, c'est bien après avoir lu toutes ces œuvres occidentales que je commence à y voir plus clair dans notre propre culture.* (Cheng 1998: 96–7)

Haolang's elaborate assertion clearly articulates May Fourth intellectuals' aspiration for a modern Chinese reincarnation of the ideas behind the European Renaissance (*renaître*) and Enlightenment (*lumière*). Hu Shi, most notably, "perceived the *vernacular movement* to be the major feature of the European Renaissance and the strongest basis for his invention of the Chinese Renaissance" (Zhou 2011: 46, italics in the original). The determination to be "reborn" through "ashes" strongly echoes Guo Moruo's important vernacular poem "Nirvana of Phoenix" 凤凰涅槃 (1920). Such an aspiration illustrates what Shu-mei Shih calls May Fourth Occidentalism, which "effectively inserted the West into the Chinese cultural imaginary as the arbiter of cultural capital, and ultimately of symbolic power." For May Fourth intellectuals, "the locus of cultural power" was "an alien Other that was to be welcomed with open arms to replace the old self and usher in its rebirth. 'Western learning' was no longer an external category, but was incorporated for the 'enlightenment' of the self, becoming an internal category" (2001: 130).

However, as a member of the post-May Fourth generation, Haolang also shows a critical sensibility to revise his predecessors' radical stance against traditional Chinese language and culture. He cautions against "blindly" (*aveuglement*) embracing the West and re-interrogates the question of whether his predecessors' absolute approach would entail the loss of an authentic Chinese self, voice, and soul: "Who are we? What is this very old, moribund country called China? Where is its soul? What is its destiny? And for us what is the proper creative *path* [*voie*]? By turning our eyes in another direction, won't we go astray? Unless we are already lost, and lost with us all inner *voice* and all true worth?" (2000: 62, my italics).[14] In a way, Cheng's exophone creative strategy addresses such an embrace of the West and many of Haolang's questions here. The French homophonic formulation of *voix-voie*, as seen in this passage, is key to understanding Cheng's translingual and transcultural enterprise. "La Voie" (the Way) is the French translation of the Chinese "dao" of Daoism (or Taoism), which means both "to walk/the way" and "to say/the speech," hence semantically joining the French word "*la voix*" (the voice).[15] And the dynamic between the

---

[14] *Qui sommes-nous? Quel est ce pays trop vieux et moribond qu'on appelle la Chine? Où est son âme? Quel est son destin? Et quelle est notre propre voie de création? À force de tourner le regard ailleurs, n'allons-nous pas nous égarer? À moins que nous ne soyons déjà perdus, et perdues avec nous toute voix intérieure et toute valeur authentique?* (Cheng 1998: 96)

[15] For another instance of Cheng's novelistic elaboration of *voix-voie*, see Li 2017: 192–3. Incidentally, this should further inform us about the French title of the novel: *Le Dit* [saying] *de Tianyi* is thus also the *dao* of Tianyi.

two notions does not stop at the level of wordplay. Haolang writes the following poem at the end of his remark:

> When nostalgia overwhelms you
> Drive it off, to the far horizon.
> Wild goose cleaving the clouds
> You carry in you the dead season
> Frozen rushes, charred trees
> Bent low beneath the hurricane.
> Wild goose that need not tarry
> Free now for flight, or death...
> Between natal soil and welcoming sky
> Your sole kingdom: your own call! (Cheng 2000: 64)[16]

This is one of Cheng's own poems directly composed in French; however, in this fictional context, it is supposed to be written in modern vernacular Chinese. Here, the vernacularity of Haolang's "new poetic language" is conveyed through style. The poetic imagery of the wild goose 雁 is not exactly "modern"; in fact, the wild goose is one of the most recurrent motifs in Classical Chinese poetry, which can be traced all the way back to the earliest Chinese anthologies, such as *Shijing* (ca. 600 BCE) and *Chu Ci*. However, its modern identification with Chinese intellectuals' complex feelings of hesitancy, struggle, disorientation, determination, homesickness, and nostalgia is famously celebrated by another May Fourth poet Wen Yiduo, particularly in his vernacular poem "Lone Wild Goose" 孤雁 (1922). Haolang's poem may feel as if it is taken directly out of Wen's twelve-stanza poem. In other words, Cheng effectively rewrites a modern vernacular Chinese poem in French and through translation.

Meanwhile, Cheng's French poetic rendition of the wild goose is redolent of Mallarméian symbolism. In Mallarmé's "*Le Cygne*" (The Swan), the magnificent *cygne*, a French homophone of *signe* (sign), is trapped in a frosted wintry lake and strives to "break free woebegone," "dismissed to futile things" (Mallarmé 2006: 66-9).[17] In comparison, Cheng's *oie* (goose), a near homophone of *voie* and *voix*, is determined to break free of its nostalgic past and leave its native soil for the far horizon for survival, following its own voice ("*ton propre cri*") and

---

[16] *Quand te submerge la nostalgie / Repousse-la vers l'horizon extrême / Oie sauvage fendant les nuages / Tu portes en toi la morte-saison / Roseaux gelés arbres calcinés / Ployés en bas sous l'ouragaon / Oie sauvage délivrée des haltes / Libre enfin de voler, ou mourir ... / Entre sol natal et ciel d'accueil / Ton royaume unique: ton propre cri!* (Cheng 1998: 97)

[17] "*qui sans espoir se délivre*"; "*parmi l'exil inutile.*"

vocation (from Latin *vocale* meaning "to call").[18] As a poet, Cheng repeatedly claims to adhere to the Mallarméian tenet of the "Orphic way of poetry" (Bertaud 2011: 237). Haolang's poem is more than an allegory; it is intended to evoke the profound predicament and fierce self-determination of Chinese intellectuals on the threshold of global modernity in the twentieth century. French symbolist poetry was indeed a very important source for the making of Chinese poetry in modern vernacular, which developed forms and contents that are distinct from what we now call "Classical Chinese poetry," including genres such as *shi, ci, qu*, and *fu*.[19] The Chinese symbolist poetry that rises to prominence during the wartime period of Haolang's left-wing literary writing adds politically and socially engaged content and tone to their French inspirations, which lean towards aestheticism and also explicitly link poets' personal commitments to national crises.[20]

Just as the character Haolang aspires to the "enrichment of new blood and new knowledge" and "salvation" from the West (Cheng 1998: 96–7; 2000: 62–3), Cheng revisits his native culture through his adopted French, creating a new poetic language that is at once vernacular and cosmopolitan. Here we find a good example of what, in the title of this chapter, I referred to as "exophone reconfiguration" of "vernacular imagination." Quite ingeniously, through such an exophone execution, Cheng is able to not only create a synchronic, translingual experiment (e.g. *voix-voie-oie* vs. *signe-cygne*), but also make a diachronic reconnection—via French—between a fictional modern vernacular Chinese poem and Classical Chinese diction, imagery, and discourse. In other words, Cheng's exophone performance further dramatizes the vernacularity of modern and contemporary Chinese and Chinese diasporic literature as a site of polyvalent translation, from language to genre, across time and space.

---

[18] It is worth pointing out that the whole novel also begins with a mysterious and mystical calling voice, a "*cri*": "*Au commencement il y eut ce cri dans la nuit*" (In the beginning there was the cry in the night) (1998: 3; 2000: 15).

[19] Up until the twentieth century, "poetry" composed in vernacular, with no explicit formal concerns over rhymes and prosodies (*yunlü*), was simply not considered poetry. In fact, it was only around this time that we could start to talk about *the* genre of poetry in Chinese, *shi*, which formerly only referred to a specific kind or genre of "rhymed writing" (*yunwen*) from the Tang dynasty (618–906) (Hockx 2016: 3–19).

[20] For a short overview of the influence of French symbolism on modern Chinese poetry, see Hockx 2016: 13, 155–8. Interestingly, in the meantime, classical Chinese poetics and writing at large also come to haunt contemporaneous Western modernist literary imaginations. For more recent discussions of this topic, see Bachner 2014: 57–89 and Bush 2010.

Politicizing the vernacular in the early history of the PRC

Just as the literary expression of modern vernacular Chinese reached its dominant status and was starting to mature after two to three generations of "making," in the 1950s it experienced another major political reform—and for that matter, "cultural revolution"—which, practically speaking, lasted until the death of Mao in 1976 and the Economic Reform and Opening Up from 1978. Whereas the kind of modern vernacular advocated by previous May Fourth intellectuals was chiefly a product of an urban and cosmopolitan literary scene, implemented by and for educated, cultural elites, this new phase of vernacular development, starting in the 1940s and remarkably guided by Mao's notorious talks at the Yen'an Forum on literature and art in 1942, was "predominantly rural, aimed at a mass audience and modeled on indigenous literary techniques" (Huters 1984: 55). While earlier May Fourth intellectuals like Hu Shi and Chen Duxiu pushed for a radical break with the past and a general adoption of Western systems and cultural values, Mao actually "warn[ed] against chopping up history and [led] the writers back to the China of yesterday and the day before yesterday" (Fokkema 1965: 27). However, regarding literary expression, the new doctrine geared the modern vernacular towards the creation of "simple language literature in a form the 'common folk of China' was used to hearing" (Fokkema 1965: 27). The theoretical idea is perhaps most succinctly captured in Ho Ch'i-fang's words in 1962, commemorating Mao's *Yen'an Talks*:

> In form, the new works, in varying degrees, have a national and mass style. Nourished by Chinese folk and classical literature, and written in the vivid language of the working people, their form is no longer foreignized or strongly intellectualized, but is one that appeals to the masses of the Chinese people. As a result, their influence and impact is the broadest and deepest of any since the new literature inspired by the May Fourth Movement began.
> (Quoted in Fokkema 1965: 33)

The foremost challenge faced by modern vernacular Chinese literature during this time was that "it must serve the new radical politics (or policies within specific temporal delineations), and the language and literary works must, at all time, express and propagate policies instead of personal feelings and experiences" (Zheng 1993: 13, my translation). T. D. Huters further explains that the political and social circumstances aggravated by the Sino-Japanese War and the Civil War of the 1940s, fought between Nationalists and Communists, "put literature and writers into a position of almost total dependence upon politics" (1984: 56). Indeed, even those writers of the May Fourth tradition seemed to acquiesce to such political functions of modern vernacular language and literature, reflecting a radically changed readership and audience. This ideology was implemented in absolute terms after the establishment of the People's Republic of China in 1949.

The new round of language reform or revolution no longer revolved around the opposition between Classical and vernacular Chinese; it aimed to unequivocally define, create, prescribe, and impose a collective, highly transparent form of literary language that would suit the purposes of proletarian revolutions, while recklessly eliminating and expunging all that may be interpreted as decadent, feudalist, corrupted, bourgeois, and, in a word, anti-revolutionary. Many of these accusations were precisely directed towards earlier May Fourth intellectuals' works. The Soviet revolutionary and political discourses, from vocabulary and syntax to theme, genre, and style of argumentation, exerted a major influence on the Chinese language and literature of this time (Zheng 1993: 13–14). This complex and drastic linguistic development from the 1950s to the end of the 1970s entailed a qualitative distinction between the modern vernacular Chinese of the PRC and that employed across the sinophone world (Zheng 1993: 13–14).[21] As far as the new literary doctrine is concerned, Fokkema authoritatively concludes:

> it must be viewed as a genuinely new phenomenon indissolvable into constituent parts. It is neither dependent of [sic] foreign influence, nor the natural outgrowth of indigenous traditions. Not being Soviet, Western, or traditional Chinese, it is a new, unprecedented species.
>
> (1965: 276)

Fortunately, contemporary Chinese literature since the 1980s has largely come well out of the shadow of this political framework for literary creation. However, mainland Chinese writers who have lived or partly lived through the preceding phase of the PRC continue to creatively engage with the "formalized"[22] or "formulist"[23] political language that permeated everyday speech and was strictly

---

[21] I should mention that it was also during this time that traditional Chinese characters were simplified, the pinyin system and the use of punctuation were firmly established.

[22] This is informed by Michael Schoenhals's study of the language in Chinese politics. "Formalized" here refers to a particular quality of linguistic "impoverishment." The politically dependent literary language of the time was also "a restricted code, one in which options with respect to formal qualities such as vocabulary, style, syntax, and trope are far more restricted than in ordinary language" (1992: 1).

[23] "Formulism" 公式主义 was initially used in the 1930s to refer to "fiction that advanced its ideological message in an overtly mechanical or schematic fashion" (Anderson 1990: 62).

imposed on literature of the time. In a similar vein, Franco-Chinese writers, whether or not they have had direct experiences with the first three decades of the PRC, have also demonstrated a keen interest to revisit and imitate the almost absurdly politicized vernacular language, themes, and writing. Yet, it is in the exophone space of articulation, essentially through translation, that they are able and willing to creatively engage and play with such stilted discourses as a cosmopolitan literary style in their novelistic fabric.

Revolutionary vernacular in fiction

François Cheng, Dai Sijie, and Shan Sa have all written about the first three decades of the PRC, especially from the Great Leap Forward (1958 to 1962) to the Cultural Revolution (1966 to 1976), in their fictional works. Only Dai had first-hand experience with (parts of) this period. As an educated urban youth, he was deemed pro-bourgeois and sent down to the countryside by force to learn from peasants and workers (1971 until 1974), which autobiographically informs his novel *Balzac et la Petite Tailleuse chinoise*. As literature becomes subordinate to politics (upon Mao's proposition), the ubiquitous, politically informed and imposed Chinese language of the time becomes a discursive and literary trope that these writers frequently employ in their translational storytelling for a cosmopolitan readership.

The most obvious example is the incorporation of Maoist sayings and political slogans into the novelistic fabric. They can be direct quotations introduced by the phrase "the President (or Chairman) says":

> "The more man power we have, the stronger we are" (Cheng 2000: 218);[24]
> "Study, study some more, keep studying" (224);[25]
> "Be both 'red and knowledgeable'" (224).[26]

This simple and plain form of language radically erases the traces of the seemingly "awkward" language and style promoted by writers following the May Fourth tradition. It exemplifies the "pure and healthy language" suited to "the propagation of the truth to the masses."[27] Schoenhals duly observes:

---

[24] *Plus on a de bras, plus on est fort* (Cheng 1998: 315).
[25] *Étudier, encore étudier, toujours étudier.* (324).
[26] *[Soyons] à la fois 'rouges et experts'* (324).
[27] These expressions are taken from a contemporaneous issue of the *People's Daily*, translated by Schoenhals (1992: 14).

> During the "Great Proletarian Cultural Revolution," language formalization was in every respect taken to its extreme. "One sentence of Chairman Mao's," Lin Biao declared, "is worth ten thousand of ours". Between 1966 and 1970, this meant that the "ten thousand" alternative sentences that an individual in the past might have chosen from to express himself or herself now had been reduced in number to "one"—and not just any "one" sentence, but one that Mao was already on record as having uttered.
>
> (1992: 19)

As the historian continues, one must show sufficient loyalty to Mao "in everything we say" in order to be socially and politically acceptable. This entailed all kinds of dialogues framed in Mao-quotes that may appear comical to us today, such as "Serve the people. Comrade, could I have two pounds of pork, please?"; "A revolution is not a dinner party. That makes 1.85 yuan altogether" (19).

Indeed, Dai's *Balzac* begins with such a dialogue. The two protagonists Ma and Luo, "city youths" (2001: 4),[28] have just arrived in their designated mountain village for "re-education." No one in the village has seen a violin before, which the village headman soon considers to be a *jouet bourgeois* ("bourgeois toy") and should therefore be burnt. Luo explains that it is a musical instrument and hastily suggests that Ma can play a Mozart sonata to prove it. By then, Western music has been banned in China for some years. Of course, these illiterate villagers, characterized as "primitive" by Dai, know neither Mozart nor sonatas. The only way to save the violin and the protagonists' dignity is to relabel and reframe the Mozart sonata within an acceptable and appropriate revolutionary discourse:

> At that instant the glint of the vigilant Communist reappeared in the headman's eyes, and his voice turned hostile.
> "What's the name of this song of yours?"
> "Well, it's like a song, but actually it's a sonata."
> "I'm asking you what it's called!" he snapped, fixing me with his gaze.
> ...
> "*Mozart* ..." I muttered.
> "*Mozart* what?"
> "*Mozart is Thinking of Chairman Mao*," Luo broke in.

---

[28] *garçons de la ville* (2000: 9).

The audacity! But it worked: as if he had heard something miraculous, the headman's menacing look softened. He crinkled up his eyes in a wide, beatific smile.

"Mozart thinks of Mao all the time," he said.

"Indeed, all the time," agreed Luo. (Dai 2001: 5, italics in the original)[29]

The formulation "*Mozart is Thinking of Chairman Mao*" is obviously intended by Dai to mimic and mock the stilted and fixed form of revolutionary discourses of the time. The content may seem playfully meaningless, but the formulation functions as a significant speech act or performance utterance; in Austinian terms, the *illocutionary* and *perlocutionary* dimensions of the formulation are highlighted in this context. The illocutionary refers to the intentional and conventional force of the speech act, the "performance of an act *in* saying something as opposed to performance of an act *of* saying something" (Austin 1962: 99). Luo's "meaningless" yet conventionally required formulation is *said* in an attempt to *save* the violin and *win* acceptance. Meanwhile, the perlocutionary refers to the consequential effects of the speech act "upon the feelings, thoughts, or actions of the audience, or of the speaker, or of other persons" (101). This is exemplified by the village headman's reaction to the formulation in the end, when his "look softened." In fact, I would argue that this notion of performance utterance is key to the understanding of the new development of the Chinese vernacular language of the time in politics, literature, and everyday speech at large, however impoverished it may seem.

Of course, the literary engagement with this vernacular goes beyond Maoist sayings and simple slogans. Franco-Chinese writers have tried to illustrate in French how this highly formalized and politicized Chinese vernacular comes to shape individual consciousness and thought processes. This is most extensively explored in the third episode of Shan's *Les Quatre Vies du saule* (1999) (*The Willow's*

---

[29] *Illico, une vigilance de bon communiste réapparut dans les yeux du chef et sa voix se fit hostile:*
—*Comment elle s'appelle, ta chanson?*
—*Ça ressemble à une chanson, mais c'est une sonate.*
—*Je te demande son nom! Cria-t-il, en me fixant droit dans les yeux.*
...
—*Mozart ..., hésitai-je.*
—*Mozart quoi?*
—*Mozart pense au président Mao, continua Luo à ma place.*
Quelle audace! Mais elle fut efficace: comme s'il avait entendu quelque chose de miraculeux, le visage menaçant du chef s'adoucit. Ses yeux se plissèrent dans un large sourire de béatitude.
—*Mozart pense toujours à Mao, dit-il.*
                                    —*Oui, toujours, confirma Luo* (Dai 2000: 12–13).

Four Lives), where a male high school student follower of Mao narrates in first person his passionate but ultimately fatal experience at the start of the Cultural Revolution. The narrative language is decidedly marked by the formal qualities of contemporaneous political discourses. Consider the following passage:

> I went from school to school to *kindle the fire of the Revolution*, and I exchanged ideas with the students. I took part in the rallies and *debates organized by the Central Committee* of the Cultural Revolution. I was received by the spouse of the President at the Fisherman's Pavillion. Full of energy and enthusiasm, she cheered us on and passed on *greetings from the great Helmsman*. I fought against those who tried to show contempt for the *greatness of our ideology*. How could I make my mother understand the *necessity and glory of such violence*?
>
> Together with some fellow classmates, the *missionaries of Maoist thought*, we would travel all over China in search of great adventures. *Magical friendships* were established among Red Guards. It was the *flame* that shot up from our emotions heightened by the events, the *warmth* that comforted the heart of the *wandering soldiers*. (My translation and italics)[30]

Those highlighted expressions, however empty, formulaic, and slogan-like they might sound to us today, are representative of the literary works of the early years of the PRC. They are constituent of "what in the eyes of the state count as 'approproriate' formulations," of a forceful discursive framework, which a "PRC citizen must employ," relate or refer to for both political protection and influence. As Schoenhals further explains, such expressions are what "a writer should employ to qualify as ideologically 'in step with the Party center'" and what "a speaker should use in order not to risk accusations of heterodoxy" (14).

In terms of narrative styles, literature of the early PRC, which Shan's episode aims to imitate here via French, is often characterized as "revolutionary romanticism combined with revolutionary realism"—another guiding principle for artistic work instituted by Mao. The "revolutionary romanticism" here is understood, not as "subjective whims, fantasy, love or imaginary freedom"

---

[30] *J'allais de lycée en lycée pour attiser le feu de la Révolution; j'échangeais des idées avec les étudiants. Je participais aux manifestations, aux débats organisés par le Comité central de la Révolution culturelle; j'étais reçu par l'épouse du Président au pavillon du Pêcheur. Femme énergique et fanatique, elle nous encourageait et nous transmettait les salutations du Timonier. Je me battais contre ceux qui cherchaient à bafouer la grandeur de notre idéologie. Comment pouvais-je faire comprendre à ma mère la nécessité et la gloire de cette violence?*
Avec quelques camarades de classe, missionnaires de la pensée maoïste, nous sillonnâmes la Chine à la recherche de grandes aventures. Des amitiés magiques se nouaient entre les gardes rouges. C'était la flamme qui jaillissait de notre sensibilité aiguisée par les événements, la chaleur qui réconfortait le cœur des soldats errants. (Shan 1999: Kindle)

but "as a power to envision and to create alternative narratives and to project different images of the world, provoking the audience to identify with those visions and to participate in their realization" (Wang 2016: 239). In many ways, it is the ideologically transparent political language, "a tool of coercion available to anybody" (Bloch 1975: 9), that empowers the teenage narrator-protagonist (who is among the first to join the Red Guards) to argue against and "re-educate" his surgeon father and to project a larger-than-life image of himself:

> But, Dad, you've forgotten the class struggle and the threat that poses to the socialist regime! If we don't eliminate the counterrevolutionaries, the country will never be at peace and we'll be able to build nothing. Please understand the urgency of the situation! … Your pessimism is dangerous! Our President has written to the Red Guards at the Tsinghua University Middle School to cheer them on in their battle against impurity. (My translation)[31]

Les Quatre Vies du saule as a whole consists of four seemingly unrelated love stories, each taking place in a different historical period, chronologically spanning from the Ming (1368 to 1644), through the Qing (1636 to 1912) and the Cultural Revolution (1966 to 1976), to contemporary China. The "weeping willow" is reincarnated as a female character in each episode, as if the eternal soul of a woman is "condemned to chase love, century after century" (back cover, my translation). Through such a mystical and transhistorical narrative, Shan showcases Chinese linguistic and literary (r)evolution in French. Of course, it is neither her goal nor technically possible to demonstrate the exact differences between Classical and modern vernacular Chinese in her exophone writing. But this highly politicized form of Chinese vernacular development in the mid-twentieth century provides Shan with a stylistic and aesthetic opportunity for a varied and imaginative exophone reconfiguration through translation.

Very few scholars today would value the quality of the blatant political propagandist literature of the first three decades of the PRC, composed in a radically impoverished vernacular that was supposed to absorb and reflect the language of the common folk of China. As Bonnie McDougall decidedly concludes: "[the quality] was mediocre to downright bad. There was hardly a single work of written literature produced in the 1950s and early 1960s that had

---

[31] *Mais, papa, vous avez oublié la lutte des classes! et la menace qui pèse sur le régime socialiste ! Si on n'élimine pas les contre-révolutionnaires, le pays ne sera jamais en paix, et on ne pourra rien construire. Comprenez l'urgence de la situation! … Votre pessimism est dangereux! Notre Président a écrit aux gardes rouges du lycée annexé à l'université de Qinghua, pour les encourager dans leur combat contre l'impureté* (Shan 1999: Kindle).

a genuine claim to literary distinction" (1984: 280). Even in China today, such stereotyped language would in all likelihood meet with contempt or be used for ironic purposes.[32]

Yet, Shan's translation of this vernacular into French and her transformation of it into one distinctive narrative and discursive style actually produce a certain literary effect, albeit with a self-conscious sense of humor and irony. For one thing, this narrative and stylistic incorporation may well be aimed at a certain Western horizon of expectations, as the French readership is likely to be curious or superficially passionate about anecdotes from "Red China." For another, such an incorporation is also consistent with Shan's broader exophone literary agenda, as she reveals in an interview, "I hope that this French language is written in such a way that, through this language, we perceive the Chinese language. And this is perhaps what characterizes the style of all my books" (cited in Croiset 2009: para. 19, my translation).[33] Therefore, revisiting and recreating this particular form of modern Chinese vernacular through French signals a political, stylistic, and aesthetic adventure that intentionally raises the cosmopolitan and exotic outlook of Shan's literary expression.[34]

Exoticisme in the francophone context, as Charles Forsdick acutely argues, has more nuanced implications than the anglophone use of the notion, which is largely overshadowed by colonial discourse and the persistent workings of "imperial nostalgia" in the twentieth century (2001: 25). Influential francophone thinkers from Victor Segalen to Edouard Glissant notably engage with the concept of exoticism in order to reconfigure "more open models of cultural interaction in which all actors are valorized, cast as both representer and represented, knower and known" (2001: 23). Franco-Chinese writers' linguistic and literary experiments are situated largely—but not exclusively—outside the postcolonial context. In Shan's case, there are certainly inherent ambiguities in her literary agenda in relation to exoticism. Is she superficially recycling Chinese cultural and political clichés to please her francophone readership and produce more marketable types of "global works"? Or is she herself looking for an alternative aesthetic possibility by intentionally rewriting and renewing clichés in a

---

[32] Nevertheless, an extensive collection of such literature in a variety of genres has been made available in English; see Hsu and Wang (1980).
[33] J'espère que cette langue française est écrite de telle manière qu'à travers elle, on aperçoit ce qu'est la langue chinoise. C'est peut-être ce qui fait le style de tous mes livres.
[34] I should point out that this whole episode of the Cultural Revolution disappears completely in Shan's own rewriting of the novel "back" into Chinese. For a detailed discussion of the Chinese version, see Li 2018: 122–4.

language and culture other than her native ones, embracing a cultural hybridity that appropriately reflects her own intellectual, artistic, and life trajectories? Such ambiguities, as Forsdick rightly concludes, "are linked closely to exoticism's persistence as a concept reflecting the inevitable ambiguities of contact between different cultures" (2001: 25–6).

From vernacular genres to an imaginary vernacular

The texts examined up to this point have illustrated a great variety of manifestations of what might count or can be related to the notion of *the vernacular* in the Chinese context, from the historical development of specific kinds of (mainly written) language, through their associated literary and political expressions and articulations, to their fictional representations in diasporic Chinese (or French exophone) literature. The notion of the vernacular may be as fluid and unstable as that of *genre*. In order to discuss "vernacular genres" more productively, some conceptual refashioning is needed. It would be particularly helpful to follow Wai Chee Dimock's formulation of genre as "not just a theory of classification but, perhaps even more crucially, a theory of interconnection. *Kin* is every bit as important as *kind*" (2006: 74). Genre, for Dimock, is an open category, a fundamentally cumulative and thickening process, as she invokes it:

> less as a law, rigid taxonomic landscape, and more as a self-obsoleting system, a provisional set that will always be bent and pulled and stretched by its many subsets. Such bending and pulling and stretching are unavoidable, for what genre is dealing with is a volatile body of material, still developing, still in transit, and always on the verge of taking flight, in some unknown and unpredictable direction.
>
> (2006: 73–4)

In many ways, this chapter is dedicated to retracing and reconstructing a contingent vernacular *kinship* or "family" network "at various distances" (2006: 75) among a number of linguistic and literary products developments, and phenomena in the Chinese and Chinese diasporic context. It reaches across and beyond our traditional, narrow, and stable classification of vernacular language and literature as *kinds*, eschewing dichotomies such as old-style vs. modern vernacular Chinese and the Ming and Qing vernacular novel vs. modern vernacular poem.

In the remainder of this chapter, I will continue to trace and expand this kinship network by exploring the exophone representation of the literary and artistic productions decisively articulated through the increasingly politicized and formalized modern vernacular Chinese from the 1940s to the end of the Cultural Revolution. Those productions have a limited number of prescribed thematic preoccupations.[35] Taxonomically, those specific vernacular genres include not only novel and poetry but also performing arts such as revolutionary theater, film, and song.

Scholars conventionally use the word "form" rather than "genre" to articulate the literary and artistic concerns of this period, due in large part to Mao's agenda of creating "national forms" 民族形式.[36] As Wang Xiaoping rightly points out, by elaborating on "form," which in this historical context has a specifically Marxist dialectical relation to "content," Mao "essentially changed the term from an issue of literary genre or style to one that pertained to the political realm" (Wang 2012: 189). No matter how vague and unspecific those "national forms" were initially, one thing was always clear to Mao: they must have proletarian origins and must engage with and mobilize "the broad masses, especially (and predominantly) the peasants who constituted more than 90% of the population" (185). Against this backdrop, traditional and native folk art and poetry as well as popular ballads and ditties became major sources for the "national forms" that were expected to help create a "revolutionary culture" and "forge a hegemonic cultural-political nation as a 'class nation'" (184). Again, different from the vernacular development during the New Culture Movement led by May Fourth intellectuals, this political phase of vernacularization of language and culture was propelled by the fierce antagonism between the cosmopolitan, urban, bourgeois elites and the indigenous, rural, proletarian masses.

This vernacular tension is at the heart of Dai's novelistic conception of *Balzac*. The novel is saturated with literary and artistic examples of "vernacular genres." Depressed by the prospect of being incarcerated in this remote mountain village for the rest of their lives, Luo sings a revolutionary tune to cheer himself up, and Ma tries to accompany that on his violin—a distinctly urban and Western musical instrument. However, Ma (the narrator) quickly remarks: "It was a Tibetan song,

---

[35] These themes include the Communist revolution up to 1949, the land reform experience, the Chinese Communist participation in the Korean War, the socialist reconstruction of the country, and the continuing need for a socialist education of the masses (Crevel 1996: 15).

[36] However, I should clarify that Mao did not initiate such a pursuit. Debates around "national forms" had already started in the 1930s, and Chen Boda was the first to propose the term (Wang 2012: 185).

which the Chinese had reworded so as to turn it into a glorification of Chairman Mao" (2001: 17).³⁷ Adapting and remaking indigenous folk cultural sources in order to serve the new political and revolutionary agenda is an ideologically required literary and artistic practice of the time. And these are the kinds of songs that Ma hopes one day to be accepted by a regional propaganda committee to play, so that he may be able to leave the "primitive" village and rejoin the city.

Similarly, in order to be sent back to the provincial capital of Sichuan, the fellow sent-down youth nicknamed Four-Eyes (or le Binoclard) is asked by his poetess mother to publish in an official journal devoted to revolutionary literature "a number of popular ballads, that is to say sincere, authentic folk songs full of romantic realism, which Four-Eyes would collect from the peasants on the mountain" (2001: 59).³⁸ Later when the mother comes to the village to fetch Four-Eyes, she is very proud to announce that her son "has assembled a collection of splendid peasant songs, which he has adapted and modified. The editor-in-chief has shown great interest in the words" (78).³⁹ Those mountain ditties are actually collected by the protagonists Ma and Luo from an old miller who does not appear to understand Mandarin. In order to draw him out, Ma disguises himself as a Communist official from Beijing on a political and literary mission and pretends not to understand Sichuanese, while Luo acts as his local interpreter. This often-commented passage draws our attention to the oral and performative aspect of the vernacular language, such as local dialect, and genre, which is further dramatized in the film adaptation (2002) of the novel by Dai himself.⁴⁰ Viewers of the film can also hear actual examples of both revolutionary songs, like "Chairman Mao's Red Guards" sung in Mandarin, and supposedly indigenous mountain ditties, such as the old miller's riddle song sung in Sichuanese.

One of the two protagonists' more pleasant tasks assigned by the village headman is to retell, in front of the whole village, the stories of the films they have been sent to watch in a bigger town nearby to put on a *cinéma oral* (oral cinema show, 2001: 18). Not surprisingly, only propagandist films are screened, such as

---

³⁷ *C'était une chanson tibétaine, dont les Chinois avaient changé les paroles pour en faire un éloge à la gloire du président Mao* (Dai 2000: 28).
³⁸ *des chants populaires recueillis in situ par le Binoclard, c'est-à-dire d'authentiques chants de montagnards, sincères et empreints d'un romantisme réaliste* (80).
³⁹ *a recueilli des chants, les a adaptés, modifiés, et les paroles de ces magnifiques chansons paysannes ont énormément plu au rédacteur en chef* (107).
⁴⁰ Deppman (2010: 141–6) and Bloom (2016: 153–4) comment extensively on the language politics of twentieth-century China reflected in both the novel and the film.

the North Korean melodrama *The Little Flower Seller* (1972). During these days, foreign-language films are conventionally dubbed in standard Mandarin with "perfect" pronunciation and enunciation.[41] It is made crystal clear in Dai's film version of *Balzac* that the two protagonists are required to translate and retell the films they have watched in the local Sichuan dialect so that they can be better understood and appreciated by the villagers, including the Little Seamstress.[42] It is therefore interesting that although the novel was originally written in French, Dai decided to shoot the film primarily in Sichuanese, his native or "vernacular" tongue, in order to return to a sense of authenticity and verisimilitude while flirting with the contemporaneous official vernacularizing developments of languages and genres.

However, the most exciting development of the novel (and film) is when the two protagonists start to performatively recount the stories of the forbidden Chinese translations of French and Western novels they have stolen from Four-Eyes and secretly read, while repackaging them as stories from Communist countries, such as Albania.[43] The two protagonists are then seen to transform the genre of nineteenth-century French novels, such as those by Balzac and Dumas, through standard, written Mandarin into local "vernacular" language and performance. Furthermore, Dai, through both textual representation and filmic mise en scène, consciously engages with the well-established Chinese cultural tradition of storytelling, known as *shuoshu* 说书, literally "book-telling," a performance genre through which the *historical* Chinese vernacular (as opposed to Classical Chinese) is used and developed.[44] Therefore, Dai's complex novelistic and filmic conception not only bridges the sometimes radically different notions of the vernacular in the Chinese context but also further nuances the concept of exophony that I have examined throughout this chapter. Not only does it demonstrate the spatio-temporal exotic appeal ("exo-") and the specifically aural-oral quality ("-phone") of the vernacular; it also develops a distinct literary

---

[41] In fact, this also applies to Chinese actors who speak with accents (Shih 2007: 2).

[42] To be clear, most sinophone speakers would have to rely on subtitles to understand the film, as Sichuanese is by no means readily intelligible to Mandarin speakers. For an in-depth study of the translational process in the novel and that between the novel and the film, see Li 2019.

[43] Albania decided to side with the PRC during the Sino-Soviet split (1956–66).

[44] For a detailed discussion of "book-telling" in *Balzac* as well as some images of storytelling from the film, see Li 2019: 363–5. For a general introduction to the centuries-old Chinese tradition of storytelling, see Børdahl 1999: 1–14.

aesthetic that renegotiates the relationship between bilingualism and diglossia cross-culturally.[45]

The politically prescribed vernacularization increasingly intensified and imposed after Mao's *Yen'an Talks* encountered resistance, even within the Communist Party. The Marxist poet and critic Hu Feng (1902–1985), a serious follower of the May Fourth tradition, was the most representative figure. He was openly concerned about "formulism" and "vulgar Marxism" as early as the 1930s. His literary theory, which stresses the centrality of the writer's subjectivity to the creative process, "was taken as a political act that not only threatened some of the basic ideological tenets of the emerging Maoist doctrine but also disrupted the CCP's efforts to gain control over writers and, more generally, the individual" (Denton 1998: 2). His advocacy for modern free verse, for example, is a direct challenge to the idea of "national forms" (Hung 2017: 586). In 1955, a nationwide anti-Hu Feng campaign was launched and the critic, together with many members of his "clique," were incarcerated. Then, during the Cultural Revolution, Hu was taken to a "re-education camp" in Sichuan.

As a historical figure, Hu also features in the Franco-Chinese novels in question. In Cheng's *Le Dit*, the anti-Hu Feng political campaign directly affects the protagonists' destinies: Tianyi's male companion Haolang is sent to a labor camp because he has previously published some poems in a journal edited by Hu (1998: 240; 2000: 167). Hu's horrific experience at River Lu camp in Sichuan, as a *criminal de la pensée* ("thought criminal," 2009: 146), receives extensive fictional treatment in Dai's *Par une nuit où la lune ne s'est pas levée* (2007). In Dai's fictional treatment, Hu is made insane by the circumstances at the camp, as shown, for example, when he is seen arguing with an invisible Mao and scared of papers. Meanwhile, Hu also has an extraordinary encounter with a fictional French Orientalist named Paul d'Ampère, a fellow prisoner who has not only been naturalized as Chinese but is also the father of the mixed-race protagonist Tumchooq. D'Ampère has come to China to research on the lost, mystical language of Tumchooq (hence his son's name). Tumchooq (meaning "bird's beak") is said to be one of the ancient and spiritual languages through which Buddhism was initially transmitted, in Pali and Sanskrit, into China. This immediately becomes a subject of passionate discussions between a delirious Hu and an obsessive D'Ampère. Here, it is perhaps worth reminding

---

[45] While bilingualism refers to two distinct languages such as Chinese and French, diglossia generally refers to "two or more varieties of the same language" (Ferguson 1959: 325). The former is often discussed within the category of psychology; the latter is seen as the former's sociological counterpart (Fishman 1967: 29).

ourselves that early written vernacular in China (as opposed to Classical Chinese) was significantly developed through "the earliest translations of Buddhist texts into Sinitic, starting from the second century of the Common Era" (Mair 1994: 709–10).

With fictional evidence, Dai initially presents Tumchooq as the indigenous language of a desert kingdom to the western region of China, along the Silk Road, buried in sand, which disappeared in the third century (2007: 159; 2009: 112). The overall narrative of *Par une nuit* revolves around the tortuous uncovering and deciphering of an ancient Buddhist manuscript written in Tumchooq, which has been torn into two parts. Through D'Ampère's cross-cultural journey, Tumchooq's peripatetic search for the manuscript, and the female French protagonist-narrator's personal and emotional entanglement with Tumchooq (language and character), this lost, indigenous, spiritual, and mystical language quickly comes to be associated and intertwined with a variety of world languages: English, Chinese Mandarin, Tibetan, Sanskrit, Pali, Burmese, Bambara, and Hebrew, spanning Europe, Asia, and Africa. Thus, Dai's imaginary vernacular allegorically reveals the fundamental, long-term translocal interactions between the vernacular and the cosmopolitan, constituting a fictional "model instance of cosmopolitan vernacularism" (Pollock 1998: 7). Again, Dai's novel demonstrates complex negotiations among various notions of the vernacular on multiple levels, from languages to genres, from history to politics, in and beyond the Chinese context.

This chapter set out to use a rather unconventional primary literary corpus, francophone Chinese literature, to examine the issue of the vernacular in the Chinese context. The focus is on the exophone literary representations and reconfigurations of the different phases of the development of modern vernacular Chinese language and literature, which are nevertheless informed by a much longer historical process in China. This deliberate exophone approach also presents an opportunity to expand our understanding of the vernacular beyond the theoretical premise of regional, indigenous, or even national languages, while helping to reveal the kind of cosmopolitanism inherent in the vernacular. As my analysis has shown, while francophone Chinese writers' literary engagement with the vernacular, from languages to genres, from politics to sensibilities, seems to be well grounded in empirical history, the literary works themselves—different from the literary works they consciously imitate and represent—do not directly contribute to the development of modern vernacular Chinese *per se*. For Cheng, Shan, and Dai, the vernacular is not their linguistic, literary, or cultural destination; rather, it signals a conceivable departure for an informed imagination that is to be reconfigured in their exophone writings. This form of vernacular imagination is not oriented towards finding or building a seemingly organic regional or national language, literature, identity, or conveying any sense of nostalgic return. On the contrary, it aspires to get outside the regional or national conceptual framework, with a sense of exoticism at times, and works towards a future literary expression that undoes the local/global dualism in a new age of world literature.

References

Anderson, M. (1990), *The Limits of Realism: Chinese Fiction in the Revolutionary Period*, Berkeley: University of California Press.

Austin, J. L. (1962), *How to Do Things with Words*, Oxford: Oxford University Press.

Bachner, A. (2014), *Beyond Sinology: Chinese Writing and the Scripts of Culture*, New York: Columbia University Press.

Bertaud, M. (2011), *François Cheng: Un cheminement vers la vie ouverte. Nouvelle édition revue et augmentée*, Paris: Hermann.

Bloom, M. E. (2016), *Contemporary Sino-French Cinemas: Absent Fathers, Banned Books, and Red Balloons*, Honolulu: University of Hawai'i Press.

Børdahl, V. (1999), "Introduction," in V. Børdahl (eds), *The Eternal Storyteller: Oral Literature in Modern China*, 1–14, Surrey: Curzon.

Bush, C. (2010), *Ideographic Modernism: China, Writing, Media*, Oxford: Oxford University Press.

Chen, P. (1999), *Modern Chinese: History and Sociolinguistics*, Cambridge: Cambridge University Press.

Cheng, F. (1998), *Le Dit de Tianyi*, Paris: Albin Michel.

Cheng, F. (2000), *The River Below*, trans. Julia Shirek Smith, New York: Welcome Rain.

Cheng, F. (2002), *Le Dialogue: Une passion pour la langue française*, Paris: Desclée de Brouwer.

Chirila, I. D. (2012), "La Littérature transculturelle franco-chinoise où comment réinventer la République des Lettres," in R. Silvester and G. Thouroude (eds), *Traits chinois/Lignes francophones: Écritures, images, cultures*, 67–83, Montréal: Les Presses de l'Université de Montréal.

Crevel, M. (1996), *Language Shattered: Contemporary Chinese Poetry and Duoduo*, Leiden: Leiden University Press.

Croiset, S. (2009), "Passeurs de langues, de cultures et de frontières: la transidentité de Dai Sijie et Shan Sa, auteurs chinois d'expression française," *TRANS: Revue de littérature générale et comparée*, accessed April 6, 2021, https://doi.org/10.4000/trans.336.

Dai, S. (2000), *Balzac et la Petite Tailleuse chinoise*, Paris: Gallimard.
Dai, S. (2001), *Balzac and the Little Chinese Seamstress: A Novel*, trans. I. Rilke, New York: Anchor Books.
Dai, S. (2008), *Par une nuit où la lune ne s'est pas levée*, Paris: Gallimard.
Dai, S. (2009), *Once on a Moonless Night*, London: Random House.
Denecke, W. and L. Zhang (2015), "Series Editors' Foreword," in J. A. Fogel (ed.), *The Emergence of the Modern Sino-Japanese Lexicon: Seven Studies*, vii–ix, Leiden: Brill.
Denton, K. A. (1998), *The Problematic of Self in Modern Chinese Literature: Hu Feng and Lu Ling*, Stanford, CA: Stanford University Press.
Deppman, H.-C. (2010), *Adapted for the Screen: The Cultural Politics of Modern Chinese Fiction and Film*, Honolulu: University of Hawai'i Press.
Dimock, W. C. (2006), *Through Other Continents: American Literature across Deep Time*, Princeton, NJ: Princeton University Press.
Dong, H. (2014), *A History of the Chinese Language*, London: Routledge.
Ferguson, C. A. (1959), "Diglossia," *word*, 15 (2): 325–40.
Fishman, J. A. (1967), "Bilingualism with and without Diglossia; Diglossia with and without Bilingualism," *Journal of Social Issues*, 23 (2): 29–38.
Fokkema, D. W. (1965), *Literary Doctrine in China and Soviet Influence, 1956–1960*, The Hague: Mouton.
Forsdick, C. (2001), "Travelling Concepts: Postcolonial Approaches to Exoticism," *Paragraph*, 24 (3): 12–29.
Hanan, P. (1981), *The Chinese Vernacular Story*, Cambridge, MA: Harvard University Press.
Hockx, M. (2016), "Introduction: The Making of Modern Chinese Poetry in the Twentieth Century," in M. Hockx (ed.), *The Flowering of Modern Chinese Poetry: An Anthology of Verse from the Republican Period*, 3–19, Montreal: McGill-Queen's University Press.
Hsu, K.-Y. and T. Wang, eds (1980), *Literature of the People's Republic of China*, Bloomington: Indiana University Press.
Hung, R. Y. Y. (2017), "Time Has Begun: Hu Feng's Poesis in Socialist China, 1937–50," *Canadian Review of Comparative Literature/Revue Canadienne de Littérature Comparée*, 44 (3): 579–93.
Li, S. (2017), "Transcultural Novels and Translating Cultures: François Cheng's *Le Dit de Tianyi* and *L'Éternité n'est pas de trop*," *Forum for Modern Language Studies*, 53 (2): 179–99.
Li, S. (2018), "Translingualism and Autoexotic Translation in Shan Sa's Franco-Chinese Historical Novels," *Essays in French Literature and Culture*, 55: 115–31.
Li, S. (2019), "Novel, Film and the Art of Translational Storytelling: Dai Sijie's Balzac Et La Petite Tailleuse Chinoise," *Forum for Modern Language Studies*, 55 (4): 359–79.
Mair, V. H. (1991), "What is a Chinese 'Dialect/Topolect'? Reflections on Some Key Sino-English Linguistic Terms," *Sino-Platonic Papers*, 29: 1–31.
Mair, V. H. (1994), "Buddhism and the Rise of the Written Vernacular in East Asia: The Making of National Languages," *Journal of Asian Studies*, 53 (3): 707–51.

Mallarmé, S. (2006), *Collected Poems and Other Verse*, trans. E. H. and A. M. Blackmore, Oxford: Oxford University Press.
McDougall, B. S. (1984), *Popular Chinese Literature and Performing Arts in the People's Republic of China, 1949–1979*, Berkeley: University of California Press.
Norman, J. (1988), *Chinese*, Cambridge: Cambridge University Press.
Pollock, S. (1998), "The Cosmopolitan Vernacular," *Journal of Asian Studies*, 57 (1): 6–37.
Schoenhals, M. (1992), *Doing Things with Words in Chinese Politics: Five Studies*, Berkeley: University of California Press.
Shan, S. (1999), *Les Quatre Vies Du Saule*, Paris: Grasset.
Shih, S.-M. (2001), *The Lure of the Modern: Writing Modernism in Semicolonial China, 1917–1937*, Berkeley: University of California Press.
Shih, S.-M. (2007), *Visuality and Identity: Sinophone Articulations Across the Pacific*, Berkeley: University of California Press.
Tageldin, S. M. (2018), "Beyond Latinity, Can the Vernacular Speak?" *Comparative Literature*, 70 (2): 114–31.
Tong, C. (2014), "Foreignized Translation and the Case Against 'Chinese Vernacular Fiction,'" *mTm*, 6: 81–97.
Venuti, L. (2008), *The Translator's Invisibility: A History of Translation*, London: Routledge.
Wang, B. (2016), "Revolutionary Realism and Revolutionary Romanticism: *Song of Youth*," in K. A. Denton (ed.), *The Columbia Companion of Modern Chinese Literature*, 237–44, New York: Columbia University Press.
Wang, J. (2013), "Fanyi wenxue, fanyi, fanyiti 翻译文学，翻译，翻译体 (Literature in Translation, Translation, Translationese)," *Contemporary Chinese Writers Criticism* 当代中国作家批评 2: 129–137.
Wang, X. (2012), "From 'Use of Old Forms' to 'Establishment of a National Form': A Re-Evaluation of Mao's Agenda of Forging a Cultural–Political Nation," *International Critical Thought*, 2 (2): 183–96.
Wong, T. C. (2011), "The Original Evolutionary Nature of Chinese Vernacular Fiction," *Comparative Literature: East & West*, 15 (1): 57–64.
Zheng, M. (1993) "Shijimo de huigu: Hanyu yuyan biange yu Zhongguo xinshi chuangzuo 世纪末的回顾：汉语语言变革与中国新诗创作 (An End-of-century Review: Sinitic Language Reforms and Chinese New Poetry)," *Wenxue pinglun* 文学评论 (*Literary Criticism*), 3: 5–20.
Zhou, G. (2011), *Placing the Modern Chinese Vernacular in Transnational Literature*, New York: Palgrave Macmillan.

Vernacular lessons: Dante, Cavafy, Gombrowicz
(Instead of an afterword)

Galin Tihanov

It is a great privilege to be writing a brief afterword to this wide-ranging, learned, and insightful collection of essays on the vernacular and its significance for conceptualizing world literature. The editors and authors have reflected on the vernacular from a multitude of intriguing and helpful perspectives; what I hope to do here is to continue their important work by offering some further considerations on the potential of the vernacular as a particular lens through which we can examine (world) literature.

The Introduction to this volume rightly singles out the role of Dante in the early European debates on the vernacular. Of course, Dante was not the first to write on the vernacular; in Europe, probably the most significant short treatise preceding Dante's is that by Raimon Vidal, written very early in the thirteenth century.[1] (Vidal wrote his piece on the poetry and grammar of the Troubadours in Occitan, a language which Dante himself would later honor in his *Divine Comedy* by composing in it a sequence of nine lines, which the Provençal poet Arnaut Daniel delivers in the *Purgatorio* in accordance with Dante's metric form.[2]) But Dante's unfinished treatise, *De vulgari eloquentia*, is remarkable in at least two respects, on which I wish to dwell in some detail here.

To begin with, Dante's is a text that still allows us—a perhaps unlikely ally in this endeavor—to complicate the habitual evolutionary scheme, according to which the vernacular succeeds the cosmopolitan. This scheme would be familiar to students of world literature from Sheldon Pollock's breath-taking book on the fortunes of Sanskrit (2006). To be sure, Pollock carefully establishes various scenarios under which the cosmopolitan and the vernacular can and do co-exist; this dialectic of the two formations (as much linguistic as they are cultural, more broadly speaking) and their overlap is also noted by Alexander Beecroft

---

[1] For an English translation, by Marianne Shapiro, see her book *De Vulgari Eloquentia: Dante's Book of Exile* (1990: 113–26).
[2] See Alison Cornish, *Vernacular Translation in Dante's Italy: Illiterate Literature* (2011: 73; 155).

in his work on the ecologies of world literature (2015). But the story Pollock tells is nonetheless that of a millennium of cosmopolitan languages disrupted by a millennium of vernaculars, which in turn is being brought to a close by the ubiquity of English. This evolutionary line may or may not be unproblematic from our modern vantage point (this question should be left for another time); but from Dante's point of view it would be a rather secular, and thus somewhat feeble, line, and one that proceeds in the context of a still somewhat rigid distinction between cosmopolitan and vernacular.

For Dante, whom we often tend to read as unadulterated champion of the vernacular (he begins his *De Vulgari Eloquentia* by declaring it "nobler" than Latin, primary, and more natural), cosmopolitan and vernacular are not such absolutes, for in the fullness of biblical time their opposition is a relatively recent occurrence. From Dante's religious perspective, the differentiation between cosmopolitan and vernacular only emerged "as the punishment of confusion" (I.8),[3] following humanity's hubris in attempting to erect the Tower of Babel. Before that, humans only had one "form of speech" (I.6), and the only question that seems to have tormented Dante with reference to that language was not how it was used (the presumption of homogeneity seemed unshaken in that regard), but who was the first to speak it: a woman or a man (I.4). The truly universal language for Dante must have been Hebrew, the rest—the long shadow the exile from Paradise casts on language—is a history of powerful transregional languages (Latin being one such language for him, Greek another), of which various vernaculars exfoliate. This proliferation of vernaculars is a process that, far from celebrating, Dante, from a Christian perspective, attributes to the woefully imperfect nature of man as "a most unstable and changeable animal," whose language "cannot be durable or lasting but must vary according to time and place" (I.9).

The lesson that emerges, I suppose, is that the pivotal discrimination for Dante is not that between vernacular and cosmopolitan (the latter is our later terminological construct; Dante does not refer to "cosmopolitan" languages), but between vernaculars and languages, such as Latin, that have "grammar … incapable of variation" (I.9), that is, codified and stable usage. No longer praising the vernacular unequivocally, Dante later in the essay stresses the capacity of codified languages to better negotiate time and space (and thus be more cosmopolitan, as

---

[3] References throughout are to Shapiro's translation of Dante's text, with the first number referring to the relevant book, the second to the relevant section in that book.

we would put it today), furnishing access to "knowledge of the opinions and deeds of the ancients, or of those whom distance makes different from ourselves" (I.9).

The vernacular is thus a language that has not been codified. Dante mentions that Italy has at least fourteen vernaculars (I.10), and he believes his mission ought to be to hunt for the "most decorous and illustrious of them" (I.11). What is on the agenda here is an elevation of the vernacular towards a certain normativity that would render the local use of any one of these fourteen vernaculars insufficiently representative of the Italian language as a whole. This yet to be identified "illustrious" vernacular is compared to an elusive "panther" (I.16) that everyone is "stalking" without finding it (for some commentators, the panther is one of Dante's similes for God); this higher vernacular "belongs to every city" but is the property of none, and by it "the municipal vernaculars of all Italy are weighed, measured, and compared" (I.16).

It is vital to realize that Dante's discourse on the vernacular is far from free of notions of hierarchy and normativity. At the end of Book One he hints at what he calls "the lesser vernaculars" (I.19), descending by degrees to the language of a single family. And the entire second (unfinished) Book is a powerful exercise in re-normativizing the vernacular by drafting a prescriptive poetics that allows and disallows its specific uses in literature. Although the "illustrious Italian vernacular" may be used for both prose and verse, Dante clearly privileges verse over prose (II.1), and so begins the second Book with an exposition of its proper use in poetry. Dante's starting point here is the quality of the poet: "the best vernacular" is "appropriate only for those who possess learning and intellect"[4] (II.1). Having established that "only the most excellent poets should use the illustrious vernacular" (II.2), Dante further introduces, explicitly following Horace's *Ars poetica*, a thematic filter: only "the highest things" (II.4) are worthy of the highest vernacular and the corresponding tragic style; these subjects are "security, love, and virtue" ("security" here stands for the thematic compass of war and defense). Lower subjects invite the comic style, for which "sometimes the lowest, sometimes the middle form of the vernacular is adopted"; and the lowest ones are the preserve of the elegiac style, which "calls for only the humblest vernacular" (II.4). This gradation of subject matter, style, and the respective vernacular (highest; middle; lowest), which Dante promised to elaborate on in the unwritten fourth Book of his treatise, is then mapped onto the repertoire of genres: *canzone* is declared nobler than the ballad, and the ballad nobler than the sonnet (II.3).

---

[4] *Ingenium* in Dante's Latin, sometimes also translated as "genius" or "natural talent."

The vernacular is thus at once liberated and trapped in renewed normativity. This is mirrored in the very material that Dante relies upon to exemplify the various uses of the vernacular. He refers to some thirty vernacular poets, most of them Italian, the rest Provençal and French, some his contemporaries, some preceding him, but none by more than about 150 years.[5] His canon of vernacular writing (if this phrase is not a contradiction in terms) is thus rather fresh; it is the literature of his own time. Projected onto that screen of contemporaneity, however, are recurrent shadows from the deeper canon: works by Aristotle, Horace, and Virgil are all directly mentioned, with Boethius and Augustine also present in the background. Dante is vernacular and classic in the same breath, embracing the potential of "vulgar speech" and seeking to realign it with examples of nobility and decorum.

This may be another way of endorsing Engels's verdict from his 1893 preface to the Italian edition of the *Communist Manifesto*, in which he concluded that Dante was "both the last poet of the Middle Ages and the first poet of modern times" (Marx and Engels 2006: 37). (Marx was also an avid reader of Dante's *Comedy*, to which he referred more than once in his writings.[6]) Gramsci would echo this formula in his prison notebooks: "Isn't the *Divine Comedy*, to some extent, the swan song of the Middle Ages but also a harbinger of the new age and the new history?" (1991–2007, vol. 3: 48).

Yet the impact of Dante's work was not immediate; *De Vulgari Eloquentia* remained virtually unknown until the sixteenth century, when both the Latin text and an Italian translation were printed (the latter before the former), and their gradual appropriation commenced. What is more, Petrarch's literary domination, which from the mid-fourteenth century helped Latin regain its authoritative position, constituted, in Martin McLaughlin's apt characterization, "a linguistic counterrevolution" (2005: 612). The neat evolutionary line of a cosmopolitan language being supplanted irrevocably by the vernacular thus proves incapable of accommodating the zig-zags of history and the staying power of Latin. To lend further emphasis to this picture of contradiction and complexity, we also need to consider that Dante wrote his treatise on eloquence in the vernacular whilst in exile; chronologically, the time of its creation is embedded within his work on

---

[5] The information here is based on Purcell (1981: 8).
[6] For a reading of Vol. 1 of *Das Kapital* that (rather metaphorically and perhaps relying too much on analogy and association) sees it as modeled on Dante's *Inferno*, see William Clare Roberts, *Marx's Inferno: The Political Theory of Capital* (2017).

another unfinished treatise, the *Convivio*, in which—contrary to what he would state in *De Vulgari Eloquentia*—Dante asserts, in Italian, the superiority of Latin over the vernacular. As noted by Albert Ascoli (who seeks to reconcile this disagreement of the poet with himself), Dante praises the vernacular in Latin and the Latin language in Italian [7]

In the end, what matters here is the overall morale of the story: whether superior or inferior to Latin, the vernacular is conceived of, in both treatises, relationally (vis-à-vis Latin), and not as a fixed substance. There are no features intrinsic to the vernacular; its characteristics only emerge in relation to another language; as Meg Worley has put it, "vernacularity is not a quality but a relationship" (2003: 19). The vernacular therefore has no political identity of its own: its energies have been manipulated and mobilized to defend both *völkisch* nationalism and left-leaning discourses of equality and popular resistance to oppression; and the tireless translation factories of world literature have often repurposed it as a conduit of marketable exoticism.

I wish to conclude by very briefly bringing into play two examples of vernacularization in world literature, in which the vernacular defines itself vis-à-vis not as a dominant cosmopolitan language, but another articulation of the same national language. Modern Greek, from the early nineteenth century into the late 1970s, presents the historian of vernacularity with a rather interesting case. The vernacular here continues to be present and recognizable as a register within an already emancipated and codified national language. The vernacular in the case of Modern Greek persists within a situation of protracted diglossia, the carving out of two different versions of the language, *katharevousa* (seeking a compromise between Modern Greek and the older cosmopolitan Greek of the Hellenistic period) and *dimotiki* (the colloquial vernacular variety of Modern Greek). Students of world literature should be particularly attentive to this self-alienation of what are usually taken to be stable, homogenous, and unitary national languages. Linguistic and cultural foreignness does not always flood in from outside; it can also be produced from within the seemingly unitary body of the national language. Constantine Cavafy, a poet born in Alexandria to Greek parents, who would spend his life in what was eventually to emerge as independent Egypt, with spells in England and Constantinople, often mixed *katharevousa* (literally, "purified") and *dimotiki* ("popular," "of the people") in his poetry (while also writing some early poems entirely in *katharevousa*). Here

---

[7] See the argument in Albert Russell Ascoli, *Dante and the Making of a Modern Author* (2008).

the question of translation looms large: how could one convey the deliberate deployment of two linguistic registers, one vernacular and one artfully bent towards the archaic? W. H. Auden, one of Cavafy's many Anglo-American admirers in the twentieth century[8] (Cavafy's poetry was discovered for the Anglophone reader by E. M. Forster), discusses this difficulty in his introduction to the 1961 selection of Cavafy's poetry in translation:

> The most original aspect of his style, the mixture, both in his vocabulary and his syntax, of demotic and purist Greek, is untranslatable. In English there is nothing comparable to the rivalry between demotic and purist, a rivalry that has excited high passions, both literary and political. We have only Standard English on the one side and regional dialects on the other, and it is impossible for a translator to reproduce this stylistic effect or for an English poet to profit from it. (1961: viii)

Note here Auden's attention to the inner temporal clash staged by *katharevousa* and *dimotiki*, which can hardly find a match in the spatial distinction between a national language and its dialects. When Cavafy chooses to combine *katharevousa* and *dimotiki*, he simultaneously writes in both the standard language and in the vernacular within it, pursuing the interplay and the tensions between them without having to resort to regional dialects to body forth the vernacular.

My second and final example of the self-alienation of national languages in ways that re-enact the vernacular comes from an exilic writer, the novelist and playwright Witold Gombrowicz (Dante wrote on the vernacular whilst in exile; Cavafy deployed its resources as a diasporic poet; Gombrowicz experimented with it after deciding to miss the boat from Argentina to his native Poland). Exilic and diasporic writings have the capacity to estrange language from its identity as a *national language*; they thus lay the foundations of world literature, which would be unthinkable without destabilizing the sacrosanct (but, in fact, historically produced and thus limited) Western model of identity between a single national language and its corresponding national literature. In a sense, the main protagonist of exilic writing is language itself; we cannot really comprehend the history of world literature, unless we understand what happens to language as it travels across political, cultural, and linguistic borders—and across itself. The two principal scenarios are well-known: either embracing the language of the new cultural milieu (Nabokov is one salient example that stands for many,

---

[8] On the Anglo-American fascination with Cavafy's poetry, see Nikolaou (2020).

even though—remarkably—his first English-language novel, *The Real Life of Sebastian Knight*, was written in France, not in the United States), or continuing to deploy the language of one's pre-exilic environment. There is, however, a third powerful way. Witold Gombrowicz, who has a place in the extended canon of Western modernism, elected to do something different. His short novel, *Trans-Atlantyk*, published in Paris in 1953, is written in a language that deliberately reactivates the resources and the ostentatious patina of the Baroque period and of Romanticism, while adding to the mix a vernacular *skaz*-like handling of language (*gawęda*). (Again, this Polish non-Polish poses significant challenges for the translator.[9]) The result is a language that emphatically liberates and estranges both Gombrowicz and his readers from the Polish that was written and spoken in Poland in the early 1950s, that is, from Polish as the language of the nation (*the national language*). This purposefully odd language, not recognizable as the national language shared by Gombrowicz's contemporaries, yet still identifiable as an iteration of Polish, is the compass his readers must use in order to be led, by Gombrowicz himself (who compares himself to Moses in his diary), out of their Polishness.[10] Exilic writing is thus inextricably bound up with, and participating in, the making of world literature—by disaggregating language and nation, and by emplotting mobility, multiplicity, and foreignness. In Gombrowicz's case, this disaggregation proceeds through the unexpected channels of archaization and vernacularity attained in the effects of secondary orality.

By way of conclusion I wish to go back to the central finding of this short essay: The vernacular is a language that has not yet been codified. There resides, it seems to me, the most powerful lesson vernacularity can teach us as we engage with world literature. The not-yet-codified is just a linguistic shorthand for a different mode of cultural production and consumption that we need to be able to name and ponder. The vernacular should become a way of referring to a particular status of language and literature: the pre-codified, the not-yet-ready, the non-finalized, that which is still in flux. The vernacular opens up the space for discussing language, literature, and culture *in statu nascendi*; this is its truly subversive potential that can begin to generate a new understanding of world literature—not as the circulation of finished works commodified in books sold

---

[9] There are two English translations by Carolyn French and Nina Karsov (1994), and by Danuta Borchardt (2014), both published by Yale University Press.

[10] Cf. Gombrowicz's diary entry: "A hundred years ago, a Lithuanian poet [Mickiewicz] forged the shape of the Polish spirit and today, I, like Moses, am leading Poles cut of the slavery of that form. I am leading the Pole out of himself" (1988–1993, vol. 1: 36).

and purchased on the global market, but as the movement of texts, genres, and artistic conventions in the making, a world literature in becoming, seen from the *longue durée* of its existence. That *longue durée* perspective would suggest that the autonomous, self-contained, and authorially stable works of literature are but a recent invention, and perhaps even a short-lived one when measured by the standards of a much longer—and today reinvigorated—tradition of texts without authors, or with more than one, often disputed, authors, texts without a secure home in a book, or sharing that home with other texts, or living in parts in multiple abodes—illustrated manuscripts, sermons, textual re-enactments through theater, recitation, and dance, dismembered and reassembled with other texts in blogs and on social media. The vernacular could serve as a symbolic pointer to this powerful and inexhaustible spring of literary creativity, unregulated and uncaptured, resisting codification and also—not always—the dubious honor of its commodification.[11]

References

Ascoli, A. R. (2008), *Dante and the Making of a Modern Author*, Cambridge: Cambridge University Press.

Auden, W. H. (1961), "Introduction," in *The Complete Poems of Cavafy*, trans. Rae Dalvin, vii–xv, London: The Hogarth Press.

Beecroft, A. (2015), *An Ecology of World Literature: From Antiquity to the Present Day*, London: Verso.

Cornish, A. (2011), *Vernacular Translation in Dante's Italy: Illiterate Literature*, Cambridge: Cambridge University Press.

Gombrowicz, W. (1988–1993), *Diary*, 3 vols., trans. Lillian Vallee, Evanston, IL: Northwestern University Press.

Gombrowicz, W. (1994), *Trans-Atlantyk*, trans. Carolyn French and Nina Karsov, New Haven and London: Yale University Press.

Gombrowicz, W. (2014), *Trans-Atlantyk: An Alternate Translation*, trans. Danuta Borchardt, New Haven and London: Yale University Press.

Gramsci, A. (1991–2007), *Prison Notebooks*, ed. Joseph Buttigieg, 3 vols., New York: Columbia University Press.

Marx, K. and F. Engels (2006), *Manifesto of the Communist Party*, New York: Cosimo.

---

[11] I discuss this processual understanding of world literature in my article "Beyond Circulation" in *Universal Localities: The Languages of World Literature* (2022).

McLaughlin, M. (2005), "Latin and Vernacular from Dante to the Age of Lorenzo (1321–c. 1500)," in A. Minnis and I. Johnson (eds), *The Cambridge History of Literary Criticism*, Vol. 2: *The Middle Ages*, 612–25, Cambridge: Cambridge University Press.

Nikolaou, P. (2020), "Translating as Re-telling: On the English Proliferation of C. P. Cavafy," in R. Chitnis et al. (eds.), *Translating the Literatures of Small European Nations*, 165–83, Liverpool: Liverpool University Press.

Pollock, S. (2006). *The Language of the Gods in the World of Men: Sanskrit, Culture, and Power in Premodern India*, Berkeley and London: University of California Press.

Purcell, S. (1981), "Introduction," in Dante, *Literature in the Vernacular*, trans. S. Purcell, 7–13, Manchester: Carcanet New Press.

Roberts, W. C. (2017), *Marx's Inferno: The Political Theory of Capital*, Princeton and Oxford: Princeton University Press.

Shapiro, M. (1990), *De Vulgari Eloquentia: Dante's Book of Exile*, Lincoln and London: University of Nebraska Press.

Tihanov, G. (2022), "Beyond Circulation," in G. Tihanov (ed.), *Universal Localities: The Languages of World Literature*, Berlin: J. B. Metzler.

Worley, M. (2003), "Using *Ormulum* to Redefine Vernacularity," in F. Somerset and N. Watson (eds), *The Vulgar Tongue*, 19–30, University Park, PA: Penn State University Press.

Index

A Brief History of Seven Killings (James) 18, 104, 203–9, 211, 216–20
   see also Jamaica; James, Marlon; Marley, Bob: portrayal in James' *Brief History*; reggae
   contradictions in 213
   and dancehall, musical idiom 205
   diaspora portrayed in 205
   excess in 204
   genre 207
   hemispheric novel 18, 205
   narrative 205, 214
   orality of 203
   and United States 206
   the vernacular in 204–6, 211
Abdelhay, A. 34
Abdul Kalam, A. P. J. 94, 95
Abellán, M. L. 60
Aboikoni, Agbago 133–4
Achebe, Chinua, *Things Fall Apart* 37
Acholi language, *Wer pa Lawino* 40–1
Adam, Naomi 218
Adejunmobi, Moradewun xvi, 16, 28
   Vernacular Palavers 15
Africa and African languages 25–50
   see also Saamaka Maroons of Suriname and Guyane (French Guiana)
   African-authored texts
      Ajami (Arabic script, writing in) 34–5, 37
      commitment to writing in the vernacular 45
      in global languages 26, 37–8, 44, 45, 46
      non-standard scripts 35, 36–8
      in vernacular languages 40, 41–2, 45, 47
      see also the vernacular in Africa below
   Central Africa 128
   diasporic songs 13
   ethnic groups, nationalisms 31, 32, 34
   mother tongue, use of term 5, 27, 29–30
   multilingualism 27
   nationalist movements 31–2, 34
   North Africa 30
   Onitsha Market Literature 31
   orthographies 35, 36, 37
   polyglotism 27
   postcolonial 31
   renouncing the larger unit for smaller spaces 29–34
   selected languages 30
   the vernacular in Africa
      advocacy for writing in the vernacular 27–8
      defining the vernacular 26–9
      experimenting with 46
      translation of texts in the vernacular 39–40, 44
      vernacular and world literatures 38–47
      vernacular languages 36, 40, 43
      vernacular literacy 25, 34, 47
      vernacularization process 25, 33, 36, 44, 47
   West Africa 4, 5, 34, 43, 128
African-American literature 4, 17–18, 20
Afrobeats 16, 28, 42–3
   mixed register 43
Aguirre, José Antonio 65
Ajami (use of Arabic script to write African languages) 34–5, 37
Alegre, Ramón González 71–2
Alier, Joan Martínez 106
Allende, Salvador 214
alter-mondialiste movement 107n4
Amazon (company) 106
Ambazonia 33
American English 17, 189, 203
Amete, Franky 146

Amharic language, Africa 26n1, 40
Anderson, Benedict 12, 13
  Imagined Communities 165
Anderson, Mark D.: *Disaster Writing* 107
Anglo-globalism 21
anglophone Cameroon 32, 33, 34
anglophone global novel 204, 206, 220
Anidjar, Gil: "On Cultural Survival" 16
Ankara Press, Nigeria 46
Annadurai, C. V. 93
Anthropocene 107
anti-caste politics 91–3
anti-imperialism 13
Aparicio, Juan 74n24
Apintii language, Saamakas 130
Apter, Emily xiii, 3
  Against World Literature xii
Apuku language, Saamakas 130
Arabic language xiv, xvi, 30
  see also Ajami (use of Arabic script to write African languages)
Arana, Sabino 68n18
Arendt, Hannah xix
Aristotle 254
Armah, Ayi Kwei 28
artefactualized languages xv, xvi
Ascoli, Albert 255
Asfaha, Y. M. 34
attachment to the smaller place, vernacular seen as *see* smaller place, vernacular seen as attachment to
Atxaga, Bernardo 70
Auden, W. H. 256
Auerbach, Erich xi
Augustine 254
authenticity and the vernacular xiv, 11–14, 194
  African texts 39n15, 44
  Chinese context 244
  cultural authenticity 11
  ethnic authenticity 195
  naming of places 196

baihua (traditional Chinese vernacular) 157, 158–61, 163
  see also China; *wenyan* (Classical Chinese)
  compared with *wenyan* 224, 226
  new-style 161–6, 169, 172, 174
  traditional versus new-style 159
  written language close to spoken form 224
Baltic region 11, 185, 187, 188
  see also Estonia; Finland; Sweden
Baltic Germans 189, 192, 195
Bao-Diop, S. 37
Barber, Karin xix, 26n2
Barthes, Roland 116n7
Basque Country (Euskadi), northern Spain
  see also ETA (*Euskadi ta Askatasuna*), Basque Country separatist group
  armed struggle 70
  Burgos trial (1970) 67
  compared with Catalonia 64, 68, 70
  compared with Galicia 71, 72
  euskera batua (unified Basque) 70
  intellectuals 67, 68
  language 59, 65, 67–9, 70, 75
    Basque-language schools (*ikastolas*) 68, 69, 76
    prohibited 52, 65, 66
  literary works post-Franco 65, 69–70
  nationalism 55, 64, 67, 68n18
  padrinos system and censorship 66
  Partido Nacionalista Vasco (PNV), political party 67
  Plan for Economic Reform (1959) 66–7
  police repression 68
  separatist movements and regional autonomy 55, 65, 67, 68, 76
  state terror 65, 67
  Statute of Autonomy 54
Bate, Bernard 92
Beecroft, Alexander x, xi, xiii, xiv, 8, 10, 18, 19, 184, 185, 197, 251–2
  An Ecology of World Literature 9
belonging, sense of 21
Beltrán, Cristina 219–20
Benet, Josep 61
Bengali language xviii
Benjamin, Walter 84
Berber languages, North Africa 30, 36
Bhabha, Homi K. xviii
  Location of Culture 14
Bharathidasan (poet) 90
Biafra 32, 33

bilingualism 60, 62, 71, 77
    and diglossia 244, 245n45
    see also monolingualism; multilingualism
Blanco, Luis Carrero 68
Blanco-Amor, Eduardo 73
blog fiction 43
Boda, Chen 242n36
Boethius 254
Botswana, Setswana language 26n1
Bourdieu, Pierre 10
Bourlet, Mélanie 36, 40n19
Brathwaite, Kamau 7, 104, 108, 113, 118, 122
    tidalectics 117
British Museum, London 37
Brouillette, Sarah 210
Buddhism 157, 158–9, 246
Buell, Lawrence 107
Buenos Aires, Argentina: Galician diaspora 73

Cameroon 32, 33, 34
Campbell, Chris 102, 107
Camus, Albert 67
Caribbean islands 101–2
    see also neoliberalism
    Caribbean language 101–2
    colonialism 104n3, 114
    contemporary poetry
        alliterative words 120
        characters in poems named after Hurricanes Irma and Maria 114, 115, 118, 119
        ecocriticism and world literature 102–3, 105–112
        "hurricane poets," categorization of 102
        labelling 102
        from Lesser Antilles 101–25
        naming and intimacy 112–16
        relationality 111, 114, 116, 122
        rhythm 17
        sound language/sound-scapes 17, 103, 111, 114, 116–22
    hurricanes in 101–125
        Hurricane Dean (2007) 107
        Hurricanes Irma and Maria (2017) 17, 102, 111, 113–15, 118, 119
        literary history 108
        resistance to being labelled as a "hurricane poet" 110
        as symbols in poetry 111
        taking on material representation 119
        see also natural catastrophes
    Lesser Antilles
        colonial context 114
        compared with the larger islands 103n2
        poetry from *see above*
        reasons for focus on 103
    native mythology 13, 113
    nature writing 108
    neoliberal turn, retrospective narrativization 204, 206
    publishing houses 4
    sense of place conveyed in literature 107
    structural adjustment programs 204
    Taino (vernacular Caribbean language) 101
    typography 114
Carpentier, Alejo 13
Casanova, Pascale xi, 3, 8, 11, 15, 31, 186
    "Faulknerian revolution" 20
    La Langue mondiale 10
    The World Republic of Letters 10
Cassava Republic, Nigeria-based publisher 46
caste, anti-caste politics 91–3
Casteel, Sarah Phillips 104–5
Castile, Spain
    importance of region 54
    language 13, 53, 55, 61, 62, 68, 70–2
        official language under Franco 52, 58, 61, 78
        variations of 59
Cat Country (Lao She) 154, 166–77
    compared with "A Madman's Diary" (Lu Xun) 173–5
Catalonia, Spain 60–5
    activism 62–4, 69
    and Barcelona 60, 64
    book sales post-Franco 59, 62–3
    bourgeoisie 60, 63

264　Index

compared with Basque Country 64, 68, 70
compared with Galicia 71
co-option by Francoist regime 63, 64
Court of Justice 60
culture 62–4, 75
Indignados movement 64
intellectuals 62, 63, 64
language 58, 59, 62, 64
  prohibited 52, 61
nationalism 55, 63, 65
non-violent action 70
Òmnium Cultural 63
Orfeó Català choir 62
Parliament 60
Plan for Economic Stabilization (1959) 63
regional autonomy 55
Renaixença cultural movement 70, 74
Statute of Autonomy 54, 60
stopping of propaganda leaflets from entered Barcelona 58, 62
category errors 220
Cavafy, Constantine 255–6
censorship of regional languages, Spain 52, 57, 58, 66
  see also Spain
centralization of power 13
Centro Galego of Buenos Aires 73
Chamoiseau, Patrick 107n4
  Les Neuf consciences du Malfini 7
  Texaco xviii
Chea, Pheng xii–xiii, 104–5
Cheng, François 230, 231–2, 235, 246
  Grand Prix de la francophonie 223
  Le Dit de Tianyi (*The River Below*) 225, 228–32, 245
  Prix Femina 223
China 5, 153–79
  see also People's Republic of China (PRC)
  and Buddhism 157, 158–9
  Chinese Civil War (1927–49) 228, 233
  Chinese Classical poetry 231, 232
  Confucianism 154, 155, 157, 158, 162, 165, 166
  cosmopolitan political-literary formation 156

Cultural Revolution *see* Chinese Cultural Revolution (1966–76)
early history of the PRC 233–5
Economic Reform and Opening Up 233
fiction
  The Book of Poetry Shijing 154
  Cat Country (Lao She) 154, 166–77
  Classical Chinese (*wenyan*) 9, 154–7, 158, 160, 224, 226, 227
  deep history 15
  exophone novels 224, 228
  Francophone Chinese diasporic literature 223–49
  The Golden Lotus 159
  Journey to the West 159
  logographic script 170
  "A Madman's Diary" (Lu Xun) xxi, 154, 161, 164, 165, 167, 174–6, 227
  Out of the Margins 159
  revolutionary vernacular in 234–5
  Romance of the Three Kingdoms 159
  textualization 159–60
  Water Margin 159, 160, 161
  Wen yi zao Dao (literature as vehicle for the Way) 165
  see also the vernacular *below*
Great Leap Forward (1958–62) 235
Han Dynasty (206 BCE–220 CE) 154, 155, 158
intellectuals 161, 165, 167, 228, 231, 232
May Fourth Movement (1919) 225, 226–7, 229, 230, 233, 234
Jinan Incident (1928) 166
and Korean War 242n35
Mandarin 243, 244
May Fourth Movement (1919) *see* May Fourth Movement (1919), China
Meji period (1868–1912) 227
Ming Dynasty (1368–1644 CE) 159, 160, 163, 226, 239, 241
nation-building 156, 162, 164, 165
New Culture Movement 9, 161, 162, 163, 165, 173, 224–5, 227, 228
Opium Wars 161
Qin Dynasty, First Emperor (221–206 BCE) 154, 155

Qing Dynasty (1644–1911/12 CE) 155–6, 161, 163, 226, 239, 241
  radical language reforms 9
  semi-colonization of 161, 165
  Sino-Japanese War (1894–5) 161
  Sino-Japanese War (1937–45) 228, 233
  Six Dynasties (317–589 CE) 158
  late Tang Dynasty (618–907 CE) 159
  the vernacular
    baihua (traditional Chinese vernacular) 9, 157, 158–66, 169, 224, 226
    Chinese context 241
    Chinese vernacular and vernacular literatures 225–8
    cultural ritual of vernacular storytelling 225
    development of a new-style vernacular 161–6
    genres 242
    modern, replacing *wenyan* 160
    politicizing in early history of the PRC 233–5
    prose fiction 165
    revolutionary vernacular in fiction 235–41
    rewriting vernacular Chinese poetry in French 231
    use of English term in Chinese context 225
    vernacular movement 154
  Yuan Dynasty (1206–1368) 160
Chinese Communist Party (CCP) 245
Chinese Cultural Revolution (1966–76) 9, 242, 245
  and fiction 233, 235, 236, 238, 239, 240n34
  "Great Proletarian" 236
climate change 7, 101
coding of languages xii, xiv, 155, 234n22
  code-switching 42
  Dante on 252
  double-coding xix
  pre-coded languages 6–7, 19
Cold War divisions 218
colonialism 9, 12, 14–15, 19, 97, 112, 115, 122, 129, 184, 206, 208, 214, 216
  anti-colonialism 67

British rule 33
colonial languages 4, 15, 16, 104n3
colonial period xviii
  in Africa 26n2, 31, 35–6
  Lesser Antilles 104n3, 114
colonization/colonial expansion 11, 12, 30, 101, 106, 107
  see also decolonization
  semi-colonization of China 161, 165
computational literary studies (CLS) xii
concept of the vernacular xiii, xvi, 1–24
  see also the vernacular
  applied as an analytical tool 197
  attachment to a place/locality 5, 25
    in Africa 29–34
  comparative analysis 8
  defining the vernacular 3–5, 6, 26–9, 181
    divergent interpretations 30, 223
  and genre 241
  highly localized forms of expression 35
  mother tongue, related to 5, 11, 27, 28, 29
  origins 5
  precodified status of language and culture 6–7
  shifting nature 6, 7
Confucianism 154, 157, 166
  abolishment 162
  Classics 155
  Confucian Way 155, 158, 165
Conversi, D. 64
Cornish, Alison 251n2
cosmopolitanism
  see also vernacular cosmopolitanism
  defined 95
  environmental 105–6
  literary modes xviii
  philosophical aspects xvii
  Sanskrit cosmopolis 156
  Tamil language 94–5
  terminology 183
  and the vernacular xviii, 3, 14
    differentiating between 252
    new cosmopolitan vernacular xiv, 137–44, 227
    vernacularization 153–4
  Westernized 175

and world literatures xi, xiii–xiv, xvii–xviii, 2
cosmopolitan-vernacular dynamic xi, xiii–xiv, xvii, xviii, xxi
   in modern Chinese fiction 153–79
Counter Reformation 186
Creole languages 6, 203, 218
creolization (language mixing) 6, 127–31
Cuesta, Raimundo Fernández 74n24
Cui Yan 168
cultural consolidation 188
cultural relativism 187
cultural revolution 203, 204, 213
cultural survival 16–17

Dai, Sijie 66, 235, 244, 246
   Balzac et la Petite Tailleuse chinoise (Balzac and the Little Chinese Seamstress) 223, 225, 235, 236–7, 242–3, 244n44
   Par une nuit où la lune ne s'est pas levée (Once on a Moonless Night) 225
   Prix Femina 223
D'Ampère, Paul 245, 246
Damrosch, David xi, 2, 18, 38, 40, 46
Daniel, Arnaut 251
Dante Alighieri 6
   Convivio 255
   Divine Comedy 251, 254
   De vulgari eloquentia 5, 251, 252, 254
      discourse on the vernacular 253, 254
      Marx on 254
      role in early European debates on the vernacular 251
Danticat, Edwidge 112
Daoism 230
De Castro, Rosalía: *Cantares gallegos* 70
De Rivera, José Antonio Primo 63n15
Deckard, Sharae 108, 113, 119, 205
decolonial rupture 213
decolonization 2, 8, 209, 210, 212, 213, 219, 220
   see also colonization/colonial expansion
deep time 9
Delegation for Press and Propaganda, Spain 51
Deleuze, Gilles 18–19, 110

DeLoughrey, Elizabeth 102, 103, 107
Denecke, Wiebke 9, 155
Denning, Michael 208–9, 211, 213, 216
   Noise Uprising 208
Derrida, Jacques 83n2
Desai, Kiran 206
dialect
   African American 20
   Arabic xiv
   Beijing 166, 168
   Spain 56, 71
   standard language 10
   writing of 207, 208
diaspora xx, 4, 20, 114
   Africa 16, 113, 144
   francophone Chinese diasporic literature 223–49
   Galicia 72, 73, 76
   and Jamaica 205
   mobility 224
Díaz, Junot 206
digital technologies 43
Dimock, Wai Chee 17–18, 105, 110, 111, 241
dimotiki (colloquial vernacular of Modern Greek) 255, 256
   see also katharevousa (purified form of Modern Greek)
Diop, Birago 36
Diop, Boubacar Boris 46, 47
   Doomi Golo (*The Hidden Notebooks*) 44, 45
disaster writing 107, 108
   see also under Caribbean islands
   genre of 121
discourses of the vernacular xvi
diglossia (division of labor) 157, 166
dislocation xx
disorientation xx
"distant reading" xii
distinctive language 29–35
   commitment to writing in, and desires for the smaller place 32
   ideal of literacy in 32
   as official language 30, 35
domain of vernacularity xv, xvi, 47
Donicie, Antoon 145
Doumerc, Eric 103

Du Bellay, Joachim: *La Deffence et illustration de la langue francoyse* 10
dub reggae 116, 205
Dungulali language, Saamakas 130
Duxiu, Chen 162, 227, 233
Dyutongo language, Suriname 128, 129

East Asia 9
ecocriticism 93–4, 96
   aesthetics of 107
   Caribbean islands, poetry from 102
   and world literatures 102–3, 105–112
ecological globalism 106
Ellis, Nadia 204
Engels, Friedrich: *Communist Manifesto* 254
English language
   global English *see* global English/globalization of English
   Modern and Old English 224
   Pidgin English 42n20
   ubiquity of 252
enlarged time frames 8–9
Enlightenment 230
Enparantza, José Alvarez 67
environmental cosmopolitanism 105–6
environmental epic 108
Eritrea, selected languages 30
Estonia
   see also Baltic region; Kallas, Aino; literary themes and vernacular literature
   archipelago 188
   bringing vernacular into modern literature 191
   independence (1918) 182
   language 182, 186
   novels 11, 190–3
   oral literatures and myths 185
   peasant language 189
   publication of the first *ABC* books 186
   Young Estonia movement 186, 189
ETA (*Euskadi ta Askatasuna*), Basque Country separatist group 67, 68, 76
Ethiopia, selected languages 30
ethnic groups, in Africa 31, 32, 34, 36, 37

ethnic nationalisms 31, 32
ethnicity and the vernacular 194–6
ethnography xix, 148–9
Ette, Ottmar xii
Eurocentrism 13, 97, 184
European Renaissance 230
Euskadi, Spain 65–70
Euzko Gogoa (literary journal) 66
existentialism 67
exophone literature 224, 228, 232

Fabian, Johannes 12
Fabra, Pompeu 57, 62
Facebook fiction 43
Fagunwa, Daniel: *Ògbójú Ọdẹ́ inú Igbó Irúnmọlẹ̀* 39, 41
Falangists, Spain 55, 59, 66
Farred, Grant: *What's My Name* 16
Fascist Italy 51
Faulkner, William 20, 205
Felski, Rita 189
Fennoman (Finnish-minded) movement 182
Ferguson, Charles A. 157
Finland
   see also Baltic region; Kallas, Aino; literary themes and vernacular literature
   civil war 187
   development of language 186
   Gulf of 181–2
   independence from imperial Russia (1917) 182, 187
   language 182
   national narratives and folk traditions 186
   nation-building 187–8, 197
   oral literatures and myths 185
   publication of the first *ABC* books 186
Fokkema, D. W. 233, 234
folklore 186, 191, 196
formulist political language 234–5, 245
Forsdick, Charles 240, 241
Forster, E. M. 256
France 1
   compared with Spain 53
   French language

as language of the "World Republic
of Letters" 3
and Latin 6, 10
libertine conception 10
translation from African languages 44
French-speaking Cameroon 33
littérature-monde xii
program of *francisation* 145
universal military service 53–4
Franco, General Francisco 76
dictatorship 51, 52, 56
Francoist monolingualism
see also Basque Country (Euskadi),
northern Spain; Castile, Spain;
Catalonia, Spain; Spain
censorship/prohibitions under Franco
52, 56–8, 61, 65, 71–3
arbitrary nature 58
book burning 52, 57, 76
as "cultural genocide" 61
"double censorship" 58
proclamations, vague language 57
production control 58
propaganda 58, 62
self-censorship 58
under resistance to 72
wartime orders 57, 59
government control 51, 52
repression and legal protection 75–8
resistance to 51–80
Euskadi 65–70
Galicia 70–5
strategies 52
functions of languages 6

Galaxia (Galician publishing house) 72, 74–5
Galicia, northwest Spain
Brotherhoods of Language 71
compared with Basque Country and
Catalonia 71, 72
denunciations of Francoist repression 73
diaspora in the US 72, 73, 76
intellectuals 73, 75, 76
manifesto (Denunciation before
UNESCO of the persecution of the
Galician language by the Spanish
State) 73
poetry 70
prohibited language 52

region of emigration 71
Rexurdimento (culture and language)
70
Statute of Autonomy 71
Galiza, Spain 70–5
Gallén, E. 62
Gan Bao 158
Ganguly, Debjani xii
Ge, Liangyan 159–60, 161, 165
Geetha, V. 92n5
Ge'ez script, Ethiopia 34
genres 153, 193, 196
Afrobeats music genre 42–3
Caribbean/Jamaican fiction 205–7
Chinese 232
and concept of the vernacular 241
conventions 189
disaster 121
global novel see global novel
historical 188–9
Jamaican/Latin American 205
narrative 158
performativity 159, 170, 174, 177
prose fiction 165
rhetorical 70
sub-genres 108
Georges, Richard 102–4, 105, 109, 110,
111, 113, 114, 121–2
Epiphaneia 102, 113
"A Mixtape for Tortola" 116
"The Transmutation of Grief" 118
Ghana, Afrobeats music genre 42
Gikuyu language, Kenya 29, 45, 47
Githiora, Chege 27, 43
Glissant, Édouard 104, 107n4, 108, 116,
122
global English/globalization of English 1,
3, 4, 9, 10, 207
see also English language
global historical perspective, the
vernacular in 7–14
global migration 31
global novel xii, 108, 219
anglophone 204, 206, 220
emphasis on the vernacular in
Caribbean/Jamaican fiction 207,
210, 212, 217, 219–20
multicultural, multilingual, and multi-
vernacular 207

global professional writer 210
global South writers 206, 210
global warming 7, 101
globalization 11, 12, 107n4, 208
    see also global English/globalization of English
    homogenous globalism 1
    recording technology 208
Goethe, Johann Wolfgang von xv, 2, 13
Gombrowicz, Witold 256
    Trans-Atlantyk 257
Google 106
Gramsci, Antonio 254
Guattari, Félix 19, 110
Guha, Ramachandra 106
Guyane
    see also Saamaka Maroons of Suriname and Guyane (French Guiana)
    changes in 145
    ethnic groups 140–1
    present-day 147–8
    Saamaka women 148
    young Saamakas in 142

Haabo, Vinije 145
Haiti earthquake (2010) 102, 108, 109
Hall, Stuart 204
    "Negotiating Caribbean Identities" 203
Harris, Wilson: *The Womb of Space* 18
Harrison, Sheri-Marie 204
Hart, George 81–2, 85, 86, 89, 92
Hasselblatt, Cornelius 186
Hausa language, Nigeria 26n1, 35, 39, 40
Hayot, Eric xiii, 104–5
    On Literary Worlds xii
Hebrew language 252
Heidegger, Martin 74
    The Essence of Truth 73
Heifetz, Hank 85, 86, 89
Heise, Ursula 105–6, 108
    Sense of Place and Sense of the Planet 106
Helgesson, Stefan xi
Herder, Johann Gottfried 11–12, 13, 187
heterochrony, vernacular language as 18
Hieroglyphics 28
hip-hop 4, 116
historical fiction 188–9
Ho Chi Minh 67

Høgel, Christian 8
homophones 231
Horace 254
    Ars poetica 253
Horta, P. xviii
Hu, Feng 245
Hu, Shi 162, 165, 227, 230, 233
Huggan, Graham 106, 107, 108
humanism 15
hurricane poetry *see under* Caribbean islands; natural catastrophes
Hurston, Zora Neale 215
    Their Eyes Were Watching God 20
Huters, T. D. 233

Igbo ethnic group, southeastern Nigeria 31, 32, 37
imagined community of nation-state 12, 13
imperialism xiv, 12, 206, 211
    see also colonialism; colonization/colonial expansion
    anti-imperialism 13, 219
    imperial languages 30, 52
    Japanese 166, 167
    trans-imperialism 8
    Western 167
India xv
    see also "Yaathum Oorey" (classical Tamil poem/song by Kanian Poongundranar)
    anti-caste politics 91–3
    North Indian Aryan identity 90
    north Indian Hindi 90
    Tamil language *see* Tamil Nadu, language and literature
indigenous languages 30, 34, 35
Institutions of World Literature (Helgesson and Vermeulen) xi
Interamerican Court for Human Rights 143
International Monetary Fund 210
IPOB (Indigenous Peoples of Biafra) 32
Irele, Abiola 41
Iribarne, Manual Fraga 59, 74
Isizulu language 37n14
Ìṣọ̀lá, Akínwùmí 45–6
    Efúnsetán Aríwúrà, Ìyálóde Ìbàdàn 39
    Tinúubu, Ìyálóde Ègbá 39
Italy
    Fascist 51

Italian language 6, 253
  regional languages 53n3
  Tuscan as national language (1870) 53n3
  unification 53n3

Jakobson, Roman 83n2
Jamaica
  Jamaican Creole 6, 203, 218
  literary tradition 204
  One Love Peace Concert of 1978 211
  People's National Party 211
  reclaiming African heritage 205
  reggae music 205, 211–12
  Standard Jamaican English 203, 218
  Tivoli Gardens ghetto, Kingston 212
  US interventions 214, 215
James, Marlon 4, 18, 104
  see also *A Brief History of Seven Killings* (James)
  Black Leopard, Red Wolf 212
  Man Booker prize (2015) 203, 206
  self-reflexive account of the vernacular 219
  vernacular within anglophone writing, use of 206
James, Tania 206
Japan
  adoption of Chinese script 9
  Meiji period (1868–1912 CE) 162
"jazz-novel" 7
Jennings, Arthur George 216, 217
Jones, Gavin 208
Jones, Gayl 207
journals, literary xxi
Juffermans, K. 34
Junco, José Álvarez 53

kaatchi (vision) 89
Kalevala mythology 191
Kaljundi, L.: *Novels, Histories and Novel Nations* 189
Kallas, Aino 181–201
  see also literary themes and vernacular literature
  archaic style 189–90, 197
  fictional and autobiographical texts 182
  folklore, use of 186, 191, 196
  on gender and class 189

  locations in stories 195
  plots 193–4
  political and nationalist themes in novels and short stories 182
  on power relations and injustice 190–1
  representation of Finland and Estonia in works 182
  sartorial markers, use of 195
  vernacular style, themes, and uses 188–90, 196–8
  works of
    Ants Raudjalg 190
    Barbara von Tiesenhusen 182, 192–3, 194, 195, 196
    "Death of old Org" 194
    Estonian novels 11, 190–3
    Imant ja hänen äitinsä (Imant and His Mother) 190
    "Ingel" (short story) 182, 191–2, 193, 194, 195
    "The Wedding" (short story) 182, 192, 193, 194
  writing as an intervention in culture and politics 184–5
Kallas, Oskar 182
Kannada (Indian language) xxi
Karayanni, Stavros, *Vernacular Worlds* 18
Karunanidhi, Nadu M. 91, 93
katharevousa (purified form of Modern Greek) 255, 256
  see also *dimotiki* (colloquial vernacular of Modern Greek)
Kelman, James 4
Kenyan languages 27, 29
Kiswahili language, Tanzania 26n1, 28–9, 40
Kivi, Aleksis, *Seven Brothers* 186
Klass, Anthony 34
Komanti language, Saamakas 130
Korea, adoption of Chinese script 9
Krohn, Kaarle 182, 191
Krutwig, Federico 67
Kullberg, Christina 223

Laanes, E.: *Novels, Histories and Novel Nations* 189
Laferrière, Dany 108, 109, 112
Laitinen, Kai 189
language boundaries xv

language nationalism 90–1
language(s)
see also coding of languages; language boundaries; language nationalism; *specific languages*
colonial 4, 15, 16, 104n3
distinctive see distinctive language
formalized 234–5
in Franco's Spain 51
indigenous 30, 34, 35
as lingua franca 27, 28, 29n6
mother tongue see mother tongue
nation language 31, 104, 118, 122
natural 87
official see official language
plurality of 6
political 234–5
pure 84
Russian 184
universalistic orders 28, 31
of wider communication 27
Lao She
Cat Country 154, 166–77
"Language and Style" 174
Latin xiv, 6, 10, 56, 252, 254
superiority over the vernacular (Dante) 255
Latin America 13, 205
see also Caribbean islands; Jamaica
Le Dit de Tianyi (The River Below), Cheng 225, 228–32, 245
Leffler, Yvonne xi
Lemke, Sieglinde xvii
The Vernacular Matters in American Literature 16
Lentz, Carola 29
Li, Shuangyi 105
Lima, José Lezama 13
lingua franca 27, 28, 29n6
Lionnet, Françoise: *Minor Transnationalism* 18
literary aesthetics 91, 97
literary practice xiii, xvi, xix, xx, xxi, 161
literary themes and vernacular literature
see also Kallas, Aino
emerging nations 186–8
ethnicity and the vernacular 194–6
and works of Aino Kallas 181–201
Estonian novels 190–3

gender and class 189, 193–4
uses of the vernaculars 196–8
vernacular themes and style 188–90, 197
literary vernacularization 39, 44, 47
literature
see also literary themes and vernacular literature; literatures of the world; Sangam Age of classical Tamil literature; Tamil Nadu, language and literature; theoretical perspectives in world literature; vernacular literature; world literature
African-American 4, 17–18, 20
exophone 224, 228, 232
major and minor 197
new media 43n23
plural conception of xiii
spatial imaginaries in xx
vernacular and world literatures 38–47
literatures of the world 38, 46, 82–3, 98
Liu, Lydia 164
Translingual Practice 165
Livonia 188
local languages
see also vernacular languages; *specific cases*
Africa 28, 29n4
concept of the vernacular 4, 10, 11, 13, 15, 20
denaturalizing by vernacularization 10–11
Francoist monolingualism, resistance to 57, 60, 72
local/global dualism 227
modern Chinese fiction 107n4, 155, 161, 176
Scandinavian countries 184, 187, 197, 198
translocal 161
the vernacular associated with the local 5, 6
location(s)
see also smaller place, vernacular seen as attachment to
disciplinary locations x–xi
literary locations xx

naming, by Aino Kallas 195, 196
  and orientation xix, xx
Longman Anthology 97
longue durée perspective 258
Lönnrot, Elias 185
Lorca, Federico García 72
Low language, China 157–8
Lu Xun 229
  "A Madman's Diary" xxi, 154, 161, 164, 165, 167, 174–6, 227
Luango language, Saamakas 130
Luganda language, Uganda 41
Lumumba, Patrice 214
Lüpke, Friedericke 29, 35, 36, 37
Luther, Martin, *Little Catechism* 186

McDougall, Bonnie 239
McGann, Jerome xi
McLaughlin, Martin 254
Machado, Elena 102
Maeztu, Ramón 68
Mahajan, Karan 206
Mallarmé, S. 232
  "*Le Cygne*" (The Swan) 231
Mandarin 243, 244
"A Madman's Diary" (Lu Xun) xxi, 154, 161, 164, 165, 167, 174–6, 227
  compared with *Cat Country* (Lao She) 173–5
Mani, Venkat xi
Manley, Michael 211, 213–15
Mao Tse-tung 9, 67, 233, 235, 236, 242
María, Manuel 71–2
market aesthetics 102
marketability of texts 2, 3
Marley, Bob: portrayal in James' *Brief History* 204, 211
  see also *A Brief History of Seven Killings* (James); Jamaica; James, Marlon; reggae
  "Buffalo Soldier" 216
  "Redemption Song" 217
Marx, Karl 254
MASSOB (Movement for the Actualization of the Sovereign State of Biafra) 32
May Fourth Movement (1919), China 158, 163, 164, 172, 245

francophone Chinese diasporic literature 225, 226–7, 233, 234, 235–6
  intellectuals 225, 226–7, 229, 230, 233, 234, 242
  see also China
Maya Codex 113–14
Meeks, Brian 214
Melamed, Jodi 204
Melkas, Kukku 189, 196
methodological globalism 183–4
methodological nationalism 183
minor literature 18, 19
Mitxelena, Koldo 75
Mitxelena, Salbatore, *Arantzazu* (*Poem of the Basque Faith*) 65
mixilingualism 42
Moberg, Ronne 18
Modern English 224
Modern Greek 255
modernity 9, 13, 15
  European 19, 20
  global 232
  late 121
  linguistic 227
  one-dimensional 175
  secular 8
  "translated modernity" 164, 165, 174
Modi, Narendra 94
monolingualism xv, 17, 62
  see also bilingualism; Francoist monolingualism; multilingualism
Montero, Alonso 72, 74n24
Monzón, Telesforo, *Urrundik* (*From Afar*) 65
Mora, Josep Ferrater 63
Moretti, Franco x, xi, xii, 2, 20
Morton, Timothy 103
mother tongue 11
  versus lingua franca 29n6
  use of in African languages 5, 27–30, 32, 33
Mufti, Aamir xv, 38, 40
Mukoma wa Ngugi 37
multiculturalism, neoliberal 204
multiglossic vernacular 154, 166, 169
multilingualism xii, xv, 4, 120
  Africa 27, 30, 33, 34, 36, 46

benefits of 207–8
concept of the vernacular 21, 22
Saamaka Maroon languages 141, 156
Muraivazhi (path of conduct) 88, 89
music idioms, vernacular 205, 209–10, 212
see also reggae
Mwangi, E. 26n2, 29
Myers-Scotton, Carol, *Duelling Languages* 42n22

Nabokov, Vladimir Vladimirovich 256–7
The Real Life of Sebastian Knight 257
Nadiminti, Kalyan 210, 211, 212
nation language 31, 104, 118, 122
national literatures xiii, xx, 197, 207
and concept of the vernacular 3, 5, 9, 10
Estonian novels 191
Finland and Estonia 183, 187
nationalism 165, 189, 190
Africa 31–2
Basque Country (Euskadi), northern Spain 55, 64, 67, 68n18
Catalonia, Spain 55, 63, 65
confrontational/violent 19, 76
contemporary 6
ethnic 31, 32
language nationalism (Tamil) 90–1
methodological 183
resurgent 1–2
völkisch 255
nation-building 11, 30
Baltic region 182, 187–8, 190, 194, 197
China 156, 162, 164, 165
and vernacularization 197
nation-state 14, 16, 17, 70, 204, 209
formation 8
modern 8, 11, 12, 13, 54, 71
multilingual 30
structural adjustment programs 204
natural catastrophes
hurricanes *see under* Caribbean islands
poems on 102, 103, 116
see also under Caribbean islands
storms, symbolism of 110
as a world literary theme 108

natural languages 87
Nazi Germany 51
Ndao, Cheikh Aliou 27
Buur Tillen 41
neoliberal multiculturalism 204
neoliberalism 18, 21, 210, 213–15
neoliberal turn in Caribbean 204, 206
Netherlands Institute for Advanced Study 131
Neumann, Birgit xiii
New Culture Movement, China 9, 161, 162, 163, 165, 173, 224–5, 227, 228, 242
new media literature 43n23
Nganang, Patrice 4
Ngũgĩ wa Thiong'o 28, 29, 39n15, 46, 47
Mũrogi wa Kagogo (*Wizard of the Crow*) 44, 45
Niblett, Michael 102, 107
Nigeria
Afrobeats music genre 42
Civil War 32
geopolitical zones 32n9
Nigerian languages 26n1, 26n2, 31
Pidgin English 42n20
separatist movements 32
southeastern 31, 32, 34
Ninaithaale Inikum (Tamil film) 94
Nixon, Rob 101, 107
Noël, James 102
non-standardized language 35–8, 40
Norman, Jerry 155, 158
North Africa 30
Norton Anthology 97
novel, contemporary 3
Noyes, John K. 11, 12
Nussbaum, Martha: "Patriotism and Cosmopolitanism" 95
Nyerere, Julius 28–9, 29n4

Obioma, Chigozie 206
official language 26n1, 29, 30, 53, 76, 141
distinctive language as 30, 35
Ohiri-Aniche, C. 36
Oil Crisis (1973) 214
Òkédìjí, Ọládẹ̀jọ 39, 45–6
Old English 224
Oloruntoba-Oju, T. 42

Olúmúyìwá, T. 36, 37
One Love Peace Concert of 1978, Jamaica 211
Ong, Aihwa 213
Onitsha Market Literature 31
orality of the vernacular 5
orientation, and location xix, xx
Orsini, Francesca xii, xiii
orthographies 35, 36, 37, 145

Pakistan xv
Panchavarna Kili (Indian film) 90
Papa language, Saamakas 130
Papagadu language, Saamakas 130
p'Bitek, Okot 41
  Song of Lawino 40
Peck, Jamie 213
People's Republic of China (PRC)
  see also China
  early history 233–5
  establishment 225
performativity xvii, 205, 217, 243, 244
  genres 159, 170, 174, 177
  and naming 112–13
  poetry 120
  textual form 43–4
Peru, oral poetry 12
Petrarch, Francesco 254
Philippines, US occupation of 17
philology 11, 170, 171
  comparative xiv, xv
phonetic transliteration 169
Pikkanen, I., *Novels, Histories and Novel Nations* 189
Piñeiro, Ramón 74, 75
Ping Chen 155, 163, 172
place, attachment to *see* smaller place, vernacular seen as attachment to
plane of equivalence 38, 40
Pléiade-group 10
plurality of languages xiii, xx, 2, 6, 17, 21
poetry
  see also Tamil Nadu, language and literature
  in Caribbean region *see* Caribbean islands
  Chinese Classical poetry 231, 232
  in India *see* "Yaathum Oorey" (classical Tamil poem/song by Kanian Poongundranar)

on natural catastrophes 102, 103
"Orphic way" 232
Polish language 257
Pollock, Sheldon xiv, 3–4, 8, 9, 15, 18–20, 25, 28, 33, 176, 184, 185, 187, 251–2
  on Chinese fiction 153, 154, 156, 161, 164–5, 227, 228n7
  "Cosmopolitan and Vernacular in History" 1
  The Language of the Gods in the World of Men 1
polyglotism 16, 27, 225
Poongundranar, Kanian 84, 87, 88, 89, 98
  "Yaathum Oorey, Yaavarum Kelir" *see* "Yaathum Oorey" (classical Tamil poem/song by Kanian Poongundranar)
Portnoy Brimmer, Ana 102
postcolonialism xvii, 9, 14–19, 210, 212, 240
  see also colonialism
  in Africa 15–16, 29, 31, 47
  in the Caribbean 104
  in India 90
  rewriting 108
  studies 2, 9, 14, 15, 106, 184
Price, Richard, *Rainforest Warriors* 143n18
print culture 10, 109
prose fiction 165
Pulaar language, Africa 35, 40n19
Pumbu language, Saamakas 130
Purcell, Sally 254n5
Puranaanuru (ancient anthology, Tamil) 87, 88
pure language 84

Qichao, Liang 165
qualitative research, world literature studies xii

Radio Biafra 32
Rafael, Vicente: *Motherless Tongues* 17
Rahman, A. R. 91
Rajadurai, S. V. 92n5
Ramanujan, A. K. 81, 85–6, 96
  The Interior Landscape 93
Rancière, Jacques 185–6
Rastafarian lyric 203, 211
  "Dread Talk" 203, 218

Reagan, Ronald 215
Reckin, Anna 114, 122
recording technology 208, 209
reggae 205, 211–12
regionalism 32, 96, 107
relationality xx, 182, 215, 220
    Lesser Antilles, poetry from 111, 114, 116, 122
    relational comparison 181
    transnational 220
    vernacular as a relational term xv, 82, 226
Republic of Cameroon 32, 33
revolutionary romanticism 238–9
Rexurdimento (Galician culture and language) 70, 74, 76
Richter, Sandra xi
Ridruejo, Dionisio 57, 61–2
Rigney, Ann 188–9
Rippl, Gabriele xiii
Robbins, Bruce xviii, 8–9
    "Prolegomena to a Cosmopolitanism in Deep Time" 8
Roberts, William Clare 254n6
Rojo, Louisa Martín 207
Romantics 187
Rosa, Hartmut 111, 121
Rovira i Virgili, Antoni 57
Russian Empire 182, 184
Russow, Balthasar 196
    Chronica der Prouintz Lyfflandt 188, 189

Saamaka Maroons of Suriname and Guyane (French Guiana) 127–51
    see also Africa and African languages; Guyane; Suriname
    in the 1960s to the 1980s 132–3
    ancestors of Saamaka Maroons 128
    assimiliationist politics 145
    battles between Saamakas and colonial armies 129
    civil war between Maroons and government 140
    collective identity 133–4
    creolization 127–31
    cults 130
    esoteric languages 130
    Fesiten ("First-Time"), seventeenth- and eighteenth-century history 131–7, 143, 144, 145
    fieldwork 131, 148
    German Moravian (Herrnhuter) missionaries 129
    historians 135, 136
    inter-African syncretism 130
    Maroon symbols 139
    multilingualism 141, 156
    new cosmopolitan vernacular 137–44
    Okanisi Maroons, eastern Suriname 131
    peace treaty with Dutch Crown (1762) 144
    speech of Komanti mediums 130–1
    traditional items of Maroon dress 149–50
    woodcarving, Maroon art of (*tembe*) 139, 145, 146–7
Saamakatongo language, Saamakas 130, 131
Saizarbitoria, Ramon 70
Sakai, Naoki 6
Sámi literature 19
Sánchez-Prado, Ignacio xi
Sangam Age of classical Tamil literature 81, 82, 87, 91, 93, 96
    see also Tamil Nadu, language and literature; "Yaathum Oorey" (classical Tamil poem/song by Kanian Poongundranar)
Sanskrit 156, 251
Santana, Stephanie Bosch 43
Saramaka People v. Suriname 143
Sartre, Jean-Paul 67
Schoenhals, Michael 234n22, 236
Scott, David 215
script language 12
scripta franca 9, 155, 224
scripts 5, 159
    Arabic 36
    indigenous 34
    non-standardized 35–8, 40
    Roman 36
    standardized 40
Sekou, Lasana M. 102–4, 105, 109, 110, 112–14, 118–19, 121–2
    Hurricane Protocol 102, 120–1
Selvamony, Nirmal, *Persona in Tolkappiyam* 93–4
Sembene, Ousmane 36
semi-periphery, literary xx–xxi

Senegal, West Africa 34, 35, 36, 37
Senghor, Leopold 36
Seoane, Luis 73
separatist movements 32, 56, 65
Setswana language, Botswana 26n1
Shaaban bin Robert 27, 29
Shan, Sa 235, 240, 246
  Les Quatre Vies du saule (*The Willow's Four Lives*) 225, 237–9
  Prix Goncourt des Lycéens 223
Shankar, S. 15, 26–7, 38, 40, 46
  Flesh and Fish Blood 15, 82, 208
Shapiro, Marianne 251n1
Sheng language, Kenya 27, 43
Shih, Shu Mei 163, 181, 185, 197, 230
  Minor Transnationalism 18
Shulman, David: *Tamil: A Biography* 81, 96
Siberia, exile writing xxi
slavery
  acts of enslavement 18
  association of the vernacular with 5
  in Suriname 127–8
  transatlantic 16
  in the United States 20
slow violence 101–2, 107
smaller place, vernacular seen as attachment to 5, 25
  in Africa 29–34
Smith, Anthony 182
Snellman, Johan Vilhelm 187
Social Darwinism 167
Sorhaindo, Celia A. 102–5, 109–112, 116, 118–19, 121–2
  Guabancex 102, 103, 113, 115
  "Invoked" 119
South Africa, post-Apartheid governments 34n13
Southern Song (1127–1279 CE) 159
Soyinka, Wole 29, 41
Spahr, Juliana: *Du Bois's Telegram* 207
Spain
  army/military service 51, 54, 57
  Basque Country (Euskadi) *see* Basque Country (Euskadi), northern Spain
  Castile *see* Castile, Spain
  Catalonia *see* Catalonia, Spain
  Catholic Church 55, 56, 60, 64
  censorship of regional languages 57.
  Civil War 56, 61, 63, 67, 71, 74
  compared with France 53
  Constitution of 1812 53
  Constitution of 1978 52, 77
  divisions in 54
  Estado Nuevo (New State) 63n15
  Falangists 55, 59, 63n15, 66
  Golden Age 55
  government decree of November 1975 77–8
  languages
    Basque Country (Euskadi) 52, 59, 65, 66, 67–9, 70, 75
    Castilian 13, 52, 53, 55, 56, 58, 59, 61, 62, 68, 69, 70–2, 78
    Catalan 52, 58, 59, 61, 62, 64
    comparative research 53–4
    Galician 70
    imperial 52
    language situation, history and development 53–4
    and Latin 6
    prohibitions by Franco *see* Francoist monolingualism
    protection of regional languages 52
    vernacular 56
  Law of Press and Printing 60
  losses in Cuba, Puerto Rico and the Philippines 54
  Ministry for National Education 58
  national crisis 54
  Opus Dei (secular Catholic order) 59
  Press Law 59–60
  regional dialects 56
  religious schools 53
  separatist movements 56
  UNESCO, entering 73
spatial imaginaries, in literature xx
speech 6, 136, 211, 224
  Cat speech in *Cat Country* (Lao She) 169, 170
  close-to-speech written language 225
  everyday 168, 234–5, 237
  formal 17
  historical single form 252
  hybrid forms 43
  localized forms 43
  metropolitan speak 210
  and modern Chinese fiction 155, 160, 162, 163, 168, 174

plain 159
of Saamaka Komanti mediums 130-1
speech acts 237
vernacular 16
vulgar 254
Srinivasa Iyengar, P. T. 92
History of the Tamils 81
Standard Jamaican English 203, 218
standardized language 10, 13, 40
Stephanides, Stephanos: *Vernacular Worlds* 18
storms, symbolism of 110
Stuelke, Patricia 215, 216, 217, 220
subalternity 7, 14
Sudan, ethnic groups 36
Suits, Gustav 190, 191
Sundaram, P. K. 89
Súñer, Ramón Serrano 63n15
suppression of vernacular languages 17
Suriname
　see also Saamaka Maroons of Suriname and Guyane (French Guiana)
　escape from plantations 128-9
　history of region 127-8
　Paramaribo (capital) 138, 141
　Saamakas living in 142
　slave plantation 127-8
　Suriname River plantations 128
Swaminatha Iyer, U. V. 87
Sweden xiii, xx
　see also Baltic region
Swift, Jonathan, *Gulliver's Travels* 157
symbolism
　color 147
　French, of Chinese poetry 231-2
　political 109, 110

Tageldin, Shaden M. xvi, 5, 26, 27, 35, 226n4
Tagore, Rabindranath xviii
Taino (vernacular Caribbean language) 101
Tamil Nadu, language and literature 14, 81-100
　see also India; "Yaathum Oorey" (classical Tamil poem/song by Kanian Poongundranar)
　comparatism 98
　Dravidian identity 90-3
　language nationalism 90-1

Sangam Age of classical literature 81, 82, 87, 91, 93, 96
　Tamil identity 90
　tinai philosophy 93, 94, 96
　transnational 82
　and world literatures 82, 96, 97
　and "Yaathum Oorey" 91
Tanzanian language 26n1, 28-9, 30
Taraborrelli, Angela 175
Texaco (Chamoiseau) xviii
textual idealism xi
textualism, excessive xix
"Thamizhukum Amudhendru Per" (film song) 90
The Tempest (Shakespeare) 97
theoretical perspectives in world literature xx, 2-5
　see also concept of the vernacular; genres; global novel; Kallas, Aino; translation
　center-periphery theories 18
　and genre 241
　global novel 108
　mainstream literary theory 155
　political 183n2
　recontextualizing 197
　renegotiating 197
　sociological 183n2
　and translation 83
　and works of Aino Kallas 182-6
Thomas, I.B., *Itan Igbesi-Aiye Emi "Ṣegilọla, Ẹlẹyin'ju Ẹge," Ẹlẹgbẹrun Ọkọ L'Aiye* 39-40
Thomsen, Mads Roosendahl 108
Tiffin, Helen 106, 107
Tifinagh script, Morocco 34
tinai philosophy 93, 94, 96
Tingliang, Qiu 162
Tone language, Saamakas 130
Tosh, Peter 211
trans-imperialism 8
translation xviii, xx
　African texts 39-40, 44, 45
　challenges 83
　Chinese texts 169
　commonality and difference 83-4, 87
　cultural 87
　and marketability 2, 3

of own vernacular language texts into global languages 45
phonetic transliteration 169
texts gaining in 2, 183
"translated modernity" 164, 165, 174
translationese 227, 229
untranslatability of certain texts xii, 3, 45, 103
works "born translated" 3
of "Yaathum Oorey" (classical Tamil poem/song) 81–2
transnational literature 82
travel writers xxi
Trilogchander, A. C. 90
Troubadours, Occitan 251
Trudell, Barbara 34
Tuglas, Friedebert 189, 191
Tumchooq (indigenous Chinese language) 246

ultra-minor languages 18, 19
Unamuno, Miguel de 68
United States
    see also *A Brief History of Seven Killings* (James); Caribbean islands; Jamaica
    African American literature 4, 17–18, 20
    dialect writing 208
    Galician diaspora 72, 73
    government agencies 212
    interventions in Jamaica 214, 215
    language policies 17
    Philippines, occupation of 17
    private foundations 212–13
    slavery in 20
    vernacular languages 20, 206
    in the world literature 97
universalism xiii, 5–6, 15
    Hebrew as universal language (Dante on) 252
    universalistic orders 28, 31

Valkenburg, Dirk 134f
Van den Bersselaar, D. 31
Vatican II 60, 64, 75
Venero, Maximiano García 61n10
Venkatachalapath, A. R. 87
Verdaguer, Jacint 62

Vermeulen, Pieter xi
the vernacular
    see also concept of the vernacular
    in Africa see Africa and African languages
    within anglophone writing 206
    in China see China
    and cosmopolitanism 3
        distinguishing between 252
        new cosmopolitan vernacular xiv, 137–44
    vernacular orientations xviii
    and culture 26
    defining 3–5, 6, 26–9, 253
    etymological roots 16
    expression of resistance to hegemony of cultural centers 4
    in global deep histories 7–14
    growth of writing in (Africa) 26
    as language that has not yet been codified 253, 257
    lesser and higher vernaculars (Dante) 253
    plurality of xx
    potentialities of 19
    rethinking 7, 19–22
    scope of form 21
    shifts in meaning and function 7
    social dimension xv, xvi
    traditional vernacular (*baihua*), rise of 158–61
    transforming into a mode of resistance 191–2
        gender and class 193–4
    uses of 196–8
vernacular cosmopolitanism xi, xviii, xix, 14, 183, 184, 228
vernacular imagination 225, 232, 241–2, 247
vernacular languages
    see also *specific countries*; vulgar languages
    demise, anxieties about 1, 2, 21
    dismissal for globally oriented writing 207
    global South 206, 210
    heterochrony 18
    and neoliberalism 204
    Standard Jamaican English 203, 218

status 76–7
suppression 17
vernacular literacy 25, 34, 47
vernacular literature
    see also literary themes and vernacular literature; vernacular languages; specific cases
    and classical literature 82
    and international publishing market 210–11
    versus transnational literature 82
vernacular millennium 8, 9
vernacular modernism 205
vernacular music idioms 205, 209–10, 212
vernacular polities 25, 28
vernacularization process xiv–xv, 8, 10–11, 14, 154
    in Africa 25, 33, 36
    characteristics of vernacularization 186
    and depoliticization 186
    literary vernacularization 39, 44, 47
Vidal, Raimon 251
Vietnam, adoption of Chinese script 9
Vila-Abadal, Vilanova i 61n10
Virgil 254
Vives, Jaume Vicens 63
Vohra, Ranbir 166, 167
Volk, notion of 12
Voorhoeve, Jan 144–5
vulgar languages 5, 56, 59, 158, 162, 174
    see also vernacular languages

Wailers (reggae band) 211
Walcott, Derek 101, 107, 108, 113
Walkowitz, Rebecca 3
Wallerstein, Immanuel x
Warner, T. 35, 44n24
Warwick Research Collective (WReC) xii, xiii
Watawenu language, Saamakas 130
Watson, David 223
Weber, Eugen 54
Wells, H. G.: *The First Men in the Moon* 166–7
Wen yi zao Dao (literature as vehicle for the Way) 165
Wen Yiduo (Chinese poet): "Lone Wild Goose" 231

Wenti language, Saamakas 130
wenyan (Classical Chinese) 9
    see also *baihua* (traditional Chinese vernacular); China
    abolishment 227
    compared with *baihua* 224, 226
    "cosmopolitan" language, East Asia 156
    development of a "cosmopolitan" *wenyan* 154–7
    replaced by modern vernacular (1920s) 160
    scripta franca of East Asian elites 224
    standardized lexical and grammatical rules 155
West Africa 4, 5, 34, 43
Westernism 184
Wolof language, Africa 35, 36, 41, 45, 47
Wood, Michael 203
World Bank 210
world literary studies 2–3, 7, 8, 21, 108, 153, 175, 184
world literature xi, xii, xxi, 3, 4, 8
    centers in Europe and North America 110
    cosmopolitanism xvii–xviii, 2–3
    cosmopolitan-vernacular dynamic xi, xiii–xiv
    critique against xvii
    defining 185
    and ecocriticism 102–3, 105–112
    enlarged time frames 8–9
    "literature for the West" 2
    and literatures of the world 38, 46, 82–3, 98
    versus postcolonialism xvii
    and Tamil language/literature 82, 96, 97, 99
    terminology 2, 183
    texts gaining in translation 2, 183
    in the United States 97
    and world history 198
    world literature theories see theoretical perspectives in world literature
world music 209
World Republic of Letters 3, 10, 74
World Tamil Conference, Tamil Nadu 91

"worlding literature" xiii
Worley, Meg 255

Xiaoping, Wang 242
Xuantong, Qian 227n5

"Yaathum Oorey" (classical Tamil poem/
  song by Kanian Poongundranar)
  81–100
  see also Tamil Nadu, language and
    literature
  in English 83–7
  first line 87
    translated as "Every city is your city.
      Everyone is your kin" 85, 86
    translated as "Everywhere is my
      home, everyone my kin" 82, 86,
      92, 94
  modern reception 82
  readings 83
    anti-caste politics 91–3
    cosmopolitanism 94–5
    distinction between inner and
      outer, difficulty of 89

diversity of 96–7
ecocriticism 93–4, 96
kelir (kinship) 86, 94
language nationalism 90–1
oorey (home/home town) 86, 87
philosophical 88–9
traditional 88
and Tamil language 91
translation 81–2
Yao, African language 29
Yen'an Forum on literature and art (1942),
  Mao's talks at 233, 245
Yoruba language, Nigeria 26n1, 26n2, 35,
  37, 37n14
  lack of translation of literature 39–40
  standardized scripts 40
Young Estonia movement 186, 189

Zhang, Longxi 9, 155
Zhou, Gang 157–8, 164
Zhou Dunyi 155
Zipitria, Elbira 69
zone of affinity 38
Zulu, South Africa 26n1

www.ingramcontent.com/pod-product-compliance
Lightning Source LLC
Chambersburg PA
CBHW052152300426
44115CB00011B/1631